SwiftUI

Apprentice

First Edition

By Audrey Tam & Caroline Begbie

SwiftUI Apprentice

By Audrey Tam & Caroline Begbie

Notice of Rights

Notice of Liability

Trademarks

ISBN: 978-1-950325-16-0

Table of Contents

Book License

By purchasing *SwiftUI Apprentice*, you have the following license:

- You are allowed to use and/or modify the source code in *SwiftUI Apprentice* in as many apps as you want, with no attribution required.

- You are allowed to use and/or modify all art, images and designs that are included in *SwiftUI Apprentice* in as many apps as you want, but must include this attribution line somewhere inside your app: "Artwork/images/designs: from *SwiftUI Apprentice*, available at www.raywenderlich.com".

- The source code included in *SwiftUI Apprentice* is for your personal use only. You are NOT allowed to distribute or sell the source code in *SwiftUI Apprentice* without prior authorization.

- This book is for your personal use only. You are NOT allowed to sell this book without prior authorization, or distribute it to friends, coworkers or students; they would need to purchase their own copies.

All materials provided with this book are provided on an "as is" basis, without warranty of any kind, express or implied, including but not limited to the warranties of merchantability, fitness for a particular purpose and noninfringement. In no event shall the authors or copyright holders be liable for any claim, damages or other liability, whether in an action of contract, tort or otherwise, arising from, out of or in connection with the software or the use or other dealings in the software.

All trademarks and registered trademarks appearing in this guide are the properties of their respective owners.

Before You Begin

This section tells you a few things you need to know before you get started, such as what you'll need for hardware and software, where to find the project files for this book, and more.

What You Need

To follow along with this book, you'll need the following:

- A **Mac computer with an Intel or ARM processor**. Any Mac that you've bought in the last few years will do, even a Mac mini or MacBook Air.

- **Xcode 12.5 or later**. Xcode is the main development environment for building iOS Apps. It includes the Swift compiler, the debugger and other development tools you'll need. You can download the latest version of Xcode for free from the Mac App Store.

- Optionally, an **iPhone, iPad or iPod Touch** running iOS 14.

Book Source Code & Forums

Where to download the materials for this book

The materials for this book can be cloned or downloaded from the GitHub book materials repository:

- https://github.com/raywenderlich/suia-materials/tree/editions/1.0

Forums

We've also set up an official forum for the book at https://forums.raywenderlich.com/c/books/swiftui-apprentice/79. This is a great place to ask questions about the book or to submit any errors you may find.

About the Cover

SwiftUI Apprentice

That's not an 18th-century writer's quill on the cover or even a gorgeous deep water plant, but a sea pen — a creature belonging to the Cnidaria family, which includes jellyfish, coral and sea anemone.

The earliest fossils date this colonial creature to the Cambrian period — some 541 million years before being featured on our book — and the pens are still thriving today in both coastal and deep temperate and tropical waters.

You can observe the soft colorful stalks of the pens lodged in the seafloor, often grouped like an underwater garden of feathers. And just as you glance at an application on your phone and take in one interface that is actually made of many working features, the sea pen isn't one creature at all, but a colony of creatures.

The main stem is one polyp — the first to take root — that then supports many other smaller polyps whose tentacles make up the fringes we see. And like the various aspects of the seamless interfaces made with SwiftUI, the delicate polyps are cleverly designed for different purposes to support the whole creature – intaking water, maintaining structure, eating and reproducing. The pens have been observed expanding and shrinking, articulating their frayed bodies, reacting to crabs and other touch, and even glowing.

A sea pen may be stationary, like any application anchored within the confines of your device. But the pens show us that with the right construction and design, you can architect something cohesive, fluid, beautiful and dynamic.

"To the raywenderlich.com community, who help create my happy place."

— *Audrey Tam*

"To my children, Robin and Kayla, who make my real life a better place."

— *Caroline Begbie*

About the Authors

 **Audrey Tam** is an author of this book. As a retired computer science academic, she's a technology generalist with expertise in translating new knowledge into learning materials. Audrey attends nearly all Melbourne Cocoaheads monthly meetings, attends many concerts at Tempo Rubato and does most of her writing and zooming at Rubato Upstairs. She also enjoys long train journeys, knitting, and trekking in the Aussie wilderness.

 **Caroline Begbie** is another author of this book. Caroline ventured out into the world as an unemployed classicist. She then taught herself to code and started up a software company in the UK and later in the US. Retiring to Australia prematurely, she performed marionette shows for pre-schools until she purchased the original iPad. She recognized the creative possibilities and became an indie iOS developer. Now she loves tinkering with vertices and watching Disney movies.

About the Editors

 **Libranner Santos** is the tech editor on this book. He's a software engineer with more than 10 years of experience. Basketball fan and player, and a decent dancer. Love learning and teaching at all levels. You can follow him on Twitter as @libranner.

 Richard Critz did double duty as editor and final pass editor for this book. He is the iOS Team Lead at raywenderlich.com and has been doing software professionally for over 40 years, working on products as diverse as CNC machinery, network infrastructure, and operating systems. He discovered the joys of working with iOS beginning with iOS 6. Yes, he dates back to punch cards and paper tape. He's a dinosaur; just ask his kids. On Twitter, while being mainly read-only, he can be found @rcritz. The rest of his professional life can be found at www.rwcfoto.com.

About the Artist

 **Vicki Wenderlich** is the designer and artist of the cover of this book. She is Ray's wife and business partner. She is a digital artist who creates illustrations, game art and a lot of other art or design work for the tutorials and books on raywenderlich.com. When she's not making art, she loves hiking, a good glass of wine and attempting to create the perfect cheese plate.

How to Read This Book

This book is designed to take you from zero to hero! Each chapter builds on the code and concepts from its predecessors, so you'll want to work your way through them in order. To help you navigate on your journey, here are some conventions we use:

- Filenames, text you enter into dialog boxes, items you look for on screen all appear in **bold**.

- Names of things you find in your code — such as variables, properties, types, protocols and method names — appear in a `monospaced typeface`.

- The ➤ icon indicates an instruction step for you to follow.

- Quick tips about Xcode are marked with **Xcode Tip**.

- Quick tips about Swift are marked with **Swift Tip**.

- Deeper explanations of Swift language topics are marked with **Swift Dive**.

- Watch for **Skills you'll learn in this section** to get a quick overview of specific new things you'll learn.

Section I: Your first app: HIITFit

At WWDC 2019, Apple surprised and delighted the developer community with the introduction of SwiftUI, a declarative way of building user interfaces. With SwiftUI, you build your user interface by combining fundamental components such as colors, buttons, text labels, lists and more into beautiful and functional views. Your views react to changes in the data they display, updating automatically without any intervention from you!

In this section, you'll begin your journey to becoming a SwiftUI developer by developing an app called HIITFit, a High Intensity Interval Training Fitness tracker. Along the way, you'll:

- Learn how to use Xcode.

- Discover how to plan and prototype an app.

- Explore the basic components of SwiftUI.

- Understand how data moves in a SwiftUI app and how to make it persist.

- Learn fundamental concepts of Swift, the programming language, needed to build your app.

Chapter 1: Checking Your Tools

By Audrey Tam

You're eager to dive into this book and create your first iOS app. If you've never used Xcode before, take some time to work through this chapter. You want to be sure your tools are working and learn how to use them efficiently.

Getting started

To develop iOS apps, you need a Mac with Xcode installed. If you want to run your apps on an iOS device, you need an Apple ID. And if you have an account on GitHub or similar, you'll be able to connect to that from Xcode.

macOS

To use the SwiftUI canvas, you need a Mac running **Catalina (v10.15)** or later. To install Xcode, your user account must have **administrator** status.

Xcode

To install Xcode, you need **29 GB** free space on your Mac's drive.

➤ Open the **App Store** app, then search for and **GET Xcode**. This is a large download so it takes a while. Plenty of time to fix yourself a snack while you wait. Or, to stay in the flow, browse Chapter 12, "Apple App Development Ecosystem".

➤ When the installation finishes, **OPEN** it from the App Store page:

Open Xcode after installing it from the App Store.

Note: You probably have your favorite way to open a Mac application, and it will work with Xcode, too. Double-click it in **Applications**. Or search for it in **Spotlight**. Or double-click a project's **.xcodeproj** file.

The first time you open Xcode after installation, you'll see this window: **Install additional required components?**:

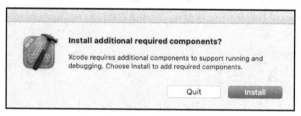

Install additional required components.

➤ Click **Install** and enter your **Mac login password** in the window that appears. This takes a little while, about enough time to make a cup of tea or coffee.

➤ When this installation process finishes, you might have to open Xcode again. The first time you open Xcode, you'll see this **Welcome** window:

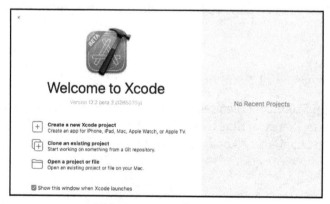

Welcome to Xcode window

If you don't want to see this window every time you open Xcode, uncheck "Show this window when Xcode launches". You can manually open this window from the Xcode menu **Window ▸ Welcome to Xcode** or press **Shift-Command-1**. And, there is an Xcode menu item to perform each of the actions listed in this window.

Creating a new Xcode project

You'll create a new Xcode project just for this chapter. The next chapter provides a starter project that you'll build on for the rest of Section 1.

➤ Click **Create a new Xcode project**. Or, if you want to do this without the Welcome window, press **Shift-Command-N** or select **File ▸ New ▸ Project...** from the menu.

A large set of choices appears:

Choose a template for your new project.

➤ Select **iOS** ▸ **App** and click **Next**. Now, you get to name your project:

Choose options for your new project:

Product Name:	FirstApp
Team:	None
Organization Identifier:	com.raywenderlich
Bundle Identifier:	com.raywenderlich.FirstApp
Interface:	SwiftUI
Life Cycle:	SwiftUI App
Language:	Swift
	☐ Use Core Data
	☐ Host in CloudKit
	☐ Include Tests

Cancel   Previous   Next

Choose options for your new project.

- For **Product Name**, type **FirstApp**.

- Skip **Team** for now.

- For **Organization Identifier**, type the *reverse-DNS* of your domain name. If you don't have a domain name, just type something that follows this pattern, like **org.audrey**. The grayed-out **Bundle Identifier** changes to **your-org-id.FirstApp**. When you submit your app to the App Store, this bundle identifier uniquely identifies your app.

- For **Interface**, select **SwiftUI**.

- For **Life Cycle**, select **SwiftUI App**.

- For **Language**, select **Swift**.

- Uncheck the checkboxes.

➤ Click **Next**. Here's where you decide where to save your new project.

Decide where to save your project.

Note: If you forget where you saved a project, you can find it by selecting **File ▸ Show in Finder** from the Xcode menu.

➤ If you're saving this project to a location that is **not** currently under source control, click the **Source Control** checkbox to create a local Git repository. Later in this chapter, you'll learn how to connect this to a remote repository.

➤ Click **Create**. Your new project appears, displaying **ContentView.swift** in the editor pane.

New project appears with ContentView.swift in the editor.

Looks like there's a lot going on! Don't worry, most iOS developers know enough about Xcode to do their job, but almost no one knows how to use *all* of it. Plus Apple changes and adds to it every year. The best (and only) way to learn it is to jump in and start using it.

Ready, set, jump!

A quick tour of Xcode

You'll spend most of your time working in a **.swift** file:

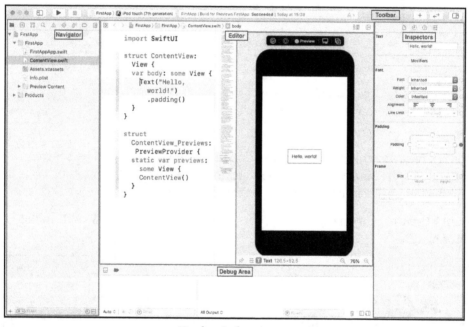

Xcode window panes

The Xcode window has three main panes: **Navigator**, **Editor** and **Inspectors**. When you're viewing a SwiftUI View file in the **Editor**, you can view the preview canvas side-by-side with the code. When the app is running, the **Debug Area** opens below the **Editor**.

You can hide or show the navigator with the toolbar button just above it, and the same for the inspectors. The debug area has a hide button in its own toolbar. You can also hide any of these three panes by dragging its border to the edge of the Xcode window.

And all three have keyboard shortcuts:

- Hide/show Navigator: **Command-0**

- Hide/show Inspectors: **Option-Command-0**

- Hide/show Debug Area: **Shift-Command-Y**

> **Note:** There's a handy cheat sheet of Xcode keyboard shortcuts in the assets folder for this chapter. Not a complete list, just the ones that many people use.

Navigator

The **Navigator** has nine tabs. When the navigator pane is hidden, you can open it directly in one of its tabs by pressing **Command-1** to **Command-9**:

1. **Project**: Add, delete or group files. Open a file in the editor.

2. **Source Control**: View Git repository working copies, branches, commits, tags, remotes and stashed changes.

3. **Symbol**: Hierarchical or flat view of the named objects and methods.

4. **Find**: Search tool.

5. **Issue**: Build-time and runtime errors and warnings.

6. **Test**: Create, manage and run unit and UI tests.

7. **Debug**: Information about CPU, memory, disk and network usage while your app is running.

8. **Breakpoint**: Add, delete, edit and manage breakpoints.

9. **Report**: View or export reports and logs generated when you build and run the project.

The **Filter** field at the bottom is different for each tab. For example, the **Project Filter** lets you show only the files you recently worked on. This is very handy for projects with a lot of files in a deeply nested hierarchy.

Editor

When you're working in a code file, the **Editor** shows the code and a **Minimap**. The minimap is useful for long code files with many properties and methods. You can hover the cursor over the minimap to locate a specific property, then click to go directly to it. You don't need it for the apps in this book, so you may want to hide it via the button in the upper right corner of the editor.

When you're working in a SwiftUI file, **Option-Command-Return** shows or hides the preview **canvas**.

The editor has browser features like tab and go back/forward. Keyboard shortcuts for tabs are the same as for web browsers: **Command-T** to open a new tab, **Shift-Command-[** or **]** to move to the previous or next tab, **Command-W** to close the tab and **Option-click** a tab's close button to close all the *other* tabs. The back/forward button shows a list of previous/next files, but the keyboard shortcuts are **Control-Command-right** or **-left arrow**.

Inspectors

The **Inspectors** pane has three or four tabs, depending on what's selected in the **Project** navigator. When this pane is hidden, you can open it directly in one of its tabs by pressing **Option-Command-1** to **Option-Command-4**:

1. **File**: Name, Full Path, Target Membership.

2. **History**: Source Control log.

3. **Quick Help**: Short form of Developer Documentation if you select a symbol in the editor.

4. **Attributes**: Properties of the symbol you select in the editor.

The fourth tab appears when you select a file in the Project navigator. If you select a folder, you get only the first three tabs.

This quick tour just brushes the surface of what you can do in Xcode. Next, you'll use a few of its tools while you explore your new project.

Navigation preferences

In this book, you'll use keyboard shortcuts to examine and structure your code. Unlike the fixed keyboard shortcuts for opening navigator tabs or inspectors, you can set preferences for which shortcut does what. To avoid confusion while working through this book, you'll set your preferences to match the instructions you'll see.

➤ Press **Command-,** to open **Preferences**. In the **Navigation** tab, set:

- **Command-click on Code** to **Selects Code Structure**

- **Option-click on Code** to **Shows Quick Help**

- **Navigation Style** to your choice of **Open in Tabs** or **Open in Place**.

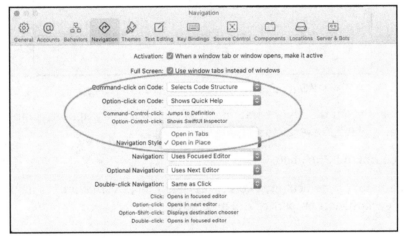

Set Navigation Preferences.

ContentView.swift

The heart of your new project is in **ContentView.swift**, where your new project opened. This is where you'll lay out the initial view of your app.

➤ If **ContentView.swift** isn't in the editor, select it in the Project navigator.

The first several lines are comments that identify the file and you, the creator.

import

The first line of code is an `import` statement:

```
import SwiftUI
```

This works just like in most programming languages. It allows your code to access everything in the built-in SwiftUI module. See what happens if it's missing.

➤ Click on the `import` statement, then press **Command-/**.

```
//import SwiftUI

struct ContentView: View {                                    ⊘  Cannot find type 'View' in scope
  var body: some View {                                        ⊘  Cannot find type 'View' in scope
    Text("Hello, world!")
      .padding()
  }
}

struct ContentView_Previews: PreviewProvider {   ⊘  Cannot find type 'PreviewProvider' in scope
  static var previews: some View {                             ⊘  Cannot find type 'View' in scope
    ContentView()
  }
}
```

What happens if import SwiftUI is missing

You commented out the `import` statement, so compiler errors appear, complaining about `View` and `PreviewProvider`.

➤ Press **Command-Z** to undo.

Below the `import` statement are two `struct` definitions. A *structure* is a named data type that encapsulates properties and methods.

struct ContentView

The name of the first structure matches the name of the file. Nothing bad happens if they're different, but most developers follow and expect this convention.

```
struct ContentView: View {
  var body: some View {
    Text("Hello, world!")
      .padding()
  }
}
```

Looking at `ContentView: View`, you might think `ContentView` *inherits* from `View`, but Swift structures don't have inheritance. `View` is a *protocol*, and `ContentView` *conforms* to this protocol.

The required component of the View protocol is the body computed property, which returns a View. In this case, it returns a Text view that displays the usual "Hello, world!" text.

> **Swift Tip**: If there's only a single code statement, you don't need to explicitly use the return keyword.

The Text view has a padding modifier — an instance method of View — that adds space around the text. You can see it in this screenshot:

Text padding and Quick Help

This also shows the **Quick Help** inspector for Text. If you don't want to use screen real estate for this inspector, **Option-click** Text in the code editor to see the same information in a pop-up window. Clicking **Open in Developer Documentation** opens a window with more information.

➤ Select the Text view in either the code editor or the canvas, then select the **Attributes inspector**. Click in the **Add Modifier** field and wait a short while until the modifiers menu appears:

Text attributes inspector and modifiers menu

Scrolling through this list goes on and on and on.

This inspector is useful when you want to add several modifiers to a View. If you just need to add one modifier, **Control-Option-click** the view to open the Attributes inspector pop-up window.

struct ContentView_Previews

Below ContentView is a ContentView_Previews structure.

```
struct ContentView_Previews: PreviewProvider {
  static var previews: some View {
    ContentView()
  }
}
```

The `ContentView_Previews` structure is what appears in the canvas on the right of the code editor. Again, see what happens if it's missing.

➤ Select the five lines of `ContentView_Previews` and press **Command-/**.

```
import SwiftUI

struct ContentView: View {
  var body: some View {
    Text("Hello, world!")
      .padding()
  }
}

//struct ContentView_Previews: PreviewProvider {
//  static var previews: some View {
//    ContentView()
//  }
//}
```

No PreviewProvider so there's nothing in the canvas.

Without `ContentView_Previews`, there's nothing in the canvas.

➤ Press **Command-Z** to undo or, if the five lines are still selected, press **Command-/** to uncomment them.

For most apps, **ContentView.swift** is just the starting point. Often, `ContentView` just defines the app's organization, orchestrating several subviews. And usually, you'll define these subviews in separate files.

Creating a new SwiftUI View file

Everything you see in a SwiftUI app is a `View`. Apple encourages you to create as many subviews as you need, to avoid redundancy (DRY or Don't Repeat Yourself) and organize your code to keep it manageable. The compiler takes care of creating efficient machine code, so your app's performance won't suffer.

➤ In the Project navigator, select **ContentView.swift** and type **Command-N**. Alternatively, right-click **ContentView.swift** then select **New File...** from the menu.

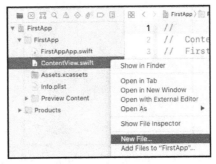

Select New File... from right-click menu.

> **Xcode Tip**: A new file appears in the project navigator below the currently selected file. If that's not where you want it, drag it to where you want it to appear in the project navigator.

The new file window displays a lot of options! The one you want is **iOS ▸ User Interface ▸ SwiftUI View**. In Chapter 5, "Organizing Your App's Data", you'll get to create a **Swift File**.

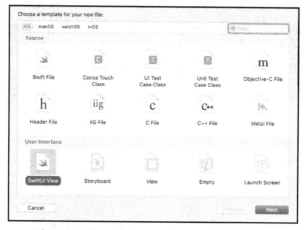

Choose iOS ▸ User Interface ▸ SwiftUI View.

Naming a new SwiftUI view

➤ Select **SwiftUI View** then click **Next**. The next window lets you specify a file name. By default, the name of the new view will be the same as the file name. You'll define the ByeView in this file, so replace **SwiftUIView** with **ByeView**.

SwiftUI view file name matches the new SwiftUI View.

> **Swift Tip**: Swift convention is to name types (like `struct`) with **UpperCamelCase** and properties and methods with **lowerCamelCase**.

This window also lets you specify where (in the project) to create your new file. The default location is usually correct: in this project, in this group (folder) and in this target.

➤ Click **Create** to finish creating your new file.

The template code for a SwiftUI view looks almost the same as the `ContentView` of a new project.

```swift
import SwiftUI

struct ByeView: View {
  var body: some View {
    Text("Hello, world!")
  }
}

struct ByeView_Previews: PreviewProvider {
  static var previews: some View {
    ByeView()
  }
}
```

Like `ContentView`, the view's body contains `Text("Hello, world!")`, but there's no padding.

Using your new SwiftUI view

Next, edit your new view's `Text` view string to look like this:

```swift
Text("Bye bye, World!")
```

Now, in **ContentView.swift**, in the code editor, delete the `Text` view, then type **bye**. Xcode suggests some auto-completions:

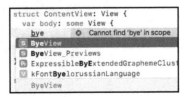

Xcode suggests auto-completions.

Notice you don't have to type the correct capitalization of `ByeView`.

> **Xcode Tip**: Descriptive names for your types, properties and methods is good programming practice, and auto-completion is one way Xcode helps you do the right thing. You can also turn on spell-checking from the Xcode menu: **Edit ▸ Format ▸ Spelling and Grammar ▸ Check Spelling While Typing**.

Select **ByeView** from the list, then add parentheses, so the line looks like this:

```
ByeView()
```

You're calling the initializer of `ByeView` to create an instance of the view.

➤ Click **Resume** or press **Option-Command-P** to refresh the preview:

```
struct ContentView: View {
  var body: some View {
    ByeView()
      .padding()
  }
}
```

Bye bye, World!

Replace Text view with ByeView.

You'll create many new SwiftUI view files and Swift files to develop the apps in this book.

What else is in your project?

The Project navigator lists several files and folders.

- **FirstAppApp.swift**: This file contains the code for your app's entry point. This is what actually launches your app.

```
@main
struct FirstAppApp: App {
  var body: some Scene {
    WindowGroup {
      ContentView()
    }
  }
}
```

The @main attribute marks FirstAppApp as the app's entry point. You might be accustomed to writing a main() method to actually launch an app. The App protocol takes care of this.

The App protocol requires only a computed property named body that returns a Scene. And a Scene is a container for the root view of a view hierarchy.

For an iOS app, the default setup is a WindowGroup scene containing ContentView() as its root view. A common customization is to set different root views, depending on whether the user has logged in.

In an iOS app, the view hierarchy fills the entire display. In a macOS or iPadOS app, WindowGroup can manage multiple windows.

- **Assets.xcassets**: Store your app's images and colors here. AppIcon is a special image set for all the different sizes and resolutions of your app's icon.

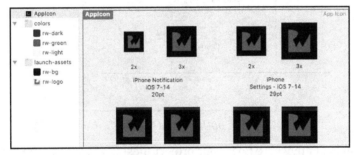

Assets: A small sample of an AppIcon set

- **Info.plist**: This configuration *property list* contains information needed to launch your app. Many of the names are environment variables derived from the options you set when you created the project. Here you can find things like the app name and version number.

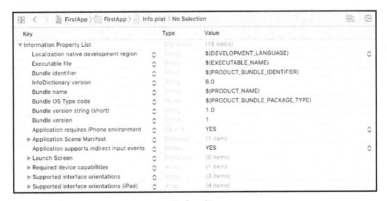

Info.plist

- **Preview Content**: If your views need additional code and sample data or assets while you're developing your app, store them here. They won't be included in the final distribution build of your app.

- **Products**: This is where Xcode stores your app after you build and run the project. A project can contain other products, like a Watch app or a framework.

In this list, the last two items are *groups*. Groups in the Project navigator appear to be folders, but they don't necessarily match up with folders in Finder. In particular, there's no **Products** folder in your project in Finder.

➤ In the Project navigator, select **Products ▸ FirstApp.app**, then show the **File inspector**:

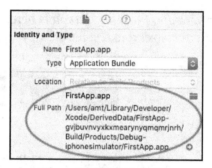

File path of FirstApp.app

FirstApp.app isn't anywhere near your project files! It's in your home directory's hidden **Library** folder.

> **Note**: Don't rename or delete any of these files or groups. Xcode stores their path names in the project's build settings and will flag errors if it can't find them.

You'll learn how to use these files in the rest of this book.

Xcode Preferences

Xcode has a huge number of preferences you can set to make your time in Xcode more productive.

Themes

You'll be spending a lot of time working in the code editor, so you want it to look good and also help you distinguish the different components of your code. Xcode provides several preconfigured font and color themes for you to choose from or modify.

➤ Press **Command-,** to open **Preferences**, then select the **Themes** tab:

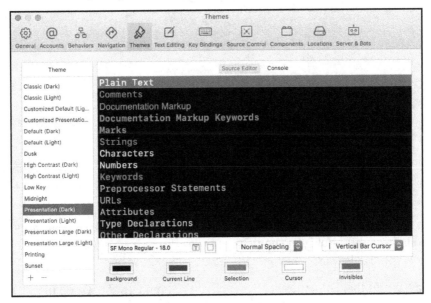

Preferences: Font and color themes

Go ahead and explore these. You can customize them or create your own. I'll wait here. ;]

Matching delimiters

SwiftUI code uses *a lot* of nested closures. It's really easy to mismatch your braces and parentheses. Xcode helps you find any mismatches and tries to prevent these errors from happening.

➤ In **Preferences**, select **Text Editing** ▸ **Editing**:

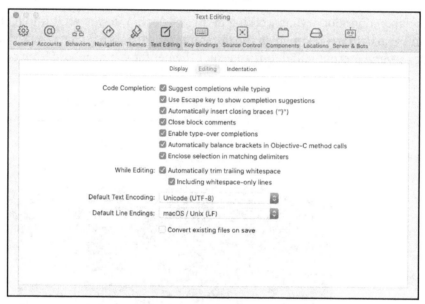

Preferences ▸ Text Editing ▸ Editing

Most of the **Code Completion** items are super helpful. Although you can copy and paste code from this book, you should try to type the code as much as possible to learn how these aids work.

Here's a big hint that something's wrong or you're typing in the wrong place: You're expecting Xcode to suggest completions while you type, but nothing (useful) appears. When this happens, it's usually because you're outside the closure you need to be in.

➤ Now select the **Text Editing ▸ Display** tab. Check **Code folding ribbon** and, if you like to see them, **Line numbers**:

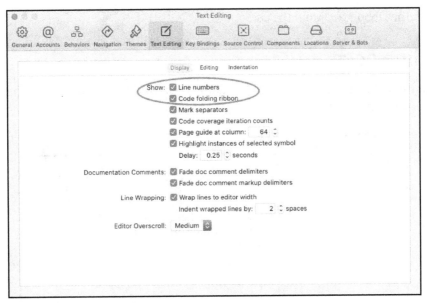

Preferences ▸ Text Editing ▸ Display

So what's a *code folding ribbon*? Between the line numbers and the code, you see darker gray vertical bars. Hover your cursor over one, and it highlights the start and end braces of that closure:

```
35   struct ContentView: View {
36     var body: some View {
37       ByeView()
38         .padding()
39     }
40   }
```

Code folding ribbon: Hover to show braces.

Other ways to see matching delimiters:

- **Option-hover** over {, (, [or a closing delimiter: Xcode highlights the start and end delimiters.

- **Double-click** a delimiter: Xcode selects the delimiters and their contents.

➤ Now click the bar (ribbon) to collapse (fold) those lines of code:

```
35   struct ContentView: View {
36     var body: some View { ••• }
40   }
```

Code folding ribbon: Click to fold code.

This can be incredibly useful when you're trying to find your way around some complex deeply-nested code.

➤ Click the ribbon to unfold the code.

Adding accounts

You can access some Xcode features by adding login information for your Apple ID and source control accounts.

➤ In **Preferences**, select **Accounts**:

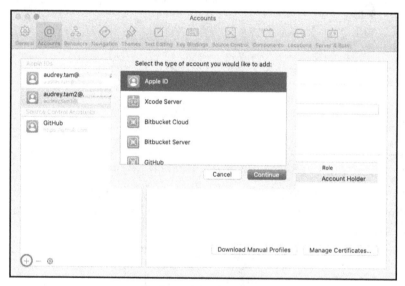

Preferences ▸ Accounts

➤ Add your Apple ID. If you have a separate paid Apple Developer account, add that too.

To run your app on a device, you'll need to select a **Team**. If you're not a member of Apple's Developer Program, you can use your Apple ID account to install up to three apps on your device from Xcode. The app works for seven days after you install it.

To add capabilities like push notifications or Apple Pay to your app, you need to set **Team** to a Developer Program account.

Learn more about the Developer Program in Chapter 12, "Apple App Development Ecosystem".

- If you have an account at Bitbucket, GitHub or GitLab, add it here if you want to push your project's local git repository to a remote repository.

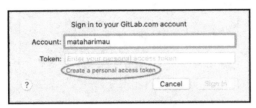

Add a source control account.

Bitbucket, GitHub and GitLab accounts require a *personal access token*. Click the link to open the site's token-creation page.

➤ To set up a remote repository, open the Source Control navigator (**Command-2**), then click the settings button and select **New "FirstApp" Remote…**:

New Remote…

➤ Select your options, then click **Create**:

Create-remote options

And here it is:

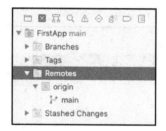

New remote created.

Running your project

So far, you've relied on Preview to see what your app looks like. In the next chapter, you'll use Live Preview to interact with your app. But some features don't work in Live Preview, so then you need to build and run your app on a simulator. And some things will only work on an iOS device. Plus, it's fun to have something on your iPhone that you built yourself!

The Xcode toolbar

First, a quick tour of the toolbar:

Xcode window toolbar

Xcode Tip: Press **Option-Command-T** to show or hide the toolbar. If this keyboard shortcut conflicts with another app, select the command from the Xcode **View** menu.

So far, you've only used the buttons at either end of the toolbar, to show or hide the navigator or inspector panes.

Working from left to right after the navigation pane button:

- **Run** button: Build and run (**Command-R**) the project.

- **Stop** button: Stop (**Command-.**) the running project.

- **Scheme** menu: This button's label is the name of the app. Select, edit or manage *schemes*. Each product has a scheme. FirstApp has only one product, so it has only one scheme.

- **Run destination** menu: This menu defaults to its last item, currently iPod touch. Select a connected device or a simulated device to run the project.

- **Activity** view: A wide gray field that shows the project name, status messages and warning or error indicators.

- **Library** button: Label is a + sign. Opens the library of views, modifiers, code snippets and media and colors stored in Assets. **Option-click** this button to keep the library open.

- **Code review** button: If this project has a local git repository, this button shows a `diff` of the current version of the current file and the most recent committed version. You can choose earlier committed versions from a menu.

Now that you know where the controls are, it's time to use some of them.

Choosing a run destination

Apple sells a lot of different iPhone models, plus iPads and even an iPod Touch. They're all different sizes, and some have a notch. How do you know if your app looks good on every screen size?

You don't need a complete collection of iOS devices. Xcode has several **Developer Tools**, and one of them is **Simulator**. The run destination menu lets you choose from a list of simulated devices.

➤ Click the run destination button and select **iPhone 12 Pro**.

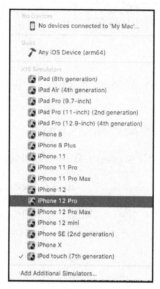

Run destination menu

➤ Refresh the preview of `ContentView` or `ByeView`:

Preview device is run destination.

The preview uses the run destination device by default. You can create more than one preview and set each to a different device with the `previewDevice` modifier.

For example:

```swift
struct ContentView_Previews: PreviewProvider {
  static var previews: some View {
    Group {
      ContentView()
      ContentView()
        .previewDevice("iPhone SE (2nd generation)")
    }
  }
}
```

Preview of two devices

The preview usually looks the same as your app running on a simulated or real device, but not always. If you feel the preview doesn't match what your code is laying out, try running it on a simulator.

Note: To zoom in or out on the preview canvas, use the + or - buttons in the canvas toolbar.

Build and run

➤ Click the run button or press **Command-R**.

The first time you run a project on a simulated device, it starts from an "off" state, so you'll see a loading indicator. Until you quit the Simulator app, this particular simulated device is now "awake", so you won't get the startup delay even if you run a different project on it.

After the simulated device starts up, the app's launch screen appears. For FirstApp, this is just a blank screen. You'll learn how to set up your own launch screen in Chapter 16, "Adding Assets to Your App".

And now, your app is running!

Debug navigator and debug area

There's not much happening in this app, but the debug toolbar appears below the editor window. For this screenshot, I showed the debug area, selected the **Debug** tab in the navigator pane, then selected the **CPU** item.

Not stopping

Here's a trick that will make your Xcode life a little easier.

➤ **Don't click** the stop button. Yes, it's enabled. But trust me, you'll like this. :]

➤ In **ByeView.swift**, replace "Bye bye" with "Hello again":

```
Text("Hello again, World!")
```

➤ Click the run button or press **Command-R**.

Up pops this message:

Check do-not-show-this-again.

➤ **Don't click Stop**, although that will work: The currently running process will stop, and the new process will run. And this will happen every time you forget to stop the app. It takes just a moment, but it jars a little. Every time. And it's easy to get rid of.

➤ Check **Do not show this message again**, *then* click **Stop**.

The app loads with your new change. But that's not what I want to show you.

➤ One more time: Click the run button or press **Command-R**.

No annoying message, no "doh!" moment, ever again! You're welcome. ;]

Running your apps on an iOS device

Sometimes, your app doesn't look or behave quite right on the simulated device. Running it on a real device is the final word: It might look just as you expect, or it might agree with the preview and simulator that you've got more work to do.

Also, there are features like motion and camera that you can't test in a simulator. For these, you must install your app on a real device.

Apple does its best to protect its users from malicious apps. Part of this protection is ensuring Apple knows who is responsible for every app on your device. Before you can install your app from Xcode onto your device, you need to select a team (your Apple ID), to get a signing certificate from Apple.

➤ In the project page, select the **target**. In the **Signing & Capabilities** tab, check **Automatically manage signing**, then select your account from the **Team** menu:

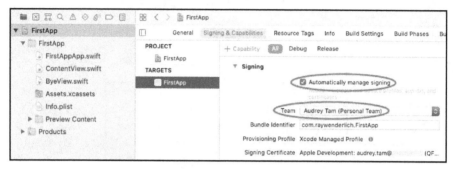

Target ▸ Signing ▸ Team

After some activity spinning, you'll see a **Provisioning Profile** and a **Signing Certificate**. Xcode has created these and stored the certificate in your Mac's keychain.

> **Note**: The **Bundle Identifier** of your project uses your organization name because you created it as a new project. The other apps in this book have starter projects with **com.raywenderlich** as the organization. If you want to run these apps on an iOS device, you need to change the organization name in the bundle ID to something that's uniquely yours. This is because one of the authors has already signed the app with the original bundle ID, and you're not a member of our teams.

To run this book's apps on your iOS device, it must have **iOS 14** installed. If it's not the absolute latest update, select the **project**, then set its **iOS Deployment Target** to match your device.

Set deployment target to match your device.

➤ Connect your device to your Mac with a cable. Use an Apple cable, as other-brand cables might not work for this purpose.

> **Note:** If your account is a paid Apple Developer account, you won't need to do the next several steps. Running your app on your device will just work.

The first time you connect a device to your Mac, the device will ask **Trust This Computer?**

Trust This Computer?

➤ Tap **Trust**, then enter the device passcode when prompted.

➤ Select your device from the run destination menu: It appears at the top, above the simulators:

Select your device as the run destination.

➤ Unlock your device, then build and run your project. Keep your device screen active until the app launches on your device.

This is the first time you're running an app on a device, so there are several extra steps that Apple makes you perform, mainly trying to make sure nothing nasty installs itself on your device.

➤ First, you need to allow **codesign** to access the certificate that Xcode stored in your keychain:

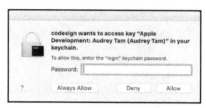

Allow access to the certificate in your keychain.

➤ Enter your password, then click **Always Allow**.

Next, you'll see FirstApp's app icon appear on the screen of your device, but this error message appears on your Mac:

Could not launch FirstApp

Of the three possible reasons, it's the last one that's holding things up: *its profile has not been explicitly trusted by the user.* Apple *really* doesn't want just anyone installing potentially malicious apps on your device. *You* have to say it's OK. The problem is, there's not much here to tell you what to do.

➤ Well, the app icon is on your device's screen, so why not tap it to see what happens?

Untrusted Developer

You can allow using these apps in Settings is a pretty minimal hint, but open **Settings** to see what's there. You'll probably never guess where to look, so here are the relevant screenshots:

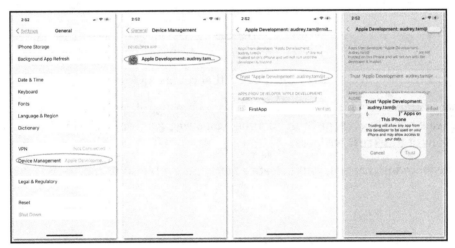

Settings ... Trust your certificate

➤ Tap **General**. Scroll down to **Device Management** — you can just see the start of your certificate name. Tap this item.

➤ Tap **Apple Development...**, then tap **Trust "Apple Development...** and finally, tap **Trust**.

You won't need to do this again unless you delete all your apps from this device.

➤ Now close **Settings** and tap the **FirstApp** icon:

FirstApp running on an iPhone

Underwhelming? Yes, well, it's the thought that counts. ;]

What matters is, you're now all set up to run your own projects on this device. When you really want to get something running *right away*, you won't have to stop and deal with any of this **Trust** business.

In the following chapters, you'll create a much more interesting app.

Key points

- The Xcode window has Navigator, Editor and Inspectors panes, a Toolbar and a Debug Area, plus a huge number of Preferences.

- You can set some navigation keyboard shortcuts in Preferences, to match the instructions in this book.

- The template project defines an App that launches with ContentView, which displays "Hello, world!" in a Text view.

- You can view Quick Help documentation in an inspector or by using a keyboard shortcut. Or, you can open the Developer Documentation window.

- When you create a new SwiftUI view file, give it the same name as the View you'll create in it.

- Xcode's auto-completion, delimiter-matching, code-folding and spell-checking help you avoid errors.

- You can choose one of Xcode's font and color themes, modify one or create your own.

- You can run your app on a simulated device or create previews of specific devices.

- You must add an Apple ID account in Xcode Preferences to run your app on an iOS device.

- The first time you run your project on an iOS device, Apple requires you to complete several "Trust" steps.

Chapter 2: Planning a Paged App

By Audrey Tam

In Section 1 of this book, you'll build an app to help you do high-intensity interval training. Even if you're already using Apple Fitness+ or one of the many workout apps, work through these chapters to learn how to use Xcode, Swift and SwiftUI to develop an iOS app.

In this chapter, you'll plan your app, then set up the paging interface. You'll start using the SwiftUI Attributes inspector to add modifiers. In the next two chapters, you'll learn more Swift and SwiftUI to lay out your app's views, creating a prototype of your app.

Making lists: views and actions

This app has several screens. Here's a sample to show you what the app will look like when you're finished.

HIITFit screens

There's a lot going on in these screens, especially the one with the exercise video.

You might feel overwhelmed, wondering where to start. Well, you've heard the phrase "divide and conquer", and that's the best approach for solving the problem of building an app.

First, you need an inventory of what you're going to divide. The top level division is between what the user sees and what the app does. Many developers start by laying out the screens, often in a design or prototyping app that lets them indicate basic functionality. For example, when the user taps *this* button, the app shows *this* screen. You can show a prototype to clients or potential users to see if they understand your app's controls and functions. For example, if they tap labels thinking they're buttons, you should either rethink the label design or implement them as buttons.

Listing what your user sees

To start, list the screens you need to create and describe their contents:

- A **Welcome** screen with text, images and a button.

- A title and page numbers are at the top of the **Welcome** screen and a **History** button is at the bottom. These are also on the screen with the exercise video. The page numbers indicate there are four numbered pages after this page. The waving hand symbol is highlighted.

- The screen with the exercise video also has a timer, a **Start/Done** button and rating symbols. One of the page numbers is highlighted.

- The **History** screen shows the user's exercise history as a list and as a bar chart. It has a title but no page numbers and no **History** button.

- The **High Five!** screen has an image, some large text and some small gray text. Like the **History** screen, it has no page numbers and no **History** button.

In this chapter and the next, you'll lay out the basic elements of these screens. In Chapter 10, "Refining Your App", you'll fine-tune the appearance to look like the screenshots above.

Listing what your app does

Next, list the functionality of each screen, starting with the last two.

- The **History** and **High Five!** screens are *modal sheets* that slide up over the **Welcome** or **Exercise** screen. Each has a button the user taps to dismiss it, either a circled "X" or a **Continue** button.

- On the **Welcome** and **Exercise** screens, the matching page number is white text or outline on a black background. Tapping the **History** button displays the **History** screen.

- The **Welcome** page **Get Started** button displays the next page.

- On an **Exercise** page, the user can tap the play button to play the video of the exercise.

- On an **Exercise** page, tapping the **Start** button starts a countdown timer, and the button label changes to **Done**. Ideally, the **Done** button is disabled until the timer reaches 0. Tapping **Done** adds this exercise to the user's history for the current day.

- On an **Exercise** page, tapping one of the five rating symbols changes the color of that symbol and all those preceding it.

- Tapping **Done** on the last exercise shows the **High Five!** screen.

- Nice to have: Tapping a page number goes to that page. Tapping **Done** on an **Exercise** page goes to the next **Exercise** page. Dismissing the **High Five!** screen returns to the **Welcome** page.

You'll implement all of these in Chapter 6, "Adding Functionality to Your App".

There's also the overarching page-based structure of HIITFit. This is quite easy to implement in SwiftUI, so you'll do it first, before you create any screens.

Creating Pages

Skills you'll learn in this section: adding a Git repository to an existing project; visual editing of SwiftUI views; using the pop-up Attributes inspector; TabView styles

The main purpose of this section is to set up the page-based structure of HIITFit, but you'll also learn a lot about using Xcode, Swift and SwiftUI. The short list of **Skills** at the start of each section helps you keep track of what's where.

Adding source control to an existing project

In Chapter 1, "Checking Your Tools", you created a new project. But HIITFit has a starter project with some assets and utility code. You'll add files and code to this starter project.

➤ Open this chapter's **starter** folder in **Finder** and locate **HIITFit/ HIITFit.xcodeproj**. **Double-click** this file to open it in Xcode.

This project doesn't have a Git repository. You could use the git init command line, but Xcode provides a quick way.

➤ In the **Xcode** menu, select **Source Control ▸ New Git Repositories....**

Xcode's Source Control menu

A window appears with your project checked.

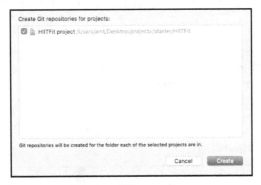

Create a Git repository.

➤ Click **Create**.

Now you'll see markers when you modify or add files, and you can commit every major addition as you build this app. I'll suggest the first few commits, then it will be up to you to make sure you commit a working copy before undertaking a new task.

Canvas and editor always in sync

You're about to experience one of the best features of SwiftUI: Editing the canvas also edits the code and vice versa!

And here's your first SwiftUI vocabulary term: Everything you can see on the device screen is a *view*, with larger views containing subviews.

Your next SwiftUI term is *modifier*: SwiftUI has an enormous number of methods you can use to modify the appearance or behavior of a view.

➤ First, in **ContentView.swift**, delete `.padding()` from the body closure: It's a modifier that adds space around the `Text` view, and you don't need it for now.

➤ In the canvas, click **Resume** if you don't see `ContentView`, then double-click the `Text` view: You've selected "Hello world" in the code:

Double-click in canvas selects text in code editor.

➤ Now type **Welcome**: You've changed the text in both the canvas and the code.

Editing code changes the view in the canvas.

> **Note:** Don't press **enter** after typing **Welcome**. If necessary, refresh the preview.

The Text view just displays a string of characters. It's useful for listing the views you plan to create, as a kind of outline. You'll use multiple Text views now, to see how to implement paging behavior.

➤ Click anywhere outside the Text view to deselect "Welcome", then select the Text view again. Press **Command-D**:

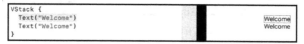

Command-D duplicates a view.

As you probably expected, you've *duplicated* the Text view. But look at the code:

```
VStack {
  Text("Welcome")
  Text("Welcome")
}
```

Your two Text views are now embedded in a VStack! When you have more than one view, you must specify how to arrange them on the canvas. Xcode knows this, so it provided the default arrangement, which displays the two Text views in a *vertical stack*.

➤ Change "V" to "H" to see the two views displayed in a *horizontal stack*:

HStack stacks its views horizontally.

➤ Type **Command-Z** to undo this change. SwiftUI's defaults tend to match up well with what most people want to do.

➤ Change the second "Welcome" to **Exercise 1**. Then duplicate "Exercise 1" and change the third string to **Exercise 2**.

```
VStack {
  Text("Welcome")
  Text("Exercise 1")
  Text("Exercise 2")
}
```

Three Text views in a VStack

Now you have three distinct views to use in a TabView.

Using TabView

Here's how easy it is to create a `TabView`:

➤ Change `VStack` to **TabView**:

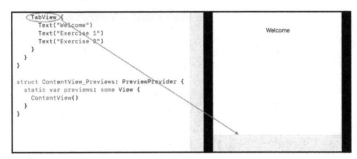

A TabView has a tab bar.

Where did your Exercises go!? Well, they're now the second and third tabs of a tab view, and there's a tab bar at the bottom of the screen. It's blank, because you haven't labeled the tabs yet.

Here's how you label the tabs. It's actually very quick to do, but it looks like a lot because you'll be learning how to use the SwiftUI Attributes inspector.

➤ In the canvas or in the editor, **Control-Option-click** the "Welcome" Text view to pop up its *Attributes inspector*:

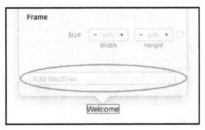

Control-Option-Click to show the Attributes inspector.

Xcode Tip: The show-inspectors button (upper right toolbar) opens the right-hand panel. The *Attributes inspector* is the right-most tab in this panel. If you're working on a small screen and just want to edit one attribute, **Control-Option-click** a view to use the pop-up inspector. It uses less space.

➤ Click in the **Add Modifier** field, then type **tab** and select **Tab Item** from the menu:

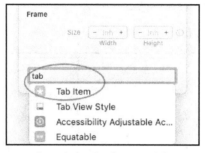

Select the Tab Item modifier.

A new `tabItem` modifier appears in the editor, with a placeholder for the *Item Label*:

```
Text("Welcome")
  .tabItem { Item Label }
```

And a blue **Label** appears in the tab bar:

```
TabView {
  Text("Welcome")
    .tabItem {             }|
```

A tab item with default label

➤ Select the *Item Label* placeholder and type **Text("Welcome")**:

```
.tabItem { Text("Welcome") }
```

And there it is in the tab bar:

```
TabView {
  Text("Welcome")
    .tabItem { Text("Welcome") }
```

Result of replacing the placeholder tab item label

➤ Replace the entire `TabView` with the following to add the labels for the other tabs:

```
TabView {
  Text("Welcome")
    .tabItem { Text("Welcome") }
  Text("Exercise 1")
    .tabItem { Text("Exercise 1") }
  Text("Exercise 2")
    .tabItem { Text("Exercise 2") }
}
```

Now you can see the three tab labels:

```
TabView {
  Text("Welcome")
    .tabItem { Text("Welcome") }
  Text("Exercise 1")
    .tabItem { Text("Exercise 1") }
  Text("Exercise 2")
    .tabItem { Text("Exercise 2") }
```

Three tab items with labels

The canvas preview is a great way to get continuous feedback on the appearance of your view but, at this point, you probably want to see it in action. That's where **Live Preview** can help.

➤ Click the **Live Preview** button to see how this would work on a device:

The Live Preview button

The first time takes a while, but subsequent live previews will refresh faster. If the **Resume** button appears, click it or press **Option-Command-P**.

➤ Now tap a tab label to switch to that tab. This is the way tab views normally operate. To make the tabs behave like pages, add this modifier to the `TabView`:

```
.tabViewStyle(PageTabViewStyle())
```

And now your tab labels are gone!

The page style uses small index dots, but they're white on white, so you can't see them.

➤ To make them show up, add this modifier below `tabViewStyle`:

```
.indexViewStyle(
  PageIndexViewStyle(backgroundDisplayMode: .always))
```

Now you can see the index dots:

TabView page style index dots

➤ Check out the **Live Preview**: Just swipe left or right and each page snaps into place.

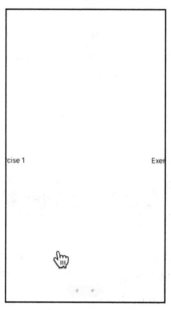

Live Preview: TabView page style in mid-swipe

➤ You won't be using `tabItem` labels for this app, so delete them. This is all the code inside the `TabView` closure:

```
TabView {
   Text("Welcome")
   Text("Exercise 1")
   Text("Exercise 2")
}
```

OK, you've set up the paging behavior, but you want the pages to be actual **Welcome** and **Exercise** views, not just text. To keep your code organized and easy to read, you'll create each view in its own file and group all the view files in a folder.

Grouping files

Skills you'll learn in this section: creating and grouping project files

You're about to create **Welcome** and **Exercise** subviews by combining smaller subviews. SwiftUI encourages you to create reusable subviews for the same reason you create functions: *Don't Repeat Yourself.* Even if you don't reuse a subview, it makes your code much easier to read. And SwiftUI compiles subviews into efficient machine code, so you can create all the subviews you need and not worry about performance.

➤ Select **ContentView.swift** in the Project navigator. Create a **new SwiftUI View file** named **WelcomeView.swift**. Then, create another **new SwiftUI View file** named **ExerciseView.swift**.

Your Project navigator now contains three view files:

Project navigator after you add two SwiftUI view files

You'll create several more view files, so now you'll create a *group folder* with these three and name it **Views**.

➤ Select the three view files, then right-click and select **New Group from Selection**:

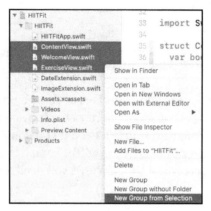

Create a group folder containing the three view files.

➤ Name the group **Views**.

Group folders just help you organize all the files in your project. In Chapter 5, "Organizing Your App's Data", you'll create a folder for your app's data models.

Passing parameters

Skills you'll learn in this section: default initializers; arrays; `let`, `var`, `Int`; **Fix** button in error messages; placeholders in auto-completions

➤ Back in `ContentView`, replace the first two `Text` placeholders with your new views:

```
TabView {
  WelcomeView()   // was Text("Welcome")
  ExerciseView()  // was Text("Exercise 1")
  Text("Exercise 2")
}
```

Swift Tip: A `View` is a *structure*, shortened to `struct` in Swift code. Like a class, it's a complex data type that encapsulates properties and methods. If a `View` has no uninitialized properties, you can create an instance of it with its default initializer. For example, `WelcomeView()` creates an instance of `WelcomeView`.

Now what? Your app will use `ExerciseView` to display the name and video for several different exercises, so you need a way to index this data and pass each index to `ExerciseView`.

Actually, first you need some sample exercise data. In the **Videos** folder, you'll find four videos:

One of the exercise videos

Note: If you prefer to use your own videos, drag them from **Finder** into the Project navigator. Be sure to check the **Add to targets** check box.

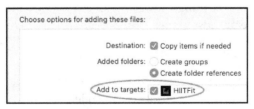

If you add your own videos, check Add to targets.

➤ In Chapter 5, "Organizing Your App's Data", you'll create an Exercise data type but, for this prototype, in **ExerciseView.swift**, simply create two arrays at the top of ExerciseView, just above var body:

```
let videoNames = ["squat", "step-up", "burpee", "sun-salute"]
let exerciseNames = ["Squat", "Step Up", "Burpee", "Sun Salute"]
```

Swift Tip: An array is an ordered collection of structure instances or class objects. All the instances or objects in an array are the same type.

The video names match the names of the video files. The exercise names are visible to your users, so you use title capitalization and spaces.

➤ Still inside ExerciseView, above the var body property, add this property:

```
let index: Int
```

Swift Tip: Swift distinguishes between creating *constants* with let and creating *variables* with var.

Xcode now complains about ExerciseView() in previews, because it's missing the index parameter.

➤ Click the red error icon to display more information:

```
struct ExerciseView_Previews: PreviewProvider {
  static var previews: some View {
    ExerciseView()
  }
}
```
⊘ Missing argument for parameter 'index' in call   ⊗
Insert 'index: <#Int#>'   Fix

Open the error to show the Fix button.

Xcode often suggests one or more ways to fix an error. Many times, its suggestion is correct, and this is one of those times.

➤ Click **Fix** to let Xcode fill in the index parameter.

➤ Now there's a placeholder for the index value — a grayed-out Int. Click it to turn it blue and type **0**. So now you have this line of code:

```
ExerciseView(index: 0)
```

> **Swift Tip**: Like other languages descended from the C programming language, Swift arrays start counting from 0, not 1.

Now use your `index` property to display the correct name for each exercise.

➤ Change `"Hello, World!"` to the exercise name for this `index` value.

```
Text(exerciseNames[index])
```

Back in **ContentView.swift**, Xcode is also complaining about the missing index parameter in `ExerciseView()`.

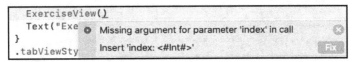

Another error to fix

➤ Fix this error the same way you did in **ExerciseView.swift**.

Now there's a placeholder for the `index` value: What should you type there?

Looping

> **Skills you'll learn in this section**: `ForEach`, `Range` vs. `ClosedRange`; developer documentation; initializers with parameters

Well, you *could* pass the first array index:

```
ExerciseView(index: 0)
```

Then copy-paste and edit to specify the other three exercises, but there's a better way. You're probably itching to use a *loop*. Here's how you scratch that itch. ;]

➤ Replace the second and third lines in `TabView` with this code:

```
ForEach(0 ..< 4) { index in
    ExerciseView(index: index)
}
```

`ForEach` loops over the *range* 0 to 4 but, because of that < symbol, **not including 4**.

Each integer value 0, 1, 2 and 3 creates an `ExerciseView` with that `index` value. The local variable name `index` is up to you. You could write this code instead:

```
ForEach(0 ..< 4) { number in
  ExerciseView(index: number)
}
```

Developer Documentation

➤ This is a good opportunity to check out Xcode's built in documentation. Hold down the **Option** key, then click `..<`:

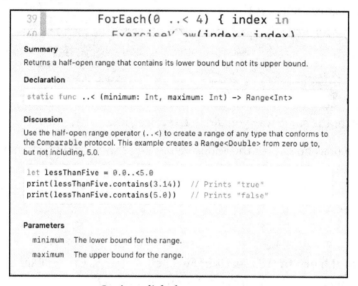

Option-click the ..< operator.

You're viewing Xcode's pop-up **Quick Help** for the *half-open range operator*. You can also view this information in the **Quick Help inspector**.

➤ Now **Option-click** `ForEach`:

Summary

A structure that computes views on demand from an underlying collection of of identified data.

Declaration

```
struct ForEach<Data, ID, Content> where Data :
RandomAccessCollection, ID : Hashable
```

Open in Developer Documentation

Quick Help for ForEach

➤ Not much information here. Click **Open in Developer Documentation** to see more detailed information.

```
init(Range<Int>, content: (Int) -> Content)
    Creates an instance that computes views on demand over a given constant range.
    Available when Data is Range<Int>, ID is Int, and Content conforms to View.

init(Data, content: (Data.Element) -> Content)
    Creates an instance that uniquely identifies and creates views across updates based on
    the identity of the underlying data.
    Available when Data conforms to RandomAccessCollection, ID is Data.Element.ID, Content
    conforms to View, and Data.Element conforms to Identifiable.

init(Data, id: KeyPath<Data.Element, ID>, content: (Data.Element) ->
Content)
    Creates an instance that uniquely identifies and creates views across updates based on
    the provided key path to the underlying data's identifier.
    Available when Data conforms to RandomAccessCollection, ID conforms to Hashable, and Content
    conforms to View.
```

Developer Documentation for ForEach: Three initializers

The topic **Creating a Collection of Views** contains three initializers. The first is the one you're using to loop over the array indices.

```
init(Range<Int>, content: (Int) -> Content)
```

➤ This ForEach initializer requires Range<Int>. Click this line to open the init(_:content:) page, then click Range in its **Declaration** to open the Range page. Sure enough, Range is "A half-open interval from a lower bound up to, but not including, an upper bound", which matches the Quick Help you saw for ..<.

➤ Close the documentation window.

➤ You won't need the TabView index dots. Open **ContentView.swift** and change:

```
.tabViewStyle(PageTabViewStyle())
.indexViewStyle(
  PageIndexViewStyle(backgroundDisplayMode: .always))
```

to:

```
.tabViewStyle(PageTabViewStyle(indexDisplayMode: .never))
```

Now, you'll never show the index dots.

This is a good place to commit the changes you've made to your project with a commit message like "Set up paging tab view."

> **Xcode Tip**: To commit changes to your local Git repository, select **Source Control ▸ Commit...** or press **Option-Command-C**. If asked, check all the changed files. Enter a commit message, then click **Commit**.

You're still in ContentView, so **Live Preview** your app. Swipe from one page to the next to see the different exercise names.

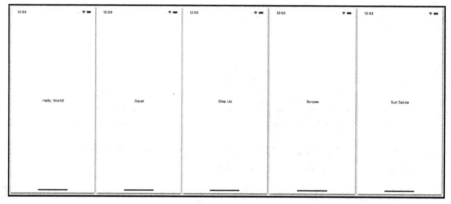

HIITFit pages

Key points

- Plan your app by listing what the user will see and what the app will do.

- Build your app with views and subviews, customized with modifiers.

- The canvas and code editor are always in sync: Changes you make in one also appear in the other.

- Layout multiple views vertically in a `VStack` or horizontally in an `HStack`.

- The Attributes inspector helps you to modify a view or a preview.

- `ForEach` lets you loop over a half-open range of numbers.

- `TabView` can behave like a tab view or like a page controller.

- You can preview or live preview your view in the canvas.

Where to go from here?

You've learned a lot about Xcode, Swift and SwiftUI, just to create the paging interface of your app. Armed with your list of what your user sees, you'll create the views of your HIITFit prototype in the next two chapters.

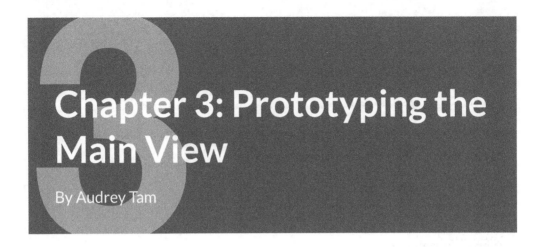

Chapter 3: Prototyping the Main View

By Audrey Tam

Now for the fun part! In this chapter, you'll start creating a prototype of your app, which has four full-screen views:

- Welcome

- Exercise

- History

- Success

Creating the Exercise view

You'll start by laying out the **Exercise** view, because it contains the most subviews. Here's the list of what your user sees in this view:

- A title and page numbers are at the top of the view and a **History** button is at the bottom.

- The page numbers indicate there are four numbered pages.

- The exercise view contains a video player, a timer, a **Start/Done** button and rating symbols.

And here's the list rewritten as a list of subviews:

- Header with page numbers

- Video player

- Timer

- Start/Done button

- Rating

- History button

You *could* sketch your screens in an app like Sketch or Figma before translating the designs into SwiftUI views. But SwiftUI makes it easy to lay out views directly in your project, so that's what you'll do.

The beauty of SwiftUI is it's declarative: You just *declare* the views you want to display, in the order you want them to appear. If you've created web pages, it's a similar experience.

Outlining the Exercise view

➤ Continue with your project from the previous chapter or open the project in this chapter's **starter** folder.

There's a lot to do in this view, so you'll start by creating an outline with placeholder Text views.

➤ Open **ExerciseView.swift**.

➤ The canvas preview uses the run destination simulated device by default. You'll start by laying out the interface for the iPad version of HIITFit, so select an **iPad simulator**:

Select an iPad simulator.

➤ If the iPad doesn't fit in the canvas, zoom out:

Zoom out to fit the iPad in the canvas.

➤ `ExerciseView` has six subviews, so duplicate the `Text(exerciseNames[index])` view, then edit the arguments — in the code or in the canvas — to create this list:

```
VStack {
   Text(exerciseNames[index])
   Text("Video player")
   Text("Timer")
   Text("Start/Done button")
   Text("Rating")
   Text("History button")
}
```

The first `Text` view is the starting point for the **Header** view. You'll create the **Header** and **Rating** views in their own files. The video player, timer and buttons are simple views, so you'll just create them directly in `ExerciseView`.

Creating the Header view

Skills you'll learn in this section: modifying views using the Attributes inspector or auto-suggestions; method signatures with internal and external parameter names; using SF Symbols; `Image` view; extracting and configuring subviews; working with previews

You'll create this **Header** view by adding code to `ExerciseView`, then you'll extract it as a subview and move it to its own file.

➤ To prepare for the later extraction, embed the first `Text` view in a `VStack`: Hold down the **Command** key, click `Text(exerciseNames[index])` then select **Embed in VStack**:

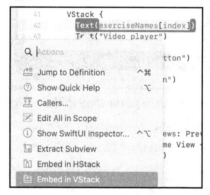

Use the Command-click menu to embed this Text view in a VStack.

Note: This version of the **Command-click** menu appears only when the canvas is open. If you don't see the **Embed in VStack** option, press **Option-Command-Return** to open the canvas.

Now this `Text` view is inside a `VStack`:

```
VStack {
  Text(exerciseNames[index])
}
```

The many ways to modify a view

➤ In the canvas, select the "Squat" Text view. To open the **Attributes inspector**, click the **inspectors** button in the toolbar, then select the **Attributes inspector**:

Open the inspectors pane and select the Attributes inspector.

This inspector has sections for the most commonly-used modifiers: Font, Padding and Frame. You *could* select a font size from the **Font ▸ Font** menu, but you'll use the search field this time. This is a more general approach to adding modifiers.

➤ Click in the **Add Modifier** field, then type **font** and select **Font** from the menu:

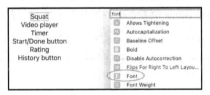

Select Font from the Add Modifier menu.

The font size of "Squat" changes in both the canvas and in code:

```
.font(.title)
```

➤ Xcode suggests the font size `title`, but this is only a placeholder. To "accept" this value, click `.title`, then press **Return** to set it as the value.

> **Note**: Xcode and SwiftUI do a good job of auto-suggesting or defaulting to an option that is probably what you want.

➤ To see other options, **Control-Option-click** font or `title`. This opens the font modifier's pop-up Attributes inspector. In the **Font** section, click the selected **Font** option **Title** to see the **Font** menu:

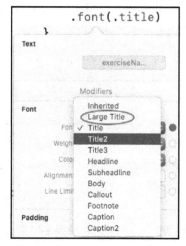

Show the Font menu in the Attributes inspector for font or title.

➤ Select **Large Title** from the menu: Now "Squat" is even bigger!

Title with Large Title font

> **Note**: Putting the modifier on its own line is a SwiftUI convention. A view often has several modifiers, each on its own line. This makes it easy to move a modifier up or down, because sometimes the order makes a difference.

➤ Here's another way to see the `font` menu. Select `.largeTitle` and replace it with `.` — Xcode's standard auto-suggest mechanism lists the possible values:

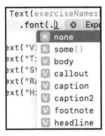

Xcode's auto-suggestions while you type code

➤ Select **largeTitle** from the menu.

➤ Once you're familiar with SwiftUI modifiers, you might prefer to just type. Delete `.font(.largeTitle)` and type **.font**. Xcode auto-suggests two `font` methods:

Xcode's auto-suggestions for methods

➤ Select either method and Xcode auto-completes with `(.title)`. Change this to **.largeTitle**.

Swift Tip: The method signature `func font(_ font: Font?) -> Text` indicates this method takes one parameter of type Font? and returns a Text view. The "_" means there's no *external parameter name* — you call it with `font(.title)`, not with `font(font: .title)`.

Creating page numbers

In addition to the name of the exercise, the header should display the page numbers with the current page number highlighted. This replaces the `TabView` index dots.

You *could* just display `Text("1")`, `Text("2")` and so on, but Apple provides a wealth of configurable icons as **SF Symbols**.

➤ The **SF Symbols app** is the best way to view and search the collection. Download and install it from apple.co/3hWxn3G. Some symbols must be used only for specific Apple products like FaceTime or AirPods. You can check symbols for restrictions at sfsymbols.com.

➤ After installing the **SF Symbols app**, open it and select the **Indices** category. Scroll down to the numbers:

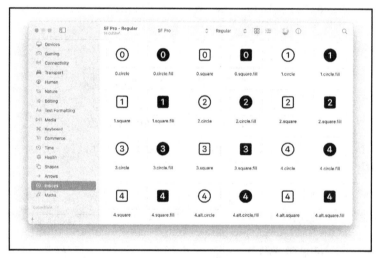

SF Symbols app: Indices category (partial)

You can choose black numbers on a white background or the other way around, in a circle or a square. The fill version is a good choice to represent the current page, with no-fill numbers for the other pages.

➤ SF Symbol names can be long, but it's easy to copy them from the app. Select a symbol, then open the app's **Edit** menu:

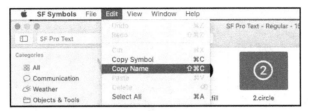

How to copy the name of an SF Symbol from the app

Note: The keyboard shortcut is **Shift-Command-C**.

➤ Select the no-fill "1.circle" symbol, press **Shift-Command-C**, then use the name to add this line of code below the title Text:

```
Image(systemName: "1.circle")
```

Image is another built-in SwiftUI View, and it has an initializer that takes an SF Symbol name as a String.

➤ Before adding more numbers, **Command-click** this Image to embed it in an HStack, so the numbers will appear side by side. Then duplicate and edit more Image views to create the other three numbers:

```
HStack {
    Image(systemName: "1.circle")
    Image(systemName: "2.circle")
    Image(systemName: "3.circle")
    Image(systemName: "4.circle")
}
```

And here's your header:

Header with title and page numbers

The page numbers look too small. Because SF Symbols are integrated into the San Francisco system font — that's the "SF" in SF Symbols — you can treat them like text and use font to specify their size.

➤ You *could* add .font(.title) to each Image, but it's quicker and neater to add it to the HStack container:

```
HStack {
    Image(systemName: "1.circle")
    Image(systemName: "2.circle")
    Image(systemName: "3.circle")
    Image(systemName: "4.circle")
}
.font(.title2)
```

The font size applies to all views in the HStack:

SF Symbols with title2 font size

➤ You can modify an Image to override the HStack modifier. For example, modify the first number to make it extra large:

```
Image(systemName: "1.circle")
    .font(.largeTitle)
```

Now only the first symbol is larger:

Overriding the stack's font size for the first symbol

➤ Delete the Image modifier, so all the numbers are the same size.

Your ExerciseView now has a header, which you'll reuse in WelcomeView. So you're about to *extract* the header code to create a HeaderView.

You'll use Xcode's refactoring tool, which works well. But it's always a good idea to commit your code before a change like this, just in case. Select **Source Control ▸ Commit…** or press **Option-Command-C**.

Extracting a subview

OK, drum roll ...

➤ **Command-click** the VStack containing the title Text and the page numbers HStack, then select **Extract Subview** from the menu:

Command-click VStack, select Extract Subview.

Xcode moves the whole VStack into the body property of a new view with the placeholder name ExtractedView. And ExtractedView() is where the VStack used to be:

Ready to rename the extracted view

➤ While the placeholders are still highlighted, type **HeaderView** and press **Return**. If you miss the moment, just edit both placeholders.

The error flag shows where you need a parameter. The index property is local to ExerciseView, so you can't use it in HeaderView. You could just pass index to HeaderView and ensure it can access the exerciseNames array. But it's always better to pass just enough information. This makes it easier to set up the preview for HeaderView. Right now, HeaderView needs only the exercise name.

➤ Add this property to HeaderView, above the body property:

```
let exerciseName: String
```

➤ And replace exerciseNames[index] in Text:

```
Text(exerciseName)
```

➤ Scroll up to ExerciseView, where Xcode is complaining about a missing argument in HeaderView(). Click the error icon to click **Fix**, then complete the line to read:

```
HeaderView(exerciseName: exerciseNames[index])
```

➤ Now press **Command-N** to create a **new SwiftUI View file** and name it **HeaderView.swift**. Because you were in **ExerciseView.swift** when you pressed **Command-N**, the new file appears below it and in the same group folder.

Your new file opens in the editor with two error flags:

1. Invalid redeclaration of 'HeaderView'.

2. Missing argument for parameter 'exerciseName'.

➤ To fix the first, in **ExerciseView.swift**, select the entire 17 lines of your new HeaderView and press **Command-X** to cut it — *copy* it to the clipboard and *delete* it from **ExerciseView.swift**.

➤ Back in **HeaderView.swift**, replace the 5-line boilerplate HeaderView with what's in the clipboard.

➤ To fix the second error, in previews, let Xcode add the missing parameter, then enter any exercise name for the argument:

```
HeaderView(exerciseName: "Squat")
```

Because you pass only the exercise name to HeaderView, the preview doesn't need access to the exerciseNames array.

Working with previews

The preview still uses the iPad simulator, which takes up a lot of space. You can modify the preview to show only the header.

➤ In HeaderView_Previews, **Control-Option-click** HeaderView(...) then type **preview** in the **Add Modifier** field:

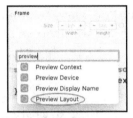

Selecting Preview Layout from the Attributes inspector for Header view

➤ Select **Preview Layout** to add this modifier:

```
.previewLayout(.sizeThatFits)
```

➤ The placeholder value is sizeThatFits, and this is what you want, but you must "accept" it. Click **sizeThatFits**, then press **Return** to set it as the value.

➤ Resume the preview to see just the header:

Preview is just big enough to show the view.

➤ Now you're all set to see the power of previews. In the preview canvas, click the **Duplicate Preview** button:

Duplicated previews, with Duplicate Preview button circled

You've made a copy of the preview in the canvas and in the code:

```
Group {
  HeaderView(exerciseName: "Squat")
    .previewLayout(.sizeThatFits)
  HeaderView(exerciseName: "Squat")
    .previewLayout(.sizeThatFits)
}
```

Just like when you duplicated the Text view, Xcode embeds the two views in a container view. This time it's a Group, which doesn't specify anything about layout. Its only purpose is to wrap multiple views into a single view.

> **Swift Tip**: The body and previews properties are *computed properties*. They must return a value of type some View, so what's inside the closure must be a *single* view.

➤ Now you can modify the second preview. Click its **Inspect Preview** button:

Inspect the second preview.

The inspector lets you set **Color Scheme** and **Dynamic Type**.

➤ Set **Color Scheme** to **Dark** and **Dynamic Type** to **accessibilityLarge**.

```
struct HeaderView_Previews: PreviewProvider {
  static var previews: some View {
    Group {
      HeaderView(exerciseName: "Squat")
        .previewLayout(.sizeThatFits)
      HeaderView(exerciseName: "Squat")
        .preferredColorScheme(.dark)
        .environment(\.sizeCategory,
          .accessibilityLarge)
        .previewLayout(.sizeThatFits)
    }
  }
}
```

Second preview with dark color scheme and accessibilityLarge font size

That's how easy it is to see how this view appears on a device with these settings.

Now return to **ExerciseView.swift**, where the header is just the way you left it.

Exercise view with Header view

Time to commit changes again: Select **Source Control ▸ Commit…** or press **Option-Command-C**. And this is the last time I'll remind you. ;]

Next, you'll set up the video player.

Playing a video

Skills you'll learn in this section: using `AVPlayer` and `VideoPlayer`; using bundle files; optional types; make conditional; using `GeometryReader`; adding padding

➤ In **ExerciseView.swift**, add this statement just below `import SwiftUI`:

```
import AVKit
```

`AVKit` is a framework in Apple's software development kits (SDKs). Importing it allows you to use high-level types like `AVPlayer` to play videos with the usual playback controls.

➤ Now replace `Text("Video player")` with this line:

```
VideoPlayer(player: AVPlayer(url: url))
```

Xcode complains it "cannot find 'url' in scope", so you'll define this value next.

Getting the URL of a bundle file

You need the URL of the video file for this exercise. The `videonames` array lists the name part of the files. All the files have file extension **.mp4**.

These files are in the project folder, which you can access as `Bundle.main`. Its method `url(forResource:withExtension:)` gets you the URL of a file in the main app bundle **if it exists**. Otherwise, it returns `nil` which means *no value*. The return type of this method is an `Optional` type, `URL?`.

> **Swift Tip**: Swift's `Optional` type helps you avoid many hard-to-find bugs that are common in other programming languages. It's usually declared as a type like `Int` or `String` followed by a question mark: `Int?` or `String?`. If you declare `var index: Int?`, index can contain an `Int` or no value at all. If you declare `var index: Int` — with no `?` — index must *always* contain an `Int`. Use `if let index = index {...}` to check whether an optional has a value. The index on the right of = is the optional value. If it has a value, the index on the left of = is an `Int` and the condition is `true`. If the optional has no value, the assignment = is not performed and the condition is `false`. You can also check `index != nil`, which returns `true` if index has a value.

> **Note**: You'll learn more about the app bundle in Chapter 8, "Saving Settings" and about optionals in Chapter 9, "Saving History Data".

So you need to wrap an `if let` around the `VideoPlayer`. Yet another pair of braces! It can be hard to keep track of them all. But Xcode is here to help. ;]

➤ **Command-click** `VideoPlayer` and select **Make Conditional**. And there's an if-else closure wrapping `VideoPlayer`!

> **Xcode Tip**: Take advantage of features like **Embed in HStack** and **Make Conditional** to let Xcode keep your braces matched. To adjust what's included in the closure, use **Option-Command-[** or **Option-Command-]** to move the closing brace up or down.

➤ Now replace `if true {` with:

```
if let url = Bundle.main.url(
    forResource: videoNames[index],
    withExtension: "mp4") {
```

➤ In the `else` closure, replace `EmptyView()` with:

```
Text("Couldn't find \(videoNames[index]).mp4")
    .foregroundColor(.red)
```

Swift Tip: The *string interpolation* code `\(videoNames[index])` inserts the value of `videoNames[index]` into the string literal.

➤ It's easy to test this `else` code: Create a typo by changing the `withExtension` argument to **np4**, then refresh the preview:

Testing the Couldn't-find message

Actually, it's squat.**np4** that isn't in the app bundle.

➤ Undo the np4 typo.

➤ Now click **Live Preview**, then click the play button to watch the video. If the play button disappears, try this: Click on the video then press **Space**.

Getting the screen dimensions

The video takes up a lot of space on the screen. You could set the width and height of its frame to some constant values that work on most devices, but it's better if these measurements adapt to the size of the device.

➤ In body, **Command-click** VStack and select **Embed...**. Change the Container { placeholder to this line:

```
GeometryReader { geometry in
```

GeometryReader is a container view that provides you with the screen's measurements for whatever device you're previewing or running on.

➤ Add this modifier to VideoPlayer:

```
.frame(height: geometry.size.height * 0.45)
```

The video player now uses only 45% of the screen height:

Video player uses 45% of screen height.

Adding padding

➤ The header looks a little squashed. **Control-Option-click** HeaderView to add padding to its bottom:

Add padding to Header view in Exercise view.

This gives you a new modifier padding(.bottom) and now there's space between the header and the video:

Exercise view with padding under Header view

> **Note**: You *could* have added padding to the VStack *in* **HeaderView.swift**, but
> HeaderView is a little more reusable without padding. You can choose whether
> to add padding and how to customize it whenever you use HeaderView in
> another view.

Now head back to **ContentView.swift** and **Live Preview** your app. Swipe from one
page to the next to see the different exercise videos.

HIITFit pages

Finishing the Exercise view

> **Skills you'll learn in this section**: Text with date and style parameters; types
> in Swift; Date(); Button, Spacer, foregroundColor; repeating a view;
> unused closure parameter

To finish off the **Exercise** view, add the timer and buttons, then create the **Ratings**
view.

Creating the Timer view

➤ Add this property to ExerciseView, above body:

```
let interval: TimeInterval = 30
```

These are high-intensity interval exercises, so the timer counts down from 30
seconds.

➤ Replace Text("Timer") with this code:

```
Text(Date().addingTimeInterval(interval), style: .timer)
    .font(.system(size: 90))
```

The default initializer Date() creates a value with the current date and time. The Date method addingTimeInterval(_ timeInterval:) adds interval seconds to this value.

➤ The Swift Date type has a lot of methods for manipulating date and time values. **Option-click** Date and **Open in Developer Documentation** to scan what's available. You'll dive a little deeper into Date when you create the **History** view.

The timeInterval parameter's type is TimeInterval. This is just an alias for Double. If you say interval is of type Double, you won't get an error, but TimeInterval describes the value's purpose more accurately.

> **Swift Tip**: Swift is a *strongly typed language*. This means that you must use the correct type. When using numbers, you can usually pass a value of a wrong type to the initializer of the correct type. For example, Double(myIntValue) creates a Double value from an Int and Int(myDoubleValue) truncates a Double value to create an Int. If you write code in languages that allow automatic conversion, it's easy to create a bug that's very hard to find. Swift makes sure you, and people reading your code, know that you're converting one type to another.

You're using the Text view's (_:style:) initializer for displaying dates and times. The timer and relative styles display the time interval between the current time and the date value, formatted as "mm:ss" or "mm min ss sec", respectively. These two styles update the display every second.

You set the system font size to 90 points to make a really big timer.

➤ Click **Live Preview** to watch the timer count down from 30 seconds:

Exercise view with 30-second timer

Because you set `date` to 30 seconds in the future, the displayed time interval decreases by 1 every second, as the current time approaches `date`. If you wait until it reaches 0 (change `interval` to 3 so you don't have to wait so long), you'll see it start counting **up**, as the current time moves away from `date`. Don't worry, this `Text` timer is just for the prototype. You'll replace it with a *real* timer in Chapter 7, "Observing Objects".

Creating buttons

Creating buttons is simple, so you'll do both now.

➤ Replace `Text("Start/Done button")` with this code:

```
Button("Start/Done") { }
  .font(.title3)
  .padding()
```

Here, you gave the Button the label **Start/Done** and an empty action. You'll add the action in Chapter 7, "Observing Objects". Then, you enlarged the font of its label and added padding all around it.

➤ Replace Text("History button") with this code:

```
Spacer()
Button("History") { }
  .padding(.bottom)
```

The Spacer pushes the History button to the bottom of the screen. The padding pushes it back up a little, so it doesn't look squashed.

You'll add this button's action in Chapter 6, "Adding Functionality to Your App".

Here's what ExerciseView looks like now:

Exercise view with buttons

Now for the last subview in ExerciseView: RatingView.

Creating the Rating view

➤ Create a new **new SwiftUI View file** named **RatingView.swift**. This will be a small view, so add this modifier to its preview:

```
.previewLayout(.sizeThatFits)
```

A rating view is usually five stars or hearts, but the rating for an exercise should reflect the user's exertion.

➤ To find a more suitable rating symbol, open the **SF Symbols** app and select the **Health** category:

SF Symbols Health category: ECG waveform

➤ The ECG wave form seems just right for rating high-intensity exercises! Select it, then press **Shift-Command-C** to copy its name.

➤ Replace the boilerplate Text with this code, pasting the symbol name in between double quotation marks:

```
Image(systemName: "waveform.path.ecg")
  .foregroundColor(.gray)
```

You've added the SF Symbol as an Image and set its color to gray.

A rating view needs five of these symbols, arranged horizontally.

➤ In the canvas or in the editor, **Command-click** the Image and select **Repeat** from the menu:

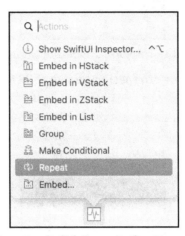

Command-click Image, select Repeat.

Xcode gives you a loop, with suggested range 0 ..< 5:

```
ForEach(0 ..< 5) { item in
  Image(systemName: "waveform.path.ecg")
    .foregroundColor(.gray)
}
```

➤ Click this range and press **Return** to accept it.

In the canvas, you see five separate previews! Xcode should have embedded them in a stack, like when you duplicated a view, but it didn't.

➤ **Command-click** ForEach and embed it in an HStack.

Now your code looks like this:

```
HStack {
  ForEach(0 ..< 5) { item in
    Image(systemName: "waveform.path.ecg")
      .foregroundColor(.gray)
  }
}
```

That's better! Now the symbols are all in a row. But they're very small.

ECG waveform symbols in HStack

➤ Remember, you can use `font` to specify the size of SF Symbols. So add this modifier to the `Image`:

```
.font(.largeTitle)
```

Bigger is better!

SF Symbols with largeTitle font size

One last detail: The code Xcode created for you contains an unused *closure parameter* `item`:

```
ForEach(0 ..< 5) { item in
```

➤ You don't use `item` in the loop code, so replace `item` with `_`:

```
ForEach(0 ..< 5) { _ in
```

Swift Tip: It's good programming practice to replace unused parameter names with `_`. The alternative is to create a throwaway name, which takes a non-zero amount of time and focus and will confuse you and other programmers reading your code.

➤ Now head back to **ExerciseView.swift** to use your new view. Replace `Text("Rating")` with this code:

```
RatingView()
  .padding()
```

Your ECG wave forms now march across the screen!

Exercise view with Rating subview

In Chapter 6, "Adding Functionality to Your App", you'll add code to let the user set a rating value and represent this value by setting the right number of symbols to red. And, in Chapter 8, "Saving Settings", you'll save the rating values so they persist across app launches.

Key points

- SwiftUI is declarative: Simply declare views in the order you want them to appear.

- Create separate views for the elements of your user interface. This makes your code easier to read and maintain.

- Use the SwiftUI convention of putting each modifier on its own line. This makes it easy to move or delete a modifier.

- Xcode and SwiftUI provide auto-suggestions and default values that are often what you want.

- Let Xcode help you avoid errors: Use the **Command**-menu to embed a view in a stack or in an if-else closure, or extract a view into a subview.

- The **SF Symbols** app provides icon images you can configure like text.

- Previews are an easy way to check how your interface appears for different user settings.

- Swift is a strongly typed programming language.

- GeometryReader enables you to set a view's dimensions relative to the screen dimensions.

Where to go from here?

Your **Exercise** view is ready. In the next chapter, you'll lay out the other three full-screen views your app needs.

Chapter 4: Prototyping Supplementary Views

By Audrey Tam

Your app still needs three more full-screen views:

- Welcome

- History

- Success

In the previous chapter, you laid out the **Exercise** view. In this chapter, you'll lay out the **History** and **Welcome** views then complete the challenge to create the **Success** view. And your app's prototype will be complete.

Creating the History view

Skills you'll learn in this section: working with dates; extending a type; Quick Help comments; creating forms; looping over a collection; layering views with ZStack; stack alignment values

In this chapter, you'll just do a mock-up of the list view. After you create the data model in the next chapter, you'll modify this view to use that data.

➤ Continue with your project from the previous chapter or open the project in this chapter's **starter** folder.

➤ Create a **new SwiftUI View file** named **HistoryView.swift**. For this mock-up, add some sample history data to HistoryView, above body:

```
let today = Date()
let yesterday = Date().addingTimeInterval(-86400)

let exercises1 = ["Squat", "Step Up", "Burpee", "Sun Salute"]
let exercises2 = ["Squat", "Step Up", "Burpee"]
```

You'll display exercises completed over two days.

➤ Replace Text("Hello, World!") with this code:

```
VStack {
  Text("History")
    .font(.title)
    .padding()
  // Exercise history
}
```

You've created the title for this view with some padding around it.

Creating a form

SwiftUI has a container view that automatically formats its contents to look organized.

➤ Inside the VStack, replace // Exercise history with this code:

```
Form {
  Section(
    header:
    Text(today.formatted(as: "MMM d"))
      .font(.headline)) {
    // Section content
  }
  Section(
    header:
    Text(yesterday.formatted(as: "MMM d"))
      .font(.headline)) {
    // Section content
  }
}
```

Inside the Form container view, you create two sections. Each Section has a header with the date, using headline font size.

This code takes yesterday and today's date as the section headers, so your view will have different dates from the one below:

History Form with two Sections

Extending the Date type

When you created the timer view, you had a quick look at the Swift Date type and used one of its methods. It's now time to learn a little more about it.

> **Swift Tip**: A Date object is just some number of seconds relative to January 1, 2001 00:00:00 UTC. To display it as a calendar date in a particular time zone, you must use a DateFormatter. This class has a few built-in styles named short, medium, long and full, described in links from the developer documentation page for DateFormatter.Style. You can also specify your own format as a String.

➤ Open **DateExtension.swift**. The first method shows how to use a DateFormatter.

```
func formatted(as format: String) -> String {
    let dateFormatter = DateFormatter()
    dateFormatter.dateFormat = format
    return dateFormatter.string(from: self)
}
```

DateFormatter has only the default empty initializer. You create one, then configure it by setting the properties you care about. This method uses its format argument to set the dateFormat property.

In HistoryView, you pass "MMM d" as format. This specifies three characters for the month — so you get SEP or OCT — and one character for the day — so you get a number. If the number is a single digit, that's what you see. If you specify "MM dd", you get numbers for both month and day, with leading 0 if the number is single digit: **09 02** instead of **SEP 2**.

Once you've configured `dateFormatter`, its `string(from:)` method returns the date string.

You don't have to worry about time zones if you simply want the user's current time zone. That's the default setting.

Formatting Quick Help comments

Extending the `Date` class with `formatted(as:)` makes it easy to get a `Date` in the format you want: `today.formatted(as: "MMM d")`.

> **Swift Tip**: You can add methods to extend any type, including those built into the software development kit, like `Image` and `Date`. Then, you can use them the same way you use the built-in methods.

➤ Look at the comment above the `formatted(as:)` method:

```
/// Format a date using the specified format.
///   - parameters:
///     - format: A date pattern string like "MM dd".
```

This is a special kind of comment. It appears in Xcode's **Quick Help** when you **Option-click** the method name:

DIY Quick Help documentation comment

It looks just like all the built-in method summaries!

It's good practice to document all the methods you write this way. Apple's documentation for Formatting Quick Help is at apple.co/33hohbk.

Looping over a collection

➤ Now, head back to **HistoryView.swift** to fill in the section content.

To display the completed exercises for each day, you'll use ForEach to loop over the elements of the exercises1 and exercises2 arrays.

➤ In the first Section, replace // Section content with this code:

```
ForEach(exercises1, id: \.self) { exercise in
  Text(exercise)
}
```

In ContentView, you looped over a number range. Here, you're using the third ForEach initializer:

```
init(Data, id: KeyPath<Data.Element, ID>, content:
(Data.Element) -> Content)
```

The exercises1 array is the Data and \.self is the key path to each array element's identifier. The \.self key path just says each element of the array is its own unique identifier.

As the loop visits each array element, you assign it to the local variable exercise, which you display in a Text view.

➤ In the second Section, replace // Section content with the almost identical code:

```
ForEach(exercises2, id: \.self) { exercise in
  Text(exercise)
}
```

This time, you display the exercises2 array.

➤ Refresh the preview to admire your exercise history:

History list for two days

Creating a button in another layer

In Chapter 6, "Adding Functionality to Your App", you'll implement this view to appear as a *modal sheet*, so it needs a button to dismiss it. You'll often see a dismiss button in the upper right corner of a modal sheet. The easiest way to place it there, without disturbing the layout of the rest of HistoryView, is to put it in its own layer.

If you think of an HStack as arranging its contents along the device's x-axis and a VStack arranging views along the y-axis, then the ZStack container view stacks its contents along the *z-axis*, perpendicular to the device screen. Think of it as a **depth** stack, displaying views in layers.

➤ **Command-click** VStack to embed it in a ZStack, then add this code at the top of ZStack:

```
Button(action: {}) {
  Image(systemName: "xmark.circle")
}
```

Here's the top part of your view now:

Dismiss button outline

The button is centered in the view, because the default stack alignment is center. Because you added the Button code *above* the VStack in the source code, it's *underneath* the VStack on screen, so you see only its outline.

The arrangement is a little counter-intuitive unless you think of it as placing the first view down on a flat surface, then layering the next view on top of that, and so on. So declaring the button as the first view places it on the bottom of the stack. If you want the button in the *top layer*, declare it *last* in the ZStack.

It doesn't matter in this case, because you'll move the button into the top right corner of the view, where there's nothing in the VStack to cover it.

You can specify an alignment value for any kind of stack, but they use different alignment values. VStack alignment values are horizontal: leading, center or trailing. HStack alignment values are vertical: top, center, bottom, firstTextBaseline or lastTextBaseline.

To specify the alignment of a ZStack, you must set both horizontal and vertical alignment values. You can either specify separate horizontal and vertical values, or a combined value like topTrailing.

➤ Replace ZStack { with this:

```
ZStack(alignment: .topTrailing) {
```

You set the ZStack alignment parameter to position the button in the top right corner of the view. Other views in the ZStack have their own alignment values, so the ZStack alignment value doesn't affect them.

The button is now visible, but it's small and a little too close to the corner edges.

➤ Add these modifiers to the Button to adjust its size and position:

```
.font(.title)
.padding(.trailing)
```

Refresh the preview to see the result:

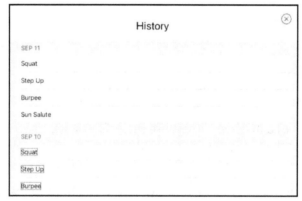

History view with dismiss button in top trailing corner

Creating the Welcome view

Skills you'll learn in this section: refactoring/renaming a parameter; modifying images; using a custom modifier; Button label with text and image

➤ Open **WelcomeView.swift**.

WelcomeView is the first page in your app's page-style TabView, so it should have the same header as ExerciseView.

➤ Replace Text("Hello, World!") with this line:

```
HeaderView(exerciseName: "Welcome")
```

You want the title of this page to be "Welcome", so you pass this as the value of the exerciseName parameter. HeaderView also displays the page numbers of the four exercises:

Welcome view header: First try

Refactoring HeaderView

Using HeaderView here raises two issues:

1. There's no page number for the **Welcome** page.

2. The parameter name exerciseName isn't a good description of "Welcome".

The first issue is easy to resolve. The app has only one non-exercise page, so you just need to add another page "number" in HeaderView.

➤ In **HeaderView.swift**, in the canvas preview, duplicate the 1.circle Image, then change the first Image to display a hand wave:

```
Image(systemName: "hand.wave")
```

➤ Refresh the preview to see how it looks:

Header with hand-wave SF Symbol for Welcome page

That'll do nicely.

Now to rename the exerciseName property. Its purpose is really to be the title of the page, so titleText is a better name for it.

You could search for all occurrences of `exerciseName` in your app, then decide for each whether to change it to `titleText`. In a more complex app, this approach almost guarantees you'll forget one or change one that shouldn't change.

Xcode has a safer way!

➤ **Command-click** the first occurrence of `exerciseName` and select **Rename...** from the menu:

Command-click exerciseName, select Rename.

> **Note**: If you **Command-click** `exerciseName` in `Text(exerciseName)`, you'll see the longer menu that includes *Embed in HStack* etc. **Rename...** is at the bottom of this menu.

Xcode displays all the code statements that need to change:

```
HeaderView.swift
35   struct HeaderView: View {
36     let exerciseName  String
37     var body: some View {
38       VStack {
39         Text(exerciseName)
40           .font(.largeTitle)
55       Group {
56         HeaderView(exerciseName: "Squat")
57           .previewLayout(.sizeThatFits)
58         HeaderView(exerciseName: "Squat")
59           .preferredColorScheme(.dark)
ExerciseView.swift
45         VStack {
46           HeaderView(exerciseName: exerciseNames[index])
47             .padding(.bottom)
WelcomeView.swift
36       var body: some View {
37         HeaderView(exerciseName: "Welcome")
38       }
```

Xcode shows code affected by name change.

➤ The first instance is highlighted differently. Type **titleText**, and all the instances change:

Change exerciseName to titleText.

➤ Click the **Rename** button in the upper right corner to confirm these changes, then head back to **WelcomeView.swift** to see the results:

Welcome view with refactored Header view: issues resolved

That's better! The user sees a page icon, and the programmer sees a descriptive parameter.

More layering with ZStack

So far, so good, but the header should be at the top of the page. There's also a **History** button that should be at the bottom of the page. The main content should be centered in the view, independent of the heights of the header and button.

In HistoryView, you used a ZStack to position the dismiss button in the upper right corner (topTrailing), without affecting the layout of the other content.

In this view, you'll use a ZStack to put the header and **History** button in one layer, to push them apart. Then you'll create the main content in another layer, centered by default.

➤ First, embed `HeaderView` in a `VStack`, then embed that `VStack` in a `ZStack`.

```
ZStack {
  VStack {
    HeaderView(titleText: "Welcome")
  }
}
```

➤ In the `VStack`, below `HeaderView`, add this code:

```
Spacer()
Button("History") { }
  .padding(.bottom)
```

You have the header and the **History** button in a `VStack`, with a `Spacer` to push them apart and some padding so the button isn't too close to the bottom edge:

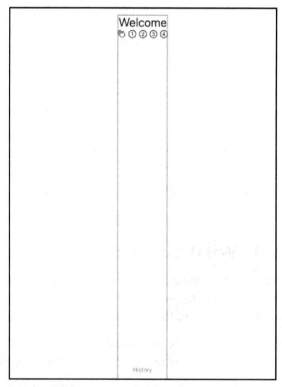

Welcome view header and footer

➤ Now to fill in the middle space. Add this layer to the ZStack:

```
VStack {
  HStack {
    VStack(alignment: .leading) {
      Text("Get fit")
        .font(.largeTitle)
      Text("with high intensity interval training")
        .font(.headline)
    }
  }
}
```

Note: You can add this VStack either above or below the existing VStack. It doesn't matter because there's no overlapping content in the two layers.

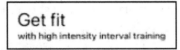

Welcome view center text

The inner VStack contains two Text views with different font sizes. You set its alignment to leading to left-justify the two Text views.

This VStack is in an HStack because you're going to place an Image to the right of the text. And the HStack is in an outer VStack because you'll add a Button below the text and image.

Modifying an Image

➤ Look in **Assets.xcassets** for the **step-up** image:

step-up image in Assets

➤ Back in **WelcomeView.swift**, open the **Library** with **Shift-Command-L** (or click the + toolbar button) and select the media tab:

Add image from canvas library.

➤ To insert **step-up** in the correct place, it's easiest to drag it into the **code editor**. Hold onto it while nudging the code with the cursor, until a line opens, just below the VStack with two Text views. Let go of the image, and it appears in your code:

```
HStack {
  VStack(alignment: .leading) {
    Text("Get fit")
      .font(.largeTitle)
    Text("with high intensity interval training")
      .font(.headline)
  }
  Image("step-up")  // your new code appears here
}
```

➤ You usually have to add several modifiers to an Image, so open the **Attributes inspector** in the **inspectors panel**:

Open Attributes inspector in the inspector panel.

Note: If you don't see **Image** with a value of **step-up**, select the image. You might have to close then reopen the inspector panel.

➤ First, you must add a modifier that lets you *resize* the image. In the **Add Modifier** field, type **resiz** then select **Resizable**.

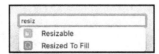

Select Resizable modifier.

Don't worry if the image stretches. You'll fix that with the next modifier.

➤ When resizing an image, you usually want to preserve the *aspect ratio*. So search for an **aspect** modifier and select **Aspect Ratio**:

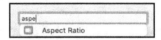

Select Aspect Ratio modifier.

➤ The suggested `contentMode` value is `fill`, which is what you usually want, so press **Return** to accept it.

➤ Now the image looks more normal, but it's too big. In the **Frame** section, set the **Width** and **Height** to **240**:

Set Frame Width and Height to 240.

That's looking pretty good! How about *clipping* it to a circle?

➤ Search for a **clip** modifier and select **Clip Shape**:

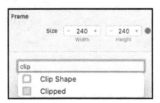

Select Clip Shape modifier.

➤ Again, the suggestion `Circle()` is what you want, so accept it.

Your `HStack` code and canvas now look like this:

```
VStack {
  HStack {
    VStack(alignment: .leading) {
      Text("Get fit")
        .font(.largeTitle)
      Text("with high intensity interval
            training")
        .font(.headline)
    }
    Image("step-up")
      .resizable()
      .aspectRatio(contentMode: .fill)
      .frame(width: 240.0, height: 240.0)
      .clipShape(Circle())
  }
}
```

Welcome view center view

➤ You need just one more tweak: The text would look better if you align it with the bottom of the image. Just change the *alignment* of the enclosing `HStack`:

```
HStack(alignment: .bottom)
```

And here's your **Welcome** page:

Welcome view center view with text aligned to bottom of HStack

You've done enough to make it look welcoming. :] In Chapter 10, "Refining Your App", you'll add a few more images.

Using a custom modifier

You'll use this triplet of `Image` modifiers *all the time*:

```
.resizable()
.aspectRatio(contentMode: .fill)
.frame(width: 240.0, height: 240.0)
```

Everyone does, although the frame dimensions won't always be 240. In **ImageExtension.swift**, you'll find `resizedToFill(width:height:)` which encapsulates these three modifiers:

```
func resizedToFill(width: CGFloat, height: CGFloat)
-> some View {
  return self
    .resizable()
    .aspectRatio(contentMode: .fill)
    .frame(width: width, height: height)
}
```

It extends the `Image` view, so `self` is the `Image` you're modifying with `resizedToFill(width:height:)`.

➤ To use this custom modifier, head back to **WelcomeView.swift**. Comment out (**Command**-/) or delete the first three modifiers of `Image("step-up")`, then add this custom modifier:

```
.resizedToFill(width: 240, height: 240)
```

And the view looks the same, but there's a little less code.

Labeling a Button with text and image

The final detail is a `Button`. The user can tap this to move to the first exercise page, but the label also has an arrow image to indicate they can swipe to the next page.

The other buttons you've created have only text labels. But it's easy to label a `Button` with text *and* an image.

➤ In the center view `VStack`, below the `HStack` with the image, add this code:

```
Button(action: { }) {
  Text("Get Started")
  Image(systemName: "arrow.right.circle")
}
.font(.title2)
.padding()
```

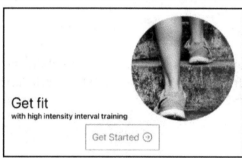

Welcome view Get Started button

This code is quite different from the other buttons you've created and requires some explanation. SwiftUI uses a lot of *syntactic sugar*: Instead of using the official method calls, SwiftUI lets you write code that's much simpler and more readable.

If you start typing **Button** in the code editor, Xcode will auto-suggest this official `Button` signature:

```
Button(action: {}, label: {
  <Content>
})
```

`Button` has two parameters: `action` is a method or a closure containing executable code; `label` is a view describing the button's `action`. Both parameter values can be closures, so `action` can be more than one executable statement, and `label` can be more than one view.

Swift Tip: You can move the last closure argument of a function call outside the parentheses into a *trailing closure*.

If you drag a `Button` into your view *from the canvas library*, you get this version of the `Button` signature with the `label` content as a trailing closure:

```
Button(action: {} ) {
   <Content>
}
```

This is the syntax used in the "Get Started" `Button` above, with the `Text` and `Image` views in an implicit `HStack`.

The other buttons you've created use an even simpler syntax for `Button`, where the button's label is just a `String`, and the button's action is in the trailing closure. For example:

```
Button("History") { }
```

➤ The `Label` view is another way to label a `Button` with text and image. Comment out (**Command**-/) the `Text` and `Image` lines, then write this line in the `label` closure:

```
Label("Get Started", systemImage: "arrow.right.circle")
```

Look closely: Do you see what changed?

Welcome view Get Started button with Label view

Note: You can modify a `Label` with `labelStyle` to show only the text or only the image.

The image is on the *left side* of the text. This looks wrong to me: An arrow pointing right should appear *after* the text. Unfortunately for this particular Button, there's no way to make the image appear to the right of the text, unless you're using a language like Arabic that's written right-to-left. Label is ideal for icon-text lists, where you want the icons nicely aligned on the leading edge.

➤ Delete the Label and uncomment the Text and Image.

➤ Just for fun, give this button a border. Add this modifier **below** padding():

```
.background(
  RoundedRectangle(cornerRadius: 20)
  .stroke(Color.gray, lineWidth: 2))
```

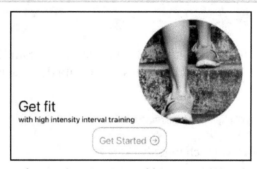

Welcome view Get Started button with border

You put a rounded rectangle around the *padded* button, specifying the corner radius, line color and line width.

Challenge

When your users tap **Done** on the last exercise page, your app will show a modal sheet to congratulate them on their success.

Your challenge is to create this SuccessView:

Challenge: Create this Success view.

Challenge: Creating the Success view

1. Create a **new SwiftUI View file** named **SuccessView.swift**.

2. Replace its Text view with a VStack containing the hand.raised.fill SF Symbol and the text in the screenshot.

3. The SF Symbol is in a 75 by 75 frame and colored purple. **Hint**: Use the custom Image modifier.

4. For the large "High Five!" title, you can use the fontWeight modifier to emphasize it more.

5. For the three small lines of text, you could use three `Text` views. Or refer to our Swift Style Guide bit.ly/30cHeeL to see how to create a *multi-line string*. `Text` has a `multilineTextAlignment` modifier. This text is colored gray.

6. Like `HistoryView`, `SuccessView` needs a button to dismiss it. Center a **Continue** button at the bottom of the screen. **Hint**: Use a `ZStack` so the "High Five!" view remains vertically centered.

Here's a close-up of the "High Five!" view:

Success view center view

You'll find the solution to this challenge in the **challenge** folder for this chapter.

Key points

- The `Date` type has many built-in properties and methods. You need to configure a `DateFormatter` to create meaningful text to show your users.

- Use the `Form` container view to quickly lay out table data.

- `ForEach` lets you loop over the items in a collection.

- `ZStack` is useful for keeping views in one layer centered while pushing views in another layer to the edges.

- You can specify vertical alignment values for `HStack`, horizontal alignment values for `VStack` and combination alignment values for `ZStack`.

- Xcode helps you to refactor the name of a parameter quickly and safely.

- `Image` often needs the same three modifiers. You can create a custom modifier so you Don't Repeat Yourself.

- A `Button` has a label and an action. You can define a `Button` a few different ways.

Where to go from here?

Your views are all laid out. You're eager to implement all the button actions. But ... you've been using hard-coded sample data to lay out your views. Before you can make everything work, you need to design your data model. The Model-View-Controller division of labor still applies. And you'll learn lots more about Swift and Xcode.

Chapter 5: Organizing Your App's Data

By Audrey Tam

In this chapter, you'll use structures and enumerations to organize your app's data. The compiler can then help you avoid errors like using the wrong type value or misspelling a string.

Your app needs sample data during development. You'll use a *compiler directive* to create this data only during development. And you'll store your development-only code and data in **Preview Content** to exclude them from the release version of your app.

You'll learn how to localize your app to expand its audience. You'll replace user-facing text with NSLocalizedString instances, generate the development language (English) **Localizable.strings** file, then use this as the reference language resource file for adding another language.

➤ Continue with your project from the previous chapter or open the project in this chapter's **starter** folder.

Creating the Exercise structure

Skills you'll learn in this section: how to use enumeration, computed property, `extension`, `static` property

For the initial layout of HIITFit, you used two arrays of strings for the exercise names and video file names. This minimalist approach helped you see exactly what data each view needs, and this helped to keep the previews manageable.

But you had to manually ensure the strings matched up across the two arrays. It's safer to encapsulate them as properties of a named type.

First, you'll create an `Exercise` structure with the properties you need. Then, you'll create an array of `Exercise` instances and loop over this array to create the `ExerciseView` pages of the `TabView`.

➤ Create a **new Swift file** and name it **Exercise.swift**. Add the following code below `import Foundation`:

```swift
struct Exercise {
  let exerciseName: String
  let videoName: String

  enum ExerciseEnum: String {
    case squat = "Squat"
    case stepUp = "Step Up"
    case burpee = "Burpee"
    case sunSalute = "Sun Salute"
  }
}
```

In the previous chapters, you've created and used structures that conform to the `View` protocol. This `Exercise` structure *models* your app's data, encapsulating the `exerciseName` and `videoName` properties.

Enumerating exercise names

`enum` is short for *enumeration*. A Swift enumeration is a named type and can have methods and computed properties. It's useful for grouping related values so the compiler can help you avoid mistakes like misspelling a string.

> **Swift Tip**: A *stored property* is one you declare with a type and/or an initial value, like `let name: String` or `let name = "Audrey"`. You declare a *computed property* with a type and a closure where you compute its value, like `var body: some View { ... }`.

Here, you create an enumeration for the four exercise names. The case names are camelCase: If you start typing `ExerciseEnum.sunSalute`, Xcode will suggest the auto-completion.

Because this enumeration has `String` type, you can specify a `String` as the *raw value* of each case. Here, you specify the title-case version of the exercise name: "Sun Salute" for `sunSalute`, for example. You access this `String` with `ExerciseEnum.sunSalute.rawValue`, for example.

Creating an array of Exercise instances

You get to use your enumeration right away to create your `exercises` array.

➤ **Below** `Exercise`, completely outside its braces, add this code:

```
extension Exercise {
  static let exercises = [
    Exercise(
      exerciseName: ExerciseEnum.squat.rawValue,
      videoName: "squat"),
    Exercise(
      exerciseName: ExerciseEnum.stepUp.rawValue,
      videoName: "step-up"),
    Exercise(
      exerciseName: ExerciseEnum.burpee.rawValue,
      videoName: "burpee"),
    Exercise(
      exerciseName: ExerciseEnum.sunSalute.rawValue,
      videoName: "sun-salute")
  ]
}
```

In an *extension* to the `Exercise` structure, you initialize the `exercises` array as a *type property*.

exerciseName and videoName are *instance properties*: Each Exercise instance has its own values for these properties. A *type property* belongs to the type, and you declare it with the static keyword. The exercises array doesn't belong to an Exercise instance. There's just one exercises array no matter how many Exercise instances you create. You use the type name to access it: Exercise.exercises.

You create the exercises array with an *array literal*: a comma-separated list of values, enclosed in square brackets. Each value is an instance of Exercise, supplying the raw value of an enumeration case and the corresponding video file name.

As the word suggests, an *extension* extends a named type. The starter project includes two extensions, in **DateExtension.swift** and **ImageExtension.swift**. Date and Image are built-in SwiftUI types but, using extension, you can add methods and computed or type properties.

Here, Exercise is your own custom type, so why do you have an extension? In this case, it's just for housekeeping, to keep this particular task — initializing an array of Exercise values — separate from the core definition of your structure — stored properties and any custom initializers.

Developers also use extensions to encapsulate the requirements for protocols, one for each protocol. When you organize your code like this, you can more easily see where to add features or look for bugs.

Refactoring ContentView and ExerciseView

Now, you'll modify ContentView and ExerciseView to use your new Exercise.exercises array.

➤ In **ContentView.swift**, replace the ForEach loop range with this:

```
ForEach(0 ..< Exercise.exercises.count) { index in
```

Instead of a magic number, you use the number of exercises elements as the upper bound of the ForEach range.

> **Note:** You *could* pass the whole Exercise item to ExerciseView but, in the next chapter, you'll use index to decide when to show SuccessView.

➤ In **ExerciseView.swift**, delete the `videoNames` and `exerciseNames` arrays. The `Exercise.exercises` array contains the same data. The error flags tell you where you need to use this array.

Replace `exerciseNames[index]` with this:

```
Exercise.exercises[index].exerciseName
```

And replace `videoNames[index]`, in two places, with this:

```
Exercise.exercises[index].videoName
```

➤ Run **live preview** in **ContentView.swift** to check everything still works:

Exercise views work after refactoring.

Refactoring `ContentView` and `ExerciseView` is *almost* everything you need to do. You don't need to modify any of the other views, except `HistoryView`.

Structuring HistoryView data

Skills you'll learn in this section: `Identifiable`, `mutating func`, initializer, compiler directive / conditional compilation, debug/release build config, Preview Content, `ForEach` with an array of `Identifiable` values

`HistoryView` currently uses hard-coded dates and exercise lists to mock up its display. You need a data structure for storing your user's activity. And, in the next chapter, you'll implement the **Done** button to add completed exercise names to this data structure.

Creating HistoryStore

➤ Create a **new Swift file** and name it **HistoryStore.swift**. Group it with **Exercise.swift** and name the group folder **Model**:

Model group with Exercise and HistoryStore

➤ Add the following code below `import Foundation`:

```swift
struct ExerciseDay: Identifiable {
  let id = UUID()
  let date: Date
  var exercises: [String] = []
}

struct HistoryStore {
  var exerciseDays: [ExerciseDay] = []
}
```

An ExerciseDay has properties for the date and a list of exercise names completed by your user on that date.

ExerciseDay conforms to Identifiable. This protocol is useful for named types that you plan to use as elements of a collection, because you usually want to loop over these elements or display them in a list.

When you loop over a collection with ForEach, it must have a way to uniquely identify each of the collection's elements. The easiest way is to make the element's type conform to Identifiable and include id: UUID as a property.

UUID is a basic Foundation type, and UUID() is the easiest way to create a unique identifier whenever you create an ExerciseDay instance.

The only property in HistoryStore is an array of ExerciseDay values you'll loop over in HistoryView.

In Chapter 9, "Saving History Data", you'll extend HistoryStore with a method to save the user's history to persistent storage and another method to load the history. Soon, you'll add a HistoryStore property to HistoryView, which will initialize it.

In the meantime, you need some sample history data and an initializer to create it.

➤ **Below** HistoryStore, completely outside its braces, add this code:

```
extension HistoryStore {
  mutating func createDevData() {
    // Development data
    exerciseDays = [
      ExerciseDay(
        date: Date().addingTimeInterval(-86400),
        exercises: [
          Exercise.exercises[0].exerciseName,
          Exercise.exercises[1].exerciseName,
          Exercise.exercises[2].exerciseName
        ]),
      ExerciseDay(
        date: Date().addingTimeInterval(-86400 * 2),
        exercises: [
          Exercise.exercises[1].exerciseName,
          Exercise.exercises[0].exerciseName
        ])
    ]
  }
}
```

This is pretty much the same sample data you had before, now stored in your new `Exercise` and `ExerciseDay` structures. In the next chapter, you'll add a new `ExerciseDay` item, so I've moved the development data to yesterday and the day before yesterday.

You create this sample data in a method named `createDevData`. This method changes, or mutates, the `exerciseDays` property, so you must mark it with the `mutating` keyword.

And you create this method in an extension because it's not part of the core definition. But there's another reason, too – coming up soon!

➤ Now, in the main `HistoryStore`, create an initializer for `HistoryStore` that calls `createDevData()`:

```
init() {
  #if DEBUG
  createDevData()
  #endif
}
```

You don't want to call `createDevData()` in the release version of your app, so you use a compiler directive to check whether the current **Build Configuration** is **Debug**:

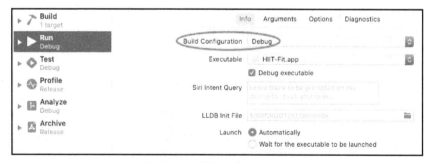

Debug build configuration

> **Note**: To see this window, click the toolbar button labeled **HIITFit**. It also opens the run destination menu alongside. Select **Edit Scheme…**, then select the **Info** tab.

Moving development code into Preview Content

In fact, you don't want `createDevData()` to ship in your release version at all. Xcode provides a place for development code and data: **Preview Content**. Anything you put into this group will not be included in your release version.

➤ In the **Preview Content** group, create a **new Swift file** named **HistoryStoreDevData.swift** and move the `HistoryStore` extension into it:

```
33   import Foundation
34
35   extension HistoryStore {
36       mutating func createDevData() {
37           // Development data
38           exerciseDays = [
39               ExerciseDay(
40                   date: Date(),
41                   exercises: [
42                       Exercise.exercises[0],
43                       Exercise.exercises[1],
44                       Exercise.exercises[2]
45                   ]),
46               ExerciseDay(
47                   date: Date().addingTimeInterval(-86400),
48                   exercises: [
49                       Exercise.exercises[1],
50                       Exercise.exercises[0]
51                   ])
52           ]
53       }
54   }
```

HistoryStore extension in Preview Content

And this is the other reason `createDevData()` is in an extension: You can store extensions in separate files. This means you never have to scroll through very long files.

Refactoring HistoryView

➤ In **HistoryView.swift**, delete the `Date` properties and the exercise arrays, then add this property:

```
let history = HistoryStore()
```

`HistoryStore` now encapsulates all the information in the stored properties `today`, `yesterday` and the exercises arrays.

The Form closure currently displays each day in a Section. Now that you have an exerciseDays array, you should loop over the array.

➤ Replace the Form closure with the following:

```
Form {
  ForEach(history.exerciseDays) { day in
    Section(
      header:
        Text(day.date.formatted(as: "MMM d"))
        .font(.headline)) {
        ForEach(day.exercises, id: \.self) { exercise in
          Text(exercise)
        }
      }
    }
}
```

Instead of today and yesterday, you use day.date. And instead of the named exercises arrays, you use day.exercises.

The code you just replaced looped over exercises1 and exercises2 arrays of String. The id: \.self argument told ForEach to use the instance itself as the unique identifier. The exercises array also contains String instances, so you still need to specify this id value.

➤ Refresh the preview to make sure it still looks the same:

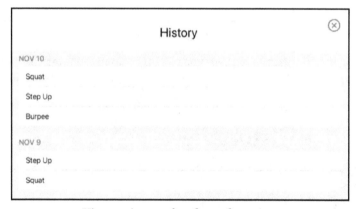

History view works after refactoring.

Congratulations, you've set up your data structures and refactored your views to use them. The final project up to this point is in the **final-no-loc** folder. The rest of this chapter shows you how to localize your app.

Localizing your app

Skills you'll learn in this section: how to localize your app; how to use `CustomStringConvertible` and `genstrings`; how to change app language

You surely want to maximize the audience for your app. A good way to do this is to translate it into languages other than English. This is called *localization*.

You need to complete the following tasks. You can do these in a different order, but this workflow will save you some time:

1. Set up localization for the project's development language (English).

2. Decide which user-facing strings you want to localize and replace these with `NSLocalizedString` instances.

3. Generate the contents of **Localizable.strings** from these `NSLocalizedString` instances.

4. Add another language, choosing the existing English **Localizable.strings** as the reference language resource file.

5. In the **Localizable.strings** file for the new language, replace English strings with translated strings.

Getting started

➤ In the Project navigator, select the top-level **HIITFit** folder. This opens the project page in the editor:

Open the project page.

If you don't see the projects and targets list, click the button in the upper left corner.

➤ Select the **HIITFit Project**, then its **Info** tab:

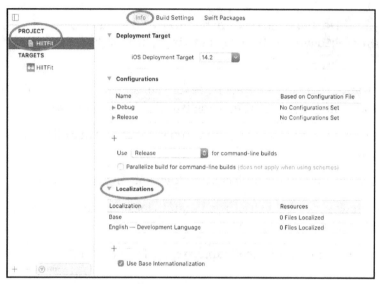

Project Info: Localizations

The **Localizations** section lists **Base** and **English — Development Language**, both with **0 Files Localized**.

UIKit projects have a **Base.lproj** folder containing **.storyboard** and/or **.xib** files. SwiftUI projects with a **LaunchScreen.storyboard** file also have this folder. These files are already marked as *localized* in the development language (English). When you add another language, they appear in a checklist of resources you want to localize in the new language. So projects like these have at least one base-localized file.

If you don't do anything to localize your app, you won't have any development-language-localized files. All the user-facing text in your app just appears the way you write it. As soon as you decide to add another language, you'll replace this text with NSLocalizedString instances. For this mechanism to work, you'll also have to localize in the development language.

> **Note**: To change **Development Language** to another language, edit **project.pbxproj** in a text editor and, for both **developmentRegion** and **knownRegions**, change **en** to the language ID for your preferred development language.

You *could* add another language now, but the workflow you'll follow below saves you some time.

Creating en.lproj/Localizable.strings

This step sets up localization for the project's development language (English). First, you'll create a **Strings** file named **Localizable.strings**.

➤ To create this file in the **HIITFit** group, but not in the **Views** group, select **Assets.xcassets** or **HIITFitApp.swift** in the Project navigator.

➤ Press **Command-N** to open the new file window, search for **string**, then select **Strings File**:

New Strings File

➤ Name this file **Localizable**. This is the default name iOS uses. Don't let your auto-correct change it to Localisable, or you'll have to type the name of this file *every* time you reference a localized string.

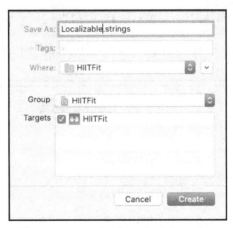

File name must be Localizable.strings.

Naming this file "Localizable" doesn't make it so. You must explicitly localize it.

➤ Select **Localizable.strings** in the Project navigator and open the File inspector (**Option-Command-1**).

Localizable.strings: File inspector

Notice the file's pathname is:

```
HIITFit/HIITFit/Localizable.strings
```

➤ Click **Localize....** Something very quick happens! If the file inspector goes blank, select **Localizable.strings** in the Project navigator again:

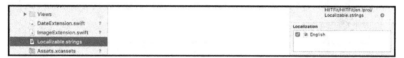

Localizable.strings is now localized.

A **Localization** section has replaced the button. And now the file's pathname has a new subdirectory:

```
HIITFit/HIITFit/en.lproj/Localizable.strings
```

This new **en.lproj** folder doesn't appear in the Project navigator, but here it is in Finder:

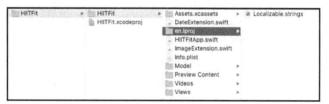

New en.lproj folder

Whenever you localize a resource, Xcode stores it in a folder named **xx.lproj**, where **xx** is the language ID (*en* for English).

That's the project-level setup done. The next two steps will populate this **Localizable.strings** file with lines like "Start" = "Start";, one for each string you want to translate into another language.

Which strings?

The next step starts with deciding which user-facing strings you want to localize.

➤ Now scan your app to find all the text the user sees:

- `WelcomeView` text: **Welcome**, **Get fit ....**

- Exercise names used as `ExerciseView` titles and in `HistoryView` lists.

- Button labels **Get Started**, **Start/Done** and **History**.

- `SuccessView` text: **High Five**, **Good job ....**

Creating NSLocalizedString instances

Next, you'll replace these strings with instances of
`NSLocalizedString(_:comment:)`, where the first argument is the English text and
`comment` provides information to clarify the string's context. If you don't know the
other language well enough to translate your text, you'll usually ask someone else to
provide translations. The `comment` should help a translator make a translation that's
accurate for your context.

➤ Start in **WelcomeView.swift**. Replace `"Welcome"` with this:

```
NSLocalizedString("Welcome", comment: "greeting")
```

Here, "Welcome" is a greeting, not a verb.

➤ Replace most of the other strings in this view:

```
NSLocalizedString("History", comment: "view user activity")
NSLocalizedString("Get Fit", comment: "invitation to exercise")
NSLocalizedString("Get Started", comment: "invitation")
```

➤ Leave "with high intensity interval training" as it is, for now.

➤ In **ExerciseView.swift**, reuse the `"History"` `NSLocalizedString` and replace
`"Start/Done"` with this:

```
NSLocalizedString(
  "Start/Done",
  comment: "begin exercise / mark as finished")
```

➤ In **HistoryView.swift**, again reuse the "History" NSLocalizedString.
DateFormatter automatically localizes dates, so you don't have to do anything to
day.date.

➤ Leave **SuccessView.swift** as it is.

That takes care of everything except the exercise names. You create these in
Exercise.swift, so that's where you'll set up the localized strings.

Localizing the Exercise structure

In **Exercise.swift**, you've been using raw values of ExerciseEnum for exerciseName.
Now you need to use NSLocalizedString("Squat", comment: "exercise")
instead. But an enumeration's raw value must be a literal string, so you can't just
replace the raw values with NSLocalizedString instances.

You need to refactor Exercise to use localized strings instead of enumeration raw
values.

➤ Delete the raw values, then make the enumeration conform to
CustomStringConvertible. This simply requires each case to have a description
string. And a description string can be an NSLocalizedString instance.

```
enum ExerciseEnum: CustomStringConvertible {
  case squat
  case stepUp
  case burpee
  case sunSalute

  var description: String {
    switch self {
    case .squat:
      return NSLocalizedString("Squat", comment: "exercise")
    case .stepUp:
      return NSLocalizedString("Step Up", comment: "exercise")
    case .burpee:
      return NSLocalizedString("Burpee", comment: "exercise")
    case .sunSalute:
      return NSLocalizedString(
        "Sun Salute", comment: "yoga stretch")
    }
  }
}
```

➤ Now, in the exercises array, use the description string for exerciseName
instead of the literal string:

```
extension Exercise {
  static let exercises = [
    Exercise(
      exerciseName: String(describing: ExerciseEnum.squat),
      videoName: "squat"),
    Exercise(
      exerciseName: String(describing: ExerciseEnum.stepUp),
      videoName: "step-up"),
    Exercise(
      exerciseName: String(describing: ExerciseEnum.burpee),
      videoName: "burpee"),
    Exercise(
      exerciseName: String(describing: ExerciseEnum.sunSalute),
      videoName: "sun-salute")
  ]
}
```

Now, when **ContentView.swift** initializes an ExerciseView with an exerciseName, ExerciseView will be able to display that name in Spanish.

> **Note**: Why not ExerciseEnum.squat.description instead of String(describing:)? Well, the CustomStringConvertible documentation says "Accessing a type's description property directly ... is discouraged."

Generating Localizable.strings content

Here's the first time-saving step.

Your **Localizable.strings** file needs to contain lines like "Start" = "Start";, but it's currently blank. You *could* type every line yourself, but fortunately Xcode provides a tool to generate these from your NSLocalizedString instances.

➤ In **Finder**, locate the **HIITFit** folder that contains the **Assets.xcassets** and **en.lproj** subfolders:

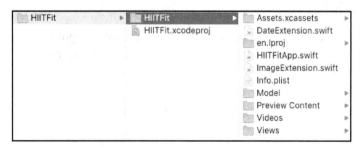

HIITFit folder to drag into Terminal

➤ Open **Terminal**, type cd followed by a space, then drag this **HIITFit** folder into **Terminal**:

```
cd <drag HIITFit folder here>
```

➤ Press **Return**. You changed directory to the folder that contains **Assets.xcassets** and **en.lproj**. Enter this command to check:

```
ls
```

You should see something like this:

```
Assets.xcassets        Info.plist        Views
DateExtension.swift    Model             en.lproj
HIITFitApp.swift       Preview Content
ImageExtension.swift   Videos
```

➤ Now enter this command:

```
genstrings -o en.lproj Views/*.swift Model/*.swift
```

You use the Xcode command line tool genstrings to scan files in **Views** and **Model** for NSLocalizedString. It generates the necessary strings for the key values and stores these in your **Localizable.strings** file.

➤ Back in Xcode, select **Localizable.strings** in the Project navigator. It contains lines like these:

```
/* view user activity */
"History" = "History";
```

That's your comment in comments and the key string assigned to itself. Aren't you glad you didn't have to type all that out yourself? ;]

Adding a language

And here's the other time-saving step. You'll add another language, choosing the existing English **Localizable.strings** as the reference language resource file. And automagic happens!

➤ In the Project navigator, select the top-level **HIITFit** folder, then the project in the projects and target list. In the **Localizations** section, click the + button and select another language:

Add Spanish localization.

This chapter uses Spanish.

Now you get to choose the file and reference language to create your localization:

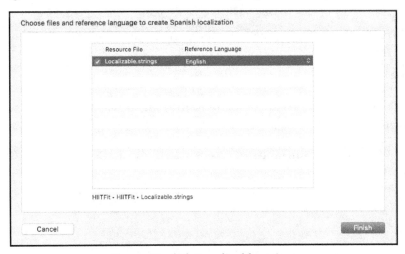

Choose English Localizable.strings.

➤ Click **Finish**.

This produces several changes. The **Localizations** section now has a **Spanish** item, which already has **1 File Localized**.

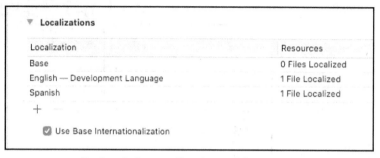

Project Info: Localizations with Spanish

Sure enough, the Project navigator shows **Localizable.strings** is now a group containing two **Localizable.strings** files.

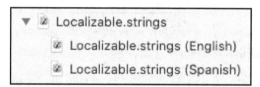

Localizable.strings group

And the Spanish file has the same contents as the English file!

Translating

Now for the final step: In the **Localizable.strings** file for the alternate language, you need to replace English strings with translated strings.

➤ Open **Localizable.strings (Spanish)** and replace the right-hand-side strings with translations:

```
/* exercise */
"Burpee" = "Burpee";

/* invitation to exercise */
"Get Fit" = "Ponte en forma";

/* invitation */
"Get Started" = "Empieza";

/* view user activity */
"History" = "Historia";
```

```
/* exercise */
"Squat" = "Sentadilla";

/* begin exercise / mark as finished */
"Start/Done" = "Empieza/Hecho";

/* exercise */
"Step Up" = "Step Up";

/* warm up stretch */
"Sun Salute" = "Saludo al Sol";

/* greeting */
"Welcome" = "Bienvenid@";
```

Note: Often, Spanish-speakers just use the English exercise names. And using '@' to mean 'a or o' is a convenient way to be gender-inclusive.

Exporting for localization (Optional)

If you use a localization service to translate your strings, Xcode has commands to export **Localizable.strings** files to **XLIFF** (XML Localization Interchange File Format) and import XLIFF translations.

Before you export, localize any media resources or assets that provide useful context information to translators.

Resources like the **.mp4** files have a **Localize** button in their file inspector.

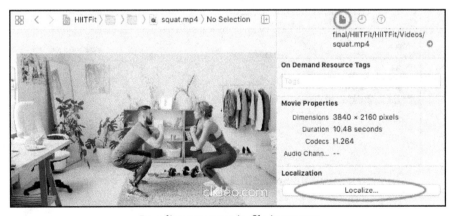

Localize resource in file inspector

Select the **Base** menu option:

Select Base localization.

This *moves* the **.mp4** file into a new **Base.lproj** folder in **Videos**.

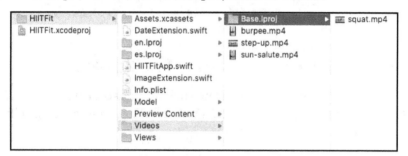

Resource moved into new Base.lproj folder

The **Localize** button for an **Assets.xcassets** item is in its Attributes inspector (**Option-Command-4**). Check the box for Spanish:

Localize asset in Attributes inspector.

To export for localization, select the project in the Project navigator, then select
Editor ▸ Export for Localization...:

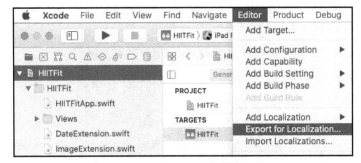

Editor ▸ Export for Localization..

Check the languages you want translations for and choose where to save the
exported folder.

Export options

Note: The **final-loc** project exported to **Preview Content** to keep it with the
project.

See what you got:

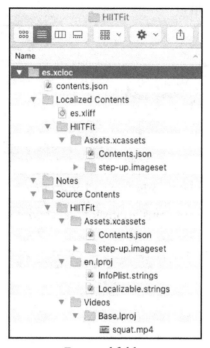

Exported folder

The exported folder has the same name as your project and contains **.xcloc** folders for the languages you checked. For each language, the **.xliff** file is in **Localized Contents**, and localized assets and resources are in **Source Contents**. You can supply additional context information in the **Notes** folder.

> **Note:** I had mixed results exporting videos. If you don't see these in the exported folder, just copy resources and assets directly to the exported **Source Contents** folder.

Testing your localization

To test your localization, you simply need to set the project's **App Language** to **Spanish**.

➤ Edit the scheme and select **Run** ▸ **Options** ▸ **App Language** ▸ **Spanish**

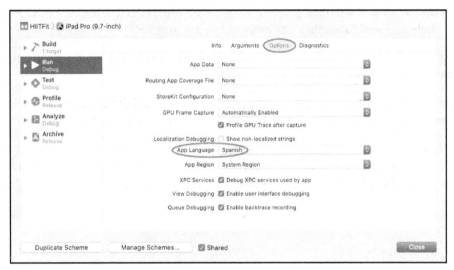

App Language: Spanish

➤ Now check your previews:

Localized app views

Note: The first three letters of November are the same in Spanish, so I changed the date format to "MMMM d" to display the full month name.

Key points

- To use a collection in a ForEach loop, it needs to have a way to uniquely identify each of its elements. The easiest way is to make it conform to Identifiable and include id: UUID as a property.

- An *enumeration* is a named type, useful for grouping related values so the compiler can help you avoid mistakes like misspelling a string.

- Use compiler directives to create development data only while you're developing and not in the release version of your app.

- **Preview Content** is a convenient place to store code and data you use only while developing. Its contents won't be included in the release version of your app.

- Localize your app to create a larger audience for your app. Replace user-facing text with NSLocalizedString instances, generate the English Localizable.strings file, then use this as the reference language resource file for adding other languages.

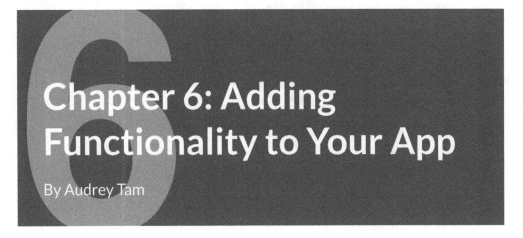

Chapter 6: Adding Functionality to Your App

By Audrey Tam

In the previous chapter, you structured your app's data to be more efficient and less error-prone. In this chapter, you'll implement most of the functionality your users expect when navigating and using your app. Now, you'll need to *manage* your app's data so values flow smoothly through the views and subviews of your app.

Managing your app's data

SwiftUI has two guiding principles for managing how data flows through your app:

- **Data access = dependency**: Reading a piece of data in your view creates a *dependency* for that data in that view. Every view is a function of its data dependencies — its inputs or state.

- **Single source of truth**: Every piece of data that a view reads has a source of truth, which is either *owned* by the view or *external* to the view. Regardless of where the source of truth lies, you should always have a *single* source of truth.

Tools for data flow

SwiftUI provides several tools to help you manage the flow of data in your app. The SwiftUI framework takes care of creating views when they should appear and updating them whenever there's a change to data they depend on.

Property wrappers augment the behavior of properties. SwiftUI-specific wrappers like @State, @Binding, and @EnvironmentObject declare a view's dependency on the data represented by the property.

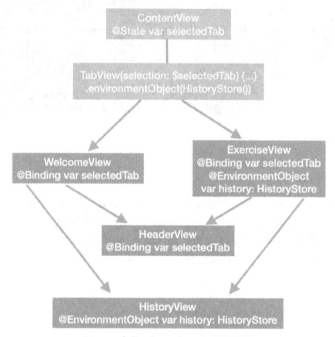

Some of the data flow in HIITFit

Each wrapper indicates a different *source of data*:

- A @State property is a source of truth. One view owns it and passes its value or reference, known as a binding, to its subviews.

- A @Binding property is a reference to a @State property owned by another view. It gets its initial value when the other view passes it a binding, using the $ prefix. Having this reference to the source of truth enables the subview to change the property's value, and this changes the state of any view that depends on this property.

- @EnvironmentObject declares dependency on some shared data — data that's visible to all views in a subtree of the app. It's a convenient way to pass data indirectly instead of passing data from parent view to child to grandchild, especially if the in-between child view doesn't need it.

You'll learn more about these, and other, property wrappers in Chapter 11, "Understanding Property Wrappers".

Navigating TabView

> **Skills you'll learn in this section**: using @State and @Binding properties; pinning a preview; adding @Binding parameters in previews

Here's your first feature: Set up TabView to use tag values. When a button changes the value of selectedTab, TabView displays that tab.

Open the starter project. It's the same as the final no-localization project from the previous chapter.

Tagging the tabs

➤ In **ContentView.swift**, add this property to ContentView:

```
@State private var selectedTab = 9
```

> **Note**: You almost always mark a State property private, to emphasize that it's owned and managed by this view specifically. Only this view's code in this file can access it directly. An exception is when the App needs to initialize ContentView, so it needs to pass values to its State properties. Learn more about access control in *Swift Apprentice*, Chapter 18, "Access Control, Code Organization & Testing" bit.ly/37EUQDk.

Declaring selectedTab as a @State property in ContentView means ContentView *owns* this property, which is the *single source of truth* for this value.

Other views will *use* the value of selectedTab, and some will *change* this value to make TabView display another page. But, you won't declare it as a State property in any other view.

The initial value of selectedTab is **9**, which you'll set as the tag value of the welcome page.

➤ Now replace the entire body closure of `ContentView` with the following code:

```
var body: some View {
  TabView(selection: $selectedTab) {
    WelcomeView(selectedTab: $selectedTab)  // 1
      .tag(9)  // 2
    ForEach(0 ..< Exercise.exercises.count) { index in
      ExerciseView(selectedTab: $selectedTab, index: index)
        .tag(index)  // 3
    }
  }
  .tabViewStyle(PageTabViewStyle(indexDisplayMode: .never))
}
```

Xcode complains you're passing an extra argument because you haven't yet added a `selectedTab` property to `WelcomeView` or `ExerciseView`. You'll do that soon.

1. You pass the *binding* `$selectedTab` to `WelcomeView` and `ExerciseView` so `TabView` can respond when they change its value.

2. You use **9** for the tag of `WelcomeView`.

3. You tag each `ExerciseView` with its index in `Exercise.exercises`.

➤ Before you head off to edit **WelcomeView.swift** and **ExerciseView.swift**, click the **pin** button to *pin* the preview of `ContentView`:

Pin the preview of ContentView.

When you change code in **WelcomeView.swift** and **ExerciseView.swift**, you'll be able to live-preview the results without needing to go back to **ContentView.swift**.

Adding a Binding to a view

➤ Now, in **ExerciseView.swift**, add this property to ExerciseView, **above** let index: Int:

```
@Binding var selectedTab: Int
```

You'll soon write code to make ExerciseView change the value of selectedTab, so it can't be a plain old var selectedTab. Views are structures, which means you can't change a property value unless you mark it with a property wrapper like @State or @Binding.

ContentView owns the *source of truth* for selectedTab. You don't declare @State private var selectedTab here in ExerciseView because that would create a *duplicate* source of truth, which you'd have to keep in sync with the selectedTab value in ContentView. Instead, you declare @Binding var selectedTab — a *reference* to the State variable owned by ContentView.

➤ You need to update previews because it creates an ExerciseView instance. Add this new parameter like this:

```
ExerciseView(selectedTab: .constant(1), index: 1)
```

You just want the preview to show the second exercise, but you can't pass 1 as the selectedTab value. You must pass a Binding, which is tricky in a standalone situation like this, where you don't have a @State property to bind to. Fortunately, SwiftUI provides the Binding type method constant(_:) to create a Binding from a constant value.

➤ Now add the same property to WelcomeView in **WelcomeView.swift**:

```
@Binding var selectedTab: Int
```

➤ And add this parameter in its previews:

```
WelcomeView(selectedTab: .constant(9))
```

➤ Now that you've fixed the errors, you can **Resume** the preview in **WelcomeView.swift**:

WelcomeView preview with pinned ContentView preview

Progressing to the first exercise

Next, you'll implement the **Welcome** page **Get Started** button action to display the first ExerciseView.

➤ In **WelcomeView.swift**, replace Button(action: { }) { with this:

```
Button(action: { selectedTab = 0 }) {
```

➤ Now turn on **live preview** for the pinned `ContentView` preview, then tap **Get Started**.

Tap Get Started to show first exercise.

Note: You can't preview this action in the `WelcomeView` preview because it doesn't include `ExerciseView`. Tapping **Get Started** doesn't go anywhere.

You've used `selectedTab` to navigate from the welcome page to the first exercise!

Next, you'll work even more magic in **ExerciseView.swift**.

Progressing to the next exercise

Your users will be exerting a lot of physical energy to perform the exercises. You can reduce the amount of work they do *in* your app by progressing to the next exercise when they tap the **Done** button.

➤ First, simplify your life by separating the **Start** and **Done** buttons in ExerciseView. In **ExerciseView.swift**, replace `Button("Start/Done") { }` with this `HStack`:

```
HStack(spacing: 150) {
  Button("Start Exercise") { }
  Button("Done") { }
}
```

Keep the `font` and `padding` modifiers on the `HStack`, so both buttons use `title3` font size, and the padding surrounds the `HStack`.

Now you're ready to implement your time-saving action for the **Done** button: Tapping **Done** goes to the next `ExerciseView`, and tapping **Done** in the last `ExerciseView` goes to `WelcomeView`.

➤ Add this to the other properties in `ExerciseView`:

```
var lastExercise: Bool {
  index + 1 == Exercise.exercises.count
}
```

You create a computed property to check whether this is the last exercise.

➤ In **ExerciseView.swift**, replace `Button("Done") { }` with the following code:

```
Button("Done") {
  selectedTab = lastExercise ? 9 : selectedTab + 1
}
```

> **Swift Tip**: The *ternary conditional operator* tests the condition specified before ?, then evaluates the first expression after ? if the condition is true. Otherwise, it evaluates the expression after :.

Later in this chapter, you'll show `SuccessView` when the user taps **Done** on the last `ExerciseView`. Then dismissing `SuccessView` will progress to `WelcomeView`.

➤ Refresh **live preview** for the pinned `ContentView` preview, then tap **Get Started** to load the first exercise. Tap **Done** on each exercise page to progress to the next. Tap **Done** on the last exercise to return to the welcome page.

Tap your way through the pages.

Next-page navigation is great, but your users might want to jump directly to their favorite exercise. You'll implement this soon.

Interacting with page numbers and ratings

Skills you'll learn in this section: passing a value vs. passing a `Binding`; making `Image` tappable

Users expect the page numbers in `HeaderView` to indicate the current page. A convenient indicator is the *fill* version of the symbol. In light mode, it's a white number on a black background.

Light mode 2.circle and 2.circle.fill

➤ In **HeaderView.swift**, replace the contents of `HeaderView` with the following code:

```
@Binding var selectedTab: Int  // 1
let titleText: String

var body: some View {
  VStack {
    Text(titleText)
      .font(.largeTitle)
    HStack {  // 2
      ForEach(0 ..< Exercise.exercises.count) { index in  // 3
        let fill = index == selectedTab ? ".fill" : ""
        Image(systemName: "\(index + 1).circle\(fill)")  // 4
      }
    }
    .font(.title2)
  }
}
```

1. `HeaderView` doesn't change the value of `selectedTab`, but it needs to redraw itself when other views change this value. You create this dependency by declaring `selectedTab` as a `@Binding`.

2. The **Welcome** page doesn't really need a page "number", so you delete the `"hand.wave"` symbol from the `HStack`.

3. To accommodate any number of exercises, you create the `HStack` by looping over the `exercises` array.

4. You create each symbol's name by joining together a `String` representing the integer `index + 1`, the text `".circle"` and either `".fill"` or the empty `String`, depending on whether `index` matches `selectedTab`. You use a ternary conditional expression to choose between `".fill"` and `""`.

➤ Now `previews` needs this new parameter, so replace the `Group` contents with the following:

```
HeaderView(selectedTab: .constant(0), titleText: "Squat")
  .previewLayout(.sizeThatFits)
HeaderView(selectedTab: .constant(1), titleText: "Step Up")
  .preferredColorScheme(.dark)
  .environment(\.sizeCategory, .accessibilityLarge)
  .previewLayout(.sizeThatFits)
```

Next, you need to update the instantiations of `HeaderView` in `WelcomeView` and `ExerciseView`.

➤ In **WelcomeView.swift**, change `HeaderView(titleText: "Welcome")` to the following:

```
HeaderView(selectedTab: $selectedTab, titleText: "Welcome")
```

➤ In **ExerciseView.swift**, change `HeaderView(titleText: Exercise.exercises[index].exerciseName)` to the following:

```
HeaderView(
  selectedTab: $selectedTab,
  titleText: Exercise.exercises[index].exerciseName)
```

➤ Refresh **live preview** for the pinned `ContentView` preview, then tap **Get Started** to load the first exercise. The **1** symbol is filled. Tap **Done** on each exercise page to progress to the next and see the symbol for each page highlight.

ExerciseView with page numbers

Making page numbers tappable

Many users expect page numbers to respond to tapping by going to that page.

➤ In **HeaderView.swift**, add this modifier to `Image(systemName:)`:

```
.onTapGesture {
  selectedTab = index
}
```

This modifier reacts to the user tapping the `Image` by setting the value of `selectedTab`.

➤ Refresh **live preview** for the pinned `ContentView` preview, then tap a page number to navigate to that exercise page:

Tap page number to jump to last exercise.

Congratulations, you've improved your app's user experience out of sight by providing all the navigation features your users expect.

Indicating and changing the rating

The `onTapGesture` modifier is also useful for making `RatingView` behave the way everyone expects: Tapping one of the five rating symbols changes the color of that symbol and all those preceding it to red. The remaining symbols are gray.

Rating view: rating = 3

➤ First, add a `rating` property to `ExerciseView`. In **ExerciseView.swift**, add this to the other properties:

```
@State private var rating = 0
```

In Chapter 8, "Saving Settings", you'll save the `rating` value along with the `exerciseName`, so `ExerciseView` needs this `rating` property. You use the property wrapper `@State` because `rating` must be able to change, and `ExerciseView` owns this property.

➤ Now scroll down to `RatingView()` and replace it with this line:

```
RatingView(rating: $rating)
```

You pass a binding to `rating` to `RatingView` because that's where the actual value change will happen.

➤ In **RatingView.swift**, in `RatingView_Previews`, replace `RatingView()` with this line:

```
RatingView(rating: .constant(3))
```

➤ Now replace the contents of `RatingView` with the following code:

```
@Binding var rating: Int  // 1
let maximumRating = 5  // 2

let onColor = Color.red  // 3
let offColor = Color.gray

var body: some View {
  HStack {
    ForEach(1 ..< maximumRating + 1) { index in
      Image(systemName: "waveform.path.ecg")
        .foregroundColor(
          index > rating ? offColor : onColor)  // 4
        .onTapGesture {  // 5
          rating = index
        }
    }
  }
  .font(.largeTitle)
}
```

1. `ExerciseView` passes to `RatingView` a binding to its `@State` property `rating`.

2. Most apps use a 5-level rating system, but you can set a different value for `maximumRating`.

3. When `rating` is an integer between 1 and `maximumRating`, the first `rating` symbols should be the `onColor`, and the remaining symbols should be the `offColor`.

4. In the `HStack`, you still loop over the symbols, but now you set the symbol's `foregroundColor` to `offColor` if its `index` is higher than `rating`.

5. When the user taps a symbol, you set `rating` to that `index`.

➤ Refresh **live preview** for the pinned `ContentView` preview, then tap a page number to navigate to that exercise page. Tap different symbols to see the colors change:

Rating view

➤ Navigate to other exercise pages and set their ratings, then navigate through the pages to see the ratings are still the values you set.

➤ Click the **pin** button to unpin the `ContentView` preview.

Showing and hiding modal sheets

Skills you'll learn in this section: more practice with @State and @Binding; using a Boolean flag to show a modal sheet; dismissing a modal sheet by toggling the Boolean flag or by using @Environment(\.presentationMode)

HistoryView and SuccessView are modal sheets that slide up over WelcomeView or ExerciseView. You dismiss the modal sheet by tapping its **circled-x** or **Continue** button, or by dragging it down.

Showing HistoryView

One way to show or hide a modal sheet is with a Boolean flag.

➤ In **WelcomeView.swift**, add this State property to WelcomeView:

```
@State private var showHistory = false
```

When this view loads, it doesn't show HistoryView.

➤ Replace Button("History") { } with the following:

```
Button("History") {
  showHistory.toggle()
}
.sheet(isPresented: $showHistory) {
  HistoryView(showHistory: $showHistory)
}
```

Tapping the **History** button toggles the value of showHistory from false to true. This causes the sheet modifier to present HistoryView.

You pass a binding $showHistory to HistoryView so it can change this value back to false when the user dismisses HistoryView.

➤ You'll edit HistoryView to do this soon. But first, repeat the steps above in **ExerciseView.swift**.

Hiding HistoryView

There are actually two ways to dismiss a modal sheet. This way is the easiest to understand. You set a flag to `true` to show the sheet, so you set the flag to `false` to hide it.

➤ In **HistoryView.swift**, add this property:

```
@Binding var showHistory: Bool
```

This matches the argument you passed to `HistoryView` from `WelcomeView`.

➤ Add this new parameter in `previews`:

```
HistoryView(showHistory: .constant(true))
```

➤ Now replace `Button(action: {})` { with the following:

```
Button(action: { showHistory.toggle() }) {
```

You toggle `showHistory` back to `false`, so `HistoryView` goes away.

➤ Go back to **WelcomeView.swift**, start live preview, then tap **History**:

Testing WelcomeView History button

`HistoryView` slides up over `WelcomeView`, as it should. Tap the dismiss button to hide it. You can also drag down on `HistoryView`.

➤ Also check the **History** button in **ExerciseView.swift**:

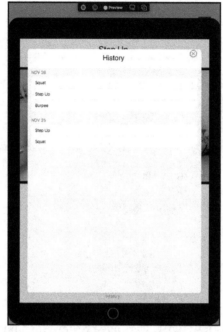

Testing ExerciseView History button

Your app has another modal sheet to show and hide. You'll show it the same way as `HistoryView`, but you'll use a different way to hide it.

Showing SuccessView

In **ExerciseView.swift**, you'll modify the action of the **Done** button so when the user taps it on the last exercise, it displays `SuccessView`.

➤ First, add the `@State` property:

```
@State private var showSuccess = false
```

➤ Then replace the **Done** button action with an `if-else` statement and add the `sheet(isPresented:)` modifier:

```
Button("Done") {
  if lastExercise {
    showSuccess.toggle()
  } else {
    selectedTab += 1
  }
}
```

```
  }
  .sheet(isPresented: $showSuccess) {
    SuccessView()
  }
```

Notice you **don't** pass $showSuccess to SuccessView(). You're going to use a different way to dismiss SuccessView. And the first difference is, it doesn't use the Boolean flag.

Hiding SuccessView

The internal workings of this way are complex, but it simplifies your code because you don't need to pass a parameter to the modal sheet. And you can use exactly the same two lines of code in every modal view.

➤ In **SuccessView.swift**, add this property to SuccessView:

```
@Environment(\.presentationMode) var presentationMode
```

@Environment(\.presentationMode) gives read access to the environment variable referenced by the key path \.presentationMode.

Every view's environment has properties like colorScheme, locale and the device's accessibility settings. Many of these are inherited from the app, but a view's presentationMode is specific to the view. It's a binding to a structure with an isPresented property and a dismiss() method.

When you're viewing SuccessView, its isPresented value is true. You want to change this value to false when the user taps the Continue button.

But the @Environment property wrapper doesn't let you **set** an environment value directly. You can't write presentationMode.isPresented = false.

Here's what you need to do.

➤ In **SuccessView.swift**, replace Button("Continue") { } with the following:

```
Button("Continue") {
  presentationMode.wrappedValue.dismiss()
}
```

You access the underlying PresentationMode instance as the wrappedValue of the presentationMode binding, then call the PresentationMode method dismiss(). This method isn't a toggle. It dismisses the view if it's currently presented. It does nothing if the view isn't currently presented.

➤ Go back to **ExerciseView.swift** and change the line in `previews` to the following:

```
ExerciseView(selectedTab: .constant(3), index: 3)
```

To test showing and hiding `SuccessView`, you'll preview the *last* exercise page.

➤ Refresh the preview and start live preview. You should see **Sun Salute**. Tap **Done**:

Tap Done on the last exercise to show SuccessView.

➤ Tap **Continue** to dismiss `SuccessView`.

One more thing

The **High Five!** message of `SuccessView` gives your user a sense of accomplishment. Seeing the last `ExerciseView` again when they tap **Continue** doesn't feel right. Wouldn't it be better to see the welcome page again?

➤ In **SuccessView.swift**, add this property:

```
@Binding var selectedTab: Int
```

`SuccessView` needs to be able to change this value.

➤ Also add it in `previews`:

```
SuccessView(selectedTab: .constant(3))
```

➤ And add this line to the **Continue** button action:

```
selectedTab = 9
```

`WelcomeView` has tag value 9.

> **Note**: You can add it either above or below the `dismiss` call, but adding it above feels more like the right order of things.

Now back to **ExerciseView.swift** to pass this parameter to `SuccessView`.

➤ Change `SuccessView()` to this line:

```
SuccessView(selectedTab: $selectedTab)
```

➤ And finally, back to **ContentView.swift** to see it work. Run live preview, tap the page 4 button, tap **Done**, then tap **Continue**:

Dismissing SuccessView returns to WelcomeView.

> **Note**: If you don't see the welcome page, press **Command-B** to rebuild the app, then try again.

Tapping **Continue** on `SuccessView` displays `WelcomeView` and dismisses `SuccessView`.

You've used a Boolean flag to show modal sheets. And you've used the Boolean flag and the environment variable `.\presentationMode` to dismiss the sheets.

In this chapter, you've used view values to navigate your app's views and show modal sheets. In the next chapter, you'll observe **objects**: You'll subscribe to a `Timer` publisher and rework `HistoryStore` as an `ObservableObject`.

Key points

- Declarative app development means you declare both how you want the views in your UI to look and also what data they depend on. The SwiftUI framework takes care of creating views when they should appear and updating them whenever there's a change to data they depend on.

- Data access = dependency: Reading a piece of data in your view creates a dependency for that data in that view.

- Single source of truth: Every piece of data has a source of truth, internal or external. Regardless of where the source of truth lies, you should always have a *single* source of truth.

- Property wrappers augment the behavior of properties: `@State`, `@Binding` and `@EnvironmentObject` declare a view's dependency on the data represented by the property.

- `@Binding` declares dependency on a `@State` property owned by another view. `@EnvironmentObject` declares dependency on some shared data, like a reference type that conforms to `ObservableObject`.

- Use Boolean `@State` properties to show and hide modal sheets or subviews. Use `@Environment(\.presentationMode)` as another way to dismiss a modal sheet.

Chapter 7: Observing Objects

By Audrey Tam

In the previous chapter, you managed the flow of values to implement most of the functionality your users expect when navigating and using your app. In this chapter, you'll manage some of your app's data *objects*. You'll use a `Timer` publisher and give some views access to `HistoryStore` as an `EnvironmentObject`.

Showing/Hiding the timer

> **Skills you'll learn in this section**: using a `Timer` publisher; showing and hiding a subview

Here's your next feature: In `ExerciseView`, tapping **Start Exercise** shows a countdown timer; the **Done** button is disabled until the timer reaches 0. Tapping **Done** hides the timer. In this section, you'll create a `TimerView`, then use a Boolean flag to show or hide it in `ExerciseView`.

Using a real Timer

Your app currently uses a Text view with style: .timer. This counts down just fine, but then it counts up and keeps going. You don't have any control over it. You can't stop it. You can't even check when it reaches zero.

Swift has a Timer class with a class method that creates a Timer *publisher*. Publishers are fundamental to Apple's new Combine concurrency framework, and a Timer publisher is much easier to work with than a plain old Timer.

> **Note**: For complete coverage of this framework, check out our book *Combine: Asynchronous Programming with Swift* at https://bit.ly/3sW1L3I.

➤ Continue with your project from the previous chapter or open the project in this chapter's **starter** folder.

➤ Create a **new SwiftUI view file** and name it **TimerView.swift**.

➤ Replace the View and PreviewProvider structures with the following:

```swift
struct TimerView: View {
  @State private var timeRemaining = 3 // 1
  @Binding var timerDone: Bool // 2
  let timer = Timer.publish( // 3
    every: 1,
    on: .main,
    in: .common)
    .autoconnect() // 4

  var body: some View {
    Text("\(timeRemaining)") // 5
      .font(.system(size: 90, design: .rounded))
      .padding()
      .onReceive(timer) { _ in // 6
        if self.timeRemaining > 0 {
          self.timeRemaining -= 1
        } else {
          timerDone = true // 7
        }
      }
  }
}

struct TimerView_Previews: PreviewProvider {
  static var previews: some View {
    TimerView(timerDone: .constant(false))
      .previewLayout(.sizeThatFits)
```

```
    }
}
```

1. timeRemaining is the number of seconds the timer runs for each exercise. Normally, this is 30 seconds. But one of the features you'll implement in this section is disabling the **Done** button until the timer reaches zero. You set timeRemaining very small so you won't have to wait 30 seconds when you're testing this feature.

2. You'll set up the **Start Exercise** button in ExerciseView to show TimerView, passing a binding to the timerDone Boolean flag that enables the **Done** button. You'll change the value of timerDone when the timer reaches zero, but this value isn't owned by TimerView so it has to be a Binding variable.

3. You call the class method Timer.publish(every:on:in:) to create a Timer publisher that publishes an event every 1 second on the run loop of the main — user interface — thread in common mode.

> **Note**: Run loops are the underlying mechanism iOS uses for asynchronous event source processing.

4. The Timer publisher is a ConnectablePublisher. It won't start firing upon subscription until you explicitly call its connect() method. Here, you use the autoconnect() operator to connect the publisher as soon as your Text view subscribes to it.

5. The actual TimerView displays timeRemaining in a large rounded system font, surrounded by padding.

6. The onReceive(_:perform:) modifier *subscribes* to the Timer publisher and updates timeRemaining as long as its value is positive.

7. When timeRemaining reaches 0, it sets timerDone to true. This enables the **Done** button in ExerciseView.

> **Note**: onReceive(_:perform:) returns a published event, but your action doesn't use it, so you acknowledge its existence with _.

Showing the timer

➤ In **ExerciseView.swift**, replace `let interval: TimeInterval = 30` with the following code:

```
@State private var timerDone = false
@State private var showTimer = false
```

You'll pass `$timerDone` to `TimerView`, which will set it to `true` when the timer reaches zero. You'll use this to enable the **Done** button.

And, you'll toggle `showTimer` just like you did with `showHistory` and `showSuccess`.

➤ Next, locate the `Text` view timer:

```
Text(Date().addingTimeInterval(interval), style: .timer)
  .font(.system(size: 90))
```

There's an error flag on it because you deleted the `interval` property.

➤ Replace this `Text` view and `font` modifier with the following code:

```
if showTimer {
  TimerView(timerDone: $timerDone)
}
```

You call `TimerView` when `showTimer` is `true`, passing it a binding to the `State` variable `timerDone`.

➤ Then, replace `Button("Start Exercise") { }` with the following code:

```
Button("Start Exercise") {
  showTimer.toggle()
}
```

This is just like your other buttons that toggle a Boolean to show another view.

Enabling the Done button and hiding the timer

➤ Now, add these two lines to the **Done** button action, *above* the if-else:

```
timerDone = false
showTimer.toggle()
```

If the **Done** button is enabled, `timerDone` is now `true`, so you reset it to `false` to disable the **Done** button.

Also, `TimerView` is showing. This means `showTimer` is currently `true`, so you toggle it back to `false`, to hide `TimerView`.

➤ Next, add this modifier to the `Button`, above the `sheet(isPresented:)` modifier:

```
.disabled(!timerDone)
```

You disable the **Done** button while `timerDone` is `false`.

Testing the timer and Done button

➤ Now check `previews` still shows the last exercise:

```
ExerciseView(selectedTab: .constant(3), index: 3)
```

This exercise page provides visible feedback. It responds to tapping **Done** by showing `SuccessView`.

➤ Start live preview:

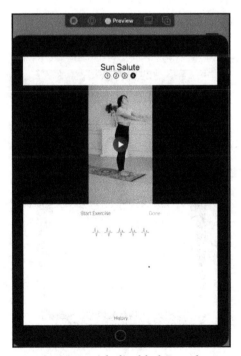

ExerciseView with disabled Done button

The **Done** button is disabled.

➤ Tap **Start Exercise** and wait while the timer counts down from three:

ExerciseView with enabled Done button

When the timer reaches 0, the **Done** button is enabled.

➤ Tap **Done**.

Tap Done to show SuccessView.

This is the last exercise, so SuccessView appears.

➤ Tap **Continue**.

ExerciseView with disabled Done button

Because you're previewing `ExerciseView`, not `ContentView`, you return to `ExerciseView`, not `WelcomeView`.

Now the timer is hidden and **Done** is disabled again.

➤ Tap **Start Exercise** to see the timer starts from 3 again.

Tweaking the UI

Tapping **Start Exercise** shows the timer and pushes the buttons and rating symbols down the screen. Tapping **Done** moves them up again. So much movement is probably not desirable, unless you believe it's a suitable "feature" for an exercise app.

To stop the buttons and ratings from doing squats, you'll rearrange the UI elements.

➤ In **ExerciseView.swift**, locate the line `if showTimer {` and the line `Spacer()`. Replace these lines, and everything between them, with the following code:

```
HStack(spacing: 150) {
  Button("Start Exercise") { // Move buttons above TimerView
    showTimer.toggle()
  }
  Button("Done") {
    timerDone = false
    showTimer.toggle()
```

```
    if lastExercise {
      showSuccess.toggle()
    } else {
      selectedTab += 1
    }
  }
  .disabled(!timerDone)
  .sheet(isPresented: $showSuccess) {
    SuccessView(selectedTab: $selectedTab)
  }
}
.font(.title3)
.padding()
if showTimer {
  TimerView(timerDone: $timerDone)
}
Spacer()
RatingView(rating: $rating) // Move RatingView below Spacer
  .padding()
```

You move the buttons above the timer and `RatingView(rating:)` below `Spacer()`.
This leaves a stable space to show and hide the timer.

➤ Run live preview. Tap **Start Exercise**, wait for the **Done** button, then tap it. The
timer appears then disappears. None of the other UI elements moves.

Show/hide timer without moving other UI elements.

There's just one last feature to add to your app. It's another job for the **Done** button.

Adding an exercise to history

> **Skills you'll learn in this section**: using @ObservableObject and
> @EnvironmentObject to let subviews access data; class vs structure

This is the last feature: Tapping **Done** adds this exercise to the user's history for the
current day. You'll add the exercise to the exercises array of today's ExerciseDay
object, or you'll create a new ExerciseDay object and add the exercise to its array.

Examine your app to see which views need to access HistoryStore and what kind of
access each view needs:

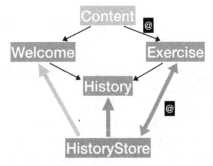

HistoryStore view tree

- ContentView calls WelcomeView and ExerciseView.

- WelcomeView and ExerciseView call HistoryView.

- ExerciseView changes HistoryStore, so HistoryStore must be either a State
  or a Binding variable in ExerciseView.

- HistoryView only needs to read HistoryStore.

- WelcomeView and ExerciseView call HistoryView, so WelcomeView needs read
  access to HistoryStore only so it can pass this to HistoryView.

More than one view needs access to HistoryStore, so you need a single source of
truth. There's more than one way to do this.

The last list item above is the least satisfactory. You'll learn how to manage
HistoryStore so it doesn't have to pass through WelcomeView.

➤ Make a copy of this project **now** and use it to start the challenge at the end of this
chapter.

Creating an ObservableObject

To dismiss SuccessView, you used its presentationMode environment property. This is one of the system's predefined environment properties. You can define your own environment object on a view, and it can be accessed by any subview of that view. You don't need to pass it as a parameter. Any subview that needs it simply declares it as a property.

So if you make HistoryStore an EnvironmentObject, you won't have to pass it to WelcomeView just so WelcomeView can pass it to HistoryView.

To be an EnvironmentObject, HistoryStore must conform to the ObservableObject protocol. An ObservableObject is a *publisher*, like Timer.publisher.

To conform to ObservableObject, HistoryStore must be a *class*, not a structure.

> **Swift Tip**: Structures and enumerations are *value types*. If Person is a structure, and you create Person object audrey, then audrey2 = audrey creates a *separate copy* of audrey. You can change properties of audrey2 without affecting audrey. Classes are *reference* types. If Person is a class, and you create Person object audrey, then audrey2 = audrey creates a *reference* to the *same* audrey object. If you change a property of audrey2, you also change that property of audrey.

➤ In **HistoryStore.swift**, replace the first two lines of HistoryStore with the following:

```
class HistoryStore: ObservableObject {
  @Published var exerciseDays: [ExerciseDay] = []
```

You make HistoryStore a class instead of a structure, then make it conform to the ObservableObject protocol.

You mark the exerciseDays array of ExerciseDay objects with the @Published property wrapper. Whenever exerciseDays changes, it publishes itself to any subscribers, and the system redraws any affected views.

In particular, when ExerciseView adds an ExerciseDay to exerciseDays, HistoryView gets updated.

➤ Now, add the following method to `HistoryStore`, below `init()`:

```
func addDoneExercise(_ exerciseName: String) {
  let today = Date()
  if today.isSameDay(as: exerciseDays[0].date) { // 1
    print("Adding \(exerciseName)")
    exerciseDays[0].exercises.append(exerciseName)
  } else {
    exerciseDays.insert( // 2
      ExerciseDay(date: today, exercises: [exerciseName]),
      at: 0)
  }
}
```

You'll call this method in the **Done** button action in `ExerciseView`.

1. The date of the first element of `exerciseDays` is the user's most recent exercise day. If `today` is the same as this `date`, you *append* the current `exerciseName` to the `exercises` array of this `exerciseDay`.

2. If `today` is a new day, you create a new `ExerciseDay` object and *insert* it at the beginning of the `exerciseDays` array.

> **Note**: `isSameDay(as:)` is defined in **DateExtension.swift**.

➤ Now to fix the error in **Preview Content/HistoryStoreDevData.swift**, delete `mutating`:

```
func createDevData() {
```

You had to mark this method as `mutating` when `HistoryStore` was a structure. You **must not** use `mutating` for methods defined in a class.

> **Swift Tip**: Structures tend to be constant, so you must mark as `mutating` any method that changes a property. If you mark a method in a class as `mutating`, Xcode flags an error. See Chapter 15, "Structures, Classes & Protocols" for further discussion of reference and value types.

Using an EnvironmentObject

Now, you need to set up `HistoryStore` as an `EnvironmentObject` in the parent view of `ExerciseView`. `ContentView` contains `TabView`, which calls `ExerciseView`, so you'll create the `EnvironmentObject` "on" `TabView`.

➤ In **ContentView.swift**, add this modifier to `TabView(selection:)` above `.tabViewStyle(PageTabViewStyle(indexDisplayMode: .never))`:

```
.environmentObject(HistoryStore())
```

You initialize `HistoryStore` and pass it to `TabView` as an `EnvironmentObject`. This makes it available to all views in the subview tree of `TabView`, including `HistoryView`.

➤ In **HistoryView.swift**, replace `let history = HistoryStore()` with this property:

```
@EnvironmentObject var history: HistoryStore
```

You don't want to create another `HistoryStore` object here. Instead, `HistoryView` can access `history` directly without needing it passed as a parameter.

➤ Next, add this modifier to `HistoryView(showHistory:)` in `previews`:

```
.environmentObject(HistoryStore())
```

You must tell `previews` about this `EnvironmentObject` or it will crash with no useful information on what went wrong.

➤ In **ExerciseView.swift**, add the same property to `ExerciseView`:

```
@EnvironmentObject var history: HistoryStore
```

`ExerciseView` gets read-write access to `HistoryStore` without passing `history` from `ContentView` to `ExerciseView` as a parameter.

➤ Replace `ExerciseView(selectedTab:index:)` in `previews` with the following:

```
ExerciseView(selectedTab: .constant(0), index: 0)
  .environmentObject(HistoryStore())
```

You'll preview the *first* exercise, and you attach `HistoryStore` as an `EnvironmentObject`, just like in **HistoryView.swift**.

➤ Now add this line at the top of the **Done** button's action closure:

```
history.addDoneExercise(Exercise.exercises[index].exerciseName)
```

You add this exercise's name to `HistoryStore`.

➤ Run live preview, then tap **History** to see what's already there:

History: before

➤ Dismiss `HistoryView`, then tap **Start Exercise**. When **Done** is enabled, tap it. Because you're previewing `ExerciseView`, it won't progress to the next exercise.

➤ Now tap **History** again:

History: after

There's your new `ExerciseDay` with this exercise!

Your app is working pretty well now, with all the expected navigation features. But you still need to save the user's ratings and history so they're still there after quitting and restarting your app. And then, you'll finally get to make your app look pretty.

Challenge

To appreciate how well @EnvironmentObject works for this feature, implement it using State and Binding.

Challenge: Use @State and @Binding to add exercise to HistoryStore

- Start from the project copy you made just before you changed HistoryStore to an ObservableObject. Or open the **starter** project in the **challenge** folder.

- Save time and effort by commenting out previews in WelcomeView, ExerciseView and HistoryView. Just pin the preview of ContentView so you can inspect your work while editing any view file.

- Initialize history in ContentView and pass it to WelcomeView and ExerciseView. Use State and bindings where you need to.

- Pass history to HistoryView from WelcomeView and ExerciseView. In HistoryView, change let history = HistoryStore() to let history: HistoryStore.

- Add addDoneExercise(_ exerciseName:) to HistoryStore as a mutating method and call it in the action of the **Done** button in ExerciseView.

My solution is in the **challenge/final** folder for this chapter.

Key points

- Create a timer by subscribing to the `Timer` publisher created by `Timer.publish(every:tolerance:on:in:options:)`.

- `@Binding` declares dependency on a `@State` variable owned by another view. `@EnvironmentObject` declares dependency on some shared data, such as a reference type that conforms to `ObservableObject`.

- Use an `ObservableObject` as an `@EnvironmentObject` to let subviews access data without having to pass parameters.

Chapter 8: Saving Settings

By Caroline Begbie

Whenever your app closes, all the data entered, such as any ratings you've set or any history you've recorded, is lost. For most apps to be useful, they have to persist data between app sessions. Data persistence is a fancy way of saying "saving data to permanent storage".

In this chapter, you'll explore how to store simple data using AppStorage and SceneStorage. You'll save the exercise ratings and, if you get called away mid-exercise, your app will remember which exercise you were on and start there, instead of at the welcome screen.

You'll also learn about how to store data in Swift dictionaries and realize that string manipulation is complicated.

Data persistence

Depending on what type of data you're saving, there are different ways of persisting your data:

- **UserDefaults**: Use this for saving user preferences for an app. This would be a good way to save the ratings.

- **Property List file**: A macOS and iOS settings file that stores serialized objects. Serialization means translating objects into a format that can be stored. This would be a good format to store the history data, and you'll do just that in the following chapter.

- **JSON file**: An open standard text file that stores serialized objects. You'll use this format in Section 2.

- **Core Data**: An object graph with a macOS and iOS framework to store objects. For further information, check out our book **Core Data by Tutorials** at https://bit.ly/39lo2k3.

Saving the ratings to UserDefaults

Skills you'll learn in this section: AppStorage; UserDefaults

UserDefaults is a class that enables storing and retrieving data in a **property list** (plist) file held with your app's sandboxed data. It's called "defaults" because you should only use UserDefaults for simple app-wide settings. You should never store data such as your history, which will get larger as time goes on.

➤ Continue with the **final** project from the previous chapter or open the project in this chapter's **starter** folder.

So far you've used iPad in previews. Remember to test your app just as much using iPhone as well. To test data persistence, you'll need to run the app in Simulator so that you can examine the actual data on disk.

➤ Click the run destination button and select **iPhone 12 Pro**.

AppStorage

@AppStorage is a property wrapper, similar to @State and @Binding, that allows interaction between UserDefaults and your SwiftUI views.

You set up a ratings view that allows the user to rate the exercise difficulty from one to five. You'll save this rating to UserDefaults so that your ratings don't disappear when you close the app.

The source of truth for rating is currently in **ExerciseView.swift**, where you set up a state property for it.

➤ Open **ExerciseView.swift** and change @State private var rating = 0 to:

```
@AppStorage("rating") private var rating = 0
```

The property wrapper @AppStorage will save any changes to rating to UserDefaults. Each piece of data you save to UserDefaults requires a unique key. With @AppStorage, you provide this key as a string in quotes, in this case **rating**.

➤ Build and run, and choose an exercise. Tap the ratings view to score a rating for the exercise. UserDefaults now stores your rating.

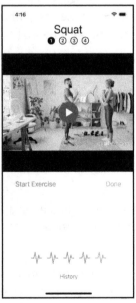

Rating the exercise

AppStorage only allows a few types: `String`, `Int`, `Double`, `Data`, `Bool` and `URL`. For simple pieces of data, such as user-configurable app settings, storing data to `UserDefaults` with `AppStorage` is incredibly easy.

> **Note**: Even though `UserDefaults` is stored in a fairly secure directory, you shouldn't save sensitive data such as login details and other authentication codes there. For those you should use the keychain: https://apple.co/3evbAkA.

➤ Stop the app in Simulator, by swiping up from the bottom. Then, in Xcode, run the app again and go to the same exercise. Your rating persists between launches.

> **Note**: When using @AppStorage and @SceneStorage, always make sure you exit the app in Simulator or on your device before terminating the app in Xcode. Your app may not save data until the system notifies it of a change in state.

You've solved the data persistence problem, but caused another. Unfortunately, as you only have one **rating** key for all ratings, you are only storing a single value in `UserDefaults`. When you go to another exercise, it has the same rating as the first one. If you set a new rating, all the other exercises have that same rating.

You really need to store an array of ratings, with an entry for each exercise. For example, an array of [1, 4, 3, 2] would store individual rating values for exercises 1 to 4. Before fixing this problem, you'll find out how Xcode stores app data.

Data directories

> **Skills you'll learn in this section**: what's in an app bundle; data directories; `FileManager`; property list files; `Dictionary`

When you run your app in Simulator, Xcode creates a **sandboxed** directory containing a standard set of subdirectories. Sandboxing is a security measure that means no other app will be able to access your app's files.

Conversely, your app will only be able to read files that iOS allows, and you won't be able to read files from any other app.

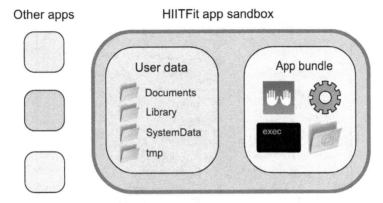

App sandbox and directories

The app bundle

Inside your app sandbox are two sets of directories. First, you'll examine the app bundle and then the user data.

➤ In Xcode, open the **Products** group at the bottom of the groups list. When you build your app, Xcode creates a product with the same name as the project.

➤ If your app's name is in red, build the project to ensure that the compiled project exists on disk.

➤ **Control-click HIITFit.app** and choose **Show in Finder**.

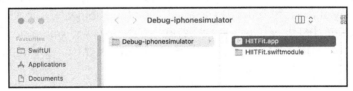

App in Finder

You see here Simulator's debug directory for the app.

➤ In Finder, **Control-click HIITFit** and choose **Show Package Contents**.

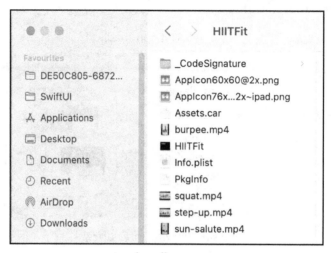

App bundle contents

The app bundle contains:

- App icons for the current simulator.

- Any app assets not in **Assets.xcassets**. In this app, there are four exercise videos.

- **HIITFit** executable.

- Optimized assets from **Assets.xcassets**, held in **Assets.car**.

- Settings files — Info.plist, PkgInfo etc.

The app bundle is read-only. Once the device loads your app, you can't change the contents of any of these files inside the app. If you have some default data included with your bundle that your user should be able to change, you would need to copy the bundle data to the user data directories when your user runs the app after first installation.

> **Note**: This would be another good use of `UserDefaults`. When you run the app, store a Boolean — or the string version number — to mark that the app has been run. You can then check this flag or version number to see whether your app needs to do any internal updates.

You've already used the bundle when loading your video files with `Bundle.main.url(forResource:withExtension:)`. Generally, you won't need to look at the bundle files on disk but, if your app fails to load a bundle file for some reason, it's useful to go to the actual files included in the app and do a sanity check. It's easy to forget to check Target Membership for a file in the File inspector, for example. In that case, the file wouldn't be included in the app bundle.

User data directories

The files and directories you'll need to check most often are the ones that your app creates and updates during execution.

The FileManager class

You interface with the file system using `FileManager`. This allows you to do all the file operations you'd expect, such as examine, move, remove and copy files and directories.

➤ Open **HIITFitApp.swift** and add this modifier to `ContentView`:

```
.onAppear {
  print(FileManager.default.urls(
    for: .documentDirectory,
    in: .userDomainMask))
}
```

Your app will run `onAppear(perform:)` every time the view initially appears.

Here you use the shared file manager object to list the URLs for the specified directory. There are many significant directories, which you can find in the documentation at https://apple.co/3pTE3U5. Remember that your app is sandboxed, and each app will have its own app directories.

➤ Build and run in Simulator. The debug console will print out an array of URLs for your **Documents** directory path in the specified domain. The domain here, `userDomainMask`, is the user's home directory.

Documents directory path

> **Swift Tip**: The result is an array of URLs rather than a single URL, because you could ask for an array of domain masks. These domains could include `localDomainMask` for items available to everyone on the machine, `networkDomainMask` for items available on the network and `systemDomainMask` for Apple system files.

➤ Highlight from `/Users..` to `/Documents/` and **Control-click** the selection. Choose **Services ▸ Show in Finder**.

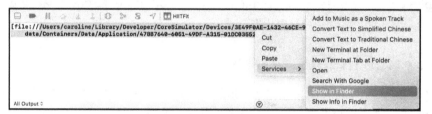

Show in Finder

This will open a new **Finder** window showing Simulator's user directories:

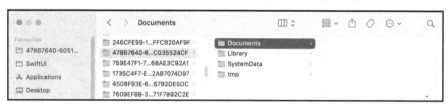

Simulator directories

➤ The parent directory — in this example, **47887…524CF** — contains the app's sandboxed user directories. You'll see other directories also named with UUIDs that belong to other apps you may have worked on. Select the parent directory and drag it to your Favorites sidebar, so you have quick access to it.

In your app, you have access to some of these directories:

- **documentDirectory**: **Documents/**. The main documents directory for the app.

- **libraryDirectory**: **Library/**. The directory for files that you don't want to expose to the user.

- **cachesDirectory**: **Library/Caches/**. Temporary cache files. You might use this if you expand a zipped file and temporarily access the contents in your app.

iPhone and iPad backups will save **Documents** and **Library**, excluding **Library/Caches**.

Inside a property list file

@AppStorage saved your rating to a UserDefaults property list file. A property list file is an XML file format that stores structured text. All property list files contain a Root of type Dictionary or Array, and this root contains a hierarchical list of keys with values.

For example, instead of distributing HIITFit's exercises in an array, you could store them in a property list file and read them into an array at the start of the app:

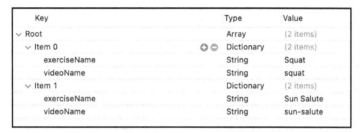

Exercises in a property list file

The advantage of this is that you could, in a future release, add an in-app exercise purchase and keep track of purchased exercises in the property list file.

Xcode formats property lists files in a readable format. This is the text version of the property list file above:

```
<?xml version="1.0" encoding="UTF-8"?>
<!DOCTYPE plist PUBLIC "-//Apple//DTD PLIST 1.0//EN" "http://
www.apple.com/DTDs/PropertyList-1.0.dtd">
<plist version="1.0">
<array>
  <dict>
    <key>exerciseName</key>
    <string>Squat</string>
    <key>videoName</key>
    <string>squat</string>
  </dict>
  <dict>
    <key>exerciseName</key>
    <string>Sun Salute</string>
    <key>videoName</key>
    <string>sun-salute</string>
  </dict>
</array>
</plist>
```

The root of this file is an array that contains two exercises. Each exercise is of type Dictionary with key values for the exercise properties.

Swift Dive: Dictionary

A `Dictionary` is a **hash table** which consists of a hashable key and a value. A hashable key is one that can be transformed into a numeric hash value, which allows fast look-up in a table using the key.

For example, you might create a `Dictionary` that holds ratings for exercises:

```
var ratings = ["burpee": 4]
```

This is a `Dictionary` of type [`String : Integer`], where burpee is the key and 4 is the value.

You can initialize with multiple values and add new values:

```
var ratings = ["step-up": 2, "sun-salute": 3]
ratings["squat"] = 5 // ratings now contains three items
```

```
> (key "sun-salute", value 3)
> (key "squat", value 5)
> (key "step-up", value 2)
```

Dictionary contents

This last image is from a Swift Playground and shows you that dictionaries, unlike arrays, have no guaranteed sequential order. The order the playground shows is different than the order of creation.

If you haven't used Swift Playgrounds before, they are fun and useful for testing snippets of code. You'll use a playground in Chapter 24, "Downloading Data".

You can retrieve values using the key:

```
let rating = ratings["squat"]  // rating = 5
```

UserDefaults property list file

➤ In **Finder**, open your app's sandbox and locate **Library/Preferences**. In that directory, open **com.raywenderlich.HIITFit.plist**. This is the UserDefaults file where your ratings are stored. Your app automatically created this file when you first stored rating.

UserDefaults property list file

This file has a single entry: rating with a Number value of 1. This is the rating value that can be from one to five.

Property list files can contain:

. Dictionary

. Array

. String

. Number

. Boolean

. Data

. Date

With all these types available, you can see that direct storage to property list files is more flexible than @AppStorage, which doesn't support dictionaries or arrays. You could decide that, to store your ratings array, maybe @AppStorage isn't the way to go after all. But hold on — all you have to do is a little data manipulation. You could store your integer ratings as an array of characters, also known as a String.

You'll initially store the ratings as a string of "0000". When you need, for example, the first exercise, you'll read the first character in the string. When you tap a new rating, you store the new rating back to the first character.

This is extensible. If you add more exercises, you simply have a longer string.

Swift Dive: Strings

Skills you'll learn in this section: Unicode; `String` indexing; nil coalescing operator; `String` character replacement

Strings aren't as simple as they may appear. To support the ever-growing demand for emojis, a string is made up of **extended grapheme clusters**. These are a sequence of Unicode values, shown as a single character, where the platform supports it. They're used for some language characters and also for various emoji tag sequences, for example skin tones and flags.

```
"\u{270C}"   "\u{270C}\u{1F3FF}"   "\u{1F1E6}\u{1F1FA}"   "\u{1F1EA}\u{1F1F8}"
```

```
"\u{1F3F4}\u{E0067}\u{E0062}\u{E0077}\u{E006C}\u{E0073}\u{E007F}"
```

Unicode tag sequences

The Welsh flag uses seven tag sequences to construct the single character ▨. On platforms where the tag sequence is not supported, the flag will show as a black flag ▪.

A `String` is a collection of these characters, very similar to an `Array`. Each element of the `String` is a `Character`, type-aliased as `String.Element`.

Just as with an array, you can iterate through a string using a `for` loop:

```swift
for character in "Hello World" {
  print(character) // console shows each character on a new line
}
```

Because of the complicated nature of strings, you can't index directly into a `String`. But, you *can* do subscript operations using indices.

```
let text = "Hello World"
let seventh = text[text.index(text.startIndex, offsetBy: 6)]
// seventh = "W"
```

`text.index(_:offsetBy:)` returns a `String.Index`. You can then use this special index in square brackets, just as you would with an array: `text[specialIndex]`.

As you will see shortly, you can also insert a `String` into another `String` at an index, using `String.insert(contentsOf:at:)`, and insert a `Character` into a `String`, using `String.insert(_:at:)`.

> **Note:** You can do so much string manipulation that you'll need Use Your Loaf's Swift String cheat sheet at https://bit.ly/3aGRjWp

Saving ratings

Now that you're going to store `ratings`, `RatingView` is a better source of truth than `ExerciseView`. Instead of storing `ratings` in `ExerciseView`, you'll pass the current exercise index to `RatingView`, which can then read and write the rating.

➤ Open **ExerciseView.swift**, and remove:

```
@AppStorage("rating") private var rating = 0
```

➤ Toward the end of body, where the compile error shows, change `RatingView(rating: $rating)` to:

```
RatingView(exerciseIndex: index)
```

You pass the current exercise index to the rating view. You'll get a compile error until you fix `RatingView`.

➤ Open **RatingView.swift** and replace `@Binding var rating: Int` with:

```
let exerciseIndex: Int
@AppStorage("ratings") private var ratings = "0000"
@State private var rating = 0
```

Here you hold `rating` locally and set up `ratings` to be a string of four zeros.

Preview holds its own version of @AppStorage, which can be hard to clear.

➤ Replace RatingViewPreviews with:

```
struct RatingView_Previews: PreviewProvider {
  @AppStorage("ratings") static var ratings: String?
  static var previews: some View {
    ratings = nil
    return RatingView(exerciseIndex: 0)
      .previewLayout(.sizeThatFits)
  }
}
```

To remove a key from the Preview UserDefaults, you need to set it to a nil value. Only optional types can hold nil, so you define ratings as String?, with the ? marking the property as optional. You can then set the @AppStorage ratings to have a nil value, ensuring that your Preview doesn't load previous values. You'll take another look at optionals in the following chapter.

You pass in the exercise index from Preview, so your app should now compile.

Extracting the rating from a string

➤ In body, add a new modifier to Image:

```
// 1
.onAppear {
  // 2
  let index = ratings.index(
    ratings.startIndex,
    offsetBy: exerciseIndex)
  // 3
  let character = ratings[index]
  // 4
  rating = character.wholeNumberValue ?? 0
}
```

Swift can be a remarkably succinct language, and there's a lot to unpack in this short piece of code:

1. Your app runs onAppear(perform:) every time the view initially appears.

2. ratings is labeled as @AppStorage so its value is stored in the UserDefaults property list file. You create a String.Index to index into the string using exerciseIndex.

3. Here you extract the correct character from the string using the `String.Index`.

4. Convert the character to an integer. If the character is not an integer, the result of `wholeNumberValue` will be an optional value of `nil`. The two question marks are known as the **nil coalescing operator**. If the result of `wholeNumberValue` is `nil`, then use the value after the question marks, in this case, zero. You'll learn more about optionals in the next chapter.

➤ Preview the view. Your stored ratings are currently `0000`, and you're previewing exercise zero.

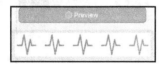

Zero Rating

➤ Change `@AppStorage("ratings") private var ratings = "0000"` to:

```
@AppStorage("ratings") private var ratings = "4000"
```

➤ Resume the preview, and the rating for exercise zero changes to four.

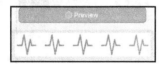

Rating of four

Storing rating in a string

You're now reading the ratings from `AppStorage`. To store the ratings back to `AppStorage`, you'll index into the string and replace the character at that index.

Add a new method to `RatingView`:

```
func updateRating(index: Int) {
  rating = index
  let index = ratings.index(
    ratings.startIndex,
    offsetBy: exerciseIndex)
  ratings.replaceSubrange(index...index, with: String(rating))
}
```

Here you create a `String.Index` using `exerciseIndex`, as you did before. You create a `RangeExpression` with `index...index` and replace the range with the new rating.

> **Note**: You can find more information about `RangeExpressions` in the official documentation at https://apple.co/3qNxD8R.

➤ Replace the `onTapGesture` action `rating = index` with:

```
updateRating(index: index)
```

➤ Build and run and replace all your ratings for all your exercises. Each exercise now has its individual rating.

Rating the exercise

➤ In Finder, examine **com.raywenderlich.HIITFit.plist** in your app's Library directory.

Key	Type	Value
⌄ Root	Dictionary	(2 items)
ratings	String	3124
rating	Number	3

AppStorage

You can remove `rating` from the property list file, as you no longer need it. The ratings stored in the above property list file are:

- Squat: 3

- Step Up: 1

- Burpee: 2

- Sun Salute: 4

Thinking of possible errors

Skills you'll learn in this section: custom initializer

You should always be thinking of ways your code can fail. If you try to retrieve an out of range value from an array, your app will crash. It's the same with strings. If you try to access a string index that is out of range, your app is dead in the water. It's a catastrophic error, because there is no way that the user can ever input the correct length string, so your app will keep failing. As you control the `ratings` string, it's unlikely this would occur, but bugs happen, and it's always best to avoid catastrophic errors.

You can ensure that the string has the correct length when initializing `RatingView`.

Custom initializers

➤ Add a new initializer to `RatingView`:

```
// 1
init(exerciseIndex: Int) {
  self.exerciseIndex = exerciseIndex
  // 2
  let desiredLength = Exercise.exercises.count
  if ratings.count < desiredLength {
    // 3
    ratings = ratings.padding(
      toLength: desiredLength,
      withPad: "0",
      startingAt: 0)
  }
}
```

Going through the code:

1. If you don't define `init()` yourself, Xcode creates a default initializer that sets up all the necessary properties. However, if you create a custom initializer, you must initialize them yourself. Here, `exerciseIndex` is a required property, so you must receive it as a parameter and store it to the `RatingView` instance.

2. `ratings` must have as many characters as you have exercises.

3. If `ratings` is too short, then you pad out the string with zeros.

To test this out, in Simulator, choose **Device ▸ Erase All Contents and Settings…** to completely delete the app and clear caches.

In `RatingView`, change `@AppStorage("ratings") private var ratings = "4000"` to:

```
@AppStorage("ratings") private var ratings = ""
```

When `AppStorage` creates `UserDefaults`, it will create a string with fewer characters than your exercise count.

➤ Build and run and go to an exercise. Then locate your app in Finder. Erasing all contents and settings creates a completely new app sandbox, so open the path printed in the console.

➤ Open **Library ▸ Preferences ▸ com.raywenderlich.HIITFit.plist**. `ratings` will be padded out with zeros.

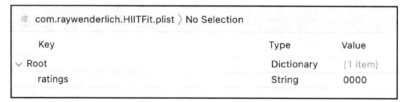

Zero padding

Multiple scenes

Skills you'll learn in this section: multiple iPad windows

Perhaps your partner, dog or cat would like to exercise at the same time. Or maybe you're just really excited about HIITFit, and you'd like to view two exercises on iPad at the same time. In iPad Split View, you can have a second window open so you can compare your Squat to your Burpee.

First ensure that your app supports multiple windows.

➤ Select the top **HIITFit** group in the Project navigator.

➤ Select the **HIITFit** target, the **General** tab and, under **Deployment Info**, locate **Supports multiple windows**.

➤ Ensure this is checked. When unchecked, you won't be able to have two windows of either your own app, or yours plus another app, side-by-side.

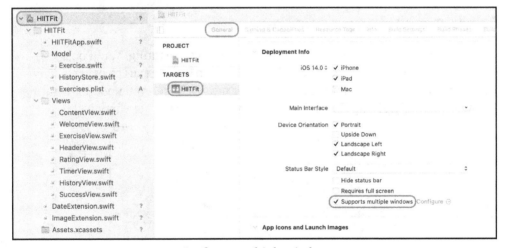

Configure multiple windows

➤ Build and run **HIITFit** either on your iPad device or in iPad Simulator.

Turn Simulator to landscape orientation using **Command-Right Arrow**. With the app open, gently swipe up from the bottom edge to reveal the Dock. You'll see the HIITFit icon in the Dock. Drag this to either the right or left edge of the screen, then drop. You can resize the windows by dragging the divider between the windows.

 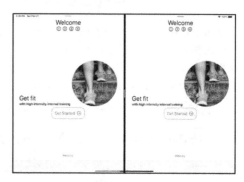

Multiple iPad Windows

You now have two sessions open.

Making ratings reactive

➤ On each window, go to Exercise 1 Squat and change the rating. You'll notice there's a problem, as, although the rating is stored in `UserDefaults` using `AppStorage`, the windows reflect two different ratings. When you update the rating in one window, the rating should immediately react in the other window.

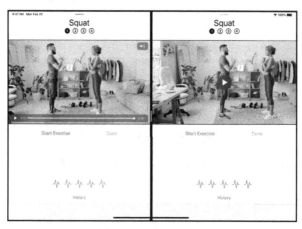

Non-reactive rating

➤ Open **RatingView.swift** and review the code.

With `AppStorage`, you hold one `ratings` value per app, no matter how many windows are open. You change `ratings` and update `rating` in `onTapGesture(count:perform:)`. The second window holds its own `rating` instance. When you change the rating in one window, the second window should react to this change and update and redraw its rating view.

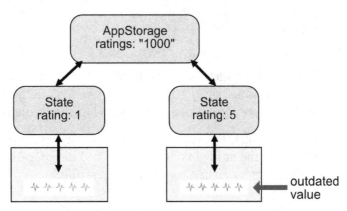

Outdated rating

If you were showing a view with the `ratings` string from `AppStorage`, not the extracted integer `rating`, `AppStorage` would automatically invalidate the view and redraw it. However, because you're converting the string to an integer, you'll need to perform that code on change of `ratings`.

The code that you perform in `onAppear(perform:)`, you'll add to a new `onChange(of:perform:)` modifier that will run whenever `ratings` changes. Instead of duplicating the code, you'll create a new method, and call the method twice.

➤ In `onAppear(perform:)`, highlight:

```
let index = ratings.index(
  ratings.startIndex,
  offsetBy: exerciseIndex)
let character = ratings[index]
rating = character.wholeNumberValue ?? 0
```

➤ **Control-click** the highlighted code and choose **Refactor ▸ Extract to Method**

➤ Name the extracted method `convertRating()`.

> **Swift tip**: Note the `fileprivate` access control modifier in the new method. This modifier allows access to `convertRating()` only inside **RatingView.swift**.

➤ Add a new modifier to `Image`:

```
.onChange(of: ratings) { _ in
  convertRating()
}
```

Here you set up a reactive method that will call `convertRating()` whenever `ratings` changes. If you were using only one window, you wouldn't notice the effect, but multiple windows can now react to the property changing in another window.

➤ Build and run the app with two windows side by side. Return to Exercise 1 in both windows and change the rating in one window. The rating view in the other window should immediately redraw when you change the rating.

Apps, Scenes and Views

> **Skills you'll learn in this section**: scenes; `@SceneStorage`

You opened two independent sessions of HIITFit in Simulator. If this app were running on macOS, users would expect to be able to open any number of HIITFit windows. You'll now take a look at how SwiftUI handles multiple windows.

➤ Open **HIITFitApp.swift** and examine the code:

```
@main
struct HIITFitApp: App {
  var body: some Scene {
    WindowGroup {
      ContentView()
      ...
    }
  }
}
```

This simple code controls execution of your app. The `@main` attribute indicates the entry point for the app and expects the structure to conform to the `App` protocol.

`HIITFitApp` defines the basic hierarchy of your app, made up of:

- **HITTFitApp**: Conforms to `App`, which represents the entire app.

- **WindowGroup**: Conforms to the `Scene` protocol. A `WindowGroup` presents one or more windows that all contain the same view hierarchy.

- **ContentView**: Everything you see in a SwiftUI app is a `View`. Although the SwiftUI template creates `ContentView`, it's a placeholder name, and you can rename it.

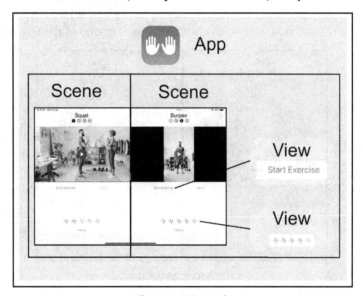

The App Hierarchy

`WindowGroup` behaves differently depending on the platform. On macOS and iPadOS, you can open more than one window or scene, but on iOS, tvOS and watchOS, you can only have the one window.

Restoring scene state with SceneStorage

Currently, when you exit and restart your app, you always start at the welcome screen. This might be the behavior you prefer, but using @SceneStorage, you can persist the current state of each scene of your app.

➤ Build and run your app in iPad Simulator, in two windows, and go to Exercise 3 in the second window. Exit the app in Simulator by swiping up from the bottom. Then stop the app in Xcode. Remember that your app may not save data unless the device notifies it that state has changed.

➤ Rerun the app and, because the app is completely refreshed with new states, the app doesn't remember that you were doing Exercise 3 in one of the windows.

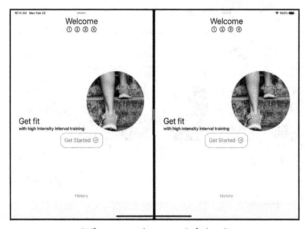

What exercise was I doing?

As you might guess, @SceneStorage is similar to @AppStorage. Instead of being persisted per app instance, @SceneStorage properties persist per scene.

➤ Open **ContentView.swift**.

The property that controls the current exercise is selectedTab.

➤ Change @State private var selectedTab = 9 to:

```
@SceneStorage("selectedTab") private var selectedTab = 9
```

➤ Build and run the app. In the first window, go to Exercise 1, and in the second window, go to Exercise 3.

➤ Exit the app in Simulator by swiping up from the bottom. Then, stop the app in Xcode.

➤ Build and run again, and this time, the app remembers that you were viewing both Exercise 1 and Exercise 3 and goes straight there.

> **Note:** To reset `SceneStorage` in Simulator, you will have to clear the cache. In Simulator, choose **Device ▸ Erase All Content and Settings…** and then re-run your app.

Although you won't realize this until the next chapter, introducing `SceneStorage` has caused a problem with the way you're initializing `HistoryStore`. Currently you create `HistoryStore` in **ContentView.swift** as an environment object modifier on `TabView`. `SceneStorage` reinitializes `TabView` when it stores `selectedTab`, so each time you change the tab, you reinitialize `HistoryStore`. If you do an exercise your history doesn't save. You'll fix this in the following chapter.

Key points

- You have several choices of where to store data. You should use `@AppStorage` and `@SceneStorage` for lightweight data, and property lists, JSON or Core Data for main app data that increases over time.

- Your app is sandboxed so that no other app can access its data. You are not able to access the data from any other app either. Your app executable is held in the read-only app bundle directory, with all your app's assets. You can access your app's **Documents** and **Library** directories using `FileManager`.

- Property lists store serialized objects. If you want to store custom types in a property list file, you must first convert them to a data type recognized by a property list file, such as `String` or `Boolean` or `Data`.

- String manipulation can be quite complex, but Swift provides many supporting methods to extract part of a string or append a string on another string.

- Manage scenes with `@SceneStorage`. Your app holds data per scene. iPads and macOS can have multiple scenes, but an app run on iPhone only has one.

Chapter 9: Saving History Data

By Caroline Begbie

@AppStorage is excellent for storing lightweight data such as settings and other app initialization. You can store other app data in property list files, a database such as SQLite or Realm, or Core Data. Since you've learned so much about property list files already, in this chapter, you'll save the history data to one.

The saving and loading code itself is quite brief, but when dealing with data, you should always be aware that errors might occur. As you would expect, Swift has comprehensive error handling, so that if anything goes wrong, your app can recover gracefully.

In this chapter, you'll learn about error checking techniques as well as saving and loading from a property list file. Specifically, you'll learn about:

- **Optionals**: nil values are not allowed in Swift unless you define the property type as Optional.

- **Debugging**: You'll fix a bug by stepping through the code using breakpoints.

- **Error Handling**: You'll throw and catch some errors, which is just as much fun as it sounds. You'll also alert the user when there is a problem.

- **Closures**: These are blocks of code that you can pass as parameters or use for completion handlers.

- **Serialization**: Last but not least, you'll translate your history data into a format that can be stored.

Adding the completed exercise to history

➤ Continue with your project from the previous chapter, or open the project in this chapter's **starter** folder.

➤ Open **HistoryStore.swift** and examine addDoneExercise(_:). This is where you save the exercise to exerciseDays when your user taps **Done**.

Currently, on initializing HistoryStore, you create a fake exerciseDays array. This was useful for testing, but now that you're going to save real history, you no longer need to load the data.

➤ In init(), comment out createDevData().

➤ Build and run your app. Start an exercise and tap **Done** to save the history. Your app performs addDoneExercise(_:) and crashes with **Fatal error: Index out of range**.

Xcode highlights the offending line in your code:

```
if today.isSameDay(as: exerciseDays[0].date) {
```

This line assumes that exerciseDays is never empty. If it's empty, then trying to access an array element at index zero is out of range. When users start the app for the first time, their history will always be empty. A better way is to use optional checking.

Using optionals

> **Skills you'll learn in this section**: optionals; unwrapping; forced unwrapping; filtering the debug console

Swift Dive: Optionals

In the previous chapter, to remove a key from Preview's UserDefaults, you needed to assign nil to ratings. So you defined ratings as an **optional** String type by adding ? to the type:

```
@AppStorage("ratings") static var ratings: String?
```

`ratings` here can either hold a string value or `nil`.

You may have learned that Booleans can be either true or false. But an optional Boolean can hold `nil`, giving you a third alternative.

> **Swift Tip**: `Optional` is actually an enumeration with two cases: `some(Wrapped)` and `none`, where `some` has a generic value of type `Wrapped` and `none` has no value.

Checking for `nil` can be useful to prevent errors. At compile time, Xcode prevents Swift properties from containing `nil` unless you've defined them as optional. At run time, you can check that `exerciseDays` is not empty by checking the value of the optional `first`:

```
if exerciseDays.first != nil {
  if today.isSameDay(as: exerciseDays[0].date) {
    ...
  }
}
```

When `first` is `nil`, the array is empty, but if `first` is not `nil`, then it's safe to access index 0 in the array. This is true, because `exerciseDays` doesn't accept `nil` values. You can have arrays with `nil` values by declaring them like this:

```
var myArray: [ExerciseDay?] = []
```

The more common way of checking for `nil` is to use:

```
if let newProperty = optionalProperty {
  // code executes if optionalProperty is non-nil
}
```

This places a non-optional **unwrapped** result into `newProperty`. Unwrapped here means that `newProperty` is assigned the contents of `optionalProperty` as long as `optionalProperty` is not `nil`.

➤ Change if `today.isSameDay(as: exerciseDays[0].date) {` to:

```
if let firstDate = exerciseDays.first?.date {
```

`if let` tells the compiler that whatever follows could result in `nil`. The property `first?` with the added `?` means that `first` is an optional and can contain `nil`.

If `exerciseDays` is empty, then `first?` will be `nil` and your app won't perform the conditional block, otherwise `firstDate` will contain the unwrapped first element in `exerciseDays`.

Swift Dive: Forced unwrapping

If you're really sure your data is non-`nil`, then you can use an exclamation mark `!` on an optional. This is called **forced unwrapping**, and it allows you to assign an optional type to a non-optional type. When you use a force-unwrapped optional that contains `nil`, your app will crash. For example:

```
let optionalDay: ExerciseDay? = exerciseDays.first
let forceUnwrappedDay: ExerciseDay = exerciseDays.first!
let errorDay: ExerciseDay = exerciseDays.first
```

- `optionalDay` is of type `ExerciseDay?` and allows `nil` when `exerciseDays` is empty.

- `forceUnwrappedDay` is not optional and could cause a runtime error if `exerciseDays` is empty and you force-unwrap `first`.

- `errorDay` causes a compile error because you are trying to put an optional which could contain `nil` into a property that can't contain `nil`.

Unless you're really certain that the value will never contain `nil`, don't use exclamation marks to force-unwrap it!

Multiple conditionals

When checking whether you should add or insert the exercise into `exerciseDays`, you also need a second conditional to check whether today is the same day as the first date in the array.

➤ Change `if let firstDate = exerciseDays.first?.date {` to:

```
if let firstDate = exerciseDays.first?.date,
  today.isSameDay(as: firstDate) {
```

You can stack up conditionals, separating them with a comma. Your second conditional evaluates the Boolean condition. If `firstDate` is not `nil`, and `today` is the same day as `firstDate`, then the code block executes.

➤ At the end of `addDoneExercise(_:)`, add:

```
print("History: ", exerciseDays)
```

This will print the contents of `exerciseDays` to the debug console after adding or inserting history.

➤ Build and run, complete an exercise and tap **Done**.

Your app doesn't crash, and your completed exercise prints out in the console.

Filtering the debug console

You may find that your debug console is filled with Apple errors, and it can be quite difficult to see your own `print` statements there.

➤ Enter part of the print output that you expect to see, in this case **History**, into **Filter** at the bottom right of the console:

Filter debug console

Your log will show up on its own:

Completed exercise log

To hide the left panel in the debug console, you can choose the icon at the bottom right. This allows you to read your debug messages more easily.

If you have a number of print statements that you wish to see, you can prefix them with particular characters, such as **>>>**.

```
print(">>>", today)
print(">>> Inserting \(exerciseName)")
```

You can then enter **>>>** into **Filter** and your logs will show up on their own. Remember to clear your filter when you're through. It can be frustrating when you forget to add **>>>**, and you filter out your own debugging logs.

Debugging HistoryStore

Skills you'll learn in this section: breakpoints

Even though the contents of `exerciseDays` appears correct at the end of `addDoneExercise(_:)`, if you tap **History**, your history data is blank. This is a real-life frustrating situation where you're pretty sure you've done everything correctly, but the history data refuses to stay put.

Time to put your debugging hat on.

The first and often most difficult debugging step is to find where the bug occurs and be able to reproduce it consistently. Start from the beginning and proceed patiently. Document what should happen and what actually happens.

➤ Build and run, complete an exercise and tap **Done**. The contents of `exerciseDays` print out correctly in the debug console. Tap **History** and the view is empty, when it should show the contents of `exerciseDays`. This error happens every time, so you can be confident at being able to reproduce it.

Error Reproduction

An introduction to breakpoints

When you place breakpoints in your app, Xcode pauses execution and allows you to examine the state of variables and, then, step through code.

➤ Still running the app, with the first exercise done, in Xcode tap in the gutter to the left of `let today = Date()` in `addDoneExercise(_:)` and click. This adds a breakpoint at that line.

```
57   func addDoneExercise(_ exerciseName: String) {
58     let today = Date()
59     if let firstDate = exerciseDays.first?.date,
60       today.isSameDay(as: firstDate) {
61       print("Adding \(exerciseName)")
62       exerciseDays[0].exercises.append(exerciseName)
63     } else {
```

Breakpoint

➤ Without stopping your app, complete a second exercise and tap **Done**.

When execution reaches `addDoneExercise(_:)`, it finds the breakpoint and pauses. The Debug navigator shows the state of the CPU, memory and current thread operations. The debug console shows a prompt — `(lldb)` — allowing you to interactively debug.

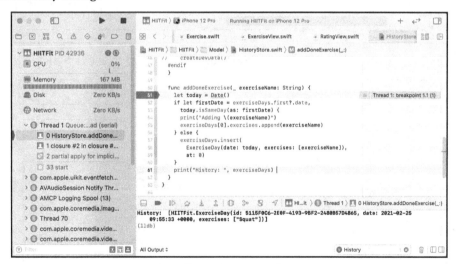

Execution paused

Above the debug console, you have icons to control execution:

Icons to control execution

1. **Deactivate breakpoints**: Turns on and off all your breakpoints.

2. **Continue program execution**: Continues executing your app until it reaches another active breakpoint.

3. **Step over**: If the next line to execute includes a method call, stop again *after* that method completes.

4. **Step into/out**: If your code calls a method, you can step into the method and continue stepping through it. If you step over a method, it will still be executed, but execution won't be paused after every instruction.

➤ Click **Step over** to step over to the next instruction. today is now instantiated and contains a value.

➤ In the debug console, remove any filters, and at the (lldb) prompt, enter:

```
po today
po exerciseDays
```

po prints out in the debug console the contents of today and exerciseDays:

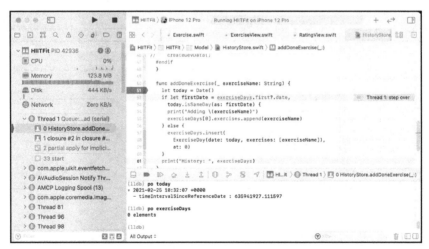

Printing out contents of variables

In this way, you can examine the contents of any variable in the current scope.

Even though `exerciseDays` should have data from the previous exercise, it now contains zero elements. Somewhere between tapping **Done** on two exercises, `exerciseDays` is getting reset.

➤ Step over each instruction and examine the variables to make sure they make sense to you. When you've finished, drag the breakpoint out of the gutter to remove it.

The next step in your debugging operation is to find the source of truth for `exerciseDays` and when that source of truth gets initialized. You don't have to look very far in this case, as `exerciseDays` is owned by `HistoryStore`.

➤ At the end of `init()` add:

```
print("Initializing HistoryStore")
```

➤ Build and run, and reproduce your error by performing an exercise and tapping **Done**. In the debug console, filter on **History**.

Your console should look like this:

```
Initializing HistoryStore
Initializing HistoryStore
History:  [HIITFit.ExerciseDay(id: B1C68848-85A1-4323-A149-A38F9CFB8E3F, date: 2021-02-25
    10:35:33 +0000, exercises: ["Squat"])]
Initializing HistoryStore


All Output ⌄                                    ⊕ History        ◁ ⊗   🗑  ⬜⬜
```

Initializing HistoryStore

Now you can see why `exerciseDays` is empty after performing an exercise. Something is reinitializing `HistoryStore`!

➤ Open **ContentView.swift**. This is where you initialize `HistoryStore` in an environment object modifier on `TabView`.

You may remember from the end of the previous chapter that `@SceneStorage` reinitializes `TabView` when it stores `selectedTab`. The redraw re-executes `environmentObject(HistoryStore())` and incorrectly initializes `HistoryStore` with all its data.

You've now successfully debugged why your history data is empty. All you have to do now is decide what to do about it.

This first step to fix this is to move the initialization of `HistoryStore` up a level in the view hierarchy. Later in the chapter, you'll set up `HistoryStore` so that you're sure that the store will initialize only once.

➤ Cut `environmentObject(HistoryStore())` from `ContentView`'s body.

➤ Open **HIITFitApp.swift** and paste the modifier to `ContentView`:

```
WindowGroup {
  ContentView()
    .environmentObject(HistoryStore())
  ...
}
```

➤ Build and run, perform all four exercises, tapping **Done** after each, and check your history:

Successful history store

Congratulations! You fixed your first bug! You can now remove all your print statements from `HistoryStore` with pride and a sense of achievement.

Now you can continue on and save your history so that it doesn't reset every time you restart your app.

Swift error checking

Skills you'll learn in this section: throwing and catching errors

Saving and loading data is serious business, and if any errors occur you'll need to know about them. There isn't a lot you can do about file system errors, but you can let your users know that there has been an error, and they need to take some action.

➤ Open **HistoryStore.swift** and add a new enumeration to `HistoryStore`:

```
enum FileError: Error {
  case loadFailure
  case saveFailure
  case urlFailure
}
```

This is a list of possible errors that you'll check for.

To create a method that raises an error, you mark it with `throws` and add a `throw` statement.

➤ Add this new method to `HistoryStore`:

```
func load() throws {
  throw FileError.loadFailure
}
```

Here, you'll read the history data from a file on disk. Currently, this method will always raise an error, but you'll come back to it later when you add the loading code. When you throw an error, the method returns immediately and doesn't execute any following code. It's the caller that should handle the error, not the throwing method.

try...catch

When calling a method that throws, you use `try`. If you don't need to handle any errors specifically, you can call the method with `try?` as, for example, `try? load()`. This will convert an error result to `nil` and execution continues. To handle an error from a throwing method, you use the expression `do { try ... } catch { }`.

➤ Add this to the end of `init()`:

```
do {
  try load()
} catch {
  print("Error:", error)
}
```

You call the throwing method and, if there's an error, the `catch` block executes.

➤ Build and run and, in the debug console, you'll see your printed error: **Error: loadFailure**. (Remember to clear your debug console filter if you have one.)

Throwing initializers

You can also throw errors when initializing an object. If your loading of the history data fails, you could either report a catastrophic error and crash the app or, preferably, you could report an error but continue with no history and an empty `exerciseDays`.

➤ Change the signature of `init()` to:

```
init(withChecking: Bool) throws {
```

You'll try to create a `HistoryStore` using this initializer, but fall back to the default initializer if necessary.

➤ Create a new default initializer:

```
init() {}
```

This is your fall-back initializer, which won't call any loading code.

➤ In `init(withChecking:)`, change `print("Error:", error)` to:

```
throw error
```

This will pass back the error to the object that initializes `HistoryStore`.

➤ Open **HIITFitApp.swift**. This is where you initialize `HistoryStore` and place it into the environment.

➤ Add a new property to `HIITFitApp`:

```
@StateObject private var historyStore: HistoryStore
```

So far you've used `@State` for mutable values. You should only use `@State` properties for temporary items, as they will disappear when the view is deleted. `@StateObject` will create an observable object which won't disappear when the view does.

`@State`, being so transient, is incompatible with reference objects and, as `HistoryStore` is a class, `@StateObject` is the right choice here.

> **Note**: In case you're confused about all the property wrappers you've used so far, you will review them in Chapter 11, "Understanding Property Wrappers".

Earlier in the chapter, you moved the initialization of `HistoryStore` from `ContentView` to `HIITFitApp`, but noted that the store must initialize only once. `@StateObject` is a read-only property wrapper. You get one chance to initialize it, and you can't change the property once you set it.

As you want to instantiate `historyStore` using a throwing method, you'll use an initializer.

➤ In `HIITFitApp`, create a new initializer:

```
init() {
  let historyStore: HistoryStore
  do {
    historyStore = try HistoryStore(withChecking: true)
  } catch {
    print("Could not load history data")
    historyStore = HistoryStore()
  }
}
```

When `ContentView` first initializes, you try loading the history. If there is no error, then `historyStore` will contain the loaded history data. If the `try` fails, then you print out an error message and use `HistoryStore`'s default initializer. `HistoryStore.init()` can't possibly fail, but will load with empty history data.

You still have to assign the local `historyStore` to the state object.

➤ Add this to the end of `init()`:

```
_historyStore = StateObject(wrappedValue: historyStore)
```

As the name suggests, a property wrapper wraps an underlying value or object. You use the `StateObject(wrappedValue:)` initializer to set the wrapped value of the state object and use an underscore prefix to assign the initialized state object to `historyStore`.

➤ Change `.environmentObject(HistoryStore())` to:

```
.environmentObject(historyStore)
```

Here you use the state object instead of creating `HistoryStore`, when setting up the environment object.

➤ Build and run and, because `load()` still throws an error, you'll see your error in the debug console: **Could not load history data**.

Alerts

Skills you'll learn in this section: `Alert` view

When you release your app, your users won't be able to see `print` statements, so you'll have to provide them with more visible communication. When you want to give the user a choice of actions, you can use an `ActionSheet` but, for simple notifications, an `Alert` is perfect. An `Alert` pops up with a title and a message and pauses app execution until the user taps **OK**.

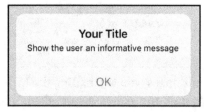

An alert

➤ Open **HIITFitApp.swift** and add a new property to `HIITFitApp`:

```
@State private var showAlert = false
```

This toggle will control whether you show the alert.

➤ In the catch block in init(), update showAlert:

```
showAlert = true
```

➤ Add a new modifier to ContentView:

```
.alert(isPresented: $showAlert) {
  Alert(
    title: Text("History"),
    message: Text(
      """
      Unfortunately we can't load your past history.
      Email support:
        support@xyz.com
      """))
}
```

When showAlert is true, you show an Alert view with the supplied Text title and message. Surround the string with three """ to format your string on multiple lines.

➤ Build and run. Because HistoryStore's initializer fails, you set showAlert to true, which causes your Alert to show.

History Alert

➤ Tap **OK**. Alert resets showAlert and your app continues with empty history data.

Now that your testing of error checking is complete, open **HistoryStore.swift** and remove `throw FileError.loadFailure` from `load()`.

> **Note**: You can find out more about error handling in our *Swift Apprentice* book, which has an entire chapter on the subject. You can find *Swift Apprentice* at: https://bit.ly/2MuhHu0.

Saving history

> **Skills you'll learn in this section**: `FileManager`

You'll first save your history data to disk and then, come back to filling out `load()` using the saved data.

➤ Add a new method to `HistoryStore` to create the URL where you will save the data:

```
func getURL() -> URL? {
  // 1
  guard let documentsURL = FileManager.default.urls(
    for: .documentDirectory, in: .userDomainMask).first else {
    // 2
    return nil
  }
  // 3
  return documentsURL.appendingPathComponent("history.plist")
}
```

This method returns an optional URL. The calling method can then decide what to do if the result of this method is `nil`.

Going through the code:

1. Using `guard`, you can jump out of a method if a condition is not met. `guard let` is similar to `if let` in that you assign an optional to a non-optional variable and check it isn't `nil`. Here you check that `FileManager.default.urls(for:in:).first` is not `nil` and, if it isn't `nil`, assign it to `documentsURL`.

2. You always provide an `else` branch with `guard` where you specify how to leave the method when the `guard` conditional test fails. Generally you return from the method, but you could also use `fatalError(_:file:line:)` to crash the app.

3. You add the file name to the documents path. This gives you the full URL of the file to which you'll write the history data.

➤ Add a new throwing method to `HistoryStore`:

```
func save() throws {
  guard let dataURL = getURL() else {
    throw FileError.urlFailure
  }
}
```

You set up your URL. If `getURL()` returns `nil`, you throw an error and `save()` stops execution.

You'll save the history data to a property list (plist) file. As mentioned in the previous chapter, the root of a property list file can be a dictionary or an array. Dictionaries are useful when you have a number of discrete values that you can reference by key. But in the case of history, you have an array of `ExerciseDay` to store, so your root will be an array.

Property list files can only store a few standard types, and `ExerciseDay`, being a custom type, is not one of them. In Chapter 19, "Saving Files", you'll learn about `Codable` and how to save custom types to files but, for now, the easy way is to separate out each `ExerciseDay` element into an array of `Any` and append this to the array that you will save to disk.

➤ Add this to save() after the previous code:

```
var plistData: [[Any]] = []
for exerciseDay in exerciseDays {
  plistData.append(([
    exerciseDay.id.uuidString,
    exerciseDay.date,
    exerciseDay.exercises
  ]))
}
```

For each element in the loop, you construct an array with a String, a Date and a [String]. You can't store multiple types in an Array, so you create an array of type [Any] and append this element to plistData.

plistData is a type [[Any]]. This is a **two dimensional** array, which is an array that contains an array. After saving two elements, plistData will look like this:

String	Date	[String]	
"4258821"	20210314	["Squat" "Burpee"]	[Any]
"2825419"	20210315	["Squat" "Step Up"]	[Any]

An array of type [[Any]]

The for loop **maps** exerciseDays to plistData. In other words, the loop transforms one set of data to another set of data. As this happens so often in code, Swift provides map(_:), an optimized method on Array, for this transforming of data.

Closures

Skills you'll learn in this section: closures; map(_:); transforming arrays

Swift Dive: Closures

map(_:) takes a **closure** as a parameter so, before continuing, you'll learn how to use closures. You've already used them many times, as SwiftUI uses them extensively.

A closure is simply a block of code between two curly braces. Closures can look complicated, but if you recognize how to put a closure together, you'll find that you use them often, just as SwiftUI does. Notice a closure's similarity to a function: Functions are closures — blocks of code — with names.

A closure

The closure is the part between the two curly braces {...}. In the example above, you assign the closure to a variable addition.

The signature of addition is (Int, Int) -> Int and declares that you will pass in two integers and return one integer.

It's important to recognize that when you assign a closure to a variable, the closure code doesn't execute. The variable addition contains the code return a + b, not the actual result.

To perform the closure code, you execute it with its parameters:

```
let result = addition(1, 2) // result contains 3
```

Closure result

You pass in 1 and 2 as the two integer parameters and receive back an integer:

Closure signature

Another example:

```
let aClosure: () -> String = { "Hello world" }
```

This closure takes in no parameters and returns a string.

Your current task is to convert each ExerciseDay element to an element of type [Any].

This is the closure that would perform this conversion for a single `ExerciseDay` element:

```
let result: (ExerciseDay) -> [Any] = { exerciseDay in
  [
    exerciseDay.id.uuidString,
    exerciseDay.date,
    exerciseDay.exercises
  ]
}
```

`result` is of type `(ExerciseDay) -> [Any]`. The closure takes in a parameter `exerciseDay` and combines the `ExerciseDay` properties into an array of type `[Any]`.

Using map(_:) to transform data

Similar to a `for` loop, `map(_:)` goes through each element individually, transforms the data to a new element and then combines them all into a single array.

You could send `result` to `map` which returns an array of the results:

```
let plistData: [[Any]] = exerciseDays.map(result)
```

`map(_:)` takes the closure `result`, executes it for every element in `exerciseDays` and returns an array of the results.

Rather than separating out into a closure variable, it's more common to declare the map operation together with the closure.

➤ Replace the previous code from `var plistData: [[Any]] = []` to the end of `save()` with:

```
let plistData = exerciseDays.map { exerciseDay in
  [
    exerciseDay.id.uuidString,
    exerciseDay.date,
    exerciseDay.exercises
  ]
}
```

The full declaration of `Array.map(_:)` is:

```
func map<T>(
  _ transform: (Self.Element) throws -> T) rethrows -> [T]
```

- If `map(_:)` finds any errors, it will throw.

- T is a generic type. You'll discover more about generics in Section 2, but here T is equivalent to [Any].

- `transform`'s signature is (Self.element) -> T. You'll recognize this as the signature of a closure to which you pass a single element of ExerciseDay and return an array of type [Any].

This is how your code matches `map(_:)`:

```
func map<T>(_ transform: (Self.Element) throws -> T) rethrows -> [T]
```

```
                    [T]: [[Any]]         Array              Array.Element
                         |                 |                     |
    let plistData: [[Any]] = exerciseDays.map { exerciseDay in
      [
        exerciseDay.id.uuidString,
        exerciseDay.date,                  ———————  T: [Any]
        exerciseDay.exercises
      ]
    }
```

Deconstructing map(_:)

This code gives exactly the same result as the previous `for` loop. Option click `plistData`, and you'll see that its type is [[Any]], just as before.

Type of plistData

One advantage of using `map(_:)` rather than dynamically appending to an array in a `for` loop, is that you declare `plistData` as a constant with `let`. This is some extra safety, so that you know that you won't accidentally change `plistData` further down the line.

An alternative construct

When you have a simple transformation, and you don't need to spell out all the parameters in full, you can use $0, $1, $2, $... as replacements for multiple parameter names.

➤ Replace the previous code with:

```
let plistData = exerciseDays.map {
  [$0.id.uuidString, $0.date, $0.exercises]
}
```

Here you have one input parameter, which you can replace with $0. When using $0, you don't specify the parameter name after the first curly brace {.

Again, this code gives exactly the same result. Option click plistData, and you'll see that its type is still [[Any]].

Type of plistData

Swift Dive: filter(_:) and reduce(_:_:)

There are other common methods that convert one array to another.

With filter(_:) you can filter one array to another array, as for example:

```
let oneToThree = [4, 2, 0, 9, 3, 1].filter {
  Range(1...3).contains($0)    // same as $0 >= 1 && $0 <= 3
}
```

The closure takes each element of the array and returns a value of true if the integer is between one and three. When the closure result is true, the element is added to the new array. After completing this code, oneToThree contains [2, 3, 1].

reduce(_:) combines all the elements in an array into one value. For example:

```
let result = [4, 2, 0].reduce(0) { runningTotal, value in
```

```
    runningTotal + value
  }
```

You call reduce(_:_:) with a starting value. Although you can substitute $0 and $1 for the parameters here, the code reads better with explicitly named parameters. The first parameter is the running total, and you add the second parameter to the first, resulting in a single value. After this code result will contain 6.

Property list serialization

Skills you'll learn in this section: property list serialization

Writing data to a property list file

You now have your history data in an array with only simple data types that a property list can recognize. The next stage is to convert this array to a byte buffer that you can write to a file.

➤ Add this code to the end of save():

```
do {
  // 1
  let data = try PropertyListSerialization.data(
    fromPropertyList: plistData,
    format: .binary,
    options: .zero)
  // 2
  try data.write(to: dataURL, options: .atomic)
} catch {
  // 3
  throw FileError.saveFailure
}
```

Going through the code:

1. You convert your history data to a serialized property list format. The result is a Data type, which is a buffer of bytes.

2. You write to disk using the URL you formatted earlier.

3. The conversion and writing may throw an error, which you catch by throwing an error.

➤ Call save() from the end of addDoneExercise(_:):

```
do {
  try save()
} catch {
  fatalError(error.localizedDescription)
}
```

If there's an error in saving, you crash the app, printing out the string description of your error. This isn't a great way to ship your app, and you may want to change it later.

➤ Build and run and do an exercise. Tap **Done** and your history file will save.

➤ In **Finder**, go to your app's **Documents** directory, and you'll see **history.plist**. Double click the file to open this file in Xcode.

Key	Type	Value
⧈ history.plist ⟩ No Selection		
Key	Type	Value
⌄ Root	Array	(1 item)
⌄ Item 0	Array	(3 items)
Item 0	String	1D352437-606A-4AF9-9D65-FE9C6BB1379A
Item 1	Date	2021-02-11T06:42:34Z
⌄ Item 2	Array	(2 items)
Item 0	String	Sun Salute
Item 1	String	Burpee

Saved history property list file

See how the property list file matches with your data:

- **Root**: The property list array you saved in plistData. This is an array of type [[Any]].

- **Item 0**: The first element in exerciseDays. This is an array of type [Any].

- **Item 0**: The id converted to String format.

- **Item 1**: The date of the exercise

- **Item 2**: The array of exercises that you have performed and tapped **Done** to save. In this example, the user has exercised on one day with two exercises: **Sun Salute** and **Burpee**.

Reading data from a property list file

You're successfully writing some history, so you can now load it back in each time the app starts.

➤ In **HistoryStore.swift**, add this code to load():

```
// 1
guard let dataURL = getURL() else {
  throw FileError.urlFailure
}

do {
  // 2
  let data = try Data(contentsOf: dataURL)
  // 3
  let plistData = try PropertyListSerialization.propertyList(
    from: data,
    options: [],
    format: nil)
  // 4
  let convertedPlistData = plistData as? [[Any]] ?? []
  // 5
  exerciseDays = convertedPlistData.map {
    ExerciseDay(
      date: $0[1] as? Date ?? Date(),
      exercises: $0[2] as? [String] ?? [])
  }
} catch {
  throw FileError.loadFailure
}
```

Loading is very similar to saving, but with some type checking to ensure that your data conforms to the types you are expecting. Going through the code:

1. First set up the URL just as you did with saving the file.

2. Read the data file into a byte buffer. This buffer is in the property list format. If **history.plist** doesn't exist on disk, Data(contentsOf:) will throw an error. Throwing an error is not correct in this case, as there will be no history when your user first launches your app. You'll fix this error as your challenge for this chapter.

3. Convert the property list format into a format that your app can read.

4. When you serialize from a property list, the result is always of type Any. To cast to another type, you use the **type cast operator** as?. This will return nil if the type cast fails. Because you wrote **history.plist** yourself, you can be pretty sure about the contents, and you can cast plistData from type Any to the [[Any]] type that you serialized out to file. If for some reason **history.plist** isn't of type [[Any]], you provide a fall-back of an empty array using the nil coalescing operator ??.

5. With convertedPlistData cast to the expected type of [[Any]], you use map(_:) to convert each element of [Any] back to ExerciseDay. You also ensure that the data is of the expected type and provide fall-backs if necessary.

➤ Build and run, and tap **History**. The history you saved out to your property list file will load in the modal.

Saved history

Challenge

Challenge: Ignore the Error

➤ Delete **history.plist** in Finder, and build and run your app. Your loading error appears because load() fails.

Load error

You're not first checking to see whether **history.plist** exists. If it doesn't, Data(contentsOf:) throws an error.

Your challenge is to ignore the error, as it's most likely that in this case the error is that the file doesn't exist. Remember that you can use try? to discard an error. When you've completed your mission, your app should load data from **history.plist** if it exists and take no action if it doesn't.

You can find the answer to this challenge in load() in the challenges directory for this chapter.

Key points

- Optionals are properties that can contain `nil`. Optionals make your code more secure, as the compiler won't allow you to assign `nil` to non-optional properties. You can use `guard let` to unwrap an optional or exit the current method if the optional contains `nil`.

- Don't force-unwrap optionals by marking them with an `!`. It is tempting to use an `!` when assigning optionals to a new property because you think the property will never contain `nil`. Instead, try and keep your code safe by assigning a fall-back value with the nil coalescing operator `??`. For example: `let atLeastOne = oldValue ?? 1`.

- Use breakpoints to halt execution and step through code to confirm that it's working correctly and that variables contain the values you expect.

- Use `throw` to throw errors in methods marked by `throws`.

- If you need to handle errors, call methods marked by `throws` with `do { try ... } catch { ... }`. `catch` will only be performed if the `try` fails. If you don't need to handle errors, you can call the method with `let result = try? method()`. `result` will contain `nil` if there is an error.

- Use `@StateObject` to hold your data store. Your app will only initialize a state object once.

- Closures are chunks of code that you can pass around just as you would any other object. You can assign them to variables or provide them as parameters to methods. A common paradigm is to pass a closure as a completion handler to be executed when an operation completes. `Array` has a number of methods requiring closures to transform its elements into a new array.

- `PropertyListSerialization` is just one way of saving data to disk. You could also use `JSON`, or Core Data, which manages objects and their persistence.

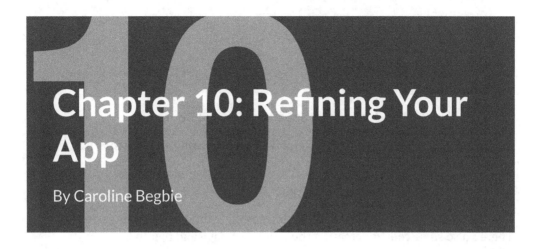

Chapter 10: Refining Your App

By Caroline Begbie

While you've been toiling on making your app functional, your designer has been busy coming up with a stunning eye-catching design. One of the strengths of SwiftUI is that, as long as you've been encapsulating views and separating them out along the way, it's easy to restyle the UI without upsetting the main functionality.

In this chapter, you'll style some of the views for iPhone, making sure that they work on all iPhone devices. The designer has moved your elements around and created a new modal screen for the timer. Essentially, the app works in the same way, though.

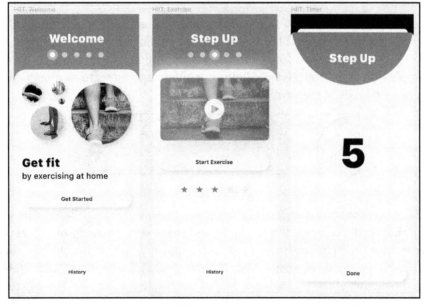

iPhone design

Creating individual reusable elements is a good place to start. Looking at the design, you'll have to style:

1. A raised button for **Get Started**, **Start Exercise** and **Done**.

2. An embossed button for **History** and the exercise rating. The **History** button is a capsule shape, while the rating is round.

3. An inset view background for the timer.

The starter app contains the colors and images that you'll need in the asset catalog. There's also some code for creating the welcome image and text in **WelcomeImages.swift**.

Neumorphism

Skills you'll learn in this section: neumorphism

This style of design, where the background and controls are one single color, is called **neumorphism**. It's a recent trend in design, and you achieve the look with shading rather than with colors.

In the old days, peak iPhone design had **skeuomorphic** interfaces with realistic surfaces, so you had wood and fabric textures with dials that looked real throughout your UI. iOS 7 went in the opposite direction with minimalistic flat design. The name **Neumorphism** comes from **New** + **Skeuomorphism** and refers to minimalism combined with realistic shadows.

Neumorphism

Essentially, you choose a theme color. You then choose a lighter tint and a darker shade of that theme color for the highlight and shadow. You can define colors with red, green, blue (RGB) or hue, saturation and lightness (HSL). When shifting tones within one color, HSL is the easier model to use as you keep the same hue. The base color in the picture above is Hue: 166, Saturation: 54, Lightness: 59. The lighter highlight color has the same Hue and Saturation, but a Lightness: 71. Similarly, the darker shadow color has a Lightness: 30.

Creating a neumorphic button

The first button you'll create is the **Get Started** raised button.

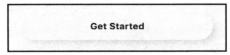

Get Started button

➤ Create a new SwiftUI View file called **RaisedButton.swift**.

Replace the two structures with:

```swift
struct RaisedButton: View {
  var body: some View {
    Button(action: {}, label: {
      Text("Get Started")
    })
  }
}

struct RaisedButton_Previews: PreviewProvider {
  static var previews: some View {
    ZStack {
      RaisedButton()
        .padding(20)
    }
    .background(Color("background"))
    .previewLayout(.sizeThatFits)
  }
}
```

Here you create a plain vanilla button with a preview sized to fit the button. **Assets.xcassets** holds the background color "background".

Plain button

The text style on all three raised buttons is the same.

➤ Add this code after `RaisedButton`:

```
extension Text {
  func raisedButtonTextStyle() -> some View {
    self
    .font(.body)
    .fontWeight(.bold)
  }
}
```

Here you style the text with a bold font.

➤ In `RaisedButton`, add the new modifier to `Text("Get Started")`:

```
.raisedButtonTextStyle()
```

Abstracting the style into a modifier makes your app more robust. If you want to change the text style of the buttons, simply change `raisedButtonTextStyle()` and the changes will reflect wherever you used this style.

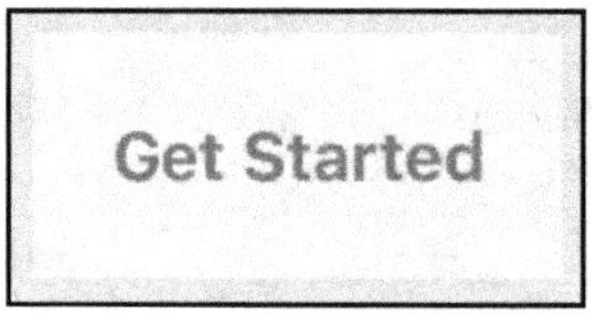

Get Started

Styled text

Styles

Skills you'll learn in this section: view styles; button style; shadows

Apple knows that you often want to style objects, so it created a range of style protocols for you to customize. You'll find the list at https://apple.co/3kzvD2e.

Styling text is not on that list, which is why you created your own view modifier.

You've already used one of these styles, the built-in `PageTabViewStyle`, on your `TabView`. In the documentation, it appears that there are a number of button styles available, however most of these apply to specific operating systems. For example you can only use `BorderedButtonStyle` on macOS, tvOS and watchOS.

You can customize buttons by setting up a structure that conforms to `ButtonStyle`.

➤ Add this new structure to **RaisedButton.swift**:

```
struct RaisedButtonStyle: ButtonStyle {
  func makeBody(configuration: Configuration) -> some View {
    configuration.label
      .background(Color.red)
  }
}
```

Here you make a simple style giving the button text a red background. `ButtonStyle` has one required method: `makeBody(configuration:)`. The configuration gives you the button's label text and a Boolean `isPressed` telling you whether the button is currently depressed.

Swift Tip: If you want to customize how the button action triggers with gestures, you can use `PrimitiveButtonStyle` instead of `ButtonStyle`.

You can use this button style to change all your buttons in a view hierarchy.

➤ Open **HIITFitApp.swift** and temporarily add this new modifier to `ContentView()`:

```
.buttonStyle(RaisedButtonStyle())
```

You tell `ContentView` that whenever there's a button in the hierarchy, it should use your custom style.

➤ Build and run.

Buttons with styled red background

All the buttons in your app will use your new style with the red background. Notice that when you use a style, the button text color changes from the default accent color of blue to the primary color. That's black in Light Mode and white in Dark Mode.

➤ The buttons in your app won't all use the same style so remove `buttonStyle(RaisedButtonStyle())` from `HIITFitApp`.

➤ Open **RaisedButton.swift** and in `RaisedButton_Previews` add a new modifier to `RaisedButton()`:

```
.buttonStyle(RaisedButtonStyle())
```

You can now preview your button style as you change it.

➤ In `RaisedButtonStyle`, change `makeBody(configuration:)` to:

```
func makeBody(configuration: Configuration) -> some View {
  configuration.label
    .frame(maxWidth: .infinity)
    .padding([.top, .bottom], 12)
    .background(
      Capsule()
    )
}
```

When you set `frame(maxWidth:)` to `.infinity`, you ask the view to take up as much of the width as its parent gives it. Add some padding around the label text at top and bottom. For the background, use a `Capsule` shape.

Initial button

When you use `Shapes`, such as `Rectangle`, `Circle` and `Capsule`, the default fill color is black, so you'll change that in your neumorphic style to match the background color.

Shadows

You have two choices when adding shadows. You can choose a simple all round shadow, with a radius. The radius is how many pixels to blur out to. A default shadow with radius of zero places a faint gray line around the object, which can be attractive.

The other alternative is to specify the color, the amount of blur radius, and the offset of the shadow from the center.

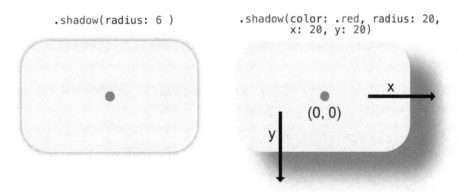

Shadows

➤ In `makeBody(configuration:)`, add new modifiers to `Capsule()`:

```
.foregroundColor(Color("background"))
.shadow(color: Color("drop-shadow"), radius: 4, x: 6, y: 6)
.shadow(color: Color("drop-highlight"), radius: 4, x: -6, y: -6)
```

Watch the button preview change as you add these modifiers. Your darker shadow is offset by six pixels to the right and down, whereas the highlight is offset by six pixels to the left and up. When you add the highlight, the button really pops off the screen.

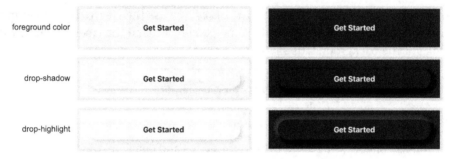

Button styling

The buttons work in Dark Mode too, because each color in the asset catalog has a value for both Light Mode and Dark Mode. You'll learn more about the asset catalog in Chapter 16, "Adding Assets to Your App".

Abstracting your button

Skills you'll learn in this section: passing closures to views

Your button is finished, so you can now replace your three buttons in your app with this one.

➤ Open **WelcomeView.swift** and locate the button code for **Get Started**. Replace the button code and all the button modifiers with:

```
Button(action: { selectedTab = 0 }) {
  Text("Get Started")
    .raisedButtonTextStyle()
}
.buttonStyle(RaisedButtonStyle())
.padding()
```

Here you use your new text and button styles to create your new button.

➤ Preview the button and, even though you haven't yet changed the background color, it looks great.

New Get Started

You could change your other two buttons in the same way, or you could make RaisedButton more abstract by passing in text and an action. You became familiar with closures in the previous chapter, and here's another way you might use one.

➤ Open **RaisedButton.swift** and change RaisedButton to:

```
struct RaisedButton: View {
  let buttonText: String
  let action: () -> Void

  var body: some View {
    Button(action: {
      action()
    }, label: {
      Text(buttonText)
        .raisedButtonTextStyle()
    })
    .buttonStyle(RaisedButtonStyle())
  }
}
```

You pass in the button text and an action closure. The action closure of type () -> Void takes no parameters and returns nothing. Inside Button's action closure, you perform action().

➤ In the preview where you have a compile error, change RaisedButton() to:

```
RaisedButton(
  buttonText: "Get Started",
  action: {
```

```
    print("Hello World")
})
```

When the user taps the button marked **Get Started**, your app prints *Hello World* in the console. (Of course a preview doesn't print anything, so nothing will show.)

When a closure is the method's last parameter, the preferred way of calling it is to use special **trailing closure** syntax.

➤ Replace the above code with:

```
RaisedButton(buttonText: "Get Started") {
  print("Hello World")
}
```

With trailing closure syntax, you remove the `action` label and take the closure out of the method's calling brackets.

Open **WelcomeView.swift** and create a new property for the **Get Started** button:

```
var getStartedButton: some View {
  RaisedButton(buttonText: "Get Started") {
    selectedTab = 0
  }
  .padding()
}
```

➤ In body, change your previous **Get Started** button code, including modifiers, to:

```
getStartedButton
```

That code is a lot more succinct but still descriptive and has the same functionality as before.

➤ Open **ExerciseView.swift** and create a new property for the **Start Exercise** button:

```
var startExerciseButton: some View {
  RaisedButton(buttonText: "Start Exercise") {
    showTimer.toggle()
  }
}
```

➤ In body, replace the **Start Exercise** button code with:

```
startExerciseButton
```

You'll move the **Done** button out of the view shortly.

Exercise Button

The embossed button

Skills you'll learn in this section: stroking a shape

The **History** button will have an embossed border in the shape of a capsule. This will be very similar to RaisedButton, except that your embossed button will be able to contain any content, not just text. For this reason, you'll only create a new button style, and not a new button structure.

➤ Create a new SwiftUI View file named **EmbossedButton.swift**.

➤ Remove EmbossedButton entirely as you won't be needing it.

➤ Copy RaisedButtonStyle from **RaisedButton.swift** to **EmbossedButton.swift**, and change the copied RaisedButtonStyle to EmbossedButtonStyle.

➤ Replace previews in EmbossedButton_Previews with:

```
static var previews: some View {
  Button(
    action: {},
    label: {
    Text("History")
      .fontWeight(.bold)
    })
  .buttonStyle(EmbossedButtonStyle())
  .padding(40)
  .previewLayout(.sizeThatFits)
}
```

You show a **History** button using the embossed button style.

➤ Add a Dark Mode preview.

History Button before embossed styling

➤ In EmbossedButtonStyle, replace makeBody(configuration:) with:

```
func makeBody(configuration: Configuration) -> some View {
  let shadow = Color("drop-shadow")
  let highlight = Color("drop-highlight")
  return configuration.label
    .padding(10)
    .background(
      Capsule()
        .stroke(Color("background"), lineWidth: 2)
        .foregroundColor(Color("background"))
        .shadow(color: shadow, radius: 1, x: 2, y: 2)
        .shadow(color: highlight, radius: 1, x: -2, y: -2)
        .offset(x: -1, y: -1)
    )
}
```

Here you use stroke(_:linewidth:) to outline the capsule instead of filling it with color. You'll learn more about shapes and fills in Chapter 18, "Paths & Custom Shapes". You offset the capsule outline by half the width of the stroke, which centers the content.

➤ Preview your button:

Embossed History Button

The padding doesn't look enough for the text, but different content may require minimal padding, so you'll add the padding to the content you provide for the button instead of inside the button style.

Your capsule-shaped button is now ready for use in your app. However, looking back at the design at the beginning of the chapter, the designer has placed the ratings in a circular embossed button. You can make your button more useful by allowing different shapes.

➤ Add a new enumeration to **EmbossedButton.swift**:

```
enum EmbossedButtonShape {
  case round, capsule
}
```

➤ In EmbossedButtonStyle, below makeBody(configuration:), add a new method:

```
func shape() -> some View {
  Capsule()
}
```

Here, you will determine the shape depending on a passed-in parameter.

➤ In makeBody(configuration:), replace Capsule() with:

```
shape()
```

You get a compile error, as stroke(_:lineWidth:) is only allowed on actual shapes such as Rectangle or Capsule, not on some View. Place your cursor on .stroke(Color("background"), lineWidth: 2), and press **Option-Command-]** repeatedly to move the line down to below Capsule() in shape(). The compile error will then go away.

➤ Add a new property to EmbossedButtonStyle:

```
var buttonShape = EmbossedButtonShape.capsule
```

If you don't provide a shape, the embossed button will be a capsule.

➤ Change shape() to:

```
func shape() -> some View {
  switch buttonShape {
  case .round:
    Circle()
      .stroke(Color("background"), lineWidth: 2)
  case .capsule:
    Capsule()
      .stroke(Color("background"), lineWidth: 2)
  }
}
```

Here you return the desired shape. Unfortunately, you get a compile error. You'll look at this problem in more depth in Section 2, but for now, you just need to understand that the compiler expects some View to be one type of view. You're returning either a Circle or a Capsule, determined at run time, so the compiler doesn't know which type some View should be at compile time.

@ViewBuilder

Skills you'll learn in this section: view builder attribute

There are several ways of dealing with this problem. One way is to return a `Group` from `shape()` and place `switch` inside `Group`.

Another way is to use the function builder `@ViewBuilder`. Various built-in views, such as `HStack` and `VStack` can display various types of views, and they achieve this by using `@ViewBuilder`. Shortly, you'll create your own container view where you can stack up other views just as `VStack` does.

➤ Add this above `func shape() -> some View {`:

```
@ViewBuilder
```

Your code now magically compiles.

Internally, `@ViewBuilder` takes in up to ten views and combines them into one `TupleView`. A **tuple** is a loosely formed type made up of several items.

`@ViewBuilder` has ten `buildBlock(...)` methods and, depending on how many contained views there are, calls the appropriate method. Have you ever tried to add more than ten views in a `VStack`? Because there are only ten methods for building up views in `ViewBuilder`, you'll get a compile error: **Extra argument in call**.

This is one of the declarations of `buildBlock(...)` that takes in seven contained views and returns one `TupleView` made up of these seven views:

```
@available(iOS 13.0, macOS 10.15, tvOS 13.0, watchOS 6.0, *)
extension ViewBuilder {

    public static func buildBlock<C0, C1, C2, C3, C4, C5, C6>(_ c0: C0, _ c1: C1, _ c2: C2, _ c3: C3, _ c4: C4,
        _ c5: C5, _ c6: C6) -> TupleView<(C0, C1, C2, C3, C4, C5, C6)> where C0 : View, C1 : View, C2 : View,
        C3 : View, C4 : View, C5 : View, C6 : View
}
```

buildBlock(...)

The other nine `buildBlock(...)` methods are the same except for the different number of views passed in.

➤ In `EmbossedButton_Previews`, change the Light Mode `.buttonStyle(EmbossedButtonStyle())` to:

```
.buttonStyle(EmbossedButtonStyle(buttonShape: .round))
```

➤ Preview the button, and this is the result for Light Mode:

Initial round button

The circle takes its diameter from the height of the button.

➤ To visualize this, in shape(), click Circle() to view the circle outline in the preview:

Size of the button

The size of the circle should be the larger of either the width or the height of the button contents. You've already used GeometryReader to find out the size of a view, and that's what you'll use here.

➤ In makeBody(configuration:), embed shape() in GeometryReader and add a size parameter to shape. This is the contents of background(_:):

```
.background(
  GeometryReader { geometry in
    shape(size: geometry.size)
      .foregroundColor(Color("background"))
      .shadow(color: shadow, radius: 1, x: 2, y: 2)
      .shadow(color: highlight, radius: 1, x: -2, y: -2)
      .offset(x: -1, y: -1)
  })
```

➤ Change func shape() -> some View to:

```
func shape(size: CGSize) -> some View {
```

You're now passing to shape(size:) the size of the contents of the button, so you can determine the larger of width or height.

➤ In shape(size:), add this modifier to Circle():

```
.frame(
  width: max(size.width, size.height),
  height: max(size.width, size.height))
```

Here you set the frame to the larger of the width or height.

➤ Preview the button, and you can see that the circle takes the correct diameter of the width of the button contents, but starts at the top.

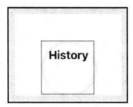

Correct diameter of the button

➤ Add this after the previous modifier:

```
.offset(x: −1)
.offset(y: −max(size.width, size.height) / 2 +
  min(size.width, size.height) / 2)
```

You offset the circle in the **x** direction by half of the width of the stroke. In the **y** direction, you offset the circle by half the diameter plus the smaller of half the width or height.

Completed round button

Your embossed button is now complete and ready to use.

➤ Open **WelcomeView.swift** and add a new property:

```swift
var historyButton: some View {
  Button(
    action: {
      showHistory = true
    }, label: {
      Text("History")
        .fontWeight(.bold)
        .padding([.leading, .trailing], 5)
    })
    .padding(.bottom, 10)
    .buttonStyle(EmbossedButtonStyle())
}
```

Here you use the other form of `Button` so that you can format the button contents. You use the default capsule shape for the button style.

➤ In body, replace:

```swift
Button("History") {
  showHistory.toggle()
}
.sheet(isPresented: $showHistory) {
  HistoryView(showHistory: $showHistory)
}
.padding(.bottom)
```

with:

```swift
historyButton
  .sheet(isPresented: $showHistory) {
    HistoryView(showHistory: $showHistory)
  }
```

➤ Copy the `var historyButton` code, open **ExerciseView.swift** and paste the code into `ExerciseView`.

➤ In body, replace:

```swift
Button("History") {
  showHistory.toggle()
}
```

with:

```swift
historyButton
```

Notice as you replace body's button code with properties describing the views, the code becomes a lot more readable.

➤ In **RatingView.swift**, in body, replace the contents of ForEach with the new round button:

```
Button(action: {
  updateRating(index: index)
}, label: {
  Image(systemName: "waveform.path.ecg")
    .foregroundColor(
      index > rating ? offColor : onColor)
    .font(.body)
})
.buttonStyle(EmbossedButtonStyle(buttonShape: .round))
.onChange(of: ratings) { _ in
  convertRating()
}
.onAppear {
  convertRating()
}
```

You embed Image inside the new embossed button as the label and this time you use the round embossed style.

➤ Build and run and admire your new buttons:

New buttons

ViewBuilder container view

Skills you'll learn in this section: container views

Looking at the design at the beginning of the chapter, the tab views have a purple/ blue gradient background for the header and a gray background with round corners for the rest of the view.

You can make this gray background into a container view and embed WelcomeView and ExerciseView inside it. The container view will be a @ViewBuilder. It will take in any kind of view content as a parameter and add its own formatting to the view stack. This is how HStack and VStack work.

➤ Create a new SwiftUI View file named **ContainerView.swift**.

➤ Change struct ContainerView: View { to:

```
struct ContainerView<Content: View>: View {
  var content: Content
```

Content is a generic. Generics make Swift very flexible and let you create methods that work on multiple types without compile errors. Here, Content takes on the type with which you initialize the view. You'll learn more about generics in Chapter 15, "Structures, Classes & Protocols".

➤ Create an initializer for ContainerView:

```
init(@ViewBuilder content: () -> Content) {
  self.content = content()
}
```

You'll recognize the argument of the initializer as a closure. It's a closure that takes in no parameters and returns a generic value Content. In the initializer, you run the closure and place the result of the closure in ContainerView's local storage.

You mark the closure method with the @ViewBuilder attribute, allowing it to return multiple child views of any type.

➤ Change body to:

```
var body: some View {
  content
}
```

The view here is the result of the content closure that the initializer performed.

Now you can test out your container view in the preview.

➤ Change `ContainerView_Previews` to:

```
struct Container_Previews: PreviewProvider {
  static var previews: some View {
    ContainerView {
      VStack {
        RaisedButton(buttonText: "Hello World") {}
          .padding(50)
        Button("Tap me!") {}
          .buttonStyle(EmbossedButtonStyle(buttonShape: .round))
      }
    }
    .padding(50)
    .previewLayout(.sizeThatFits)
  }
}
```

You create a `VStack` of two buttons. You send `ContainerView` the `VStack` as the content closure parameter. `ContainerView` then shows the result of running the closure content.

Preview of ContainerView

Obviously, this container view only returns the `VStack`, so it's not a lot of use at the moment. You can make view builders quite complex though. In supporting code in Chapter 21, "Delightful UX — Final Touches", you can find a `RenderableView` view builder that observes the contained views and takes a screenshot of the views when triggered.

Your view builder here will format the background.

➤ In `ContainerView` replace body with:

```swift
var body: some View {
  ZStack {
    RoundedRectangle(cornerRadius: 25.0)
      .foregroundColor(Color("background"))
    VStack {
      Spacer()
      Rectangle()
        .frame(height: 25)
        .foregroundColor(Color("background"))
    }
    content
  }
}
```

Here you create a rounded rectangle using the background color from the asset catalog. You don't want the bottom corners to be rounded, so you add a rectangle with sharp corners at the bottom to cover up the corners.

➤ Preview the view, and your container view is finished. It's a good idea not to add unnecessary padding to the actual container view, as that reduces the flexibility. Here you have padding in the preview. When you use the container view shortly, you'll make it go right to the edges.

Finished ContainerView

Designing WelcomeView

Skills you'll learn in this section: refactoring with view properties; the safe area

➤ Open **WelcomeImages.swift**. This is a file included in your starter project which contains some images and formatted text to use in `WelcomeView`.

Welcome images and text

One interesting formatting tip to note in `welcomeText` is the text **kerning** in the modifier `.kerning(2)`. This gives you control over the spacing between the letters.

➤ Open **WelcomeView.swift** and replace body with:

```
var body: some View {
  GeometryReader { geometry in
    VStack {
      HeaderView(
        selectedTab: $selectedTab,
        titleText: "Welcome")
      Spacer()
      // container view
      VStack {
        WelcomeView.images
        WelcomeView.welcomeText
        getStartedButton
        Spacer()
        historyButton
      }
    }
    .sheet(isPresented: $showHistory) {
      HistoryView(showHistory: $showHistory)
```

```
      }
    }
  }
```

Here you use the images and text from **WelcomeImages.swift**. Wherever you can refactor your code into smaller chunks, you should. This code is much clearer and easier to read. You embed the top VStack in GeometryReader so that you'll be able to determine the size available for the container view.

➤ Embed the second VStack — the one containing the images and text — in your ContainerView and add the modifier to determine its height:

```
// container view
ContainerView {
  VStack {
    ...
  }
}
.frame(height: geometry.size.height * 0.8)
```

Using the size given by GeometryReader, the container view will take up 80% of the available space. You'll take a further look at GeometryReader in Chapter 20, "Delightful UX - Layout".

➤ Open **ContentView.swift** and preview your app on both iPhone 12 Pro Max and iPod Touch. These are the biggest and smallest screens (not taking into account iPad), and you want to make sure that your app looks great on all iPhones.

Preview on iPhone 12 Pro Max and iPod Touch

The safe area

On iPhone 12, there is a gap at the bottom for the safe area, and the gray background color does not extend to the bottom edge. Any iPhone without a physical home button has this safe area for the black bar at the bottom where you swipe up to leave the app.

When you're layering background colors, it's often safe to use the modifier `edgesIgnoringSafeArea(_:)`. But if you use this modifier on your `TabView` here, this will be the result:

Ignoring safe edges

The **History** button will be too close to the bottom edge to swipe up. You could go to `WelcomeView` and pad the history button, but then the button will also be padded on iPod Touch which doesn't need a safe area. There are several solutions. You could layer a `Rectangle` underneath `TabView` just as you did in `ContainerView` to cover up the hidden area and ignore the safe edge.

As you're going to be adding a gradient background behind `TabView`, you can include the gray background color in the gradient and then ignore safe edges on the layered background color.

Gradients

> **Skills you'll learn in this section**: gradient views

SwiftUI makes using gradients really easy. You simply define the gradient colors in an array. You're going to use a lovely purple to blue gradient, using the predefined colors in the asset catalog.

➤ Create a new SwiftUI View file called **GradientBackground.swift**.

➤ Change the preview to:

```
struct GradientBackground_Previews: PreviewProvider {
  static var previews: some View {
    GradientBackground()
      .frame(width: 300, height: 300)
      .previewLayout(.sizeThatFits)
  }
}
```

You only need a small preview of the gradient.

➤ Add a new property to `GradientBackground`:

```
var gradient: Gradient {
  Gradient(colors: [
    Color("gradient-top"),
    Color("gradient-bottom")
  ])
}
```

This defines the gradient colors.

➤ Change body to:

```
var body: some View {
  LinearGradient(
    gradient: gradient,
    startPoint: .top,
    endPoint: .bottom)
    .edgesIgnoringSafeArea(.all)
}
```

You start the gradient at the top and continue down to the bottom. If you want the gradient to be diagonal, you can use `.topLeading` as the start point and `.bottomTrailing` as the end point. Because this gradient will only be used as a background color, you can ignore the safe area, and the gradient will stretch to all screen edges.

Initial Gradient

➤ You're also going to cover up the safe area with gray, so include that in the list of colors:

```
Gradient(colors: [
  Color("gradient-top"),
  Color("gradient-bottom"),
  Color("background")
])
```

This result gives a less pleasant purple to blue gradient.

Gray added to gradient

You can control where the gradient changes using stops.

➤ Replace `gradient` with:

```
var gradient: Gradient {
  let color1 = Color("gradient-top")
  let color2 = Color("gradient-bottom")
  let background = Color("background")
  return Gradient(
    stops: [
      Gradient.Stop(color: color1, location: 0),
      Gradient.Stop(color: color2, location: 0.9),
      Gradient.Stop(color: background, location: 0.9),
      Gradient.Stop(color: background, location: 1)
    ])
}
```

Here you use purple to blue for 90% of the gradient. At the 90% mark, you switch to the background color for the rest of the gradient. As you have two stops right next to each other, you get a sharp line across instead of a gradient. If you want a striped background, you can achieve this using color stops in this way.

Gradient with background color

➤ Open **ContentView.swift** to add your gradient background.

➤ Embed `TabView` in a `ZStack` and add your background:

```
ZStack {
  GradientBackground()
  TabView(selection: $selectedTab) {
    ...
  }
  ...
}
```

➤ Preview your result on several iPhone sizes. Also make sure that you check that your layout works as far as possible with accessibility dynamic type. With this layout, iPod Touch is still usable even set to Accessibility Large.

Accessibility Large Dynamic Type

Challenge

Challenge: Continue Styling

Your challenge is to continue styling. First style HeaderView.

Finished HeaderView

Functionality will remain the same, but instead of numbers, you'll have circles. A faded circle behind the circle indicates the current page. You can achieve transparency with the modifier opacity(:), where opacity is between zero and one. You may need to build and run to see your changes in Simulator if they don't show up in preview.

ExerciseView doesn't look so hot with the gradient background, so embed this in ContainerView just as you did in WelcomeView.

Before and after styling

The project supplied in the challenge directory contains a fully designed app which makes full use of the buttons you styled in this chapter. Check out:

- The **Get Started** button which appears to indent when you tap it.

- The **History** views. There are two of them, one a list and one a bar chart. To make the history bar chart, there are some extension methods on `Date()` to work out an array for the last seven days, as well as formatting day and month.

- The **Timer** view, now a modal with a circular cut-out for the title.

Key points

- It's not always possible to spend money on hiring a designer, but you should definitely spend time making your app as attractive and friendly as possible. Try various designs out and offer them to your testers for their opinions.

- Neumorphism is a simple style that works well. Keep up with designer trends at https://dribbble.com.

- Style protocols allow you to customize various view types to fit in with your desired design.

- Using `@ViewBuilder`, you can return varying types of views from methods and properties. It's easy to create custom container views that have added styling or functionality.

- You can layer background colors in the safe area, but don't place any of your user interface there.

- Gradients are an easy way to create a stand-out design. You can find interesting gradients at https://uigradients.com.

Chapter 11: Understanding Property Wrappers

By Audrey Tam

In your SwiftUI app, every data value or object that can change needs a single source of truth and a mechanism to enable views to change or observe it. SwiftUI's property wrappers enable you to declare how each view interacts with mutable data.

In this chapter, you'll review how you managed data values and objects in HIITFit with `@State`, `@Binding`, `@Environment`, `ObservableObject`, `@StateObject` and `@EnvironmentObject`. And, you'll build a simple app that lets you focus on how to use these property wrappers. You'll also learn about `TextField`, the `environment` modifier and the `@ObservedObject` property wrapper.

To help answer the question "struct or class?", you'll see why `HistoryStore` should be a class, not a structure, and learn about the natural architecture for SwiftUI apps: Model-View-ViewModel (MVVM).

Getting started

➤ Open the **TIL** project in the starter folder. The project name "TIL" is the acronym for "Today I Learned". Or, you can think of it as "Things I Learned". Here's how the app should work: The user taps the + button to add acronyms like "YOLO" and "BTW", and the main screen displays these.

TIL in action

This app embeds a VStack in a NavigationView. This gives you the navigation bar where you display the title and the + button. You'll learn more about NavigationView in Section 3.

This project has a ThingStore, like HistoryStore in HIITFit. This app is much simpler than HIITFit, so you can focus on how you manage the data.

Remember how you managed changes to HistoryStore in HIITFit:

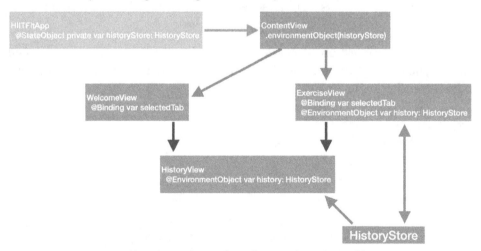

HIITFit: HistoryStore shared as EnvironmentObject

In Chapter 6, "Adding Functionality to Your App", you converted HistoryStore from a structure to a class conforming to ObservableObject, then set it up as an @EnvironmentObject so ExerciseView and HistoryView could access it directly. HistoryView is a subview of WelcomeView, but you saw how using

`@EnvironmentObject` allowed you to avoid passing `HistoryStore` to `WelcomeView`, which doesn't use it. If you did the challenge in that chapter, you also managed `HistoryStore` with `@State` and `@Binding`.

In Chapter 9, "Saving History Data", you moved the initialization of `HistoryStore` from `ContentView` to `HIITFitApp` to initialize it with or without saved history data.

`ThingStore` has the property `things`, which is an array of `String` values. Like the `HistoryStore` in the first version of HIITFit, it's a structure.

In this chapter, you'll first manage changes to the `ThingStore` structure using `@State` and `@Binding`, then convert it to an `ObservableObject` class and manage changes with `@StateObject` and `@ObservedObject`:

TIL: ThingStore shared as Binding and as ObservedObject

You'll learn that these two approaches are very similar.

> **Note**: Our tutorial *Property Wrappers* (bit.ly/3vLOpbl) extends this project to use `ThingStore` as an `@EnvironmentObject`.

Tools for managing data

You already know that a `@State` property is a *source of truth*. A view that owns a `@State` property can pass either its value or its binding to its subviews. If it passes a binding to a subview, that subview now has a reference to the source of truth. This allows it to update that property's value or redraw itself when that value changes. When a `@State` value changes, any view with a reference to it invalidates its appearance and redraws itself to display the new state.

Your app needs to manage changes to two kinds of data:

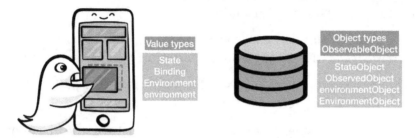

Managing UI values and model objects

- User interface values, like Boolean flags to show or hide views, text field text, slider or picker values.

- Data model objects, often collections of objects that model the app's data, like daily logs of completed exercises.

Property wrappers

Property wrappers wrap a value or object in a structure with two properties:

- `wrappedValue` is the underlying value or object.

- `projectedValue` is a binding to the wrapped value or a projection of the object that creates bindings to its properties.

Swift syntax lets you write just the name of the property, like `showHistory`, instead of `showHistory.wrappedValue`. And, its binding is `$showHistory` instead of `showHistory.projectedValue`.

SwiftUI provides tools — mostly property wrappers — to create and modify the single source of truth for values and for objects:

- User interface *values*: Use `@State` and `@Binding` for values like `showHistory` that affect the view's appearance. The underlying type must be a *value* type like `Bool`, `Int`, `String` or `Exercise`. Use `@State` to create a source of truth in one view, then pass a `@Binding` to this property to subviews. A view can access built-in `@Environment` values as `@Environment` properties or with the `environment(_:_:)` view modifier.

- Data model *objects*: For objects like `HistoryStore` that model your app's data, use either `@StateObject` with `@ObservedObject` or `environmentObject(_:)` with `@EnvironmentObject`. The underlying object type must be a *reference* type — a class — that conforms to `ObservableObject`, and it should *publish* at least one value. Then, either use `@StateObject` and `@ObservedObject` or declare an `@EnvironmentObject` with the same type as the environment object created by the `environmentObject(_:)` view modifier.

While prototyping your app, you can model your data with structures and use `@State` and `@Binding`. When you've worked out how data needs to flow through your app, you can refactor your app to accommodate data types that need to conform to `ObservableObject`.

This is what you'll do in this chapter to consolidate your understanding of how to use these property wrappers.

Saving/Persisting app or scene state

There are two other property wrappers you've used. `@AppStorage` wraps `UserDefault` values. In Chapter 8, "Saving Settings", you used `@AppStorage` to save exercise ratings in `UserDefaults` and load them when the app launches.

In the same chapter, you used `@SceneStorage` to save and restore the state of scenes — windows in the iPad simulator, each showing a different exercise.

Managing UI state values

`@State` and `@Binding` value properties are mainly used to manage the state of your app's user interface.

A view is a structure, so you can't change a property value unless you wrap it as a `@State` or `@Binding` property.

The view that owns a `@State` property is responsible for initializing it. The `@State` property wrapper creates persistent storage for the value outside the view structure and preserves its value when the view redraws itself. This means initialization happens exactly once.

You already got lots of practice with @State and @Binding in Chapter 6, "Adding Functionality to Your App":

- selectedTab controls TabView.

- showHistory, showSuccess, showTimer, timerDone show or hide views.

- rating and timeRemaining values must be able to change.

In the challenge for that chapter, you used @State and @Binding to manage changes to HistoryStore. That was just an exercise to demonstrate it's possible, and it's one approach you can take to prototyping. For most apps, your final data model will involve ObservableObject classes.

Managing ThingStore with @State and @Binding

TIL is a very simple app, making it easy to examine different ways to manage the app's data. First, you'll manage ThingStore the same way as any other mutable *value* you share between your app's views.

➤ In **ContentView.swift**, run live preview and tap the + button:

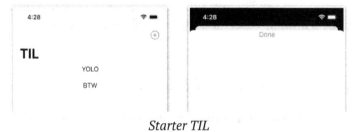

Starter TIL

TIL uses a Boolean flag, showAddThing, to show or hide AddThingView. It's a @State property because its value changes when you tap the + button, and ContentView owns it.

➤ In **ContentView.swift**, add this line to ContentView:

```
@State private var myThings = ThingStore()
```

You'll add items to myThings.things, so myThings must be a wrapped property. In this case, it's @State, because ContentView owns it and initializes it.

➤ Now, delete the temporary array:

```
let tempThings = ["YOLO", "BTW"]  // delete this line
```

You'll store strings in `myThings.things`, so you no longer need this array.

➤ Then, update the `ForEach` argument:

```
ForEach(myThings.things, id: \.self) { thing in
```

You loop over the `things` array instead of `tempThings`.

➤ Refresh the preview:

Nothing to see here

Now, there's nothing to show because `myThings` initializes with an empty `things` array. It's a better user experience if you display a message, instead of this blank page, the first time your user launches your app.

➤ In **ContentView.swift**, add this code at the top of the `VStack`, before the `ForEach` line:

```
if myThings.things.isEmpty {
   Text("Add acronyms you learn")
      .foregroundColor(.gray)
}
```

First-time empty-array screen

You give your users a hint of what they can do with your app. The text is grayed out so they know it's just a placeholder until they add their own data.

AddThingView needs to modify myThings, so you need a @Binding in AddThingView.

➤ In **AddThingView.swift**, add this property to AddThingView:

```
@Binding var someThings: ThingStore
```

You'll soon pass this binding from ContentView.

➤ You'll also add a text field, but for now, just to have something happen when you tap **Done**, add this line to the button action, before you dismiss this sheet:

```
someThings.things.append("FOMO")
```

You append a specific string to the array.

➤ Fix this view's previews:

```
AddThingView(someThings: .constant(ThingStore()))
```

You create a binding for the constant initial value of ThingStore.

➤ Now, go back to **ContentView.swift** and fix the call to AddThingView():

```
AddThingView(someThings: $myThings)
```

You pass a binding to the ContentView @State property to AddThingView.

> **Note**: Passing a binding gives the subview write access to everything in ThingStore. In this case, ThingStore has only the things array but, if it had more properties and you wanted to restrict write access to its things array, you could pass $myThings.things — a binding to only the things array. You'd need to initialize an array of String for the preview of AddThingView.

➤ Start live preview, tap + then tap **Done**:

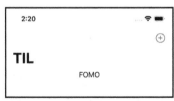

Adding a string works.

Great, you've got data flowing from AddThingView to ContentView via ThingStore!

Now to get input from your user, you'll add a TextField to AddThingView.

➤ First, pin the preview of ContentView so it's there when you're ready to test your TextField.

Using a TextField

Many UI controls work by binding a parameter to a @State property of the view: These include Slider, Toggle, Picker and TextField.

To get user input via a TextField, you need a mutable String property to store the user's input.

➤ In **AddThingView.swift**, add this property to AddThingView:

```
@State private var thing = ""
```

It's a @State property because it must persist when the view redraws itself. AddThingView owns this property, so it's responsible for initializing thing. You initialize it to the empty string.

➤ Now, add your TextField in the VStack, above the **Done** button:

```
TextField("Thing I Learned", text: $thing)  // 1
  .textFieldStyle(RoundedBorderTextFieldStyle())  // 2
  .padding()  // 3
```

1. The label "Thing I Learned" is the *placeholder* text. It appears grayed out in the TextField as a hint to the user. You pass a binding to thing so TextField can set this value to what the user types.

2. You dress up this TextField with a rounded border.

3. You add padding so there's some space from the top of the view and also to the button.

➤ Then, edit what the button action appends:

```
if !thing.isEmpty {
  someThings.things.append(thing)
}
```

Instead of "FOMO", you append the user's text input to your things array after checking it's not the empty string.

➤ Refresh live-preview in the `ContentView` preview and tap **+**. Type an acronym like **YOLO** in the text field. It automatically capitalizes the first letter, but you must hold down the **Shift** key for the rest of the letters. Tap **Done**:

TextField input

`ContentView` displays your new acronym.

Sometimes the app auto-corrects your acronym: FTW to GET or FOMO to DINO.

➤ Add this modifier to `TextField`:

```
.disableAutocorrection(true)
```

Accessing environment values

A view can access many environment values like `accessibilityEnabled`, `colorScheme`, `lineSpacing`, `font` and `presentationMode`. Apple's SwiftUI documentation has a full list of environment values at <u>apple.co/37cOxak</u>.

A view's environment is a kind of inheritance mechanism. A view inherits environment values from its ancestor views, and its subviews inherit its environment values.

➤ To see this, open **ContentView.swift** and click anywhere in this line:

```
Text("Add acronyms you learn")
```

➤ Now, open the Attributes inspector:

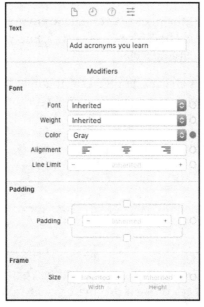

Text view attributes: Many are inherited.

Font, Weight, Line Limit, Padding and Frame Size are *Inherited*. Font Color would also be inherited if you hadn't set it to Gray.

A view can override an inherited environment value. It's common to set a default font for a stack then override it for the text in a subview of the stack. You did this in Chapter 3, "Prototyping the Main View", when you made the first page number larger than the others:

```
HStack {
  Image(systemName: "1.circle")
    .font(.largeTitle)
  Image(systemName: "2.circle")
  Image(systemName: "3.circle")
  Image(systemName: "4.circle")
}
.font(.title2)
```

Modifying environment values

AddThingView already uses the presentationMode environment value, declared as a view property the same as in HIITFit's SuccessView. But, you can also set environment values by modifying a view.

Acronyms should appear as all caps, but it's easy to forget to hold down the **Shift** key. You can actually set an environment value to automatically convert text to upper case.

➤ In **TILApp.swift**, add this modifier to ContentView():

```
.environment(\.textCase, .uppercase)
```

You set uppercase as the default value of textCase for ContentView and all its subviews.

> **Note:** textCase(.uppercase) also works, but the .environment syntax highlights the fact that textCase is an environment value.

➤ To see it in live-preview, also add this modifier in **ContentView.swift** to ContentView() in previews.

➤ Refresh live-preview, add acronyms without bothering to keep all the letters upper case. Just type **yolo** or **fomo**. Tap **DONE**. Notice this label and the placeholder text are now all uppercase:

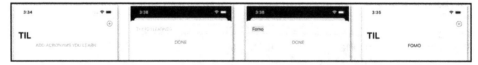

Automagic uppercase

> **Note:** If the placeholder text isn't all upper case, press **Shift-Command-K** to clean the build folder.

Your strings are automatically converted to uppercase.

The environment value applies to *all* text in your app, which looks a little strange. No problem — you can override it.

➤ In **AddThingView.swift**, add this modifier to the VStack:

```
.environment(\.textCase, nil)
```

You set the value to nil, so none of the text displayed by this VStack is converted to uppercase.

➤ Refresh live-preview, tap **+**, type **icymi** then tap **Done**:

No upper case conversion in AddThing

Now, the button label and placeholder text are back to normal. The uppercase environment default still converts your strings to all caps on the main screen.

Managing model data objects

@State, @Binding and @Environment only work with value data types. Simple built-in data types like Int, Bool or String are useful for defining the state of your app's user interface.

You can use custom value data types like struct or enum to model your app's data. And, you can use @State and @Binding to manage updates to these values, as you did earlier in this chapter.

Most apps also use *classes* to model data. SwiftUI provides a different mechanism to manage changes to class *objects*: ObservableObject, @StateObject, @ObservedObject and @EnvironmentObject. To practice using @ObservedObject, you'll refactor TIL to use @StateObject and @ObservedObject to update ThingStore, which conforms to ObservableObject. You'll see a lot of similarities, and a few differences, to using @State and @Binding.

> **Note:** You *can* wrap a class object as a @State property, but its "value" is its address in memory, so dependent views will redraw themselves only when its address changes — for example, when the app reinitializes it.

Class and structure

But, this section isn't just to practice managing objects. `ThingStore` actually *should* be a class, not a structure.

`@State` and `@Binding` work well enough to update the `ThingStore` source of truth *value* in `ContentView` from `AddThingView`. But `ThingStore` isn't the most natural use of a structure. For the way your app uses `ThingStore`, a class is a better fit.

A class is more suitable when you need *shared* mutable state like a `HistoryStore` or `ThingStore`. A structure is more suitable when you need multiple *independent* states like `ExerciseDay` structures.

For a class object, change is normal. A class object expects its properties to change. For a structure instance, change is exceptional. A structure instance requires advance notice that a method might change a property.

A class object expects to be shared, and any reference can be used to change its properties. A structure instance lets itself be copied, but its copies change independently of it and of each other.

You'll find out more about classes and structures in Chapter 15, "Structures, Classes & Protocols".

Managing ThingStore with StateObject and ObservedObject

You've already used `@EnvironmentObject` in Chapter 6, "Adding Functionality to Your App", to avoid passing `HistoryStore` through `WelcomeView` to reach `HistoryView`.

To use it as an `@EnvironmentObject`, you converted `HistoryStore` from a structure to class that conforms to `ObservableObject`. This is also the first step before you can use `@StateObject` and `@ObservedObject` with `ThingStore`. Once that's done, you'll create it as a `@StateObject` and pass it to a subview that uses it as an `@ObservedObject`. Sounds a lot like "create a `@State` property and pass its `@Binding`", doesn't it?

> **Note**: You can pass a @State value or a @StateObject to a subview as a @Binding or @ObservedObject property, even if that subview needs only read access. This enables the subview to redraw itself whenever the @State value or ObservableObject changes. You did this with selectedTab in HeaderView, in Chapter 6, "Adding Functionality to Your App".

➤ In **ContentView.swift**, replace the ThingStore structure with the following:

```
final class ThingStore: ObservableObject {
  @Published var things: [String] = []
}
```

Just like you did with HistoryStore, you make ThingStore a class instead of a structure, then make it conform to ObservableObject. You mark this class final to tell the compiler it doesn't have to check for any subclasses overriding properties or methods.

Like HistoryStore, ThingStore publishes its array of data. A view *subscribes* to this publisher by declaring it as a @StateObject, @ObservedObject or @EnvironmentObject. Any change to things notifies subscriber views to redraw themselves.

You used @EnvironmentObject in Chapter 7, "Observing Objects". In HIITFit, ExerciseView and HistoryView declared a dependency on a HistoryStore object:

```
@EnvironmentObject var history: HistoryStore
```

If a view uses an @EnvironmentObject, you must create the model object by calling the environmentObject(_:) modifier on an *ancestor* view. You first created the HistoryStore object in ContentView, applying the modifier to the TabView:

```
TabView(selection: $selectedTab) {
...
}
.environmentObject(HistoryStore())
```

Then, in Chapter 9, "Saving History Data", you elevated its initialization up one level to HIITFitApp and declared it as a @StateObject.

> **Note**: Initializing `HistoryStore` in the `environmentObject` modifier works while you're prototyping. To make sure the app never reinitializes an environment object, declare and initialize it as a `@StateObject`, then pass the property in the `environmentObject` modifier.

In TIL, `AddThingView` will use an `@ObservedObject`, so you must instantiate the model object as a `@StateObject` in an ancestor view, then pass it as a parameter to its subviews. The owning view creates the `@StateObject` exactly once.

➤ In `ContentView`, replace `@State private var myThings = ThingStore()` with this line:

```
@StateObject private var myThings = ThingStore()
```

`ThingStore` is now a class, not a structure, so you can't use the `@State` property wrapper. Instead, you use `@StateObject`.

The `@StateObject` property wrapper ensures `myThings` is instantiated only once. It persists when `ContentView` redraws itself.

➤ In the call to `AddThingView(someThings:)`, remove the binding symbol `$`:

```
AddThingView(someThings: myThings)
```

You don't need to create a reference to `myThings`. As a class object, it's already a reference.

➤ In **AddThingView.swift**, replace `@Binding` in `AddThingView` with `@ObservedObject`:

```
@ObservedObject var someThings: ThingStore
```

> **Note**: If `ThingStore` had more properties and you wanted to restrict write access to its `things` array, you could pass `$myThings.things` to `AddThingView`, which would have a `@Binding someThings: [String]` property.

➤ And fix its `previews`:

```
AddThingView(someThings: ThingStore())
```

The argument isn't a binding anymore.

➤ Refresh live-preview, tap **+**, type **yolo** then tap **Done**:

TIL in action

No surprise: The app still works the same as before.

MVVM

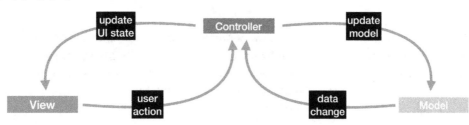

Model-View-Controller

You may be familiar with Model-View-Controller (**MVC**) architecture for apps in other settings, like web apps. Your data model knows nothing about how your app presents it to users. The view doesn't own the data, and the controller mediates between the model and the view.

A commonly used architecture for SwiftUI apps is Model-View-View Model (**MVVM**). There's no controller, so the view model prepares model data for the view to display.

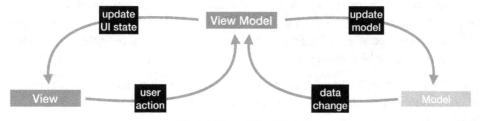

Model-View-ViewModel

A view model's properties can include the current text for a text field or whether a specific button is enabled. In a view model, you can also specify actions the view can perform, like button taps or gestures.

A user action is an *event* that triggers the view model to update the model. If the model connects to a back-end database, data can change independently of user actions. The view model uses these to update the view's state.

When a view displays a collection of objects or values, its view model manages the data collection. In simple apps like HIITFit and TIL, this is the view model's only job. So the view model's name often includes the word "Store".

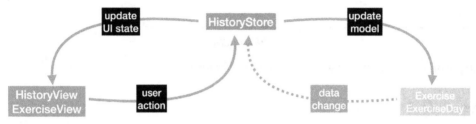

MVVM in HIITFit

HIITFit's view model, `HistoryStore`, saves and loads the user's exercise history. The model consists of the `Exercise` and `ExerciseDay` structures. `HistoryStore` publishes the `exerciseDays` array. `ExerciseView` and `HistoryView` subscribe to `HistoryStore`. The `ExerciseView`'s tap-Done event updates the `exerciseDays` array, which changes the state of `HistoryView`.

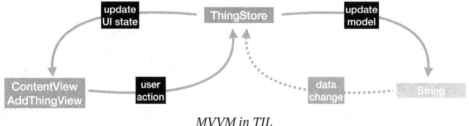

MVVM in TIL

TIL's view model, `ThingStore`, saves the user's array of acronyms. The model is simply a `String` and the view model publishes the `things` array. `ContentView` and `AddThingView` subscribe to `ThingStore`. The `AddThingView` tap-Done event updates the `things` array, which changes the state of `ContentView`.

In the Section 3 app, RWFreeView, the view model stores a collection of `Episode` instances. It's responsible for downloading data from raywenderlich.com and decoding the data into `Episodes`.

Wrapping up property wrappers

Here's a summary to help you wrap your head around property wrappers.

First, decide whether you're managing the state of a value or the state of an object. Values are mainly used to describe the state of your app's user interface. If you can model your app's data with value data types, you're in luck because you have a lot more property wrapper options for working with values. But at some level, most apps need reference types to model their data, often to add or remove items from a collection.

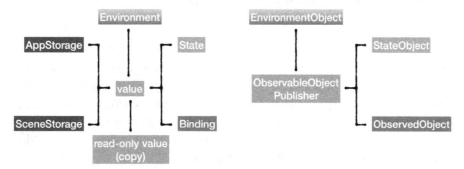

Property wrappers for values and objects

Wrapping values

@State and @Binding are the workhorses of value property wrappers. A view owns the value if it doesn't receive it from any parent views. In this case, it's a @State property — the single source of truth. When a view is first created, it initializes its @State properties. When a @State value changes, the view redraws itself, resetting everything except its @State properties.

The owning view can pass a @State value to a subview as an ordinary read-only value or as a read-write @Binding.

When you're prototyping an app and trying out a subview, you might write it as a stand-alone view with only @State properties. Later, when you fit it into your app, you just change @State to @Binding for values that come from a parent view.

Your app can access the built-in @Environment values. An environment value persists within the subtree of the view you attach it to. Often, this is simply a container like VStack, where you use an environment value to set a default like font size.

> **Note:** You can also define your own custom environment value, for example to expose a view's property to ancestor views. This is beyond the scope of this book, but check out Chapter 9, "State & Data Flow – Part II" of *SwiftUI by Tutorials* (bit.ly/39bz5vv).

You can store a few values in the `@AppStorage` or `@SceneStorage` dictionary. `@AppStorage` values are in `UserDefaults`, so they persist after the app closes. You use a `@SceneStorage` value to restore the state of a scene when the app reopens. In an iOS context, scenes are easiest to see as multiple windows on an iPad.

Wrapping objects

When your app needs to change and respond to changes in a reference type, you create a class that conforms to `ObservableObject` and publishes the appropriate properties. In this case, you use `@StateObject` and `@ObservedObject` in much the same way as `@State` and `@Binding` for values. You instantiate your publisher class in a view as a `@StateObject` then pass it to subviews as an `@ObservedObject`. When the owning view redraws itself, it doesn't reset its `@StateObject` properties.

If your app's views need more flexible access to the object, you can lift it into the environment of a view's subtree, still as a `@StateObject`. You **must** instantiate it here. Your app will crash if you forget to create it. Then you use the `.environmentObject(_:)` modifier to attach it to a view. Any view in the view's subtree can *subscribe* to the publisher object by declaring an `@EnvironmentObject` of that type.

To make an environment object available to every view in your app, attach it to the root view when the `App` creates its `WindowGroup`.

Key points

- Every data value or object that can change needs a single source of truth and a mechanism to enable views to update it.

- Use @State and @Binding to manage changes to user interface values.

- Access @Environment values as @Environment view properties or by using the environment view modifier.

- Use @StateObject and @ObservedObject to manage changes to data model objects. The object type must conform to ObservableObject and should *publish* at least one value.

- If only a few subviews need access to an ObservableObject, instantiate it as a @StateObject then pass it in the environmentObject view modifier. Declare an @EnvironmentObject property in any subviews that need access to it.

- When prototyping your app, you can use @State and @Binding with structures that model your app's data. When you've worked out how data needs to flow through your app, you can refactor your app to accommodate data types that need to conform to ObservableObject.

- A commonly used architecture for SwiftUI apps is Model-View-View Model (MVVM), where the view model is an ObservableObject. Changes to the view model's published properties cause updates to the model and view.

Chapter 12: Apple App Development Ecosystem

By Audrey Tam

Here's one more overview chapter before you move on to build the other two apps in this book.

While building HIITFit, you learned a lot about Xcode, Swift and SwiftUI at a detailed level. In the previous chapter, you got a kind of "balcony view" of how the various property wrappers help you manage the state of your app's data. This chapter provides a bird's eye view of the whole Apple app development ecosystem, demystifying many of the terms you might hear when iOS developers get together for a chat. You'll start to build your own mental model of how all the parts fit together, creating your own framework for all the new things that Apple adds every year.

A brief history of SwiftUI

You've been using SwiftUI to build HIITFit, but this is only the most recent app development paradigm from Apple.

Apple announced **SwiftUI** at its World Wide Developers Conference in June 2019. SwiftUI builds on the Swift programming language, which Apple announced in June 2014. SwiftUI is a **Domain Specific Language** (DSL), written in Swift using these new Swift features:

- Property wrappers, like @State to monitor the state of properties.

- Result builders, like @ViewBuilder to create view hierarchies.

- Opaque result types, like some View to avoid explicitly writing out the view hierarchy.

Swift creates faster, safer apps than Objective-C and is more *protocol-oriented* than object-oriented. Chapter 15, "Structures, Classes & Protocols", explains the difference between class inheritance and protocols.

By March 2018, the Redmonk Programming Language Rankings (bit.ly/3rsZmwq) ranked Swift and Objective-C in a tie at number 10.

Objective-C entered Apple history when Apple bought NeXT in 1997, which also brought Steve Jobs back to Apple. Jobs had resigned from Apple in 1985 after losing a boardroom battle with CEO John Sculley over the future of the Macintosh computer. Jobs, with five other former Apple executives, then founded **NeXT Computers**.

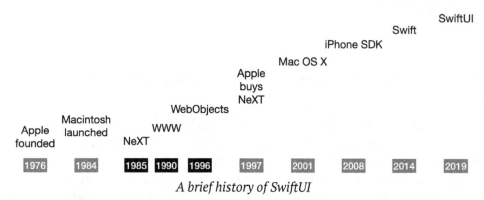

A brief history of SwiftUI

The NeXTSTEP operating system, written in Objective-C, formed the basis of **Mac OS X**, released in 2001. Apple provided the **Cocoa API** for developers to create apps for OS X. Cocoa consists of three frameworks reflecting the Model-View-Controller principles: **Core Data**, **AppKit** and **Foundation**. The "NS" prefix in AppKit and Foundation acknowledges their NeXTSTEP heritage.

Apple announced the **iPhone** in 2007 and the **iPhone SDK** (Software Development Kit) in 2008. This included **Cocoa Touch**, with **UIKit** replacing AppKit. Now called the **iOS** SDK, it helps you create apps that appear and behave the way users expect.

Fun facts

- The first World Wide Web server was a NeXT Computer, and id Software developed the video games Doom and Quake on machines running the NeXT operating system **NeXTSTEP**. In 1996, NeXT Software, Inc. released **WebObjects**, a framework for Web application development. Apple used WebObjects to build and run the Apple Store, MobileMe services and the iTunes Store.

- Cocoa != Java for kids: Before Jobs returned to Apple, the Apple Advanced Technology Group created KidSim, an app to teach kids to program. KidSim programs were embedded in web pages to run, so they renamed and trademarked the app as **Cocoa** — "Java for kids". The Cocoa program was one of the many axed in 1997, and Apple reused the name for the OS X API to avoid the delay of registering a new trademark.

- While developing the iPhone, Steve Jobs didn't want non-Apple developers to build native iPhone apps. They were supposed to be content making web applications for Safari. This stance changed in response to a backlash from developers, and the iPhone SDK was released on March 6, 2008.

SwiftUI vs. UIKit

Although you've used only SwiftUI to create HIITFit, UIKit has a lot of resources that can help you add features to your app or fine-tune how it looks and functions.

Most popular episode

As you'll see in Section 3 of this book, "SwiftUI vs. UIKit" (bit.ly/2PGuNFy) is the most popular free episode at raywenderlich.com. Presented by Ray himself, it's worth watching, but here's a TL;DW summary.

> **Note:** Like a lot of the content on this site, this episode is aimed at people who want to work for iOS app development companies. If this isn't you, skip to the next section. Also, this is the 2019 episode. There's a newer one, but it hasn't had time to accumulate the number of views to overtake the original.

Three reasons why there are still more developers using UIKit than SwiftUI:

1. SwiftUI only works on iOS 13 or later. Some companies still need to support iOS 12 or earlier, so they can't switch to SwiftUI quite yet.

2. SwiftUI is still not as mature as UIKit. Apple released UIKit in 2008, and it built on macOS AppKit, which came from NeXTSTEP, so there was a lot of time to get things right. SwiftUI still has missing features or rough edges, so some companies want to give SwiftUI a little more time to mature.

3. Many companies have already written their apps using UIKit, and it would simply be too much work at this point to rewrite the entire thing in SwiftUI, so a lot of that old UIKit legacy code will remain.

SwiftUI or UIKit?

Q: Which should you learn: SwiftUI or UIKit?

A: *If you're serious about being a professional iOS developer*, our recommendation is to learn both SwiftUI and UIKit. If you end up working at a company that already has shipped an iOS app, there's a high chance that it's been made with UIKit. So if you want to work at one of those companies, it's important for you to be able to work with those codebases, too. We created a special and optional learning path, called "iOS User Interfaces with UIKit" (bit.ly/2OaK4ye). If you need to learn UIKit development for your job, you should definitely check that out. But if you only care about SwiftUI, you can safely skip it.

It's not all or nothing: It's possible to make a certain part of your app with SwiftUI and the rest with UIKit. As companies begin to transition from UIKit to SwiftUI, we expect to see many codebases with a mixture of both SwiftUI and UIKit code in the years ahead.

Thanks, Ray! That's the perfect segue into the next section…

Integrating new and old

Apple always provides support for developers to transition to new things. The Carbon API enabled developers to port "classic" Mac OS apps to OS X. Bridging headers enable developers to use Objective-C code in Swift apps and vice versa.

Developers can still create Objective-C apps without Swift and Swift apps without SwiftUI. UIKit has many more features than SwiftUI and provides much more control over the appearance and operation of user interface elements.

But no FOMO (fear of missing out)! You can use UIKit views in your SwiftUI apps:

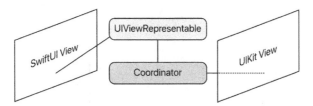

Integrating a UIKit view

You'll use the new `PHPickerViewController` in Chapter 17, "Interfacing With UIKit" and `UIActivityViewController` in Chapter 21, "Delightful UX — Final Touches".

UIActivityViewController in Cards app

And in Chapter 22, "Lists & Navigation", you'll control the appearance of the navigation bar and segmented control with `UINavigationBarAppearance` and `UISegmentedControl.appearance()`.

Using UIKit to control appearances

It's also really easy to use `UIColor` to access system and UI element colors, and you can create an `Image` view from a `UIImage`.

Apple Developer

Despite Steve Jobs' initial intentions, Apple would like everyone to be an Apple developer. Your needs and interests might be shared by a few other people or by a lot of other people. But maybe not by professional iOS developers. If you create an app *you* need or want, it becomes available to those other people too. Even better if your app uses some technology that only works on the newest Apple gadgets, so they have to upgrade to use your app. ;]

So Apple provides tons of resources at developer.apple.com to help you become a developer and stay up to date.

- **Documentation** at apple.co/3v9YVcL and Xcode's **Help ▸ Developer Documentation** (**Shift-Command-0**)

- **Human Interface Guidelines** at apple.co/3cgQJPk and Xcode's **Help ▸ Human Interface Guidelines** (**Shift-Command-H**)

WWDC

Every June, Apple holds the 5-day **World Wide Developers Conference**. The keynote on day 1 shows off all the features planned for the new versions of iOS, macOS and all the other OSes. These launch later in the year, around September or October.

For iOS developers, the more important presentation is the **Platforms State of the Union** on day 2, where you get your first look at the APIs for adding these new features to your apps, as well as improvements to developer tools like Xcode. During the rest of the week, you can watch presentations that introduce and dive deeper into the new features.

Apple provides the multi-platform **Apple Developer** app (apple.co/3eoIfs1), where you can view WWDC videos and bookmark or download your favorites.

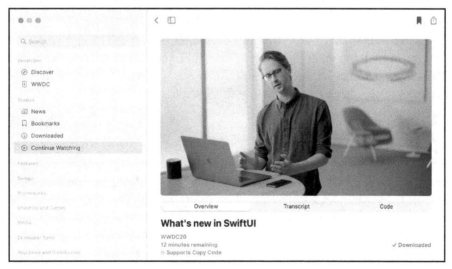

Apple Developer app

If you're a paid-up member of the **Apple Developer Program**, you can download the beta versions of Xcode and the operating systems and immediately start exploring all the new things. Your goal is to include the new features in new or existing apps, all set to go into the App Store when the new iOS launches.

A word of caution: The WWDC presenters use a special in-house version of Xcode. It's different from the Xcode beta you can download, so not everything you see in the presentations actually works in beta 1. Or beta 2. Or ever. Details of the API often change by the time Apple releases the final version, and some promised features quietly disappear.

Platforms

Using SwiftUI to build new iOS apps makes it easier to create similar apps on Apple's other platforms: macOS, watchOS and tvOS. It's not that your iOS app will "just work" on another platform. It probably won't.

You can use many SwiftUI views on other platforms, but how they look or function might be a little different. And other platforms have views that don't exist for iOS. Also, some features of your iOS app won't make sense on a more stationary platform like tvOS or on a smaller screen like watchOS.

The way you assemble a SwiftUI app remains the same, no matter which platform you're targeting. Apple expresses it this way: Learn once, apply anywhere.

Mac Catalyst is Apple's program to make it easier to create a native Mac app from an iPad app. You turn on Mac Catalyst in the iPad app's project settings, then modify the user interface to be more Mac-like. Some iPad UI elements aren't quite right for the Mac user experience, and some iPad frameworks just aren't available in macOS. Your code controls what to include using this compiler directive:

```
#if targetEnvironment(macCatalyst)
...
#endif
```

Check out Apple's tutorial for Mac Catalyst (apple.co/3qPaen7). For an even more in-depth look, browse our book *Catalyst by Tutorials* (bit.ly/32ppGwM).

> **Note**: What about **Apple Silicon**? It's Apple's program to design and manufacture its own Mac processors. Since its launch in 1984, the Mac has used Motorola 68000, PowerPC and Intel CPU chips. The Apple M1 Chip integrates Apple's new CPU with its new GPU, neural engine and more. You can install Rosetta 2 on an Apple Silicon Mac to run apps written for Intel Macs.

Frameworks

The SDK has *a lot* of frameworks, and Apple adds new ones every year. The ones every app needs are modernized versions of the original Cocoa:

- Core Data or some other database technology for data persistence.

- SwiftUI and/or UIKit for user interface.

- Foundation to manipulate and coordinate data and views.

> **Note**: Core Data is a massive topic and, if you'd like to learn more, we have a book, *Core Data by Tutorials* ([bit.ly/39lo2k3](bit.ly/39lo2k3)) and video courses *Beginning Core Data* (bit.ly/2OGjuwG) and *Intermediate Core Data* ([bit.ly/3bE2H6z](bit.ly/3bE2H6z)) to help you on your way.

The apps in this book use these frameworks:

In HIITFit and RWFreeView, `AVKit` for the `AVPlayer` in `VideoPlayer`:

AVKit for AVPlayer in VideoPlayer

In Chapter 17, "Interfacing With UIKit", `PhotosUI` for `PHPickerViewController`:

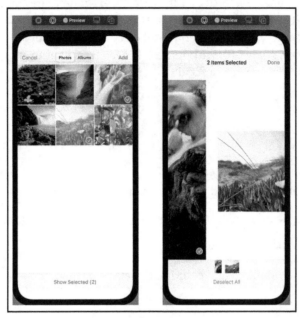

PhotosUI for photo picker

In the Chapter 17 challenge, `PencilKit` for `PKCanvasView`:

Using PencilKit to create a canvas

In Chapter 26, "Widgets", `WidgetKit` to create widgets:

Using WidgetKit to create widgets

These next two frameworks are important, but beyond the scope of this book:

- **Accessibility**: Paying attention to accessibility is one of the easiest ways to grow the audience for your apps. See Chapter 12, "Accessibility", in *SwiftUI by Tutorials* (bit.ly/32oFTCs) and our three-part tutorial "iOS Accessibility in SwiftUI Tutorial" (starting at bit.ly/2WYD9sI).

- **Combine**: You used a `Timer` publisher in Chapter 6, "Adding Functionality to Your App", but there's so much more to learn about Combine. This new framework is a major change to the way iOS apps handle concurrency. See *Combine: Asynchronous Programming in Swift* (bit.ly/3l7VqPq) and the video course *Reactive Programming in iOS with Combine* (bit.ly/3rGsL6D).

Some other frameworks you might want to explore:

MapKit to add maps, user location, routing or overlay views to your apps:

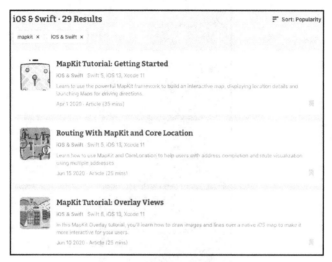

Popular MapKit tutorials

WatchKit to create apps for Apple Watch: *Watch* for the update to our book *watchOS by Tutorials*.

ARKit for augmented reality: See *Apple Augmented Reality by Tutorials* (bit.ly/ 3tabJxZ) and our video course "Beginning ARKit" (bit.ly/3qJ2a7n). Be prepared for Apple's mixed reality headset, predicted for mid-2022 (bit.ly/38rEE8K).

Apple Augmented Reality by Tutorials

Explore all the **Technologies** at <u>apple.co/3rwyxrj</u>:

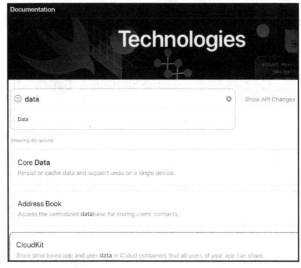

Apple Developer Technologies filtered for 'data'

And you can browse framework-specific videos in the Apple Developer app:

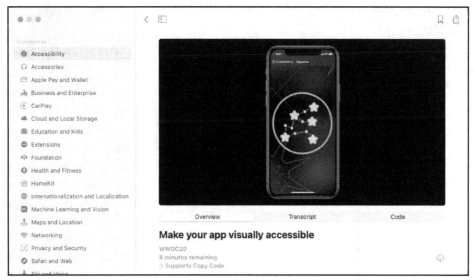

Apple Developer app: Videos classified by framework

Capabilities

Many of the frameworks are for adding special features to your apps. Apple calls these *capabilities*.

➤ To see a list of capabilities, open one of your Xcode projects or create a new one. On the project page, select a target, click the **Signing & Capabilities** tab, then click **+ Capability**:

Capabilities

You'll use an **App Group** to share data between your app and its widget in Chapter 26, "Widgets".

If you're not in the **Apple Developer Program**, you can add only some of these capabilities to your apps. They're listed in the third column on this page: apple.co/3rOhlNW.

Capabilities Available to Developers

➤ Scroll down the page to see all the capabilities you can add if you join the Apple Developer Program.

Developer Programs

So what are the three types of Developer?

Apple Developer:

- No annual fee.

- Access to documentation and videos.

- Free provisioning to install Xcode projects on your devices: Xcode creates a *provisioning profile* that lets you install a few apps. The provisioning profile expires after seven days, so the apps will stop working on your device. Simply delete the profile and reinstall your app.

Apple Developer Program (apple.co/3emR2ur):

- Annual fee approximately equivalent to US$99 in your currency.

- Access to beta operating systems and applications.

- A web interface for managing your certificates, identifiers and profiles.

- Access to **App Store Connect**: Distribute your beta apps to testers with **TestFlight**; submit your apps to the App Store.

- During virtual WWDC: You can request a lab appointment or post forum questions to Apple engineers about WWDC content. When in-person WWDCs resume, you can register for the ticket lottery.

What if you have apps in the App Store but you don't renew your membership? Here's Apple's answer:

> **Expired Memberships**: If your Apple Developer Program membership expires, your apps will no longer be available for download and you will not be able to submit new apps or updates. You will lose access to pre-release software, Certificates, Identifiers & Profiles, and Technical Support Incidents.

Apple Enterprise Program is for companies that want to distribute apps only to employees. The fee is US$299 or equivalent per year. Enterprise apps aren't submitted to the App Store so don't have to comply with Apple's requirements. But there are a lot of legal requirements (apple.co/3coUHVU), and it's probably easier to just use TestFlight.

App Distribution

The actual procedure for getting your app into the App Store changes a little bit every year. Apple's documentation can be confusing.

Check out our book *iOS App Distribution & Best Practices* (bit.ly/3al3Hez) or video course *Publishing to the App Store* (bit.ly/3tckW8Z).

Housekeeping & trouble-shooting

Hopefully, you haven't run into any issues while creating HIITFit. Xcode's error and warning messages are often helpful, but sometimes they're just wrong. At first, you won't be sure if it's something you need to fix but, as you gain more experience, you'll get a feeling for when Xcode is wrong or confused. It does happen. When this happens to an iOS developer, one of the first things they do is **Clean Build Folder**. Read on to find out what this involves.

DerivedData/Build

Xcode maintains a lot of files in **~/Library/Developer/Xcode**. Of particular interest is **DerivedData**, where Xcode creates a folder for every project you've ever created or opened. This is where Xcode stores intermediate build results, indexes and logs.

The easiest way to locate your project's derived data folder is with the new Xcode menu item **Reveal Build Products Folder**.

➤ Open one of your Xcode projects or create a new one. If it's new, press **Command-B** or refresh a preview to build it. Then select **Product ▸ Reveal Build Products Folder**:

Show .app file in Finder.

➤ In the **Finder** column view, scroll left to see your project's folder in **DerivedData**:

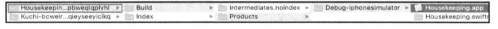

Scroll left in Finder.

The folder name starts with the name of your project followed by a hash value.

➤ Select this folder, then view it as a list and open the **Build** folder:

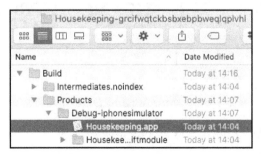

Open Build folder.

➤ Open **Intermediates.noindex** and drill down through its **.build**, **Debug** and **.build** folders to find **Objects-normal/x86_64** or, for you lucky M1 owners, **arm64**:

Locate x86_64 or arm64 folder.

➤ Double-click **x86_64** or **arm64** to open it, then sort on **Date Modified**:

Name	Date Modified
Housekeeping_dependency_info.dat	Today at 14:37
Housekeeping-master.swiftdeps	Today at 14:37
Housekeeping-mast...wiftdeps~moduleonly	Today at 14:37
Housekeeping-Swift.h	Today at 14:37
Housekeeping.swiftsourceinfo	Today at 14:37
Housekeeping.swiftdoc	Today at 14:37
Housekeeping.swiftmodule	Today at 14:37
ContentView.dia	Today at 14:37
ContentView.o	Today at 14:37
ContentView~partial.swiftsourceinfo	Today at 14:37
ContentView~partial.swiftdoc	Today at 14:37
ContentView~partial.swiftmodule	Today at 14:37
ContentView.swiftdeps	Today at 14:37
ContentView.d	Today at 14:37

Sort x86_64 or arm64 by Date Modified.

➤ Note the location and timestamp of **ContentView.o**.

➤ In Xcode, make a change in **ContentView.swift**, press **Command-B** to rebuild, then look at **ContentView.o** in **x86_64** or **arm64**:

Name	Date Modified
Housekeeping_dependency_info.dat	Today at 15:03
Housekeeping-mast...wiftdeps~moduleonly	Today at 15:03
Housekeeping-master.swiftdeps	Today at 15:03
Housekeeping.swiftsourceinfo	Today at 15:03
Housekeeping.swiftmodule	Today at 15:03
ContentView.dia	Today at 15:03
ContentView.o	Today at 15:03
ContentView~partial.swiftsourceinfo	Today at 15:03
ContentView~partial.swiftmodule	Today at 15:03
ContentView.swiftdeps	Today at 15:03
ContentView.d	Today at 15:03
Housekeeping-master.swiftdeps~	Today at 14:37
h Housekeeping-Swift.h	Today at 14:37
Housekeeping.swiftdoc	Today at 14:37

Build after code change

Xcode updated about half the files, including most of the **ContentView** files. Xcode recompiled **ContentView.swift** but not **HousekeepingApp.swift**. It knows (most of the time) which files have changed and doesn't recompile files that haven't changed. But sometimes, something goes wrong with this system, and Xcode complains about code that is correct, or weird errors appear for no apparent reason. Then it's time to *clean the build folder*.

➤ In Xcode, press **Shift-Command-K** or select **Product ▸ Clean Build Folder** from the Xcode menu:

Empty Build folder

This command deletes everything in your project's **Build** folder, giving you a fresh start.

DerivedData/Index

The **Index** folder stores data Xcode uses for search, Open Quickly and refactoring. Again, sometimes the indexes get mixed up, causing strange Xcode behavior. There's no menu command to delete the indexes. You just have to delete the whole derived data folder and let Xcode re-create it.

➤ Press **Command-up-arrow** to get back to your derived data folder or double-click its name in the path bar:

Go to derived data folder.

➤ In **Finder**, press **Command-delete** to delete the whole folder, then in Xcode, press **Command-B** to rebuild:

New derived data folder

Xcode creates a new derived data folder, with the same name.

When Xcode behaves strangely

Xcode is a hugely complex app, and sometimes it needs a nudge or something stronger to "clear its head".

Here are the escalating levels of intervention that most developers follow:

1. Clean Build Folder.

2. Delete the project's DerivedData folder.

3. Restart Xcode.

4. Restart Mac.

> **Strange but true**: Deleting earlier versions of Xcode can fix some weird issues, like no color-coding in the editor or **Command-/** not working.

Reclaiming disk space

Weird Xcode behavior isn't the only reason to delete derived data folders. Long after you've finished working on a project — or even deleted it — its derived data folder is still there, taking up disk space. Many developers routinely delete the entire DerivedData folder every month or so, reclaiming gigabytes of space. If you're running low on disk space, it's certainly the first place you should look.

Command-delete just moves it to Trash, where it still takes up space. To really delete the folder, you can enter this command in **Terminal**:

```
rm -rf ~/Library/Developer/Xcode/DerivedData/*
```

Or, if you're running **Big Sur**, you can open **Trash** and selectively erase the folder. But Big Sur's storage management provides an easier way to clear even more space.

➤ In the Apple menu, select **About this Mac** and click **Storage**. Then click **Manage** and select **Developer**. Select **Xcode Caches** and **Project Build Data and Indexes** then click **Delete...**

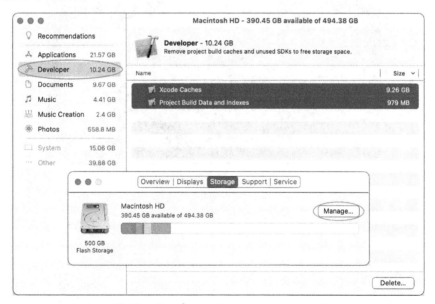

Big Sur Developer storage management

Seeking help from the community

SwiftUI's error messages can be mysterious. If you get an error message and can't figure out what it wants you to do, select the whole message, then select **Search With Google** from the right-click menu.

Many search results will be Stack Overflow or Apple developer forum questions, hopefully with answers.

Also check out raywenderlich.com forums (bit.ly/3rHLXRj) and Discord (bit.ly/3lajOjf).

The raywenderlich.com team and members are a terrific resource, but there's also a large worldwide community of iOS developers. They're almost universally friendly, welcoming and generous with their time and expertise.

An easy path to join this community is to follow @codeine_coding on Twitter and attend his monthly #iOSDevHappyHour events:

iOS Dev Happy Hour

Key points

- SwiftUI is a Domain Specific Language built on Swift, a faster and safer programming language than Objective-C.

- "SwiftUI vs. UIKit" is the most popular free episode at raywenderlich.com and answers the big question: Which should you learn?

- You can use UIKit views and view controllers in your SwiftUI apps.

- Apple provides a lot of resources to help you become a developer and stay up to date: Documentation and human interface guidelines are available on the website and in Xcode. Use the Apple Developer app to watch WWDC videos.

- The SDK has a lot of frameworks, many for adding special features (capabilities) to your apps.

- Members of the Apple Developer Program can add all the capabilities and also get early access to beta operating systems and developer tools. And only members can participate fully in WWDC.

- Xcode stores intermediate build results, indexes and logs in your project's derived data folder. Sometimes you need to Clean Build Folder or delete the entire derived data folder. To reclaim disk space, periodically delete the whole DerivedData directory.

Section II: Your second app: Cards

Now that you've completed your first app, it's time to apply your knowledge and build a new app from scratch. In this section, you'll build a photo collage app called Cards and you'll start from a blank template. Along the way, you'll:

- Dive more deeply into Swift's ways of representing data.

- Learn how to support user gestures.

- Discover how Xcode and iOS manage app assets such as images and colors.

- Learn to use UIKit components in your SwiftUI app.

- Explore more robust ways of saving and restoring data.

- Translate a designer's vision into reality in your app.

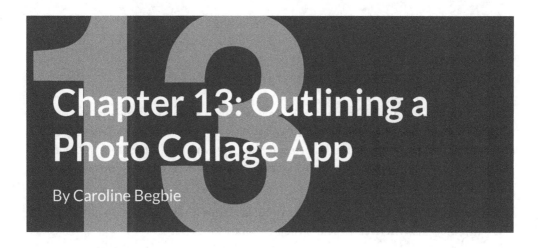

Chapter 13: Outlining a Photo Collage App

By Caroline Begbie

Congratulations — you've written your first app! HIITFit uses standard iOS user interaction with lists and swipeable page views. Now you'll get your teeth into something a bit more complex with custom gestures and custom views.

Photo collage apps are very popular, and you're going build your own collaging app to create cards to share. You'll be able to add images, from your photos or from the internet, and add text and stickers too. This app will be real-world with real-world problems to match.

In this chapter, you'll take a look at a sketch outline of the app idea and create a view hierarchy that will be the skeleton of your app.

At the end of Section 2, your finished app will look like this:

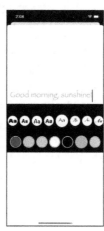

Final app

Initial app idea

The first step to creating a new app is having the idea. Before writing any code, you should do research as to whether your app is going to be a hit or a miss. Work out who your target audience is and talk to some people who might use your app. Find out what your competition is in the App Store and explore how your app can offer something new and different.

Once you've decided that you have a hit on your hands, sketch your app out and work out feasibility and where technical difficulties may lie.

Your photo collaging app will have a primary view — where you list all the cards — and a detail view for the selected card — where you can add photos and text. This might be the back-of-the-napkin sketch:

Back of the napkin sketch

In the next chapters, you'll set up the data model and data storage, but for now, examine the design and think about possible implementation difficulties that you'll need to overcome. Always take a modular approach and test out each aspect of the app as separately from the main app as possible.

SwiftUI is great for this, because you can construct views and controls independently using SwiftUI's live preview. When you're happy with how a view works, add it to your app.

Creating the project

In the previous section, you began with a starter app containing all the assets you needed to create HIITFit. In this section, you'll start with a new app, and you'll find out how to add assets as you move through the next few chapters.

➤ Open Xcode and choose **File ▸ New ▸ Project...** and create a new project called **Cards** using the **iOS App** template. If you need a refresher on how to create a new SwiftUI project, you'll find all the information in Chapter 1, "Checking Your Tools".

➤ Click the **run destination** button and select **iPhone 12 Pro**. Build and run your app using **Command-R** to make sure that everything works OK. Your iPhone 12 Pro simulator should start and show ContentView's "Hello, world!" text.

Initial screen

You should take these steps every time you create a new app just in case something in your environment has changed.

Creating the first view for your project

Skills you'll learn in this section: ScrollView

➤ Create a SwiftUI View file called **CardsListView.swift**.

This view will show a scrolling thumbnail list of all the cards you create in your app.

Creating a list of cards

➤ Open **CardsListView.swift**. Instead of cards, for the moment, you'll show a placeholder list of rounded rectangles.

➤ Replace body with:

```
var body: some View {
  ScrollView {
    VStack {
      ForEach(0..<10) { _ in
        RoundedRectangle(cornerRadius: 15)
          .foregroundColor(.gray)
          .frame(width: 150, height: 250)
      }
    }
  }
}
```

This places ten shapes in a scrollable VStack.

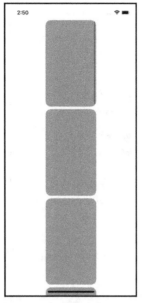

Placeholder thumbnails

A ScrollView can be vertical or horizontal. The default, which you use here, is vertical, but you can specify a horizontal axis with ScrollView(.horizontal).

➤ Live Preview the view, and you'll be able to scroll the list. When you scroll, you can see an ugly scroll bar by the side of the cards.

➤ In case you can't see the canvas, you can enable it using the icon at the top right of Xcode:

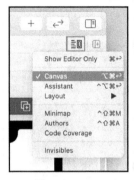

Show canvas

➤ Change ScrollView { to:

```
ScrollView(showsIndicators: false) {
```

This turns the scroll bar off.

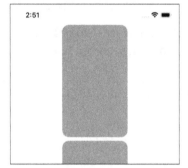

With and without the scroll bar

Refactoring the view

> **Skills you'll learn in this section**: refactoring views; view state in an environment object

As you add views, you'll recognize that later on, some views will become more complex. The RoundedRectangle is such a view. You've given it basic styling, but you'll probably want to style it a bit further down the line. It's much easier to refactor views early on, so you'll create a new view for the placeholder card now. You extracted a view in Chapter 3, "Prototyping the Main View", so this should be a refresher for you.

➤ Create a new SwiftUI View file called **CardThumbnailView.swift**.

➤ Back in **CardsListView.swift**, **Command-click** RoundedRectangle and choose **Extract Subview**.

```
var body: some View {
    ScrollView (showsIndicators: false) {
        VStack {
            ForEach(0..<10) { _ in
                ExtractedView )
            }
        }
    }
}
```

Name the subview

➤ Rename ExtractedView to **CardThumbnailView**.

The extracted view is now at the end of the current file and looks like this:

```
struct CardThumbnailView: View {
    var body: some View {
        RoundedRectangle(cornerRadius: 15)
            .foregroundColor(.gray)
            .frame(width: 150, height: 250)
    }
}
```

➤ Cut this code and open **CardThumbnailView.swift**.

➤ Select the entire `CardThumbnailView` structure and paste in the cut code.

➤ Open **CardsListView.swift**. Your list still looks the same, but it will be easier for you to add colors and shadows to the thumbnails later.

Set up the single card view

➤ Create a SwiftUI View file called **SingleCardView.swift**.

➤ A card will have a colored background to which you'll add photos, stickers and text.

➤ Replace body with:

```
var body: some View {
  Color.yellow
}
```

This color will eventually come from the card data, but for the moment you'll just make the card yellow.

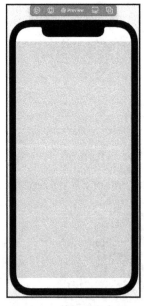

A yellow card

Transitioning from list to card

When you tap a card in the scrolling list in CardsListView, you want to show SingleCardView. You can achieve this in several ways:

- A modal view. SingleCardView will have a row of buttons that link to modal views, and it's not good practice to have modal views inside modal views.

- A NavigationView with a NavigationLink destination that pushes SingleCardView to the front. This could be a good choice, but currently you can't customize an animated transition inside a NavigationView, so it reduces your opportunities for styling your app.

- Replace CardsListView in the view hierarchy. With this option, when you return to the thumbnails after editing the card, you'd lose your current scrolling position in the cards list.

- Place SingleCardView in a new layer in front of CardsListView. This is the option you'll choose, so that you can experiment with transitions later on.

In HIITFit, you used a state property toggle to show the History view and passed a binding when you showed the modal sheet. Navigation in Cards will be spread over multiple files, so it's easier to centralize the property with a view state environment object that will be shared throughout the app.

Creating an environment object

➤ Create a new Swift file called **ViewState.swift** and replace the code with:

```
import SwiftUI

class ViewState: ObservableObject {
  @Published var showAllCards = true
}
```

showAllCards will control display of SingleCardView, and you'll change it when you tap a card. You make it published so that views that use showAllCards will react when the value changes.

You'll remember from Chapter 7, "Observing Objects", that an ObservableObject is a publisher, and ViewState must be a class to conform to it.

➤ In **CardsListView.swift**, add a new property:

```
@EnvironmentObject var viewState: ViewState
```

You'll add the environment object wherever you need to check the view state.

➤ In previews, change CardsListView() to:

```
CardsListView()
  .environmentObject(ViewState())
```

This instantiates the environment object for the preview. If you don't do this, the canvas will crash, without a specific error, when your code tries to access viewState.

➤ Now that you've set up the environment, add a modifier to CardThumbnailView():

```
.onTapGesture {
  viewState.showAllCards.toggle()
}
```

This will toggle the Boolean when you tap a card thumbnail. When showAllCards is false, you'll show the selected single card in front of the list of cards.

➤ Create a new SwiftUI View file called **CardsView.swift**.

This view will be the initial view that controls which full screen views currently show.

➤ Replace the code with:

```
import SwiftUI

struct CardsView: View {
  @EnvironmentObject var viewState: ViewState

  var body: some View {
    ZStack {
      CardsListView()
    }
  }
}

struct CardsView_Previews: PreviewProvider {
  static var previews: some View {
    CardsView()
      .environmentObject(ViewState())
  }
}
```

Here you show CardsListView and set up the environment object viewState.

➤ After `CardsListView()`, add this:

```
if !viewState.showAllCards {
    SingleCardView()
}
```

Your `ZStack` contains `CardsListView` and, in front of that, `SingleCardView`, which will only show when you've tapped a thumbnail to trigger the Boolean state change.

➤ Live Preview and tap a card. The yellow `SingleCardView` shows on top of the list of cards.

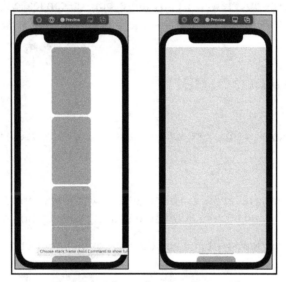

Transition from thumbnail to card

To return to the thumbnail list from `SingleCardView`, you'll need to create a **Done** button.

Before tackling the button, set up your app to run in Simulator, so that if Live Preview fails, you can still see your app.

➤ Open **CardsApp.swift** and initialize `ViewState` as a state object:

```
@StateObject var viewState = ViewState()
```

You do this so that `viewState` persists as long as your app does. If you simply initialize it as an environment object in `CardsApp`, occasionally the app will reinitialize it, and, if you're editing a card, you'll mysteriously land back at the first screen.

➤ Change `ContentView()` to:

```
CardsView()
  .environmentObject(viewState)
```

You call the view that will show the list of cards instead of `ContentView`, making sure that you put `viewState` into the app environment.

➤ Build and run and make sure that your app works in Simulator, just as it does in the preview.

You aren't using **ContentView.swift** any more, but you can leave it in the project to experiment with other SwiftUI layouts.

Navigation toolbar

Skills you'll learn in this section: toolbars; `NavigationView`; navigation bar; tuples

A **Done** button in `SingleCardView` will toggle `showAllCards` in `viewState`. You can set up buttons at top and bottom of the screen using a navigation toolbar.

➤ Open **SingleCardView.swift** and add the environment object to `SingleCardView`:

```
@EnvironmentObject var viewState: ViewState
```

➤ Remember to update `previews`:

```
SingleCardView()
  .environmentObject(ViewState())
```

➤ Add a new toolbar modifier to `Color.yellow`:

```
.toolbar {
  ToolbarItem(placement: .navigationBarTrailing) {
    Button(action: { viewState.showAllCards.toggle() }) {
      Text("Done")
    }
  }
}
```

You place a **Done** button at the top right of the screen. When the user taps this button, SingleCardView toggles showAllCards. Because this is a published property, any view that needs to react to showAllCards will, and CardsView won't show SingleCardView any more.

toolbar(content:) allows multiple ToolbarItems. placement can be:

- navigationBarLeading: The leading edge of the top navigation bar.

- navigationBarTrailing: The trailing edge of the top navigation bar.

- principal: On iOS, the principal placement is in the center of the navigation bar.

- bottomBar: The bottom toolbar.

You'll use the bottom toolbar placement shortly.

➤ Preview SingleCardView.

No Done button

Notice that the button doesn't show up. This is because ToolbarItem(placement:) is using navigationBarTrailing, so any item will only show up if the view is inside a NavigationView.

NavigationView

➤ In SingleCardView, **Command-click** Color and choose **Embed…**.

➤ Change the placeholder Container to NavigationView.

➤ Resume the preview and your button will show up.

Navigation bar Done button

Adding a navigation bar

When you use `Lists`, you often use `NavigationView` and `NavigationLink` together, which have built-in push and pop transitions and titles. You'll explore this more in Section 3. Currently, you're using a `NavigationView`, not for transitions, but to make the **Done** button show up in the `navigationBarTrailing` placement for `SingleCardView`'s toolbar. Using a `NavigationView` means that you can take advantage of the navigation bar style to design the top of the screen.

You're going to add another modifier to `Color.yellow`, so now's the time to take the opportunity to refactor it into a separate view.

➤ **Command-click** `Color` and choose **Extract Subview**.

➤ Name the extracted view **CardDetailView**.

➤ Create a new SwiftUI View file called **CardDetailView.swift** and cut and paste the extracted `CardDetailView` structure into **CardDetailView.swift**, replacing the boilerplate `CardDetailView`.

You'll get a compile error because `viewState` is missing.

➤ Add the environment object to `CardDetailView`:

```
@EnvironmentObject var viewState: ViewState
```

➤ Update `previews`, as usual, to instantiate the environment object:

```
CardDetailView()
  .environmentObject(ViewState())
```

Your code should now compile.

Back in **SingleCardView.swift**, your code is looking a lot simpler:

```
var body: some View {
  NavigationView {
    CardDetailView()
  }
}
```

➤ Add a new modifier to `CardDetailView`:

```
.navigationBarTitleDisplayMode(.inline)
```

This sets the navigation bar style.

Other styles include `automatic` and `large`. If you want to give the view a title as well, you can use `.navigationTitle("Title goes here")`.

➤ Preview `SingleCardView` to see the styled navigation bar.

Styling the navigation bar

➤ Build and run on an iPad simulator in portrait orientation. You can press **Command-Right Arrow** and **Command-Left Arrow** to rotate the simulator, or choose **Device ▸ Orientation** and pick the desired orientation.

➤ Tap a card.

You'll see that you get a white screen with a **Back** button. When you tap **Back**, you see a portion of SingleCardView with the **Done** button. Tapping **Done** takes you back to the first screen. This is due to the NavigationView which behaves differently with different size configurations.

iPad navigation view

In Chapter 16, "Adding Assets to Your App", you'll learn that different devices have different size classes. As well as an iPad simulator, you can reproduce this on an iPhone 12 Pro Max simulator in landscape orientation, as this also has a larger size class.

➤ In SingleCardView, add a modifier to NavigationView:

```
.navigationViewStyle(StackNavigationViewStyle())
```

This navigation view style ensures that you only see a single top view at a time.

➤ Build and run, and the iPad version of your app will now behave the same way as the iPhone 12 Pro version.

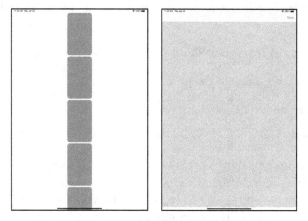

iPad single navigation view

> **Note**: NavigationView can cause issues when you're doing your own custom transitions and animations, so you have to decide whether using NavigationView is worth it. You could lay out the **Done** button in ZStack layers without using a NavigationView as you did in HIITFit.

➤ Set your run destination back to iPhone 12 Pro, as it's easier to preview in the canvas.

The bottom toolbar

The single card view is going to have four buttons at the bottom to add elements to your card:

- **Photos**: Pick photos from your Photo Library

- **Frames**: Change the shape of the photo element

- **Stickers**: Add some fun to your card with app stickers

- **Text**: Add words

Each of these buttons will show a separate modal view. When you have discrete values, such as these four destinations, you can use an enumeration to create your set of values. Enumerations make your code easy to read and ensure that values are restricted to those defined in the enumeration.

➤ Create a new Swift file called **CardModal.swift**.

➤ Add this code:

```
enum CardModal {
  case photoPicker, framePicker, stickerPicker, textPicker
}
```

These cases correspond to each of the buttons.

➤ Create a new SwiftUI View file called **CardBottomToolbar.swift**.

In this view you'll set up the four bottom buttons.

➤ Above `CardBottomToolbar`, add a new `View` for a single toolbar button:

```
struct ToolbarButtonView: View {
  var body: some View {
    VStack {
      Image(systemName: "heart.circle")
        .font(.largeTitle)
      Text("Stickers")
    }
    .padding(.top)
  }
}
```

Each modal button will use this view, and you'll style this to be more generic shortly.

➤ In `CardBottomToolbar`, add a binding for the current modal:

```
@Binding var cardModal: CardModal?
```

➤ Replace body with:

```
var body: some View {
  HStack {
    Button(action: { cardModal = .stickerPicker }) {
      ToolbarButtonView()
    }
  }
}
```

Here you create an `HStack` containing a button that will change the modal state. You'll add more toolbar items in a moment to this `HStack`.

➤ Fix up the preview to send a card modal binding:

```
struct CardBottomToolbar_Previews: PreviewProvider {
  static var previews: some View {
    CardBottomToolbar(cardModal: .constant(.stickerPicker))
      .previewLayout(.sizeThatFits)
      .padding()
  }
}
```

➤ Resume the preview, and you'll see your **Stickers** button and icon:

Stickers button

Adding the bottom toolbar

➤ Open **CardDetailView.swift** and add a new property to `CardDetailView`:

```
@State private var currentModal: CardModal?
```

When you tap a button on the bottom bar, the button will update this property. Later on, you'll show the corresponding modal view.

➤ Locate .toolbar {. This is where you currently have the **Done** button.

➤ Add a new toolbar item inside toolbar(content:), under the previous toolbar item:

```
ToolbarItem(placement: .bottomBar) {
  CardBottomToolbar(cardModal: $currentModal)
}
```

Here you add your new toolbar at the bottom of the screen.

➤ To see the toolbar, either preview **SingleCardView.swift** or build and run the app:

Bottom toolbar

Adding the other buttons

➤ Open **CardBottomToolbar.swift** and add a new property to ToolbarButtonView:

```
let modal: CardModal
```

ToolbarButtonView is the view that displays the toolbar button. You'll send in the modal that the button is tied to and show the correct image for that button. You'll get a compile error until you fix up CardBottomToolbar.

You already set up body to show an image and text for the **Stickers** button. You could do a switch in body and show the appropriate image for all the CardModal options. However, it's more succinct to set a dictionary of all the possible options with the text and image name. In case you need a refresher on dictionaries, you first used them in Chapter 8, "Saving Settings".

➤ Add this property to ToolbarButtonView:

```
private let modalButton:
  [CardModal: (text: String, imageName: String)] = [
    .photoPicker: ("Photos", "photo"),
    .framePicker: ("Frames", "square.on.circle"),
    .stickerPicker: ("Stickers", "heart.circle"),
    .textPicker: ("Text", "textformat")
  ]
```

Here you set up a dictionary of type [CardModal: (String, String)] containing values for all the possible button states. You could have set up a structure that contains text and imageName, but if you're only using a type once in an object with not much code, you can set up an "ad hoc" data type called a **tuple**.

Tuples

A tuple is a group of values. For example, you could initialize a tuple with three elements like this:

```
let button = ("Stickers", "heart.circle", 1)
```

And access the data:

```
let text = button.0
let number = button.2
```

It's obviously good practice to name your types rather than using numbers to access the data, which is why you defined your modalButton tuple with (text: imageName:)

➤ In ToolbarButtonView, replace body with:

```
var body: some View {
  if let text = modalButton[modal]?.text,
    let imageName = modalButton[modal]?.imageName {
  VStack {
    Image(systemName: imageName)
      .font(.largeTitle)
    Text(text)
```

```
    }
  .padding(.top)
  }
}
```

Using your dictionary, you access the text and image name and then use those for the button instead of the hard coded Stickers values.

➤ In `CardBottomToolbar`, replace `HStack` and its contents with:

```
HStack {
  Button(action: { cardModal = .photoPicker }) {
    ToolbarButtonView(modal: .photoPicker)
  }
  Button(action: { cardModal = .framePicker }) {
    ToolbarButtonView(modal: .framePicker)
  }
  Button(action: { cardModal = .stickerPicker }) {
    ToolbarButtonView(modal: .stickerPicker)
  }
  Button(action: { cardModal = .textPicker }) {
    ToolbarButtonView(modal: .textPicker)
  }
}
```

These are the four buttons that your view needs. Each button shows the correct image and text for the modal, and the action sets the new card modal state.

➤ Resume the preview, or build and run to see your new buttons:

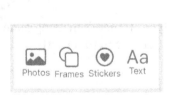

Button Preview

As of now, the buttons don't do anything, but over the next few chapters, you'll attach a new modal view to each button.

You now have a prototype of the main views of your app and can visualize how they will fit together. A prototype is useful, even at this early stage, so that you can show it to other people to find out what they think of it and whether the interface is intuitive enough for them to navigate without help. It's better to find out that your app is not useful as early as possible in its development so that you can either incorporate feedback or pivot entirely.

Challenge

Challenge: Tidy up

Make it a habit to regularly tidy up the files in your app. Look down the list of files and see which ones you can group together. **Command-click** each file that you want to group together, then **Control-click** the selected files and choose **New Group from Selection**. Name the group. If you miss any files, just drag them into the group later.

As an example, you can group all the files with **View** in their name a group called **Views**. You can then have a sub group for the views used for a single card.

You'll find suggested groups in the **challenge** project for this chapter.

Key points

- Prototypes are always worth doing. With a prototype it's easier to see what's missing and what the next steps should be. They don't have to be complicated. So far you aren't creating or saving any data, but you can tell how the app will flow. Writing an app is more than just writing code. It's finding your target audience, creating a good design and overcoming technical problems.

- When you have a button at the top of your screen, whether it's leading or trailing, you can choose to use a navigation bar. The `NavigationView` has the advantage of being a standard, built-in control, however, it can reduce your options of custom transitions.

- Dictionaries are useful for holding disparate values. For example, you can use them to hold options to format views. Using tuples, you can create ad hoc types.

Chapter 14: Gestures

By Caroline Begbie

Gestures are the main interface between you and your app. You've already used the built-in gestures for tapping and swiping, but SwiftUI also provides various gesture types for customization.

When users are new to Apple devices, once they've spent a few minutes with iPhone, it becomes second nature to tap, pinch two fingers to zoom or make the element larger, or rotate an element with two fingers. Your app should use these standard gestures. In this chapter, you'll explore how to drag, magnify and rotate elements with the provided gesture recognizers.

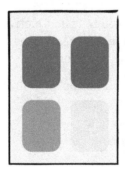 

Back of the napkin design

Looking at the single card view, you're going to drag around and resize photo and text elements. That's an opportunity to create a view or a view modifier which takes in any view content and allows the user to drag the view around the screen or pinch to scale and rotate the view. Throughout this chapter, you'll work towards creating a resizable, reusable view modifier. You'll be able to use this in any of your future apps.

Creating the resizable view

To start with, the resizable view will simply show a colored rectangle but, later on, you'll change it to show any view content.

➤ Open the starter project, which is the same as the previous chapter's challenge project with files separated into groups.

➤ Create a new SwiftUI View file named **ResizableView.swift**.

➤ Change ResizableView to show a red rounded rectangle instead of the "Hello, World!" Text:

```
struct ResizableView: View {
  // 1
  private let content = RoundedRectangle(cornerRadius: 30.0)
  private let color = Color.red

  var body: some View {
    // 2
    content
      .frame(width: 250, height: 180)
      .foregroundColor(color)
  }
}
```

Going through the code:

1. Create a RoundedRectangle view property. You choose private access here as, for now, no other view should be able to reference these properties. Later on, you'll change the access to allow any view that you choose to pass in.

2. Use content as the required View in body and apply modifiers to it.

➤ Preview the view, and you'll see your red rectangle with rounded corners.

Preview rounded rectangle

Creating transforms

Skills you'll learn in this section: transformation

Each card in your app will hold multiple images and pieces of text called, generically, **elements**. For each element, you'll need to store a size, a location on the screen and a rotation angle. In mathematics, you refer to these spatial properties collectively as a **transformation** or **transform**.

➤ In the **Model** group, create a new Swift file called **Transform.swift** to hold the transformation data.

➤ Replace the code in the file and create a structure with initialized spatial properties:

```
import SwiftUI

struct Transform {
  var size = CGSize(width: 250, height: 180)
  var rotation: Angle = .zero
  var offset: CGSize = .zero
}
```

You set up defaults for size, rotation and offset. Angle is a SwiftUI type which conveniently works with both degrees and radians.

Notice the use of .zero here. Angle.zero and CGSize.zero are both **type properties** that return zero values. You'll discover more about type properties later in this chapter. When the type is obvious to the compiler, as it is here, you can leave the Type off .zero, and the compiler will work out which type to use.

Often, transforms hold a scale value too, but in this case you'll update the size of the element instead of holding a scale value.

➤ Open **ResizableView.swift** and add a new property:

```
@State private var transform = Transform()
```

You hold the transform that you will apply to ResizableView as a state property. Later on, you'll be passing the element's saved transform in, but for now, just hold the transform locally.

➤ Change frame(width:height:alignment:) to use transform instead of the hard-coded size:

```
.frame(
  width: transform.size.width,
  height: transform.size.height)
```

Because `transform` holds the same default size, the view does not change. Now you're ready to create gestures to move your view around.

Rounded rectangle with transform sizing

Creating a drag gesture

Skills you'll learn in this section: drag gesture; operator overloading

You'll start off with the **drag** gesture, where the user moves one finger across the screen. This is also called a **pan** gesture. When the user touches down on a `ResizableView` and drags her finger, the view will follow her finger. When she lifts her finger, the view will remain in in that location.

You'll give the view a modifier which will update the offset of `ResizableView` from the center of its parent view. To position the view, you have a choice of using either `position(_:)` or `offset(_:)` view modifier. You're saving an `offset` value into `transform`, so that's what you'll use here.

➤ At the top of body, add a new DragGesture instance:

```
let dragGesture = DragGesture()
  .onChanged { value in
    transform.offset = value.translation
  }
```

The gesture will update transform's offset property as the dragging takes place.

onChanged(_:) has one parameter of type Value, which contains the gesture's current touch location and also the translation since the start of the touch.

The center of the screen is at offset.zero.

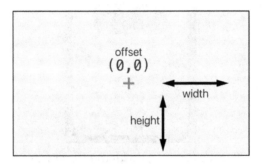

Offset and translation

The amount of translation is the amount to offset the view. The translation is a CGSize, so when you travel across the screen, that's translation.width, and up and down the screen is translation.height.

➤ Add new modifiers to content at the end of body:

```
.offset(transform.offset)
.gesture(dragGesture)
```

Order of modifiers is important — gesture(_:) needs to go after any positioning modifiers.

➤ Live preview the view and drag it around the screen.

Dragging the view

The first drag works well, but on second and subsequent drags, the view does a jump at the start of the drag. This is because the drag gesture sets value.translation to zero at the start of the drag, so you'll need to take into account any previous translations.

➤ Add a new state property to ResizableView to hold the transform's offset before you start dragging:

```
@State private var previousOffset: CGSize = .zero
```

➤ Change `dragGesture` to:

```
let dragGesture = DragGesture()
  .onChanged { value in
    transform.offset = CGSize(
      width: value.translation.width + previousOffset.width,
      height: value.translation.height + previousOffset.height)
  }
  .onEnded { _ in
    previousOffset = transform.offset
  }
```

In `onChanged(_:)`, you update `transform` with the user's drag translation amount and include any previous dragging.

In `onEnded(_:)`, you replace the old `previousOffset` with the new offset, ready for the next drag. You don't need to use the `value` provided, so you use _ as the parameter for the action method.

➤ Try it out in the live preview again.

This works well. You can now drag your view around and position it wherever you want.

The `CGSize` code is a bit long-winded though, with having to do the math on both `width` and `height`. You can shorten this code by overloading the + operator.

Operator overloading

Operator overloading is where you redefine what operators such as +, −, ∗ and / do.

To add `translation` to `offset`, you're going to add `width` to `width` and at the same time, add `height` to `height`. So you're going to redefine + with a special method.

➤ Create a new Swift file called **Operators.swift**. Any time you want to overload an operator for a particular type, you can add the method in this file.

➤ Replace the code with the new method:

```
import SwiftUI

func + (left: CGSize, right: CGSize) -> CGSize {
  CGSize(
    width: left.width + right.width,
    height: left.height + right.height)
}
```

Here you specify what the + operator should do for a `CGSize` type. The parameters are `left` and `right`, being the items to the left and right of the + sign. You return the new `CGSize`.

This is a simple example of how you want the + sign to work for `CGSize`. It makes sense here to add the `width` and `height` together. However, you can redefine this operator to do anything, and you should be very careful that the method makes sense. Don't do things like redefining a multiply sign to do division!

➤ Now, return to **ResizableView.swift** and change `dragGesture` to:

```
let dragGesture = DragGesture()
  .onChanged { value in
    transform.offset = value.translation + previousOffset
  }
  .onEnded { _ in
    previousOffset = transform.offset
  }
```

You can see how overloading the + operator reduces the code and increases clarity.

Creating a rotation gesture

Skills you'll learn in this section: rotation gesture

Now that you can move your view around the screen, it's time to rotate it. You'll use two fingers on the view and set up a `RotationGesture` to track the angle of rotation.

Just as you did with tracking the previous offset of the view, you'll track the previous rotation.

➤ In **ResizableView.swift**, set up a new state property for this:

```
@State private var previousRotation: Angle = .zero
```

This will hold the angle of rotation of the view going into the start of the gesture.

➤ At the top of body add the new gesture:

```
let rotationGesture = RotationGesture()
  .onChanged { rotation in
    transform.rotation += rotation - previousRotation
    previousRotation = rotation
```

```
    }
    .onEnded { _ in
      previousRotation = .zero
    }
```

onChanged(_:) provides the gesture's angle of rotation as the parameter for the action you provide. You add the current rotation, less the previous rotation, to transform's rotation.

onEnded(_:) takes place after the user removes his fingers from the screen. Here, you set any previous rotation to zero.

➤ Replace .gesture(dragGesture) with:

```
    .rotationEffect(transform.rotation)
    .gesture(dragGesture)
    .gesture(rotationGesture)
```

To test out your rotation effect in the live preview, because you don't have a touch screen available to you, you can simulate two fingers by holding down the **Option** key. Two dots will appear, representing two fingers. (You may have to click the preview before they show up.)

Two fingers to rotate

Move your mouse or trackpad to change the distance between the two dots. Make sure that they are both on the rectangle `View`, and click and drag. Your view should rotate. If you have the distance between the dots correct, but you want the dots to be elsewhere on the screen, you can hold down the **Shift** key as well as **Option** to move the dots. Still holding **Option**, let go the **Shift** key when they are in the right place.

Order of modifiers is again important here. The pivot point of the rotation is around the center of the view without taking any offset into consideration.

➤ Drag the view and then rotate it, and you'll see that the view's pivot point is around the center of the screen. This is the view's center point without the offset applied.

Sometimes this may be what you want. But in your case here, you want to rotate the view before offsetting it.

> **Swift Tip**: `rotationEffect(_:anchor:)` by default rotates around the center of the view, but you can change that to another point in the view by changing `anchor`.

➤ Move `.offset(transform.offset)` to *after* `rotationEffect(transform.rotation)`, but *before* `gesture(dragGesture)`.

> **Note**: The shortcut keys **Option-Command-[** and **Option-Command-]** move lines of code up and down.

The order of gestures is also important. If you place the drag gesture after the rotation gesture, then the rotation gesture will swallow up the touches.

➤ Try rotating the view in the live preview

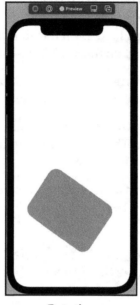

Rotation

➤ Gestures always feel better on a real device, so to run this on a device, open **CardsApp.swift**

➤ Temporarily, change `CardsView()` to:

```
ResizableView()
```

➤ Change the run destination to your device.

> **Note**: If you haven't yet run an app on your device, take a look at **Running your project** in Chapter 1, "Checking Your Tools". You'll need an Apple developer account set up in Preferences to run the app on a device.

➤ Set your team identifier on the Cards app's **Signing & Capabilities** tab.

➤ Build and run and try out your gestures to see how fluid they feel. Two fingers on the device feels much more natural than trying to manipulate the simulator gesture dots.

Creating a scale gesture

Skills you'll learn in this section: magnification gesture; simultaneous gestures

Finally, you'll scale the view up and down. MagnificationGesture operates as a pinch gesture, so you'll be able to rotate and scale at the same time, using two fingers.

You'll do the scale slightly differently from rotate and offset. The view will always be at a scale of 1 unless the user is currently scaling. At the end of the scale, you'll calculate the new size of the view and set the scale back to 1.

➤ Open **ResizableView.swift**, and create a state property to hold the current scale:

```
@State private var scale: CGFloat = 1.0
```

➤ At the top of body, create the scale gesture:

```
let scaleGesture = MagnificationGesture()
  .onChanged { scale in
    self.scale = scale
  }
  .onEnded { scale in
    transform.size.width *= scale
    transform.size.height *= scale
    self.scale = 1.0
  }
```

onChanged(_:) takes the current gesture's scale and stores it in the state property scale. To differentiate between the two properties called the same name, use self to describe ResizableView's property.

When the user has finished the pinch and raises his fingers from the screen, onEnded(_:) takes the gesture's scale and changes transform's width and height. You then reset the state property to 1.0 ready for the next scale.

➤ After .rotationEffect(transform.rotation), add the scale modifier:

```
.scaleEffect(scale)
```

Creating a simultaneous gesture

Whereas the drag is a specific gesture with one finger, you can do rotation and scale at the same time with two fingers. To do this, change `.gesture(rotationGesture)` to:

```
.gesture(SimultaneousGesture(rotationGesture, scaleGesture))
```

You can now perform the two gestures at the same time.

➤ Try out your three gestures in the live preview. Then, build and run your app and try them out in Simulator or, if possible, on a device.

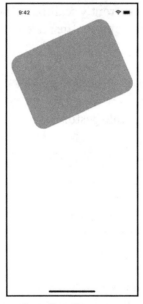

Completed gestures

Creating custom view modifiers

Skills you'll learn in this section: creating a `ViewModifier`; `View` extension; using a view modifier; advantages of a view modifier

You've made a very useful view, one that can be used in many app contexts. Rather than hard-coding the view you want to resize, you can change this view and make it a modifier that acts on other views.

➤ In **ResizableView.swift**, change `struct ResizableView: View {` to:

```
struct ResizableView: ViewModifier {
```

Here, you declare the new view modifier. For the moment, ignore all the compile errors until you've completed the modifier.

➤ Change `var body: some View {` to:

```
func body(content: Content) -> some View {
```

Because `ViewModifier` takes in an existing view, instead of a `var`, it requires a method with the view content as a parameter. The content will be a view, such as a `Rectangle` or an `Image` or any custom view you create.

`ResizableView` should only operate on expected properties of a view. For resizing, you would expect a `Transform` property, but `color` has nothing to do with resizing. You'll set up color and content outside of the modifier.

➤ Remove:

```
private let content = RoundedRectangle(cornerRadius: 30.0)
private let color = Color.red
```

➤ Also remove `.foregroundColor(color)` from `content`.

Your `content` with modifiers should be:

```
// ... define gesture variables here
content
  .frame(
    width: transform.size.width,
    height: transform.size.height)
  .rotationEffect(transform.rotation)
  .scaleEffect(scale)
  .offset(transform.offset)
  .gesture(dragGesture)
  .gesture(SimultaneousGesture(rotationGesture, scaleGesture))
```

➤ To preview the modifier, change the preview provider at the end of
ResizableView.swift

```
struct ResizableView_Previews: PreviewProvider {
  static var previews: some View {
    RoundedRectangle(cornerRadius: 30.0)
      .foregroundColor(Color.red)
      .modifier(ResizableView())
  }
}
```

Here, you set up the content that the view should use and add the `modifier(_:)`
with your custom view modifier.

It's always a good idea to keep your previews working. With view modifier previews,
you can provide an example to future users of your code how to use the modifier.
Always remember that "future users" includes you in a few weeks' time! :]

➤ In **CardsApp.swift**, revert `ResizableView()` back to:

```
CardsView()
```

Your project should now compile.

➤ In **ResizableView.swift**, resume your live preview and check out your new modifier.

View Modifier preview

It works exactly the same as ResizableView, but you can now apply the modifier to any view and make it resizable.

Using your custom view modifier

In the preview, you used .modifier(ResizableView()). You can improve this by adding a "pass-through" method to View.

➤ Create a new group and name it **Extensions**.

➤ In **Extensions**, create a new Swift file and name it **ViewExtensions.swift**.

➤ Replace the code in the file with:

```swift
import SwiftUI

extension View {
  func resizableView() -> some View {
    return modifier(ResizableView())
  }
}
```

You're extending the `View` protocol with a default method. `resizableView()` is now available on any object that conforms to `View`. The method simply returns your modifier, but it does make your code easier to read.

➤ Open **CardDetailView.swift** and add a new view property:

```
var content: some View {
  ZStack {
    Capsule()
      .foregroundColor(.yellow)
      .resizableView()
    Text("Resize Me!")
      .font(.largeTitle)
      .fontWeight(.bold)
      .resizableView()
    Circle()
      .resizableView()
      .offset(CGSize(width: 50, height: 200))
  }
}
```

➤ In body, replace `Color.yellow` with:

```
content
```

Eventually `content` will show card elements, but for now you can test out your new resizable view. Here you test out your modifier with two different types of views — two `Shapes` and one `Text`. The `Circle`'s offset is applied on top of the offset in `resizableView()`. Everything is put together inside a `ZStack`, which is a container view that allows its children to use absolute positioning.

➤ Live Preview to check out your new resizing abilities.

Resize multiple views

There is a problem with the Text. Capsule remembers its size, because of the frame(width:height:alignment:) modifier inside ResizableView. However, Text has a font(_:) modifier. Because the modifier is applied directly to the view, it takes priority over frame(width:height:alignment:).

There is a trick to scaling text on demand. Give the font a huge size, say 500. Then apply a minimum scale factor to it, to reduce it in size.

➤ Remove .font(.largeTitle).

➤ After .fontWeight(.bold), add:

```
.font(.system(size: 500))
.minimumScaleFactor(0.01)
.lineLimit(1)
```

.lineLimit(1) ensures the text stays on one line and doesn't wrap around.

➤ Try resizing the text again in live preview. This time the text retains its size.

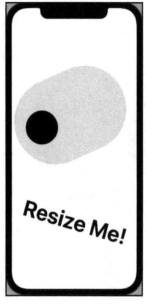

Resize the text

View modifier advantage

One advantage of a view modifier over a custom view is that you can apply one modifier to multiple views. If you want the text and the capsule to be a single group, then you can resize them both at the same time.

➤ Group `Capsule` and `Text` together inside the `ZStack`, and apply `resizableView()` to `Group` instead of the two views:

```
Group {
  Capsule()
    .foregroundColor(.yellow)
  Text("Resize Me!")
    .fontWeight(.bold)
    .font(.system(size: 500))
    .minimumScaleFactor(0.01)
    .lineLimit(1)
}
.resizableView()
```

Here, you grouped the two views together so they combine to a single view.

➤ Live preview the view.

Grouped Views

When you resize now, you're dragging and resizing both capsule and text at the same time. This could be useful where you have a caption or a watermark on an image and you want them both at the same scale.

Other gestures

- **Tap gesture**

You used `onTapGesture(count:perform:)` in the previous chapter when tapping a card. There is also a `TapGesture` structure where you can use `onEnded(_:)` in the same way as with the other gestures in this chapter.

- **Long press gesture**

Similarly, you can use either the structure `LongPressGesture` to recognize a long-press on a view, or use
`onLongPressGesture(minimumDuration:maximumDistance:pressing:perform:)`
if you don't need to set up a separate gesture property.

Type properties

Skills you'll learn in this section: type properties; type methods

So far, you've hard coded the size of the card thumbnail, and also the default size in Transform. In most apps, you'll want some global settings for sizes or color themes.

You do have the choice of holding constants in global space. You could, for example, create a new file and add this code at the top level:

```
var currentTheme = Color.red
```

currentTheme is then accessible to your whole app. However, as your app grows, sometimes it's hard to immediately identify whether a particular constant is global or whether it belongs to your current class or structure. An easy way of identifying globals, and making sure that they only exist in one place, is to set up a special type for them and add **type properties** to the type.

Swift Dive: Stored property vs type property

To create a type property, rather than a stored property, you use the static keyword.

You already used the type property CGSize.zero. CGPoint also has a type property of zero and defines a 2D point with values in x and y. Examine part of the CGPoint structure definition to see both stored and type properties:

```
public struct CGPoint {
  public var x: CGFloat
  public var y: CGFloat
}

extension CGPoint {
  public static var zero: CGPoint {
    CGPoint(x: 0, y: 0)
  }
}
```

This is an example of using a CGPoint:

```
var point = CGPoint(x: 10, y: 10)
point.x = 20
```

When you create an instance of the structure `CGPoint`, you set up x and y properties on the structure. These x and y properties are unique to every `CGPoint` you instantiate.

`CGPoint` also has a type property: `zero`, which describes a point at `(0, 0)`. To use this type property, you use the name of the type:

```
let pointZero = CGPoint.zero  // pointZero contains (x: 0, y: 0)
```

This sets up an instance of a `CGPoint`, named `pointZero`, with x and y values of zero.

When you instantiate a new structure, that structure stores its properties in memory separately from every other structure. A `static` or type property, however, is constant over all instances of the type. No matter how many times you instantiate the structure, there will only be one copy of the `static` type property.

In the following diagram, there are two copies of `CGPoint`, `pointA` and `pointB`. Each of them has its own memory storage area. `CGPoint` has a type property `zero` which is stored once.

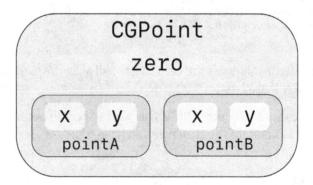

Type property storage

Swift Tip: `CGPoint.zero` is defined as a computed property. It has a return value of `CGPoint(x: 0, y: 0)`, and you can't set it to any other value. There is no effective difference between defining `.zero` as a computed property or as `static let zero = CGPoint(x: 0, y: 0)`. It is a stylistic choice.

Creating global defaults for Cards

Skills you'll learn in this section: type methods

Going back to your hard coded size values, you'll now create a file that will hold all your global constants.

➤ Create a new group called **Config**.

➤ In **Config**, create a new Swift file called **Settings.swift** and replace the code with:

```swift
import SwiftUI

struct Settings {
  static let thumbnailSize =
    CGSize(width: 150, height: 250)
  static let defaultElementSize =
    CGSize(width: 250, height: 180)
  static let borderColor: Color = .blue
  static let borderWidth: CGFloat = 5
}
```

Here you create default values for the card thumbnail size, the card element size and for a border that you'll use later.

Notice that you created a structure. While this works, it could become problematic, because you could instantiate the structure and have copies of `Settings` throughout your app.

```swift
let settings1 = Settings()
let settings2 = Settings()
```

However, if you use an enumeration, you can't instantiate it, so it ensures that you will only ever have one copy of `Settings`.

➤ Change `struct Settings {` to:

```swift
enum Settings {
```

Using an enumeration and type properties in this way future-proofs your app. Later on, someone else might want to add another setting to your app. They won't need to change the enumeration itself, but they'll just be able to create an extension.

For example, they could add a new type property like this:

```
extension Settings {
  static let aNewSetting: Int = 0
}
```

Extensions can hold type properties, but not stored properties.

➤ Open **CardThumbnailView.swift**. Instead of defining the frame size here, you can rely on your settings defaults.

➤ Change .frame(width: 150, height: 250) to:

```
.frame(
  width: Settings.thumbnailSize.width,
  height: Settings.thumbnailSize.height)
```

➤ Similarly, open **Transform.swift** and change var size = CGSize(width: 250, height: 180) to:

```
var size = CGSize(
  width: Settings.defaultElementSize.width,
  height: Settings.defaultElementSize.height)
```

If you want to change these sizes later on, you can do it in Settings.

Creating type methods

As well as static properties, you can also create static methods. To illustrate this, you'll extend SwiftUI's built-in Color type. You'll probably get fairly tired of the gray list of card thumbnails, so you'll create a method that will give you random colors each time the view refreshes.

➤ In the **Extensions** group. create a new Swift file called **ColorExtensions.swift**.

➤ Replace the code with:

```
import SwiftUI

extension Color {
  static let colors: [Color] = [
    .green, .red, .blue, .gray, .yellow, .pink, .orange, .purple
  ]
}
```

You created an array of Colors that's available throughout the app by referencing Color.colors.

➤ Create a new method inside `Color`:

```
static func random() -> Color {
  colors.randomElement() ?? .black
}
```

This method returns a random element from the colors array and, if the colors array is empty, returns black.

> **Swift Tip**: Astute readers will notice that this method could just as easily have been a `static var` computed property. However, conventionally, if you're returning a value that may change often, or there is complex code, use a method.

➤ Open **CardThumbnailView.swift**.

➤ Change `.foregroundColor(.gray)` to:

```
.foregroundColor(.random())
```

Here you're using the `static` method that you created on `Color`. Each time you list the thumbnails, they will use different colors.

➤ Preview **CardsView.swift** and see your random card colors. Each time you press Live Preview, the colors change.

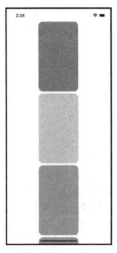

Random color

Challenge

Challenge: Make a new view modifier

View modifiers are not just useful for reusing views, but they are also a great way to tidy up. You can combine modifiers into one custom modifier. Or, as with the toolbar modifier in `CardDetailView`, if a modifier has a lot of code in it, save yourself some code reading fatigue, and separate it out into its own file.

Your challenge is to create a new view modifier that takes the toolbar code and moves it into a modifier called `CardToolbar`.

To do this, you'll:

1. Create a new file to hold the view modifier.

2. Create a structure `CardToolbar: ViewModifier` and create a new method body that just returns `content`, as you did when you made `ResizableView` a `ViewModifier`.

3. Remove the preview, as it doesn't make sense to have one for this modifier.

4. For body, cut the toolbar modifier code from `CardDetailView` and paste the modifier on `CardToolbar`'s content.

5. In `CardToolbar`, you'll need to have the `ViewState` environment object, and `currentModal` as a binding.

6. In `CardDetailView`, add to content your new custom modifier: `.modifier(CardToolbar(currentModal: $currentModal))`.

When you've completed the challenge, your code should work the same, but, with this refactoring, `CardDetailView` is easier to read.

As always, you'll find the solution in the **challenge** folder for this chapter.

Key points

- Custom gestures let you interact with your app in any way you choose. Make sure the gestures make sense. Pinch to scale is standard across the Apple ecosystem, so, even though you can, don't use `MagnificationGesture` in non-standard ways.

- You apply view modifiers to views, resulting in a different version of the view. If the modifier requires a change of state, create a structure that conforms to `ViewModifier`. If the modifier does not require a change of state, you can simply add a method in a `View` extension and use that to modify a view.

- `static` or type properties and methods exist on the type. Stored properties exist per instance of the type. `Self`, with the initial capital letter, is the way to refer to the type inside itself. `self` refers to the instance of the type. Apple uses type properties and methods extensively. For example, `Color.yellow` is a type property.

Where to go from here?

By now you should be able to understand a lot of technical jargon. It's time to check out Apple's documentation and articles. At https://apple.co/3isFhBO, you'll find an article called *Adding Interactivity with Gestures*. This article describes updating state during a gesture. Read this article and check your understanding of the topic so far.

The Apple article *Composing SwiftUI Gestures*, at https://apple.co/36meaVo describes combining gestures in various ways.

Create your own modifiers. Any time you repeat your view's design, you should look at creating a method or a modifier that encapsulates that code.

Think about parts of your app in modules. In this chapter, you created a useful resizable view modifier which you can now use in any app that you create. When creating views, consider how you could abstract them and make them more generic.

In the next chapter, you'll start planning how to structure the app data and work out how to pass data and actions through your view hierarchy.

Chapter 15: Structures, Classes & Protocols

By Caroline Begbie

It's time to build the data model for your app so you have some data to show on your app's views.

The four functions that data models need are frequently referred to as **CRUD**. That's **C**reate, **R**ead, **U**pdate, **D**elete. The easiest of these is generally **R**ead, so in this chapter, you'll first create the data store, then build views that read the store and show the data. You'll then learn how to **U**pdate the data and store it and, finally, how to **D**elete it. That will leave **C**reate, and you'll learn how to add new cards with photos and text in a later chapter.

Starter project changes

There are a few differences between the challenge project from the last chapter and the starter project of this chapter:

- **Operators.swift**: contains a new operator to multiply a `CGSize` by a scalar.

- **Preview Assets.xcassets**: contains three cute hedgehogs from http://pexels.com.

- **PreviewData.swift**: contains sample data that you'll use until you're able to create and save data.

- **TextExtensions.swift**: contains a new view modifier to scale text.

➤ If you are continuing with your own project, be sure to copy these files into your project.

Data structure

Take another look at the back of the napkin sketch:

Back of the napkin sketch

Even with this rough sketch, you can get an idea of how to shape your data.

You'll need a top level data store that will hold an array of all the cards. Each card will have a list of elements, and these elements could be an image or text.

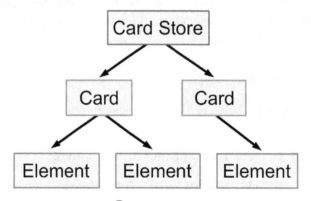

Data structure

You don't want to constrain yourself to image or text though, as you might add new features to your app in the future. Any data model you create now should be *extensible*, meaning as flexible as possible, to allow future capabilities.

Value and reference types

> **Skills you'll learn in this section**: differences between value and reference types

Before creating the data model, you'll need to decide what types to use to store your data. Should you use structures or classes?

A Swift data type is either a value type or a reference type. Value types, like structures and enumerations, contain data, while reference types, like classes, contain a reference to data.

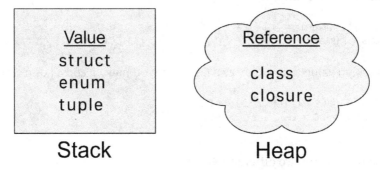

Value and reference types

At runtime, your app instantiates properties and assigns them to separate areas of memory, called the **stack** and the **heap**. Value types go on the stack, which the CPU manages and optimizes, so it's very fast and efficient. You can instantiate structures, enumerations and tuples without counting the cost. The heap, however, is much more dynamic and allows an app to allocate and deallocate areas of memory, while maintaining reference counts. This makes reference types less efficient. When you instantiate a class, that piece of data should stick around for a while.

Swift Dive: Structure vs class

Skills you'll learn in this section: how to use structures and classes

When initializing classes and structures in code, they look very similar. For example:

```
let iAmAStruct = AStruct()
let iAmAClass = AClass()
```

The important difference here is that `iAmAStruct` contains immutable data, whereas `iAmAClass` contains an immutable reference to the data. The data itself is still mutable and you can change it.

```
iAmAStruct.number = 10   // compile error
iAmAClass.number  = 10   // no error — `number` will update to 10
```

When you assign value types, such as a `CGPoint`, you make a copy. For example:

```
let pointA = CGPoint(x: 10, y: 20)
var pointB = pointA    // make a copy
pointB.x = 20          // pointA.x is still 10
```

`pointA` and `pointB` are two different objects.

With a reference type, you access the same data. For example:

```
let iAmAClass = AClass()
let iAmAClassToo = iAmAClass
iAmAClassToo.number = 20   // this updates iAmAClass
print(iAmAClass.number)    // prints 20
```

Swift keeps a count of the number of references to the `AClass` object created in the heap. The reference count here would be two, and Swift won't deallocate the object until its reference count is zero.

Changing the data like this can be a source of errors for unwitting developers. One of Swift's principles is to prevent accidental errors, and if you favor value types over reference types, you'll end up with fewer of those accidents. In this app, you'll favor structures and enumerations over classes where possible.

Creating the card store

> **Skills you'll learn in this section**: when to use classes and structures

Returning to the complex matter of deciding how to store your data, you need to choose between a structure and a class.

In general, when you hold a simple piece of data, such as a Card or a CardElement, those are lightweight objects that you won't need forever. You'd make those a structure. However, when you hold a data store that you're going to use throughout your app, that would be a good candidate for a class. In addition, if your piece of data has publisher properties, it must conform to ObservableObject, where the requirement is that the data type is a class.

Now you'll get started creating your data model, beginning at the bottom of the data hierarchy, with the element.

➤ In the **Model** group, create a new Swift file called **CardElement.swift**.

➤ Replace the code with:

```
import SwiftUI

struct CardElement {
}
```

This is the file where you'll describe the card elements. You'll come back to this shortly to define the data you'll hold.

➤ Create a new Swift file called **Card.swift** and replace the code with:

```
import SwiftUI

struct Card: Identifiable {
  let id = UUID()
  var backgroundColor: Color = .yellow
  var elements: [CardElement] = []
}
```

You set up Card to conform to Identifiable, with the protocol's required property id. Later, you can use this unique id to locate a card and to iterate through the cards.

You're also holding a background color for the card and an array of elements for all the images and text that you'll place on the card.

➤ Create a new Swift file named **CardStore.swift** and replace the code:

```
import SwiftUI

class CardStore: ObservableObject {
  @Published var cards: [Card] = []
}
```

CardStore is your main data store and your single *source of truth*. As such, you'll make sure that it stays around for the duration of the app. It isn't, therefore, a lightweight object, and you choose to make it a class.

There is a second reason for it to be a class. The protocol ObservableObject requires any type that conforms to it to be a class.

ObservableObject is part of the **Combine** framework. A class that conforms to ObservableObject can have published properties in it. When any changes happen to these properties, any view that uses them will automatically refresh. So when any card in the published array changes, views will react.

You've now set up a data model that SwiftUI can observe and write to. There is a difficulty with card elements, however. These can be either an image or text.

Class inheritance

Skills you'll learn in this section: class inheritance; composition vs inheritance

You might have come across **object oriented programming** (OOP) in Swift or other languages. This is where you have a base object, and other classes derive, or **inherit**, from this base object. Swift classes allow inheritance. Swift structures do not.

You might set up your card element data in this way:

```
class CardElement {
  var transform: Transform
}

class ImageElement: CardElement {
  var image: Image?
}
```

```
class TextElement: CardElement {
  var text: String?
}
```

Here you have a base class `CardElement` with two sub-classes inheriting from `CardElement`. `ImageElement` and `TextElement` both inherit the `transform` property, but each type has its own separate relevant data.

As discussed earlier, however, lightweight objects such as card elements should be value types, not classes.

Composition vs Inheritance

With **inheritance**, you have tightly coupled objects. Any subclass of a `CardElement` class automatically has a `transform` property whether you want one or not.

You might possibly decide in a future release to require some elements to have a color. With inheritance, you could add `color` to the base class, but you'd then be holding redundant data for the elements that don't use a color.

An alternative scenario is to use **composition** with protocols, where you add only relevant properties to an object. This means that you can hold your data in structures.

This diagram shows a `CardElement` protocol with `ImageElement` and `TextElement` structures. It also shows a possible future expansion if you want to include a new `ColorElement`. This would be much harder with inheritance.

Card Element	Protocols	Colorized
transform		color

Structs

ImageElement	TextElement	ColorElement
transform image	transform text	transform
	color	color

Composition

Traditionally, inheritance is considered to be an "is a" relationship, while composition is a "has a" relationship. But, you should avoid tightly-coupled objects as much as you can, and composition gives you much more freedom in design.

Protocols

> **Skills you'll learn in this section**: create protocol; conform structures to protocol; protocol method

You've used several protocols so far, such as View and Identifiable and, possibly, been slightly mystified as to what they actually are.

Protocols are like a contract. You create a protocol that defines requirements for a structure, a class or an enumeration. These requirements may include properties and whether they are read-only or read-write. A protocol might also define a list of methods that any type adopting the protocol must include. Protocols can't hold data; they are simply a blueprint or template. You create structures or classes to hold data and they, in turn, conform to protocols.

View is the protocol that you've used most. It has a required property body. Every view that you've created has contained body and, if you don't provide one, you get a compile error.

Identifiable is another protocol that you've used. id is a required property, so every time you've conformed to Identifiable, you have created an id property that is guaranteed to be unique. Generally you use a **universally unique identifier**, or **UUID**, to provide a unique 128-bit number.

In your app, every card element will have a transform, so you'll change CardElement to be a protocol that requires any structure adopting it to have a transform property.

➤ Open **CardElement.swift** and replace the structure with:

```
protocol CardElement {
  var id: UUID { get }
  var transform: Transform { get set }
}
```

Here you create a blueprint of your CardElement structure. Every card element type will have an id and a transform. id is read-only, and transform is read-write.

➤ In the same file as `CardElement`, create the image element:

```
struct ImageElement: CardElement {
  let id = UUID()
  var transform = Transform()
  var image: Image
}
```

`ImageElement` conforms to `CardElement` with its required `id` and `transform`. It also holds an image.

➤ Create the text element after the image element:

```
struct TextElement: CardElement {
  let id = UUID()
  var transform = Transform()
  var text = ""
  var textColor = Color.black
  var textFont = "San Fransisco"
}
```

`TextElement` also conforms to `CardElement` and holds a string for text, the text color and the font.

With protocols, you are future-proofing the design. If you later want to add a new card element that is just a solid color, you can simply create a new structure `ColorElement` that conforms to `CardElement`.

`Card` holds an array of `CardElements`. `Card` doesn't care what type of `CardElement` it holds in its `elements` array, so it's easy to add new element types.

Creating a default protocol method

Part of a protocol blueprint might be requiring the conforming type to implement a method. For example, this protocol requires all types that conform to it to implement `find()`:

```
protocol Findable {
  func find()
}
```

But sometimes you want a default method that is the same across all conforming types. For example, in your app, a card is going to hold an array of card elements. Later, you're going to want to find the index for a particular card element.

The code for this would be:

```
let index = card.elements.firstIndex { $0.id == element.id }
```

This is quite hard to read and you have to remember the closure syntax. Instead, you can create a new method in CardElement to replace it.

➤ In **CardElement.swift**, under the protocol declaration, add a new method in an extension:

```
extension CardElement {
  func index(in array: [CardElement]) -> Int? {
    array.firstIndex { $0.id == id }
  }
}
```

This method takes in an array of CardElement and passes back the index of the element. If the element doesn't exist, it passes back nil in the optional Int. The way you'll use it is:

```
let index = element.index(in: card.elements)
```

This is a lot easier to read than the earlier code, and the complicated closure syntax is abstracted away in index(in:). Any type that conforms to CardElement can use this method.

Now that you have your views and your data model implemented, you have reached the exciting point of showing the data in the views. Your app doesn't allow you to add any data, so your starter project has some preview data to work with until you can add your own.

The preview data

Skills you'll learn in this section: using preview data

➤ In the **Preview Content** group, take a look at **PreviewData.swift** and remove the comment tags /* */. If this code weren't commented, it wouldn't have compiled until you built your data model.

There are five cards. The first card uses the array of four elements, which are a mixture of images and text. You'll use this data to test out new views. The card elements are positioned for portrait orientation on an iPhone 12 Pro. As they are hard-coded, if you run the app in landscape mode or on a smaller device, some of the elements will be off the screen. Later, your card will take on a fixed size, and the elements will scale to fit in the available space.

➤ Open **CardStore.swift** and add an initializer to `CardStore`:

```
init(defaultData: Bool = false) {
  if defaultData {
    cards = initialCards
  }
}
```

When you first instantiate `CardStore`, the initializer will load the preview data when `defaultData` is `true`.

Later, when you can save and load cards from file, you'll update this to use saved cards. For the moment, you'll use the preview data.

You'll need to instantiate `CardStore`, and the best place to do that is at the start of the app.

➤ Open **CardsApp.swift** and add a new property to `CardsApp`:

```
@StateObject var store = CardStore(defaultData: true)
```

You use `@StateObject` to ensure that the data store persists throughout the app.

➤ Add a modifier to `CardsView()` so you can address the data store through the environment:

```
.environmentObject(store)
```

➤ Open **CardsView.swift** and add the new environment object to `CardsView`:

```
@EnvironmentObject var store: CardStore
```

Whenever you create an environment object property, you should make sure that the SwiftUI preview instantiates it. If you don't do this, your preview will crash mysteriously with no error message.

➤ In `previews`, add a modifier to `CardsView`:

```
.environmentObject(CardStore(defaultData: true))
```

Listing the cards

Skills you'll learn in this section: didSet property observer; mutability

➤ Open **CardsListView.swift** and, again, add the data store to CardsListView:

```
@EnvironmentObject var store: CardStore
```

➤ In previews, add a modifier to CardsListView:

```
.environmentObject(CardStore(defaultData: true))
```

You can now access the data store with the preview data in CardsListView.

➤ Change ForEach(0..<10) { _ in to:

```
ForEach(store.cards) { card in
```

Here you iterate through store.cards. Remember that ForEach in this format requires Card to be Identifiable.

➤ Open **CardThumbnailView.swift** and add a new property to CardThumbnailView:

```
let card: Card
```

You don't need card to be mutable here, as you'll only read from it to get the card's background color for the thumbnail.

➤ Replace .foregroundColor(.random()) with:

```
.foregroundColor(card.backgroundColor)
```

Instead of a random color, you use the background color of the card for the thumbnail.

➤ Update the preview to use the first card in the provided preview data:

```
struct CardThumbnailView_Previews: PreviewProvider {
  static var previews: some View {
    CardThumbnailView(card: initialCards[0])
  }
}
```

➤ Back in **CardsListView**, change `CardThumbnailView()` to:

```
CardThumbnailView(card: card)
```

You pass the current card to the thumbnail view.

➤ Preview the view and check that the scrolling card thumbnails use the background colors from the preview data:

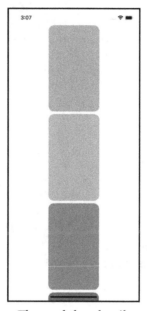

The card thumbnails

Choosing a card

When you tap a card, you toggle `viewState.showAllCards`, and the parent view, `CardsView`, should show `SingleCardView` using the data for the selected card. Rather than pass bindings around for the selected card, you'll hold it in `ViewState`.

➤ Open **ViewState.swift** and add the new property to `ViewState`:

```
var selectedCard: Card?
```

Any view with access to the environment object `ViewState` can now find out what the currently selected card is.

➤ In **CardsListView.swift**, add this to `onTapGesture(count:perform:)`:

```
viewState.selectedCard = card
```

The didSet observer

Of course, when you are listing all cards and no card is currently selected, `viewState.selectedCard` should be `nil`. You control display of this list with `viewState.showAllCards`. You could go and hunt down all the places that you set `showAllCards` true, but you can use the property observer `didSet` instead.

➤ Open **ViewState.swift** and replace `@Published var showAllCards = true` with:

```
@Published var showAllCards = true {
  didSet {
    if showAllCards {
      selectedCard = nil
    }
  }
}
```

Whenever you assign a new value to `showAllCards`, `didSet` will observe the change. You take action when you set `showAllCards` to `true` and set `selectedCard` to `nil`. If you need to access the previous value of `showAllCards` within the `didSet` closure, you can use `oldValue`.

> **Swift Tip**: There's another property observer called `willSet`. This fires before the change is made whereas `didSet` fires after the change is made. Within the `willSet` closure, the property contains the old value, but you can access `newValue`, which contains the new value of the property after the closure.

Displaying the single card

You can now pass the selected card to the single card view.

➤ Open **SingleCardView.swift** and surround `NavigationView` with this conditional: (Don't do **Command-click** and **Make Conditional** on `NavigationView`, as that would embed the view in a `VStack` and add an `else` part.)

```
if let selectedCard = viewState.selectedCard {
  NavigationView {
```

```
      ...
  }
  .navigationViewStyle(StackNavigationViewStyle())
}
```

Here you check that `selectedCard` isn't `nil` before showing `NavigationView`.

➤ Change `CardDetailView()` to:

```
CardDetailView(card: selectedCard)
```

You pass the card to `CardDetailView`. You'll get a compile error until you update `CardDetailView` to take in a card property.

But wait! Is `selectedCard` mutable? You'll want to add stickers and text to the card later on, so it does need to be mutable.

The answer, of course, is that you created `selectedCard` with a `let` and therefore it is read-only. To get a mutable card, you need to access the selected card in the data store's cards array by index. You can then pass that to `CardDetailView` as a binding.

➤ Open **CardStore.swift** and create a new method:

```
func index(for card: Card) -> Int? {
  cards.firstIndex { $0.id == card.id }
}
```

This finds the first card in the array that matches the selected card's id and returns the array index, if there is one.

➤ Open **SingleCardView.swift** and add the card store to `SingleCardView`:

```
@EnvironmentObject var store: CardStore
```

➤ Remember to instantiate it in `previews`. Add the modifier to `SingleCardView`:

```
.environmentObject(CardStore(defaultData: true))
```

Remember that `store` is your single source of truth for all data that your views display.

➤ Change `if let selectedCard = viewState.selectedCard {` to:

```
if let selectedCard = viewState.selectedCard,
  let index = store.index(for: selectedCard) {
```

Here you use the selected card's id to locate the index for the card in `store`'s cards array. You can then use the index to pass the card as a mutable object to `CardDetailView`.

➤ Change `CardDetailView(card: selectedCard)` to:

```
CardDetailView(card: $store.cards[index])
```

Now, you're passing a mutable property to `CardDetailView`, where you can add a binding to receive it.

➤ Open **CardDetailView.swift** and add the new binding:

```
@Binding var card: Card
```

This makes `card` mutable inside `CardDetailView`.

`previews` now complains that it's expecting an argument type of `Binding<Card>`.

➤ In `previews`, change `CardDetailView()` to:

```
CardDetailView(card: .constant(initialCards[0]))
```

This creates a binding from `initialCards[0]`. Your app should now compile.

➤ Build and run, or live preview `CardsView`, and make sure that everything is still working.

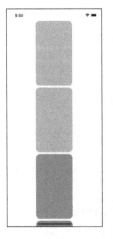

A working app

Convenience initializer

➤ Open **SingleCardView.swift**.

The preview no longer works. This is because when you initialize ViewState in the preview, selectedCard is nil, so the view doesn't show. For this preview, you'll have to initialize ViewState with the selectedCard.

All classes and structures have a designated initializer. Generally this is init(), and if nothing needs to be initialized, then you don't have to include it.

In ViewState, if you create an initializer: init(card:), then this becomes the designated initializer, and whenever you initialize ViewState, you'll have to supply a card. That's not the behavior you want.

Swift allows you to create a **convenience initializer** — one or more, actually — that calls the designated initializer, but can also take extra parameters.

➤ Open **ViewState.swift** and add the initializer:

```
convenience init(card: Card) {
  self.init()
  showAllCards = false
  selectedCard = card
}
```

You take in a specific card, use the designated initializer to instantiate a ViewState and, then, fill the properties with the values you require.

The initializer has the keyword convenience. Try leaving this off and see how many compile errors you get when the compiler thinks that this is ViewState's designated initializer.

➤ Back in **SingleCardView.swift** previews,
change .environmentObject(ViewState()) to:

```
.environmentObject(ViewState(card: initialCards[0]))
```

You initialize `ViewState` with its convenience initializer, and the preview now works.

Card conveniently initialized

Adding elements to the card detail view

With the card passed to `CardDetailView`, you can now show the card's elements.

➤ In **CardDetailView.swift**, replace content with:

```
var content: some View {
  ZStack {
    card.backgroundColor
      .edgesIgnoringSafeArea(.all)
  }
}
```

Here, you use the background color from the card. The safe area of a device screen is where navigation bars and toolbars might be. When you supply a background color to a view, the view renderer does not color these areas. You can override this by specifying which edges of the safe area you want to ignore. In this case, you ignore all the safe area and color the whole screen.

➤ Preview the view to see the background color from the first card in your preview data.

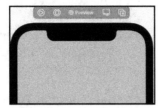

Card background from the preview data

Creating the card element view

➤ In the **Single Card Views** group, create a new SwiftUI View file named **CardElementView.swift**. This view will show a single card element.

➤ Under the existing `CardElementView`, create a new view for an image element:

```
struct ImageElementView: View {
  let element: ImageElement

  var body: some View {
    element.image
      .resizable()
      .aspectRatio(contentMode: .fit)
  }
}
```

This simply takes in an `ImageElement` and uses the stored image as the view.

➤ Create a new view for text:

```
struct TextElementView: View {
  let element: TextElement

  var body: some View {
    if !element.text.isEmpty {
      Text(element.text)
        .font(.custom(element.textFont, size: 200))
        .foregroundColor(element.textColor)
        .scalableText()
    }
  }
}
```

In the same way, this view takes in a `TextElement` and uses the stored text, color and font.

> **Swift Tip**: To find out what fonts are on your device, first list the font families in `UIFont.familyNames`. A font family might be "Avenir" or "Gill Sans". For each family, you can find the font names using `UIFont.fontNames(forFamilyName:)`. These are the weights available in the family, such as "Avenir-Heavy" or "GillSans-SemiBold".

`scalableText(font:)` is in your starter project in **TextExtensions.swift** and is the same code as you used for scaling text in the previous chapter, refactored into a method for easy reuse.

Depending on whether the card element is text or image, you'll call one of these two views. Note the `!` in front of `!element.text.isEmpty`. `isEmpty` will be `true` if text contains `""`, and `!` reverses the conditional result. This way you don't create a view for any blank text.

With these two views as examples, when future-you adds a new type of element, it will be easy to add a new view specifically for that element.

➤ Change `CardElementView` to this code:

```
struct CardElementView: View {
  let element: CardElement

  var body: some View {
    if let element = element as? ImageElement {
      ImageElementView(element: element)
    }
    if let element = element as? TextElement {
      TextElementView(element: element)
    }
  }
}
```

When presented with a `CardElement`, you can find out whether it's an image or text depending on its type.

➤ Change the preview to:

```
struct CardElementView_Previews: PreviewProvider {
  static var previews: some View {
    CardElementView(element: initialElements[0])
  }
}
```

Here you show the first element which contains a hedgehog image. To test the text view, change the parameter to `initialElements[3]`.

➤ Preview the view.

The card element view

Showing the card elements

➤ Open **CardDetailView.swift**, locate var `content` and add this after `.edgesIgnoringSafeArea(.all)`:

```
ForEach(card.elements, id: \.id) { element in
  CardElementView(element: element)
    .resizableView()
    .frame(
      width: element.transform.size.width,
      height: element.transform.size.height)
}
```

With this `ForEach`, because `CardElement` doesn't conform to `Identifiable`, you specify the `id`. A protocol can't conform to another protocol. However, a card element's `id` is always unique, so you can use the key path `\.id` as the element's identifier.

Always be aware of whether your data is mutable or not. Here `element` is immutable, but instead of passing a mutable element, you'll update element data at a later point.

➤ Preview the view and see the elements all in the center of the view:

The card elements

You've now completed the **R** in **CRUD**. Your views read and display all the data from the store. You'll now move on to **U** — updating the model when you resize, move and rotate card elements.

Understanding @State and @Binding property wrappers

Skills you'll learn in this section: @State; binding; generics

At the moment, you're using a state property transform inside ResizableView. You'll replace this with a binding to the current element's Transform property.

As you've learned already, inside a View, all properties are immutable unless they are created with a special property wrapper. A state property is the owner of a piece of data that is a source of truth. A binding connects a source of truth with a view that changes the data.

Your source of truth for all data is `CardStore`. When you select a particular card, you pass a binding to the card to `SingleCardView`.

➤ Open **SingleCardView.swift** and locate where you call `CardDetailView`. **Option-click** the `card` parameter to see the declaration.

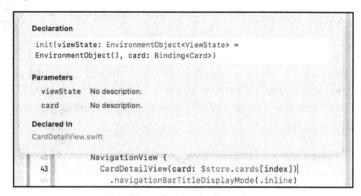

Declaration

```
init(viewState: EnvironmentObject<ViewState> =
EnvironmentObject(), card: Binding<Card>)
```

Parameters

viewState   No description.

card   No description.

Declared In
CardDetailView.swift

```
42          NavigationView {
43            CardDetailView(card: $store.cards[index])|
44              .navigationBarTitleDisplayMode(.inline)
```

CardDetailView declarations

`CardDetailView` expects an environment object and a binding. The type of these are in angle brackets. `viewState` is an environment object of type `ViewState`, and `card` is a binding of type `Card`.

Swift Dive: A very brief introduction to generics

Swift is a strongly typed language, which means that Swift has to understand the exact type of everything you declare. `Binding` has a **generic** type parameter `<Value>`. A generic type doesn't actually exist except as a placeholder. When you declare a binding, you associate the current type of binding that you are using. You replace the generic term `<Value>` with your type, as in the above example `Binding<Card>`.

Another common place where you might find this language construct is an `Array`. You defined an array in `CardStore` like this:

```
var cards: [Card] = []
```

That is actually syntactic sugar for:

```
var cards: Array<Card> = []
```

Array is a structure defined as Array<Element>. When you declare an array, you specify what the generic type Element actually is. In this example, Element is a Card. If you try and put anything other than a Card into that array, you'll get a compile error.

Binding transform data

Now that you've seen how generics work when composing a binding declaration, you'll be able to extract a binding transform from the immutable card element in CardDetailView. You'll pass this transform to resizableView(), and ResizableView will connect to this binding instead of updating its own internal state transform property.

➤ Open **CardDetailView.swift** and create a new method in CardDetailView:

```
// 1
func bindingTransform(for element: CardElement)
  -> Binding<Transform> {
  // 2
  guard let index = element.index(in: card.elements) else {
    fatalError("Element does not exist")
  }
  // 3
  return $card.elements[index].transform
}
```

Going through this code:

1. bindingTransform(for:) takes in an immutable element and returns a binding of type Transform.

2. Find the index of the element in card.elements.

3. Return a binding transform for the correct element in the card's array. card is a binding in this view, and is connected to the store environment object, which is the source of truth.

➤ In content, locate the modifier resizableView() on CardElementView.

➤ Change resizableView() to:

```
.resizableView(transform: bindingTransform(for: element))
```

You send ResizableView the transform binding from the current element. You'll get a compile error until you have updated all the dependent code.

➤ Open **ResizableView.swift** and replace `@State private var transform = Transform()` with:

```
@Binding var transform: Transform
```

`transform` is now connected to the transform property in the parent view.

➤ In `ResizableView_Previews`, change `.modifier(ResizableView())` to:

```
.resizableView(transform: .constant(Transform()))
```

This passes in a new transform instance as a binding.

➤ Open **ViewExtensions.swift** and replace `resizableView()` with:

```
func resizableView(transform: Binding<Transform>) -> some View {
  return modifier(ResizableView(transform: transform))
}
```

You're taking in a binding that is a `Transform` and passing it on to the view modifier. Your code should now compile.

Updating CardDetailView preview

The live preview in `CardDetailView` will no longer allow you to move or resize elements.

Open **CardDetailView.swift** and replace the preview with:

```
struct CardDetailView_Previews: PreviewProvider {
  struct CardDetailPreview: View {
    @State private var card = initialCards[0]
    var body: some View {
      CardDetailView(card: $card)
        .environmentObject(ViewState(card: card))
    }
  }

  static var previews: some View {
    CardDetailPreview()
  }
}
```

`CardDetailPreview` is not a type property, and therefore allows instantiation of card and updates of the transform. With transform being updated, you can now resize elements in live preview.

➤ Build and run, and choose the first green card. You'll see that the card elements are now in their correct position. Any changes you make in position or size will save to the data store.

Elements in their correct position

There is still one problem. When you first reposition an element, it jumps to a different position.

➤ Open **ResizableView.swift** and look at dragGesture.

dragGesture relies on previousOffset being set to any existing offset. So on first loading the view, you should copy transform.offset to previousOffset.

➤ Add a new modifier to content:

```
.onAppear {
  previousOffset = transform.offset
}
```

When the view first appears, you initialize previousOffset. This will happen only once.

➤ Build and run and choose the first card. In the detail view, the initial position jump has gone away, and you can now move, rotate and resize the card elements.

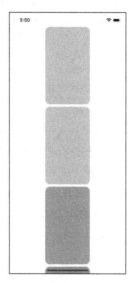 

Updating the card

Deletion

Skills you'll learn in this section: context menu; deletion; remove from array

You have now achieved both **R**ead and **U**pdate in the **CRUD** functions. Next you'll tackle **D**eletion.

You'll do this with `contextMenu(menuItems:)` modifiers on both cards and card elements. You activate the context menu with a long press. Your app will then remove the selected card or card element from the appropriate array. You'll delete card elements here and, in a challenge at the end of the chapter, you'll delete a card in the same way.

➤ Open **Card.swift** and add this code to Card:

```
func remove(_ element: CardElement) {
  if let index = element.index(in: elements) {
    elements.remove(at: index)
  }
}
```

Here you retrieve the index of the card element. You then remove the element from the array using the index.

➤ Build the app, and you get a compile error: `Cannot use mutating member on immutable value: 'self' is immutable`. Even though you have created `elements` with a var, for any method inside `Card`, the properties are immutable.

Fortunately, all you have to do is tell the compiler that you really do want to change one of the properties by marking the method as `mutating`.

➤ Change the method header to this:

```
mutating func remove(_ element: CardElement) {
```

Your app should now compile.

➤ Open **CardDetailView.swift** and locate `var content`.

➤ Add a new modifier to `CardElementView(element:)`. Because the existing modifiers alter the element transform, this modifier must be the first in the modifier list. (Later, try placing it after the other modifiers to see what happens.)

```
.contextMenu {
  Button(action: { card.remove(element) }) {
    Label("Delete", systemImage: "trash")
  }
}
```

This context menu will pop up when you perform a long press on a card element. You can have multiple buttons in a context menu, but yours will just have one, with the `trash` SFSymbol next to "Delete".

➤ Build and run, choose the first card, and long press on an element. You'll see the context menu pop up. Tap Delete to delete the element, or tap away from the menu if you decide not to delete it.

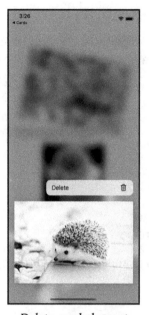

Delete card element

When you delete the element, you're deleting from `card.elements`. `card` is bound to `cards` in the data store, and `cards` is a published property. Thus all views containing `cards` will redisplay their contents.

Challenge

Challenge: Delete a card

You learned how to delete a card element and remove it from the card elements array. In this challenge you'll add a context menu so that you can delete a card.

1. In `CardStore`, create a similar remove method as the one in `Card` to remove a card from the cards array.

> **Swift Tip**: When using a `class`, you don't add `mutating` to a method. In a class, all properties declared with `var` are mutable.

2. In `CardsListView`, add a new context menu to a card with a delete option that calls your new method to remove the card.

You'll find the solution to this challenge in the **challenge** folder for this chapter.

Key points

- Use value types in your app almost exclusively. However, use a reference type for persistent stored data. When you create a value type, you are always copying the data. Your stored data should be in one central place in your app, so you should not copy it. Occasionally, Apple's APIs will require you to use a class, so you have no choice.

- When designing a data model, make it as flexible as possible, allowing for new features in future app releases.

- Use protocols to describe data behavior. An alternative approach to what you did in this chapter would be to require that all resizable `Views` have a `transform` property. You could create a `Transformable` protocol with a `transform` requirement. Any resizable view must conform to this protocol.

- You had a brief introduction to generics in this chapter. Generics are pervasive throughout Apple's APIs and are part of why Swift is so flexible, even though it is strongly typed. Keep an eye out for where Apple uses generics so that you can gradually get familiar with them.

- When designing an app, consider how you'll implement CRUD. In this chapter, you implemented Read, Update and Delete. Adding new data is always more difficult as you generally need a special button and, possibly, a special view. You'll add photos from your photos collection to your cards later on.

Where to go from here?

You covered a lot of Swift theory in this chapter. The book *Swift Apprentice* https://bit.ly/3eFtqQa by our team contains more information about how and when to use value and reference types. It also covers generics and protocol oriented programming.

If you're still confused about when to use class inheritance and OOP, watch this classic WWDC video https://apple.co/3k9GUEM where the protagonist, Crusty, firmly states "I don't do object-oriented".

Chapter 16: Adding Assets to Your App

By Caroline Begbie

Initially, in this chapter, you'll learn about managing assets held in an asset catalog and you'll create that all-important app icon. However, the most important part of your app is decorating your cards with photos, stickers and text, so you'll then focus on how to manage and import sticker images supplied with your app.

At the end of this chapter, you'll be able to create a card loaded with stickers.

Make a fun picture!

The starter project

➤ Open the starter project for this chapter.

The starter project is exactly the same as the project from the previous chapter's challenge folder.

Asset catalog

Skills you'll learn in this section: managing images in asset catalogs; app icons; screen resolution; vector vs bitmap

Asset catalogs are by far the best place to manage image and color sets.

Within an asset catalog, under one image set, you can define multiple images for different themes, different devices, different scales and even different color gamuts. When you use the name of the image set in your code, the app will automatically load the correct image for the current environment. When you supply differently scaled images for different devices in an asset catalog, the app store will automatically do **app thinning** and only download the relevant images for that particular device.

The asset catalog also holds the app icon, the launch screen image and launch screen background color.

Adding the app icon

➤ Click the project name **Cards** at the top of the Project navigator. Choose the target **Cards**. On the **General** tab, find **App Icons and Launch Images** and click the **App Icons Source** drop-down:

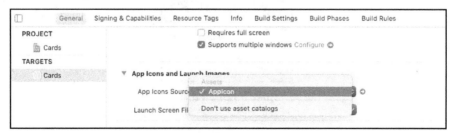

Source for app icons

This is where you can specify which icon to use for your app. You can choose to hold the icons in folders instead of asset catalogs, but it's much easier to keep them in the asset catalog as Apple intended.

➤ Click the arrow to the right of the drop-down. This will take you to the app icon set in the asset catalog. The iOS app template created this empty icon set when you first created your project.

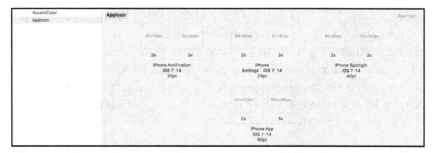

Waiting for icons

These are all the possible icon sizes and scales for all Apple iOS devices.

If you're lucky enough to have a designer for your app, as we are, they will distribute a design file, not code. This might be Sketch files or, as in our case, a Figma file.

The designer for this app, Lea Marolt (https://twitter.com/hellosunschein), created all the assets for the app in Figma, a "freemium" vector graphics prototyping tool. You can use Figma in the web interface at https://www.figma.com or download the companion app available from that link. In the **assets** folder for this chapter, you'll find a .fig file, which you can import into Figma. As you will see, some design suggestions don't always make it to the shipped product.

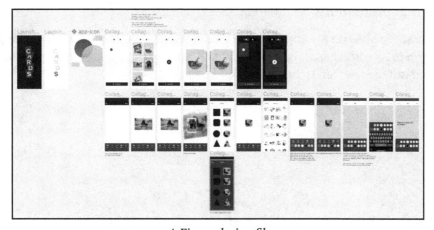

A Figma design file

This design includes the app icon. This is a single size, but for the app icon, you'll need multiple sizes for the different devices. Fortunately, Figma is a vector app, and you can export the icon design to various sizes of PNG format. You can also create icons from a single image at https://appicon.co.

Device resolutions and image scale

Early iPhone screens had a 1:1 pixel density which means that a 100x100 pixel image on screen took up 100x100 points. iPhone 4 introduced the **retina** screen. Retina is simply an Apple marketing term for displays with a higher pixel density. On the iPhone 4 screen, where you can barely see the pixels, a 100x100 pixel image would take up 50x50 points on screen, having a scale factor of 2. iPhone 6s Plus came along, introducing a 3:1 pixel density. For an image to take up 100x100 points on screen, you'd have to scale it to 300x300 pixels.

Apple resolved this scaling difficulty with an @ suffix. An image that is scaled by 2 has a suffix of @2x, and one scaled by 3 has @3x.

➤ In Finder, open the **assets** folder for this chapter and open the **App Icon** subfolder. This holds the icons in PNG format, exported from Figma.

App icon files

Each file name includes the point size and scale. For example, you can see the first icons are 20 points with three different scales.

➤ With Xcode open on the app icon and Finder open at the App Icon folder, drag each icon to its correct spot. Where iPad and iPhone use the same pixel and point size, you can use the same icon image.

Note: Even though there are now no supported non-retina devices, for iPad you should still provide 1x icons. iPadOS sometimes uses these when running iPhone apps scaled to iPad.

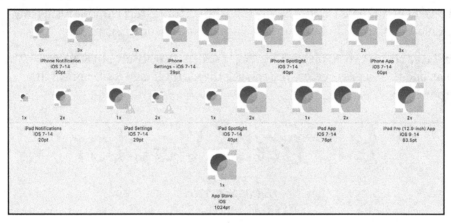

App icons

The image above has the 29 pt icons swapped around, showing a yellow exclamation mark as an error. If you see errors, you should correct them. This usually happens when you drag multiple assets at the same time and Xcode doesn't know where to put them. Consider dragging them one by one or in small groups.

➤ Build and run, and swipe up from the bottom to exit your app. You'll see your new icon takes the place of the old placeholder icon.

App icon in use

Vector vs bitmap

You imported bitmap PNG images for the icons. For other assets, you can use vector formats, such as PDF or SVG. When possible, it's always better to use vector formats. These are made up of lines, curves and fills. For a vector line, you can set a start point and an end point. When you scale the line, the vector resizes without losing any of its resolution. With a bitmap line, you must stretch or compress pixels.

This image shows two 50 pixel wide images scaled up by twelve to 600 pixels. One is bitmap and the other is vector. You can see the vector image loses none of its sharpness.

Bitmap Vector

Bitmap vs vector

Adding a vector image

Later, your app will need a placeholder image to show whether there are any errors in loading an image.

➤ In Finder, open your assets folder for this chapter and drag in **error-image.svg** to the asset catalog panel under **AppIcon**.

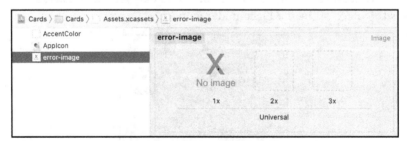

Error image

error-image.svg is a vector format image with a native size of 512x512. You don't need to scale it by 2x and 3x as Xcode can do this for you.

➤ Open the **Attributes inspector** and change **Scales** to Single Scale.

Single scale

Xcode removes the 2x and 3x options in the center panel. When you build for iPhone 12 Pro, which is 2x resolution, Xcode will automatically add to your app bundle a 512x512 optimized bitmap image scaled to the correct 2x resolution. Bundle images are held in a .car file, the format of which is not publicly available, so you can't inspect what Xcode has done.

Launch screen

Skills you'll learn in this section: launch screen; size classes

Another use for the asset catalog is to hold a launch screen image and background color that shows while your app is launching. You've already come across **Info.plist** in Chapter 8, "Saving Settings". This .plist file is where you'll set the launch image and color.

➤ Click **Cards** at the top of the Project navigator and choose the **Cards** target. Choose the **Info** tab, and you'll see the contents of **Info.plist** in the **Custom iOS Target Properties** section.

You can add new items to this either by right-clicking an entry and choosing Add Row or by selecting an object and clicking the + sign that appears. You can delete items by clicking the - sign.

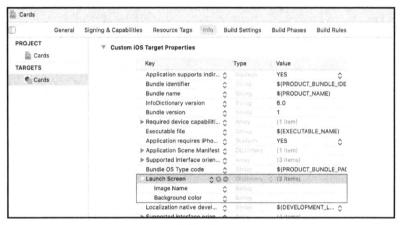

Info.plist

➤ Under **Launch Screen**, add items for **Image Name** and for **Background color**. You'll probably need to resize the columns to show Value.

➤ Double-click in the **Value** field for **Image Name** and enter:

```
LaunchImage
```

➤ Double-click in the **Value** field for **Background color** and enter:

```
LaunchColor
```

➤ Open **Assets.xcassets**, click the + sign at the bottom of the assets panel and choose **Image Set**. Rename **Image** to **LaunchImage**.

➤ Click the + sign at the bottom of the assets panel again and choose **Color Set**. Rename **Color** to **LaunchColor**.

When you run your app now, the app will use these for the launch screen. Unfortunately, the simulator doesn't clear launch screen caches, so if you change your launch image or color, in Simulator, you'll have to go to **Device > Erase All Contents and Settings…** and clear the simulator completely. On a device, deleting the app should be sufficient, but you might have to restart the device as well.

➤ Click **LaunchImage** in the catalog. You have the option of filling the three images. However, just as with the error image, you're going to use a single scale SVG image.

➤ In Finder, open **assets/Launch Screen**. Drag in **launch-screen-light.svg** to the 1x spot.

➤ In the **Attributes inspector**, change **Scales** to **Single Scale**.

Launch Image

This SVG with a transparent background has a native size of 200x500px. Xcode will create the appropriately scaled bitmap image from this and display it in the center of the screen. Landscape iPhones need an image with a smaller height, so you'll use size classes to decide which image to load.

Size classes

Size classes represent the content area available using horizontal and vertical traits. These two traits can be either regular or compact. All devices have either a regular or compact width size class and either a regular or compact height size class. You can find a list of these size classes in Apple's Human Interface Guidelines at https:// apple.co/348lVx0 under the section **Size Classes**.

This is an illustration of iPhones and iPads laid on top of each other:

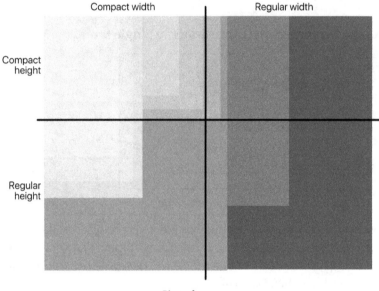

Size classes

For height in portrait mode, all devices fit into the regular height section. For height in landscape mode, all iPhones fit into the compact height section. In landscape, most iPhones fall into the compact width section. The max size iPhones and iPhone 11 and 12 use regular width in landscape.

iPads are always regular width and regular height. However, you still have to take into account size classes on iPad, because of split screen. When in portrait mode, split screen apps are both compact width. In landscape mode, the user can size between compact width and regular width.

For your app, the current launch image will fit on all devices except for iPhones in landscape. So you'll specify a sideways image for compact height.

➤ In the **Attributes inspector**, change **Height Class** to **Any & Compact**.

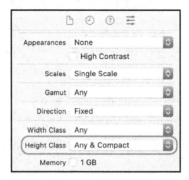

Any & Compact height size class

➤ In Finder, from **assets/Launch Screen**, drag in **launch-screen-landscape-light.svg**.

➤ Build and run, and your launch screen should show up briefly before your app does. Try rotating the simulator to get the different landscape launch screen. If your launch screen does not show up, remember to erase the simulator contents.

Launch screen in landscape

Now that you've got the hang of adding new images for checked conditions in the Attributes inspector, you'll be able to complete the challenge for Dark Mode at the end of the chapter.

> **Note**: At the time of writing, there appears to be a bug in scaling. The SVG image sometimes stretches to full screen. If this bug persists, you would have to resize the image yourself to fit an iPad screen, instead of relying on the asset catalog to manage scaling.

Adding sticker images to your app

Skills you'll learn in this section: present multiple modals; hashing

There's one thing that an asset catalog does not allow you to do, and that is enumerate through all the images contained in it.

When you release your cards app, one way of making it stand out from the crowd is to have some excellent stickers.

You could still add the stickers to an asset catalog, but you'd have to keep track of how many there are and ensure that you have a strict naming convention. All items in asset catalogs need to have names that are unique in the app bundle.

As your app becomes more popular, you'll probably add more stickers and, maybe, categorize them into themes. It would be cumbersome to list each asset by name. You might have multiple artists working on stickers, and you wouldn't want them to have access to your project.

A solution to this is to use **reference folders**. Instead of using an asset catalog, you'll keep your sticker folder outside of your project and access it from the project as a reference folder.

➤ In Finder, take a look at the **assets/Stickers/Camping** folder. Shortly, you'll add all these PNG files to your app.

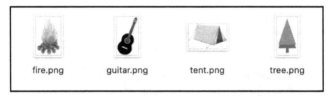

Camping stickers

Note: These stickers are from Pixabay: https://bit.ly/3vojAJf. There are several sites, such as https://unsplash.com and https://www.pexels.com, where creators share their work and allow reuse of images. Before adding an image to your app, always check that the license allows commercial use and follow the license instructions. The stickers use Pixabay's license: free for commercial use with no attribution.

Adding the stickers modal view

Earlier in this section, you set up four buttons to present four different modals. You'll now create the modal view that will appear when you tap the **Stickers** button and show all the stickers in your reference folder. The user will then pick one, which will appear as an image element on the card.

In Section 1, you used .sheet(isPresented:onDismiss:content:), where you passed a Boolean state property. When you have multiple sheets to show conditionally, you can choose a different method of presentation, by passing an optional Item. In your case, the generic Item will be a CardModal.

➤ Open **CardDetailView.swift**.

➤ In body, underneath the toolbar modifier, add this:

```
.sheet(item: $currentModal) { item in
  switch item {
  case .stickerPicker:
    EmptyView()
  default:
    EmptyView()
  }
}
```

You'll get a compile error because sheet(item:) requires its parameter to be a type that conforms to Identifiable. This seems reasonable, as under the hood, the system should track which modal you're currently using.

➤ Open **CardModal.swift** and make CardModal conform to Identifiable in the way that you did for your Card structure:

```
enum CardModal: Identifiable {
  var id = UUID()
  case photoPicker, framePicker, stickerPicker, textPicker
}
```

You'll immediately get a compiler error, saying "Enums must not contain stored properties". Remember that you can't make a copy of an enumeration by instantiating it, so you can't add stored vars to an enumeration. Yet, you need to include var id in order to conform to Identifiable.

Making an object Hashable

You need a value that uniquely identifies an object. That describes a **hash value**. Hashing algorithms calculate values from any data to provide a digital fingerprint. Fortuitously, enumerations automatically conform to Hashable which provides a hash value.

➤ Replace var id = UUID() with:

```
var id: Int {
  hashValue
}
```

Your app will now compile.

Instead of a stored property, this var is a computed property. Now, when you create a CardModal object, each object will have a different id calculated from the enumeration's hash value.

➤ Open **SingleCardView.swift** and try out your **Stickers** button in the live preview. Swipe down to dismiss the modal.

New modal view for stickers

You now have a view to show your stickers, so it's time to add them to your app.

Reference folders

> **Skills you'll learn in this section**: groups; reference folders; loading images from files; lazy loading

When you look in your Project navigator, currently all your groups, except for the asset catalogs, have yellow folder icons.

➤ Click the **Views** group and open the **File inspector**.

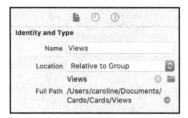

Identity and Type for group

Location describes how to store the group. **Relative to Group** means that Xcode traverses up the hierarchy of groups and folders to find an Absolute path. In your app's case, this is the very top Cards item in your Project navigator.

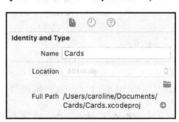

Absolute location

When you create a new group, you can choose to mirror that group with a folder on disk. If you have a file selected inside a group connected to a disk folder, and you create a new group with **File ▸ New ▸ Group,** then Xcode will create both a new group and a new folder.

If your current selection is inside a logical group without a mirrored folder on disk, then Xcode won't create a new folder for a new group. The option under **File ▸ New ▸ Group** will do the opposite. It changes between **Group with Folder** or **Group without Folder** depending upon whether your currently selected file is inside a mirrored group or not.

If your current file is in a logical group, the yellow icon has a small triangle at the bottom left.

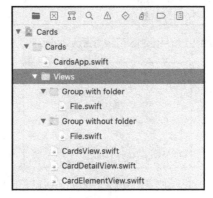

Groups

On the other hand, Xcode does not organize reference folders at all. When you bring a reference folder into the project, it will have a blue icon and its hierarchy will reflect the disk hierarchy.

➤ In Finder, locate **assets/Stickers**.

You're going to treat this folder as the master folder for your sticker assets. Any stickers that your artists create should go into this folder.

➤ Drag the Stickers folder into the Xcode Project navigator.

Generally, when you import files, you'll check **Copy items if needed**, and you'll choose **Create groups** rather than **Create folder references**. Just for this time, you'll uncheck **Copy items if needed** and choose **Create folder references**.

➤ Fill out the import screen with the following:

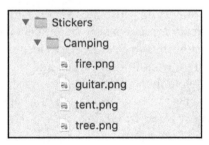

Choose options for adding these files:

Destination: ⬜ Copy items if needed

Added folders: ⬜ Create groups
🔘 Create folder references

Add to targets: ☑️ ⬜ Cards

Cancel   Finish

Add a reference folder

> **Warning**: Whenever you drag a file or folder into Xcode, make sure you
> examine these settings. You'll usually check **Copy items if needed**, and
> generally, you want to create groups, not folder references.

You now have a blue folder called **Stickers** in your project, with a blue sub-folder of
Camping. The blue folder marks it as a reference folder. Xcode will only allow you to
create folders inside this folder, not groups.

▼ 📁 Stickers

    ▼ 📁 Camping

        🖼 fire.png

        🖼 guitar.png

        🖼 tent.png

        🖼 tree.png

Reference folder

➤ In Finder, create a new folder inside Stickers called **Nature** and copy **Camping/
tree.png** to this folder. Xcode will immediately update its hierarchy to reflect what's
happening on disk.

If you tried this with yellow groups (**don't!**), Xcode wouldn't be able to find any files you moved in Finder.

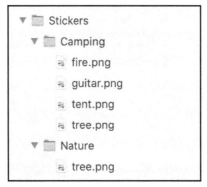

Reference folder with new sub-folder

In this folder hierarchy, you have two images with the same name **tree.png**. In an app bundle or in an asset catalog, you can't have images with the same name, but this works here because the app contains the reference folder hierarchy.

An advantage with reference folders, is that with **Stickers** as the top level folder, your artists can create new themes in different folders without touching the Xcode project.

➤ Delete the **Nature** folder as you don't need it.

> **Note**: Sometimes your project may lose the reference to the Stickers folder of images. In this case, **Stickers** will appear in the Project navigator in red. Choose the red folder name and, in the Attributes inspector, tap the folder icon under Location. Navigate to your Stickers folder and click **Choose**. Alternatively, you can delete this red item and re-import the Stickers folder as a reference folder. If you ever want confirmation of where the folder is, right-click the folder and choose **Show in Finder**.

Loading files from reference folders

Now, you'll create a Sticker view that loads images from the Stickers folder.

➤ In **Single Card Views**, create a new sub-group called **Card Modal Views**, and in this group, create a new SwiftUI View file called **StickerPicker.swift**.

➤ Open **CardDetailView.swift** and locate `.sheet(item: $currentModal)`.

➤ In case `.stickerPicker:`, replace `EmptyView()` with:

```
StickerPicker()
```

➤ Open **SingleCardView.swift**, preview it, and pin the preview, so that you can access it from other views.

➤ Try out your new stickers modal by tapping **Stickers** in live preview.

New Sticker Picker modal

Loading a SwiftUI `Image` from a folder is not as easy as loading from an asset catalog. Asset catalogs do a lot of the heavy lifting. For example, if you add a vector file to an asset catalog, Xcode will convert to a native pixel format automatically, whereas it's not an easy task to load a vector file from a folder.

When you load an image from a folder, you load it into an instance of UIKit's `UIImage`. You also need to provide the full app bundle resource path.

➤ Open **StickerPicker.swift** and replace body with:

```
var body: some View {
  // 1
  Group {
    // 2
    if let resourcePath = Bundle.main.resourcePath,
      // 3
      let image = UIImage(named: resourcePath +
```

```
      "/Stickers/Camping/fire.png") {
      Image(uiImage: image)
    } else {
      EmptyView()
    }
  }
}
```

Going through the code:

1. As you're going to return either an Image or an EmptyView, wrap the conditional in a Group.

2. Get the full resource path of the app bundle.

3. Load the UIImage using the full name and path of the sticker and use the uiImage parameter for creating the Image view.

➤ Resume the live preview, tap **Stickers**, and you'll see the sticker image.

Fire sticker

However, you don't only want one sticker, you want to see all of them. Depending on how many stickers you have, you shouldn't load up all the UIImages at once, as loading images is resource heavy and will block the user interface. You can load the file names up front and, as the user scrolls, load the image when it's needed. This is called **lazy loading**.

➤ Create a new property in `StickerPicker` to hold the file names:

```
@State private var stickerNames: [String] = []
```

➤ Create a new method to load the sticker names:

```
func loadStickers() -> [String] {
  var themes: [URL] = []
  var stickerNames: [String] = []
}
```

You'll first load the folder names in the top level in the **Stickers** folder. These will be themes. You'll be able to add new themes to your app in the future simply by adding a new folder inside the **Stickers** folder in **Finder**. You won't have to change any code to do this.

➤ Add this code after the previous code:

```
// 1
let fileManager = FileManager.default
if let resourcePath = Bundle.main.resourcePath,
  // 2
  let enumerator = fileManager.enumerator(
    at: URL(fileURLWithPath: resourcePath + "/Stickers"),
    includingPropertiesForKeys: nil,
    options: [
      .skipsSubdirectoryDescendants,
      .skipsHiddenFiles
    ]) {
    // 3
    for case let url as URL in enumerator
    where url.hasDirectoryPath {
      themes.append(url)
    }
}
```

Going through the code:

1. Load the default file manager and bundle resource path.

2. Get a directory enumerator, if it exists, for the **Stickers** folder. For the `options` parameter, you skip subdirectory descendants and hidden files. Unless you skip the subdirectories, an enumerator will continue down the hierarchy. You currently just want to collect the top folder names as the themes.

3. If the URL is a directory, add it to `themes`.

An alternative to the `for case let` code is:

```
while let url = enumerator.nextObject() as? URL {
  if url.hasDirectoryPath {
    themes.append(url)
  }
}
```

This will perform the loop in exactly the same way, but the given code is more succinct.

Now, you'll iterate through all the theme directories and retrieve the file names inside.

➤ Add this code after the previous code:

```
for theme in themes {
  if let files = try?
  fileManager.contentsOfDirectory(atPath: theme.path) {
    for file in files {
      stickerNames.append(theme.path + "/" + file)
    }
  }
}

return stickerNames
```

For each theme folder, you retrieve all the files in the directory and append the full path to `stickerNames`. You then return this array from the method.

➤ Create a new method to load a `UIImage` from a path:

```
func image(from path: String) -> UIImage {
  print("loading:", path)
  return UIImage(named: path)
    ?? UIImage(named: "error-image")
    ?? UIImage()
}
```

You temporarily print out the path name so that you can check whether you're lazily loading the image. You then return the `UIImage` loaded from the path name. If you can't load the image, return the error image from the asset catalog that you created earlier. As this is still optional and you need to return a non-optional, if everything fails, create a blank `UIImage`.

➤ Change body to:

```
var body: some View {
```

```
ScrollView {
  ForEach(stickerNames, id: \.self) { sticker in
    Image(uiImage: image(from: sticker))
      .resizable()
      .aspectRatio(contentMode: .fit)
  }
}
.onAppear {
  stickerNames = loadStickers()
}
}
```

Instead of just showing one sticker, you're iterating through all the sticker names and creating an Image from the UIImage. Using onAppear(perform:), you can load the stickers when StickerPicker first loads.

➤ To see the print output, build and run. Choose the first card and tap **Stickers**. Watch the debug console output, and you'll see all the images are loading up front, ending with the tree and the guitar. As mentioned before, with a lot of stickers, this will block the user interface.

Stickers loaded

```
loading:
    /Users/caroline/Library/Developer/CoreSimulator/Devices/AF6C374F-808C-471E-B778-E90CD80DD537/data/Containe
    rs/Bundle/Application/385304E2-5574-46DE-AB64-7CA967D6694A/Cards.app/Stickers/Camping/tree.png
loading:
    /Users/caroline/Library/Developer/CoreSimulator/Devices/AF6C374F-808C-471E-B778-E90CD80DD537/data/Containe
    rs/Bundle/Application/385304E2-5574-46DE-AB64-7CA967D6694A/Cards.app/Stickers/Camping/guitar.png
```

Debug console output

➤ To get the stickers to load lazily, in body, **Command-click** ForEach and embed it in a VStack.

➤ Change VStack { to:

```
LazyVStack {
```

➤ Build and run, and display the stickers modal screen again. Now, only the images that show on screen, plus the one just after, load. Scroll down, and you'll see in the debug console that the guitar image loads as you approach it. Your images are now loading lazily.

These images are much too big and would look much better in a grid. Fortunately, as well as lazy VStack and HStacks, SwiftUI provides a lazy loading grid view.

Using lazy grid views

Skills you'll learn in this section: grids

LazyVGrid and LazyHGrid provide vertical and horizontal grids. With the LazyVGrid, you define how to layout columns and, with the LazyHGrid, you layout rows.

➤ Add a new property to StickerPicker:

```
let columns = [
  GridItem(spacing: 0),
  GridItem(spacing: 0),
  GridItem(spacing: 0)
]
```

➤ Change LazyVStack { to:

```
LazyVGrid(columns: columns) {
```

You're still using the same ForEach and Image views but they now fit into the available space in the grid instead of taking up the whole width of the screen. The grid uses all the horizontal available space and divides it equally among the specified GridItems.

➤ To visualize this, in the design canvas, stop the live preview, if there is one, and scroll down to **Sticker Picker Previews**. In code, place the cursor just after the Image modifiers. The outlines of the Images will show in the preview.

Vertical grid

Swift Tip: If this were a LazyHGrid, you would define rows in the same way as you have columns, and the grid would divide up the available *vertical* space. To scroll horizontally, add a horizontal axis: ScrollView(.horizontal).

➤ Add a landscape preview to StickerPicker_Previews after StickerPicker():

```
StickerPicker()
  .previewLayout(PreviewLayout.fixed(width: 896, height: 414))
```

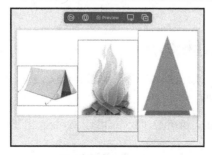

Grid in landscape

Although the grid looks good in portrait mode, it would look better with more images horizontally when in landscape.

➤ Change the `columns` property declaration to:

```
let columns = [
  GridItem(.adaptive(minimum: 120), spacing: 10)
]
```

The columns will size to 120 points, separated by ten points.

➤ Preview both portrait and landscape.

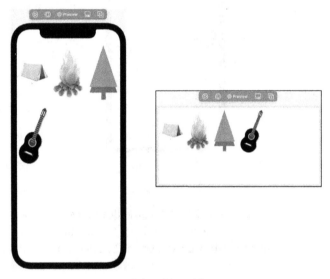

Adaptive grid

Swift Tip: As well as `adaptive`, `GridItem.size` can be `fixed` with a fixed size, or `flexible`, which sizes to the available space.

Selecting the sticker

Now that you have the stickers showing, you'll tap one to select it, dismiss the modal and add the sticker to the card as a card element.

➤ In `StickerPicker`, add a property to hold the selected image:

```
@Binding var stickerImage: UIImage?
```

The parent of the modal will pass in a state property to hold the selected image.

➤ Add the environment property that holds the presentation state:

```
@Environment(\.presentationMode) var presentationMode
```

You'll use this property to dismiss the modal.

➤ Add a modifier to Image:

```
.onTapGesture {
  stickerImage = image(from: sticker)
  presentationMode.wrappedValue.dismiss()
}
```

When the user taps an image, you'll update the bound sticker image and dismiss the modal.

➤ Update the preview:

```
struct StickerPicker_Previews: PreviewProvider {
  static var previews: some View {
    StickerPicker(stickerImage: .constant(UIImage()))
  }
}
```

You can now select a sticker and at the same time dismiss the modal. CardDetailView will then take over and store and show the selected sticker.

➤ Open **CardDetailView.swift** and add a new state property:

```
@State private var stickerImage: UIImage?
```

This will hold the current sticker chosen from StickerPicker.

➤ Locate the sheet(item:) with the stickerPicker case. This will have a compile error as you're not yet passing the state property to StickerPicker.

➤ Change StickerPicker() to:

```
StickerPicker(stickerImage: $stickerImage)
```

Now that you've bound the state property, your app should compile again.

➤ After the previous code, add this:

```
.onDisappear {
  if let stickerImage = stickerImage {
```

```
    card.addElement(uiImage: stickerImage)
  }
  stickerImage = nil
}
```

On dismissal of the modal, you should store the sticker as a card element and reset the sticker image to `nil`. You'll get a compile error until you've written `addElement(uiImage:)`.

➤ Open **Card.swift** in the **Model** group and add this new method:

```
mutating func addElement(uiImage: UIImage) {
  let image = Image(uiImage: uiImage)
  let element = ImageElement(image: image)
  elements.append(element)
}
```

Here you take in a new `UIImage` and add a new `ImageElement` to the card. In the following chapter, you'll be able to use this method for adding photos too.

➤ Build and run, select the orange second card and add some stickers to it. Resize and reposition the stickers as you want and create a masterpiece :].

Make a fun picture!

Challenges

Challenge 1: Set up a Dark Mode launch screen

Your app currently has different launch screens for portrait and also landscape, when the height size class is compact. Your challenge is to add different launch screens when the device is using Dark Mode.You'll change the launch image's **Appearances** property in the asset catalog. You'll find the dark launch screen images in the assets folder. Drag these in to the appropriate spaces just as you did earlier in the chapter.

When you test on the simulator, to get the new launch screen to show, you'll need to erase all device contents and settings.

Challenge 2: Set up launch colors

This chapter did not cover colors specifically, but you can change appearance and device in the same way as with images. You've already set up a launch color in **Info.plist** to use as the launch background color. Change the launch color in the asset catalog. Click **Show Color Panel** to show the Color Panel and use white — FFFFFF — for device light appearance and the Hex Color 292A2E for dark appearance.

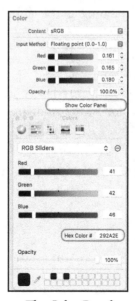

The Color Panel

If you get stuck, the asset catalog in the project in the challenge project will show you what to do.

Key points

- Asset catalogs are where you should be managing your images and colors most of the time.

- If the asset catalog is not suitable for purpose, then use reference folders.

- In asset catalogs, favor vector images over bitmaps. They are smaller in file size and retain sharpness when scaled. Xcode will automatically scale to the appropriate dimensions for the current device.

- Think about how you can make your app special. Good app design together with artwork can really make you stand out from the crowd.

Where to go from here?

In this chapter you used app icons and launch screens. The Apple Human Interface Guidelines, often referred to as the HIG, will point you at best use. You can find the HIG for iOS here: https://developer.apple.com/design/human-interface-guidelines/ios/visual-design/launch-screen/.

For example, rather than using branding on the launch screen, they suggest making your launch screen similar to the first screen in your app, so that it appears that the app loads quickly.

You should study the HIG so that you know what Apple is looking for in an app. People who use Apple devices enjoy clean, crisp interfaces, and the guidelines will help you follow this quest. If you follow the guidelines diligently, you might even be featured by Apple in the app store.

Chapter 17: Interfacing With UIKit

By Caroline Begbie

Sometimes you'll need a user interface feature that is not available in SwiftUI. **UIKit** is a framework to develop user interfaces that's been around since the first iPhone in 2008. Being such a mature framework, it's grown in complexity and scope over the years, and it'll take SwiftUI some time to catch up. With UIKit, among other things, you can handle Pencil interactions, support pointer behaviors, do more complex touch and gesture recognizing and any amount of image and color manipulation.

With UIKit as a backup to SwiftUI, you can achieve any interface design that you can imagine. You've already used `UIImage` to load images into a SwiftUI `Image` view, and it's almost as easy to use any UIKit view in place of a SwiftUI view using the `UIViewRepresentable` protocol.

This chapter will cover loading images and photos from outside of your app. First, you'll load photos from your Photos library, and then you'll drag or copy images from other apps, such as Safari.

UIKit

UIKit has a completely different data flow paradigm from SwiftUI. With SwiftUI, you define Views and a source of truth. When that source of truth changes, the views automatically update. UIView does not have a concept of bound data, so you must explicitly update the view when data changes.

UIKit	SwiftUI
design with Storyboards	design with code and previews
layout constraint system	iOS 13 and later
class based	View is a protocol
everything inherits from NSObject	chain modifiers
UIViewController handles events	manage themes easily
UIView describes interface	data bound to views

UIKit vs SwiftUI

Whenever you can for new apps, you should stick with SwiftUI. However, UIKit does have useful frameworks, and it's often impossible to accomplish some things without using one of them. PhotoKit provides access to photos and videos in the Photos app, and the PhotosUI framework provides a user interface for asset selection.

Using the Representable protocols

Representable protocols are how you insert UIKit views into your SwiftUI apps. Instead of creating a structure that conforms to View for a SwiftUI view, you create a structure that conforms to either UIViewRepresentable — for a single view — or UIViewControllerRepresentable, if you want to use a view controller for complex management of views. To receive information from the UIKit view, you create a Coordinator.

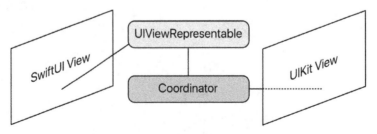

UIViewRepresentable and Coordinator

To get started with `UIViewRepresentable`, you'll first show a basic, colored `UIView` on top of a simple SwiftUI `View`.

➤ In the group **Card Modal Views**, create a new Swift file named **PhotoPicker.swift**.

➤ Replace the code with:

```
import SwiftUI

struct PhotoPicker: UIViewRepresentable {
}
```

Here you create a structure that will conform to the protocol `UIViewRepresentable`.

➤ There are two required methods, so add these:

```
func makeUIView(context: Context) -> UILabel {
  let label = UILabel()
  label.text = "Hello UIKit!"
  return label
}

func updateUIView(_ uiView: UILabel, context: Context) {
}
```

`makeUIView(context:)` is where you create and return a `UIView` — in this case, a `UILabel`, which simply shows some text.

`updateUIView(_:context:)` is where the parent view can communicate with the child view. In this case, the child view is a read-only label, and there's no communication.

➤ Create a preview that shows the SwiftUI `Text` view:

```
struct PhotoPicker_Previews: PreviewProvider {
  static var previews: some View {
    Text("Hello SwiftUI!")
      .background(Color.yellow)
  }
}
```

➤ Preview this and then replace `Text("Hello SwiftUI!")` with:

```
PhotoPicker()
```

➤ Preview the view.

Compare previews

Whereas the SwiftUI text view takes up just enough space to show itself, a UIKit view will take up the whole of the available space.

UIKit delegate pattern

Many of the UIKit classes use protocols that ask for a **delegate** object to deal with events. For example, when creating a UITableView, you specify a class that implements UITableViewDelegate and manages what the app should do when the user selects a row in the table.

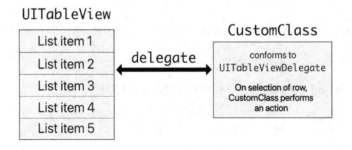

Delegate pattern

Using delegation, you can change the behavior of the table without having to subclass `UITableView`.

In `PhotoPicker`, your code will use the system photo picker: `PHPickerViewController`. This class shows the user's photos in a `UIView` and allows users to select photos from their library. An event occurs when the user taps **Add** or **Cancel**. When this happens, `PHPickerViewController` will inform the delegate object, and the delegate can take any action. This delegate must be a class that is a subclass of `NSObject` and conforms to `PHPickerViewControllerDelegate`.

`PhotoPicker` is a structure, so it can't conform to `PHPickerViewControllerDelegate`. Inside `PhotoPicker`, you'll create a coordinator class that will interface with the system photo picker and return all the selected images to `CardDetailView` via `PhotoPicker`.

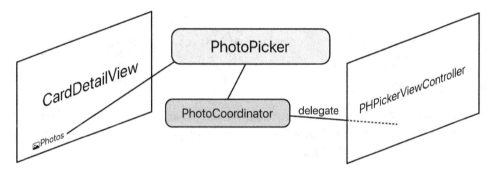

Representable PhotoPicker with delegation

Picking photos

As the system photo picker is a subclass of `UIViewController`, your Representable structure will be a `UIViewControllerRepresentable`.

➤ At the top of **PhotoPicker.swift** import the photos framework:

```
import PhotosUI
```

➤ Replace `PhotoPicker` with:

```
struct PhotoPicker: UIViewControllerRepresentable {
  func makeUIViewController(context: Context)
    -> some UIViewController {
  }
```

```
    func updateUIViewController(
      _ uiViewController: UIViewControllerType,
      context: Context
    ) {
    }
  }
```

These are the two methods required to conform to
`UIViewControllerRepresentable`.

➤ In `makeUIViewController(context:)`, add the photo picker:

```
// 1
var configuration = PHPickerConfiguration()
configuration.filter = .images
// 2
configuration.selectionLimit = 0
// 3
let picker =
  PHPickerViewController(configuration: configuration)
return picker
```

Going through the code:

1. You create a `PHPickerConfiguration`. This configuration has a filter where you
    can specify the types of photos for the user to select. As well as `images`, you can
    select `livePhotos` and `videos`.

2. Specify the number of photos a user is allowed to pick. Use 0 to allow selection of
    multiple photos.

3. Create a `PHPickerViewController` using the previously created `configuration`.

➤ Create a new class inside `PhotoPicker`:

```
class PhotosCoordinator: NSObject,
  PHPickerViewControllerDelegate {
}
```

The class doesn't need to be internal to `PhotoPicker`, but you probably won't want
to use it on its own and making it internal means that it can only be in scope inside
`PhotoPicker`.

`PhotosCoordinator` is a subclass of `NSObject`. This is the class that most Objective-
C objects inherit from, so when you're using class delegates from `UIKit` objects,
you'll usually inherit from `NSObject`.

➤ Add the required method for `PHPickerViewControllerDelegate`:

```
func picker(
  _ picker: PHPickerViewController,
  didFinishPicking results: [PHPickerResult]
) {
}
```

When the user taps **Add** after selecting photos, `PHPickerViewController` will call this delegate method and pass the selected photos as `UIImages` in an array of `PHPickerResult` objects. You'll process each of these images.

➤ Add a new property to `PhotoPicker` (not `PhotosCoordinator`):

```
@Binding var images: [UIImage]
```

`CardDetailView` will pass an empty array to `PhotoPicker`, and the delegate method will fill this array with the picked results.

➤ Update the preview:

```
struct PhotoPicker_Previews: PreviewProvider {
  static var previews: some View {
    PhotoPicker(images: .constant([UIImage]()))
  }
}
```

The preview won't be acting on the images array, so pass a constant array to the binding.

➤ Add a new property and initializer to `PhotosCoordinator`:

```
var parent: PhotoPicker

init(parent: PhotoPicker) {
  self.parent = parent
}
```

When you initialize `PhotosCoordinator` from `PhotoPicker`, you'll pass the `PhotoPicker` instance, so that you can access the `images` array.

➤ Add this method to `PhotoPicker`:

```
func makeCoordinator() -> PhotosCoordinator {
  PhotosCoordinator(parent: self)
}
```

`makeCoordinator()` saves the coordinator class in the Representable context. If you need to access the coordinator class in `updateUIViewController(_:context:)`, you can do so with `context.coordinator`.

`UIViewControllerRepresentable` calls `makeCoordinator()` before it calls `makeUIViewController(context:)`. This method exists solely to instantiate the coordinator class that coordinates with UIKit classes. If you don't need data returning from UIKit, then you don't need to create a coordinator.

Setting the delegate

➤ Add this to `makeUIViewController(context:)` at the end of the method, before returning `picker`:

```
picker.delegate = context.coordinator
```

`picker` now knows that `PhotosCoordinator` is its delegate. `PhotosCoordinator` implements `delegate?.picker(_:didFinishPicking:)` when the user taps the **Add** button on the system photo picker modal.

NSItemProvider

You've now set up the interface between the SwiftUI `PhotoPicker` and the UIKit `PHPickerViewController`. All that's left is to load the images array from the modal results.

➤ In `picker(_:didFinishPicking:)`, add this code:

```
let itemProviders = results.map(\.itemProvider)
for item in itemProviders {
  // load the image from the item here
}
```

Each `PHPickerResult` holds an `NSItemProvider`. Using the key path `\.itemProvider`, you extract the item providers from all the results into an array and then iterate through that array.

> **Swift Tip**: Using `map` with the key path `\.itemProvider` is syntactic sugar for
> `let itemProviders = results.map { $0.itemProvider }`

Any class with the NS prefix is an Objective-C class which inherits from NSObject. So NSItemProvider ultimately inherits from NSObject. When you want to transfer data around your app, or between apps, you use item providers. You can ask the item provider whether it can load a particular type and then asynchronously load it. Later in this chapter, you'll be dragging images from Safari into your app — again using item providers.

➤ Inside the for loop, add the code to load the image:

```
// 1
if item.canLoadObject(ofClass: UIImage.self) {
  // 2
  item.loadObject(ofClass: UIImage.self) { image, error in
    // 3
    if let error = error {
      print("Error!", error.localizedDescription)
    } else {
      // 4
      DispatchQueue.main.async {
        if let image = image as? UIImage {
          self.parent.images.append(image)
        }
      }
    }
  }
}
```

Going through the code:

1. Check whether the item can load a UIImage.

2. Load the UIImage. The closure parameters provide an object that conforms to NSItemProviderReading and an error object.

3. If the error is not nil, print out the description. In a full app, you would provide error handling.

4. Ensure that the passed object is a UIImage and add the image to PhotoPicker's image array asynchronously. You must do so on the main queue because it will cause an update to the UI. All NSItemProvider completion closures execute on an internal system queue in the background.

With the images loading, you should dismiss the system modal.

➤ Add a property to PhotoPicker:

```
@Environment(\.presentationMode) var presentationMode
```

➤ At the end of `picker(_:didFinishPicking:)`, add this:

```
parent.presentationMode.wrappedValue.dismiss()
```

This will tell the environment to close the modal. `PhotoPicker` is now all ready for use in SwiftUI.

➤ Live preview `PhotoPicker` to see how the system photo picker works. You can select multiple photos and also select from your photo albums. You can also show all the selected images.

System photo picker

Adding PhotoPicker to your app

To use `PhotoPicker`, you'll need hook it up to your **Photos** toolbar button and save the loaded photos as `ImageElements`.

➤ Open **CardDetailView.swift** and add this new property to `CardDetailView`:

```
@State private var images: [UIImage] = []
```

This is the array you'll hand over to `PhotoPicker`.

➤ Locate `.sheet(item:)`. Inside `switch item`, add the new modal:

```
case .photoPicker:
  PhotoPicker(images: $images)
  .onDisappear {
    for image in images {
      card.addElement(uiImage: image)
    }
    images = []
  }
}
```

Here you show the modal, passing in the array to hold the photos the user will select. When the modal disappears, you process the array and add the photos to the card elements. Finally, you clear the images array to make it ready for the next time.

➤ Build and run, and choose the second orange card. Add a couple of photos using the system photo picker. The app adds the photos to the card elements so that you can resize and reposition them.

Added photos

Note: At the time of writing, the simulator pink flowers photo causes an error. This appears to be an Apple bug, but it does give you the chance to make sure that your `PhotoPicker` error checking works. In the console, you should see `Error! Cannot load representation of type public.jpeg`.

Adding photos to the simulator

If you want more photos than the ones Apple supplies, you can simply drag and drop your photos from Finder on to the simulator. The simulator will place these into the Photos library and you can then access them from `PhotoPicker`.

Drag and drop from other apps

As well as adding photos from the ones on your device, you'll add drag and drop of images from any app. Similar to the photos system modal, you do this using an item provider.

First set up Simulator so that you'll be able to do the drag and drop.

➤ Build and run your app on an iPad simulator and turn the iPad to landscape mode. You can use the icon on the top bar, or use **Command-Right Arrow**. With your mouse cursor just touching the black bevel at the bottom of the app, drag upward slowly to show the dock. One of the apps on the dock should be Safari.

➤ Hold down the Safari icon and drag it off the dock to the right of the Cards app. A space will open up for you to drop the icon.

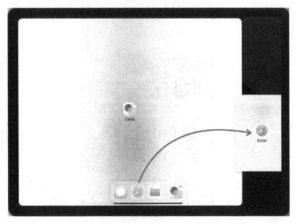

Drop Safari

➤ Use the bar in the middle to resize each app to take up half the iPad screen area.

➤ In the Cards app, tap the orange card. In Safari, Google your favorite animal and tap Images. Long press an image until it gets slightly larger and drag it onto your orange card.

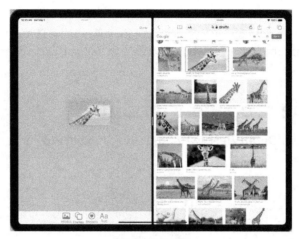

Drag a giraffe

Cards is not ready to receive a drop yet, so nothing happens. If the drop area were able to receive an item, you would get a plus sign next to the image.

Uniform Type Identifiers

Your app needs to distinguish between dropping an image and dropping another format, such as text. Most apps have associated data formats. For example, when you right-click a macOS file and choose **Open With**, the menu presents you with all the apps associated with that file's data format. When you right-click a .png file, you might see a list like this:

.png app list

These are the apps that are able to open .png files.

Uniform Type Identifiers, or UTIs, identify file types. For example, PNG is a standard UTI, with the identifier `public.png`. It's a subtype of the image data base type `public.image`.

> **Note:** There are many standard system UTIs which you can find at https://apple.co/3xASdxD.

If you have a custom data format, you can create your own UTI and include it in **Info.plist**. For this app, however, you only need to use `public.image` to receive any image format.

Adding the drop view modifier

In Xcode, open **CardDetailView.swift**. Add a new modifier to `content` above the toolbar modifier:

```
// 1
.onDrop(of: [.image], isTargeted: nil) {
  // 2
  itemProviders, _ in
  // 3
  return true
}
```

Going through the code:

1. This is where you specify the identifier of the file type you wish to process; in your case `.image`. There are several `onDrop...` modifiers. This one takes an array of `UTTypes` and a Boolean binding to indicate whether there is a drag and drop operation currently happening.

2. The closure presents the dropped items in an array of `NSItemProviders` and the drop location. For the moment you won't use the location, so you replace the parameter with `_`.

3. Returning `true` indicates to the system that the drop was successful.

➤ Build and run and repeat dragging an image on to the card.

This time, even though the drop does nothing, you get the plus sign.

Drop is active

➤ Inside `onDrop(of:isTargeted:perform:)`, before `return true`, add this code:

```
for item in itemProviders {
  if item.canLoadObject(ofClass: UIImage.self) {
    item.loadObject(ofClass: UIImage.self) { image, _ in
      if let image = image as? UIImage {
        DispatchQueue.main.async {
          card.addElement(uiImage: image)
        }
      }
    }
  }
}
```

This code is almost exactly the same as the code you wrote earlier for the photo picker. Iterate through the items and load them as a `UIImage`. Here, you add the image directly to the card's elements.

➤ Build and run. Repeat dragging an image on to the orange card and this time the drop action saves the image to the card elements.

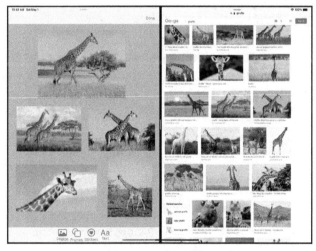

A tower of giraffes

In Simulator, to select multiple images in Safari at the same time, pick up an image and start dragging it. That small drag is important — you won't be able to multiple select without it. Then hold down **Control**. Release the click and then Control. A gray dot appears on the image representing your finger on a device. Click other images to add them to the drag pile. When you've collected all the images, drag them to Cards.

Currently, no matter where you drop images, the card adds the new elements at the center. You can use the drop location to place the element where you dropped it.

However, to calculate the `offset` for the element's `transform`, you'll need to convert the location point on the card to an offset from the center of the card. This involves knowing the screen size of the card. You'll revisit this problem in Chapter 20, "Delightful UX — Layout".

Refactoring the code

`CardDetailView` is getting quite large and complex now, and you should start to think about how you can refactor it and split out as much code as you can. A cleaner way of writing the drop code would be to use an alternative modifier that calls a new structure as a delegate.

➤ Create a new Swift file called **CardDrop.swift** to contain this delegate.

➤ Replace the code with the following:

```swift
import SwiftUI

struct CardDrop: DropDelegate {
  @Binding var card: Card
}
```

You create a new structure that will conform to `DropDelegate` and receive the card that the drop delegate should update. You need to implement one required method to conform to `DropDelegate`.

➤ Add this method to `CardDrop`:

```swift
func performDrop(info: DropInfo) -> Bool {
  let itemProviders = info.itemProviders(for: [.image])

  for item in itemProviders {
    if item.canLoadObject(ofClass: UIImage.self) {
      item.loadObject(ofClass: UIImage.self) { image, _ in
        if let image = image as? UIImage {
          DispatchQueue.main.async {
            card.addElement(uiImage: image)
          }
        }
      }
    }
  }
  return true
}
```

At the start of the method, you extract the item providers from the drop info, and then the rest of the code is the same as you have in `CardDetailView`.

DropDelegate has several other required methods that have default implementations, so you don't need to define them in your app.

- dropEntered(info:): A potential drop has entered the view.

- dropExited(info:): A potential drop has exited the view.

- dropUpdated(info:): A potential drop has moved inside the view.

If you need to have complete control of where in the screen your user is dragging items, then implement these methods.

➤ Open **CardDetailView.swift**. Replace onDrop(of:isTargeted:perform:) and all its code with:

```
.onDrop(of: [.image], delegate: CardDrop(card: $card))
```

Here you still use the image UTI, but you offload the code into CardDrop.

With this one line of code, you have reduced the apparent complexity. The CardDrop code is difficult to read, and you don't need to be viewing it every time you're updating your card detail code. It's a good idea to reduce brain overload whenever you can. :]

➤ Build and run and your app works the same as it did before.

Final drag and drop

Challenge

Challenge: Leverage PencilKit

Now that you know how to host UIKit views in SwiftUI, you have access to a wide range of Apple frameworks. One fun framework is PencilKit where you can draw into a canvas.

Your challenge is to write a few lines of code and run a live preview in which you can scribble.

- Create a new `View` and import PencilKit. Create a `PKCanvasView` state property. Pass this property to a `UIViewRepresentable` object.

- Create the two required methods in the `UIViewRepresentable` object.

- There's only two extra lines of code needed. In `makeUIView(context:)`, set the canvas `drawingPolicy` to `anyInput` to allow input from both finger and Pencil and return the canvas.

A scribble using PencilKit

You won't integrate this view in your current version of Cards, but this could be a feature in a later version where you can extract an image from the scribble.

If you have any difficulty, you'll find the solution to this challenge in the **challenge** folder for this chapter in the file **PencilView.swift**.

Key points

- SwiftUI and UIKit can go hand in hand. Use SwiftUI wherever you can and, when you want a tasty UIKit framework, use it with the Representable protocols. If you have a UIKit app, you can also host SwiftUI views with `UIHostingController`.

- The delegate pattern is common throughout UIKit. Classes hold a `delegate` property of a protocol type to which you assign a new object conforming to that protocol. The UIKit object performs methods on its delegate.

- `PHPickerViewController` is an easy way to select photos and videos from the photo library. Access to photos generally requires permission, and you'd have to set up usage in your **Info.plist**. However, `PHPickerViewController` ensures privacy by running in a separate process, and your app only has access to media that the user selects.

- Item providers enable passing data more easily between apps.

- Using Uniform Type Identifiers and the `onDrop` modifier, you can support drag and drop in your app.

Chapter 18: Paths & Custom Shapes

By Caroline Begbie

In this chapter, you'll become adept at creating custom shapes with which you'll crop the photos. You'll tap a photo on the card, which enables the Frames button. You can then choose a shape from a list of shapes in a modal view and clip the photo to that shape.

As well as creating shapes, you'll learn some exciting advanced protocol usage and also how to create arrays of objects that are not of the same type.

The starter project

The starter project moves on from hedgehogs to giraffes.

A new published property in ViewState, called selectedElement, holds the currently selected element. In CardDetailView, tapping an element updates selectedElement and CardElementView shows a border around the selected element.

In CardBottomToolbar, the **Frames** button is disabled when selectedElement is nil, but enabled when you tap an element. Tapping the background color deselects the element and disables **Frames** again.

Currently when you tap **Frames**, a modal pops up with an EmptyView. You'll replace this modal view with a FramePicker view where you'll be able to select a shape.

➤ Build and run the project to see the changes.

A selected element enables the Frames button

Shapes

Skills you'll learn in this section: predefined shapes

➤ In the **Model** group, create a new SwiftUI View file called **Shapes.swift**. This file will hold all your custom shapes.

➤ Replace body with

```
var body: some View {
  VStack {
    Rectangle()
    RoundedRectangle(cornerRadius: 25.0)
```

```
      Circle()
      Capsule()
      Ellipse()
    }
    .padding()
  }
```

These are the five built-in shapes, which fill as much space as they can.

➤ Preview the view.

Five predefined shapes

These shapes conform to the Shape protocol, which inherits from View. Using the Shape protocol, you can define any shape you want using **paths**.

Paths

Skills you'll learn in this section: paths; lines; arcs; quadratic curves

This is the triangle shape you'll draw first. You'll create a **path** made up of lines that go from point to point.

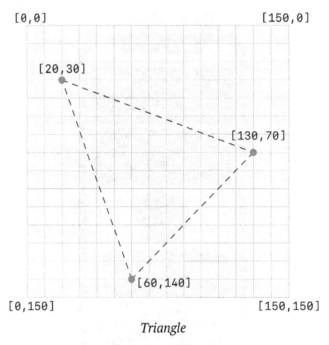

Triangle

Paths are simply abstract until you give them an outline stroke or a fill. SwiftUI defaults to filling paths with the primary color, unless you specify otherwise.

➤ At the end of **Shapes.swift**, add a new shape with this code:

```
struct Triangle: Shape {
  func path(in rect: CGRect) -> Path {
    var path = Path()
    return path
  }
}
```

Shape has one required method which returns a Path. path(in:) receives a CGRect containing the drawing canvas size in which to draw the path.

Lines

➤ Create a triangle with the same coordinates as in the diagram above. Add this to path(in:) before return path:

```
//1
path.move(to: CGPoint(x: 20, y: 30))
// 2
path.addLine(to: CGPoint(x: 130, y: 70))
path.addLine(to: CGPoint(x: 60, y: 140))
// 3
path.closeSubpath()
```

Going through the code:

1. You create a new subpath by moving to a point. Paths can contain multiple subpaths.

2. Add straight lines from the previous point. You can alternatively put the two points in an array and use addLines(_:).

3. Close the subpath when you've finished to create the polygon.

➤ Change Shapes to:

```
struct Shapes: View {
  let currentShape = Triangle()

  var body: some View {
    currentShape
      .background(Color.yellow)
  }
}
```

➤ Preview Shapes.

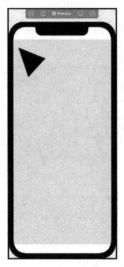

Triangle Shape

Shapes fill as much space as they can. The filled path is using the fixed numbers from `path(in:)`. But `Triangle` itself is filling the whole yellow area. Your code only replicates the triangle in the previous diagram when you add `.frame(width: 150, height: 150)` to `currentShape`.

Fixed Triangle

If you want the triangle to retain its shape, but size with the available size, you must use relative coordinates, rather than absolute values.

➤ In `Triangle`, replace `path(in:)` with:

```
func path(in rect: CGRect) -> Path {
  let width = rect.width
  let height = rect.height
  var path = Path()
  path.addLines([
    CGPoint(x: width * 0.13, y: height * 0.2),
    CGPoint(x: width * 0.87, y: height * 0.47),
    CGPoint(x: width * 0.4, y: height * 0.93)
  ])
  path.closeSubpath()
  return path
}
```

Here you use `addLines(_:)` with an array of points to make up the triangle. You replace the hard coded coordinates with relative ones that depend upon the width and height. You can calculate these coordinates by dividing the hard coded coordinate by the original frame size. For example, 20.0 / 150.0 comes out at about 0.13.

➤ In Shapes, change the contents of body to:

```
currentShape
  .aspectRatio(1, contentMode: .fit)
  .background(Color.yellow)
```

You maintain the square aspect ratio, and the triangle will now resize to the available space.

Resizable Triangle

➤ In `Shapes_Previews`, add this modifier to `Shapes`:

```
.previewLayout(.sizeThatFits)
```

Now the preview will only show the part of `Shapes` that holds the triangle.

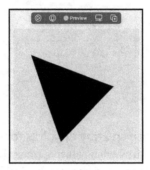

Resized preview

Arcs

Another useful path component is an arc.

➤ At the bottom of **Shapes.swift**, add this code to create a new shape:

```
struct Cone: Shape {
  func path(in rect: CGRect) -> Path {
    var path = Path()
    // path code goes here
    return path
  }
}
```

Here you create a new shape in which you'll describe a cone. To draw the cone, you'll draw an arc and two straight lines.

➤ Add the arc to `path(in:)` before `return path`

```
let radius = min(rect.midX, rect.midY)
path.addArc(
  center: CGPoint(x: rect.midX, y: rect.midY),
  radius: radius,
  startAngle: Angle(degrees: 0),
  endAngle: Angle(degrees: 180),
  clockwise: true)
```

Here you set the center point to be in the middle of the given rectangle with the radius set to the smaller of width or height.

➤ In Shapes, replace `currentShape` with:

```
let currentShape = Cone()
```

➤ Preview the top of the cone.

The arc

Forget everything you thought you knew about the clockwise direction. In iOS, angles always start at zero on the right hand side, and clockwise is reversed. So when you go from a start angle of 0° to an end angle of 180° with `clockwise` set `true`, you start at the right hand side and go anti-clockwise around the circle.

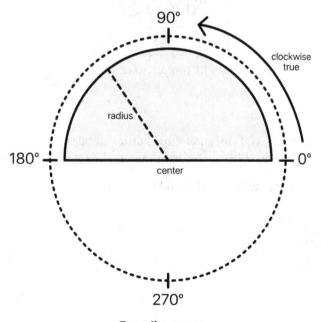

Describe an arc

This is for historical reasons. In macOS, the origin — that's coordinate (0, 0) — is at the bottom left, as in the standard Cartesian coordinate system. When iOS came out, Apple flipped the iOS drawing coordinate system on the Y axis so that (0, 0) is at the top left. However, much of the drawing code is based on the old macOS drawing coordinate system.

➤ In Cone's `path(in:)`, add two straight lines to complete the cone before the `return`:

```
path.addLine(to: CGPoint(x: rect.midX, y: rect.height))
path.addLine(to: CGPoint(x: rect.midX + radius, y: rect.midY))
path.closeSubpath()
```

You start the first line where the arc left off and end it at the middle bottom of the available space. The second line ends at the middle of the right hand side.

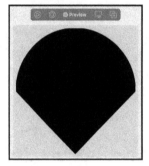

The completed cone

Curves

As well as lines and arcs, you can add various other standard elements to a path, such as rectangles and ellipses. With curves, you can create any custom shape you want.

➤ At the end of **Shapes.swift**, add this code to create a new shape:

```
struct Lens: Shape {
  func path(in rect: CGRect) -> Path {
    var path = Path()
    // path code goes here
    return path
  }
}
```

The lens shape will consist of two quadratic curves, like an ellipse with a point at each end.

If you have used vector drawing applications, you'll have used control points to draw curves. To create a quadratic curve in code, you set a start point, an end point and a control point that defines where the curve goes.

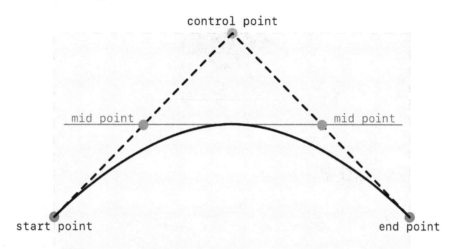

Quadratic curve

The two mid points shown are calculated and define the curvature. It can take some practice to work out the control point for the curve.

➤ In path(in:), add this code before the return:

```
path.move(to: CGPoint(x: 0, y: rect.midY))
path.addQuadCurve(
  to: CGPoint(x: rect.width, y: rect.midY),
  control: CGPoint(x: rect.midX, y: 0))
path.addQuadCurve(
  to: CGPoint(x: 0, y: rect.midY),
  control: CGPoint(x: rect.midX, y: rect.height))
path.closeSubpath()
```

The first curve here is the same as in the above diagram, and the second curve mirrors it.

➤ In Shapes, replace currentShape to use this shape:

```
let currentShape = Lens()
```

➤ Preview the shape.

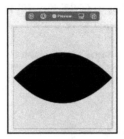

Lens shape

Strokes and fills

> **Skills you'll learn in this section**: stroke; stroke style; fill

SwiftUI is currently filling the paths with a solid **fill**. You can specify the fill color or, alternatively, you can assign a **stroke**, which outlines the shape.

Stroke and fill

In the body of Shapes, add this to currentShape:

```
.stroke(lineWidth: 5)
```

You can only use stroke(_:) on objects conforming to Shape, so you must place the modifier directly after currentShape.

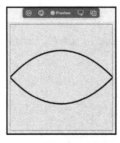

Stroke

Stroke style

When you define a stroke, instead of giving it a `lineWidth`, you can give it a `StrokeStyle` instance.

For example:

```
currentShape
    .stroke(style: StrokeStyle(dash: [30, 10]))
```

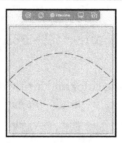

StrokeStyle with dash

With a stroke style, you can define what the outline looks like — whether it is dashed, how the dash is formed and how the line ends look.

To form a dash, you create an array which defines the number of horizontal points of the filled section followed by the number of horizontal points of the empty section.

▮ ▯▮ ▯▮ ▯▮ ▯▮ ▯▮ ▯▮ ▯▮ ▯▮ ▯▮
StrokeStyle(lineWidth: 10, dash: [5, 10, 1, 5]))

The example above describes a dashed line where you have a 5 point vertical line, followed by a 10 point space, followed by a one point vertical line, followed by a 5 point space.

▯▮ ▯▮ ▯▮ ▯▮ ▯▮ ▯▮ ▯▮ ▯▮ ▯▮ ▯▯
StrokeStyle(lineWidth: 10, dash: [5, 10, 1, 5], dashPhase: 15)

This second example adds a dash phase, which moves the start of the dash to the right by 15 points, so that the dash starts with the one point line.

Swift tip: You haven't done much animation so far as you'll cover this later in Chapter 21, "Delightful UX — Final Touches", but these dashed line parameters are animatable, so you can easily achieve the "marching ants" marquee look.

You can choose to change how the ends of lines look with the `lineCap` parameter:

Line caps

`lineCap:` `.square` is similar to `.butt`, except that the ends protrude a bit further.

➤ In `Shapes`, replace `.stroke(lineWidth:)` with:

```
.stroke(
  Color.primary,
  style: StrokeStyle(lineWidth: 10, lineJoin: .round))
.padding()
```

Here you give the stroke an outline color and, using the `lineJoin` parameter, the two sections of lens shape are now nicely rounded at each side:

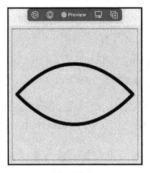

Line join

Clip shapes modal

You've now created a few shapes and feel free to experiment with more. The challenge for this chapter will suggest a few shapes for you to try.

As well as displaying a shape view, you can use a shape to clip another view. You're going to list all your shapes in a modal so that the user can select a photo and clip it to a chosen shape.

➤ In the **Card Modal Views** group, create a new SwiftUI View file called **FramePicker.swift**. This will be very similar to **StickerPicker.swift**, but will load your custom shapes into a grid instead of stickers.

First, you'll set up an array of all your shapes for the modal to iterate through.

Initially, you might think you can define the array in Shapes like this:

```
static let shapes: [Shape] = [Circle(), Rectangle()]
```

However, this will give you a compile error:

```
Protocol 'Shape' can only be used as a generic constraint
because it has Self or associated type requirements.
```

So, how can you solve this? Read on!

Associated types

Skills you'll learn in this section: protocols with associated types; type erasure

Swift Dive: Protocols with associated types

Protocols with associated types (**PAT**s) are advanced black magic Swift and, if you haven't done much programming with generics, the subject will take some time to learn and absorb. Apple APIs use them everywhere, so it's useful to have an overview.

Shape inherits from View, and this is how View is defined:

```
public protocol View {
    associatedtype Body : View
    @ViewBuilder var body: Self.Body { get }
}
```

associatedType makes a protocol generic. When you create a structure that conforms to View, the requirement is that you have a body property, and you tell the View the real type to substitute. For example:

```
struct ContentView: View {
  var body: some View {
    EmptyView()
  }
}
```

In this example, body is of type EmptyView.

Earlier, you created the protocol CardElement. This doesn't use an associated type, and so you were able to set up an array of type CardElement. This is how you defined CardElement:

```
protocol CardElement {
    var id: UUID { get }
    var transform: Transform { get set }
}
```

All of the property types in CardElement are **existential types**. That means they are types in their own right and not generic. However, you might have a requirement for id to be either a UUID or an Int or a String. In that case you can define CardElement with a generic type of ID:

```
protocol CardElement {
    associatedtype ID
    var id: ID { get }
    var transform: Transform { get set }
}
```

When you create a structure conforming to CardElement, you tell it what type ID actually is. For example:

```
struct NewElement: CardElement {
    let id = Int.random(in: 0...1000)
    var transform = Transform()
}
```

In this case, whereas the other CardElement ids are of type UUID, this id is of type Int.

Once a protocol has an associated type, because it is now a generic, the protocol is no longer an existential type. The protocol is constrained to using another type, and the compiler doesn't have any information about what type it might actually be. For this reason, you can't set up an array containing protocols with associated types, such as View or Shape.

Going back to the code at the start of this section which doesn't compile:

```
static let shapes: [Shape] = [Circle(), Rectangle()]
```

Even though Circle and Rectangle both conform to Shape, they are Shapes with different associated types and, as such, you can't put them both in the same Shape array.

Type erasure

You are able to place different `Views` in an array by converting the `View` type to `AnyView`:

```
// does not compile
let views: [View] = [Text("Hi"), Image("giraffe")]
// does compile
let views: [AnyView] = [
  AnyView(Text("Hi")),
  AnyView(Image("giraffe"))
]
```

`AnyView` is a **type-erased** view. It takes in any type of view and passes back an existential, non-generic type of `AnyView`.

Unfortunately, there isn't a built-in `AnyShape` for your array of `Shapes`, but it's quite easy to make one, when you know what the requirements for a `Shape` are.

➤ Create a new Swift file called **AnyShape.swift**.

➤ Replace the code with:

```
import SwiftUI

struct AnyShape: Shape {
  func path(in rect: CGRect) -> Path {
  }
}
```

`AnyShape` conforms to `Shape` with the required `path(in:)`. You'll get a compile error until you return a path from the method.

To convert your custom shape to an `AnyShape`, you'll use an initializer which takes in a generic `Shape`. This initializer will create a closure that uses this shape to create a path. You'll store this closure as a property, and when a view calls for the `path`, you'll perform the closure.

If you need to review closures, take a look at Chapter 9, "Saving History Data".

➤ Add a property to hold the closure:

```
private let path: (CGRect) -> Path
```

You'll perform the custom shape's `path(in:)` when it's required. `path(in:)` takes in a `CGRect` and returns a `Path`.

➤ Add the initializer:

```
// 1
init<CustomShape: Shape>(_ shape: CustomShape) {
  // 2
  self.path = { rect in
    // 3
    shape.path(in: rect)
  }
}
```

You take in the custom shape when you create the structure. To explain the code:

1. Because `CustomShape` is a generic type — in angled brackets — you tell the initializer that `CustomShape` is some sort of `Shape`.

2. You define the closure to receive a `CGRect` with `{ rect in }`

3. When you execute the closure, it calls the shape's `path(in:)` using the supplied `rect`.

You're still getting a compile error because `path(in:)` needs a return.

➤ Add this code to `path(in:)`:

```
path(rect)
```

You call your `path` closure supplying the current `rect` as the parameter. The method now returns the custom shape's path as the `Path`.

Your code now compiles, and `AnyShape` is ready to convert any custom shape to itself.

A type erased array

➤ In **Shapes.swift**, add a new extension to `Shapes`:

```
extension Shapes {
  static let shapes: [AnyShape] = [
    AnyShape(Circle()), AnyShape(Rectangle()),
    AnyShape(Cone()), AnyShape(Lens())
  ]
}
```

This holds a type-erased list of all your defined shapes. When you create more shapes, add them to this array.

Shape selection modal

Now that you have all your shapes in an array, you can create a selection modal, just as you did for your stickers.

➤ Open **FramePicker.swift** and replace `FramePicker` with:

```
struct FramePicker: View {
  @Environment(\.presentationMode) var presentationMode

  // 1
  @Binding var frame: AnyShape?
  private let columns = [
    GridItem(.adaptive(minimum: 120), spacing: 10)
  ]
  private let style = StrokeStyle(
    lineWidth: 5,
    lineJoin: .round)

  var body: some View {
    ScrollView {
      LazyVGrid(columns: columns) {
        // 2
        ForEach(0..<Shapes.shapes.count, id: \.self) { index in
          Shapes.shapes[index]
            // 3
            .stroke(Color.primary, style: style)
            // 4
            .background(
              Shapes.shapes[index].fill(Color.secondary))
            .frame(width: 100, height: 120)
            .padding()
            // 5
            .onTapGesture {
              frame = Shapes.shapes[index]
              presentationMode.wrappedValue.dismiss()
            }
        }
      }
    }
    .padding(5)
  }
}
```

This is almost exactly the same code as you wrote for `StickerPicker`. The exceptions are:

1. You pass in a frame that will hold the selected shape.

2. You iterate through the array of shapes by index.

3. Outline the shape with the primary color.

4. You need to fill the shape so that you have a touch area. If you don't fill the shape, the tap will only work on the stroke.

5. When you tap the shape, you update frame and dismiss the modal.

➤ Change the preview to:

```
struct FramePicker_Previews: PreviewProvider {
  static var previews: some View {
    FramePicker(frame: .constant(nil))
  }
}
```

➤ Preview FramePicker to see all your shapes in a grid:

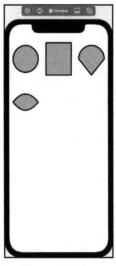

Shapes Listing

Add the frame picker modal to the card

➤ Open **CardDetailView.swift** and add a new property:

```
@State private var frame: AnyShape?
```

This is the frame that you'll pass to FramePicker.

➤ Locate .sheet(item:) and add a new case to the switch statement:

```
case .framePicker:
  FramePicker(frame: $frame)
    .onDisappear {
      if let frame = frame {
        card.update(
          viewState.selectedElement,
          frame: frame)
      }
      frame = nil
    }
```

Here you call the modal and then update the card element with the frame. As you haven't written `update(_:frame:)` yet, you'll get a compile error.

Add the frame to the card element

➤ Open **CardElement.swift** and add a new property to `ImageElement`:

```
var frame: AnyShape?
```

This will hold the element's frame. You add it only to `ImageElement`, because the frame will only clip images.

➤ Open **Card.swift** and add the new update method to `Card`:

```
mutating func update(_ element: CardElement?, frame: AnyShape) {
  if let element = element as? ImageElement,
    let index = element.index(in: elements) {
    var newElement = element
    newElement.frame = frame
    elements[index] = newElement
  }
}
```

Here you pass in the element and the frame. Because `element` is immutable and you need to update its `frame`, you create a new mutable copy and update `elements` with this new instance.

All that's left to do now, is to clip the image element.

➤ Open **CardElementView.swift** and locate `ImageElementView`.

The modifier you'll add is `.clipShape(_:)`, but you only want to add it if the element's frame is not `nil`. Surprisingly, it's not easy to add a conditional modifier in SwiftUI, but the following is a solution when the existing code is quite simple.

Add a modifier conditionally

➤ In `ImageElementView`, rename body to `bodyMain`.

➤ Add a new property to `ImageElementView`:

```
var body: some View {
  if let frame = element.frame {
    bodyMain
      .clipShape(frame)
  } else {
    bodyMain
  }
}
```

You recreate body and use `bodyMain` in both parts of the conditional. If there is a frame, add the modifier.

➤ Build and run the app, and choose the green card. Tap the giraffe and choose **Frames**. Select a frame and the giraffe photo gets clipped to that shape.

Clipped giraffe

Challenges

Challenge 1: Create new shapes

Practice creating new shapes and place them in the frame picker modal. Here are some suggestions:

Try these shapes

The last two are a Polygon shape with a number of sides property, so try that out, and take a look at the code in the challenge folder.

Challenge 2: Clip the selection border

Currently, when you tap an image, it gets a rectangular border around it. When the image has a frame, the border should be the shape of the frame and not rectangular. To achieve this, you'll replace the border with the stroked frame in an overlay.

1. In **CardElementView.swift**, in CardElementView, remove the border modifier on ImageElementView. Place it in each part of the conditional inside ImageElementView's body.

2. Pass selected from CardElementView to ImageElementView.

3. When the image has a frame, replace the border modifier with an overlay of the stroked frame.

4. When you tap the space outside the frame, but within the original unclipped image, SwiftUI still thinks you're tapping the image. After the overlay, add the modifier .contentShape(frame). This will clip the tap area to the frame.

Check your changes out by running the app or by live previewing SingleCardView.

A selected giraffe

Key points

- The Shape protocol provides an easy way to draw a 2D shape. There are some built-in shapes, such as Rectangle and Circle, but you can create custom shapes by providing a Path.

- Paths are the outline of the 2D shape, made up of lines and curves.

- A Shape fills by default with the primary color. You can override this with the fill(_:style:) modifier to fill with a color or gradient. Instead of filling the shape, you can stroke it with the stroke(_:lineWidth:) modifier to outline the shape with a color or gradient.

- With the clipShape(_:style:) modifier, you can clip any view to a given shape.

- Associated types in a protocol make a protocol generic, making the code reusable. Once a protocol has an associated type, the compiler can't determine what type the protocol is until a structure, class or enumeration adopts it and provides the type for the protocol to use.

- Using type erasure, you can hide the type of an object. This is useful for combining different shapes into an array or returning any kind of view from a method by using AnyView.

Chapter 19: Saving Files

by Caroline Begbie

You've set up most of your user interface, and it would be nice at this stage to have the card data persist between app sessions. There are a number of ways to save data that you could choose.

You've already looked at `UserDefaults` and property list (plist) files in Section 1. These are more suitable for simple data structures, whereas, when you save your card, you'll be saving images and sub-arrays of elements. While Core Data could handle this, another way is to save the data to files using the JSON format. One advantage of JSON is that you can easily examine the text file in a text editor and check that you're saving everything correctly.

This chapter will cover saving JSON files to your app's **Documents** folder by encoding and decoding the JSON representation of your cards.

The starter project

To assist you with saving UIImages to disk, the starter project contains methods in a UIImage extension to resize an image, and save, load and remove image files. These are in **UIImageExtensions.swift**.

FileManagerExtensions.swift holds a static property that contains the **Documents** folder URL.

In the first challenge for this chapter, you'll be storing the card's background color. **ColorExtensions.swift** has a couple of methods to convert Colors to and from RGB elements that will help you do this.

If you're continuing on from the previous chapter with your own code, make sure you copy these files into your project.

The saved data format

When you save the data, each card will have a JSON file with a **.rwcard** extension. This file will contain the list of elements that make up the card. You'll save the images separately. The data store on disk will look like:

Data store

When your app first starts, you'll read in all the **.rwcard** files in the **Documents** folder and show them in a scroll view. When the user taps a selected card, you'll process the card's elements and load the relevant image files.

When to save the data

> **Skills you'll learn in this section**: when to save data; ScenePhase

There are two ways you can proceed, and each has its pros and cons.

You can choose to save the card file every time you change anything, such as adding, moving, or deleting elements. This means that your data on disk is always up-to-date. The downside is that your saving is spread out all over your app.

Alternatively, you could choose to save when you really need to:

1. When CardDetailView disappears, which happens when the user taps **Done**.

2. When the app becomes inactive through the user switching apps or an external event such as a phone call.

The downside of this method is that if your app crashes before you've done the save, then the last few changes the user made might not be recorded. You'll also need to remember when testing that the app doesn't save in the simulator until you press **Done**.

In this app you'll choose a hybrid approach. You'll perform the first method of saving whenever you create or delete card data. This is primarily because of saving the image element's UIImage. You'll save the UIImage when you choose it from the **Photos** or **Stickers** modal, and you'll store the file id in the ImageElement struct. To maintain data integrity, it's a good idea to store the ImageElement at the same time as the UIImage.

However, moving and resizing elements happens regularly, and saving every time can be an overhead. To save the transform data, you'll choose the second method: saving when the user taps **Done** or leaves the app.

Saving when the user taps Done

➤ Open **Card.swift** and create a new method in Card:

```
func save() {
  print("Saving data")
}
```

You'll come back to this method to perform the saving later in this chapter.

➤ Open **CardDetailView.swift** and add a new modifier to `content` inside `body`:

```
.onDisappear {
  card.save()
}
```

➤ Build and run, tap a card, then tap **Done**. You'll see "Saving data" appear in the console.

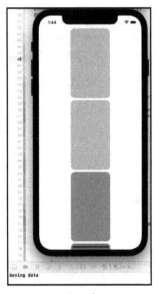

Saving data

Using ScenePhase to check operational state

When you exit the app, surprisingly, the view does not perform `onDisappear(_:)`, so the card won't get saved. However, you can check what state your app is in through the environment.

➤ Still in `CardDetailView`, add a new environment property:

```
@Environment(\.scenePhase) private var scenePhase
```

scenePhase is a useful member of `EnvironmentValues`. It's an enumeration of three possible values:

- `active`: the scene is in the foreground.

- `inactive`: the scene should pause.

- `background`: the scene is not visible in the UI.

You'll do the save when `scenePhase` becomes `inactive`.

➤ Add a new modifier to `content` before the `.onDisappear` you added earlier:

```
.onChange(of: scenePhase) { newScenePhase in
  if newScenePhase == .inactive {
    card.save()
  }
}
```

`onChange(of:)` is called whenever `scenePhase` changes. If the change is to `inactive`, then save the card.

➤ Build and run, tap a card to open it, and exit your app by swiping up from the bottom. You should see the console message **"Saving data"**.

Saving data

➤ Return to the app in the simulator. It will resume inside the card where you left it.

There is no way to simulate a phone call on the simulator, but you can activate Siri to test external events. Choose **Device ➤ Siri** and, once again, you'll see the console message **"Saving data"**.

You've now implemented the skeleton for the saving part of your app. The rest of the chapter will take you through encoding and decoding data, so you can perform save().

JSON files

> **Skills you'll learn in this section**: the JSON format

JSON is an acronym for JavaScript Object Notation. JSON data is formatted like this:

```
{
  "identifier1": [data1, data2, data3],
  "identifier2": data4
}
```

Each data item can be a nested chunk of JSON.

To find out how easy it is save simple data to JSON files, you'll create a temporary structure and save it.

Codable

> **Skills you'll learn in this section**: Encodable; Decodable

The Codable protocol is a type alias for Decodable & Encodable. When you conform your structures to Codable, you conform to both these protocols. As its name suggests, you use Codable to encode and decode data to and from external files.

➤ Open **CardsApp.swift** and add this code to the end of the file:

```
struct Team: Codable {
  let names: [String]
```

```
    let count: Int
  }

let teamData = Team(
  names: [
  "Richard", "Libranner", "Caroline", "Audrey", "Manda"
  ], count: 5)
```

After you've seen how Codable works, you'll delete this code and apply your knowledge to the more complex data in your app.

This structure contains straightforward data of types that JSON supports — an array of Strings and an Int. Team conforms to Codable and makes Team a type that can encode and decode itself.

Encoding

➤ In Team, create a new method:

```
static func save() {
  do {
  // 1
    let encoder = JSONEncoder()
    encoder.outputFormatting = .prettyPrinted
    // 2
    let data = try encoder.encode(teamData)
    // 3
    if let url = FileManager.documentURL?
      .appendingPathComponent("TeamData") {
      try data.write(to: url)
    }
  } catch {
    print(error.localizedDescription)
  }
}
```

Going through this code:

1. Initialize the JSON encoder. prettyPrinted means that the encoded data will be easier for you to read.

2. Encode the data from teamData to a byte buffer of type Data.

3. Write the data to a file called TeamData in the **Documents** folder.

➤ In `CardsApp`, create a temporary initializer:

```
init() {
  Team.save()
}
```

This will save the team data at the very start of the app so that you can examine it.

➤ In body, add a new modifier to `CardsView()`:

```
.onAppear {
  print(FileManager.documentURL ?? "")
}
```

You print out the URL of the **Documents** folder so you can find the file you've saved.

➤ Build and run the app. Highlight the **Documents** URL that shows up in the debug console, then right-click it and choose **Services ➤ Show in Finder**. Drag the parent folder to your **Favorites** sidebar as you'll be visiting this folder often while you're testing.

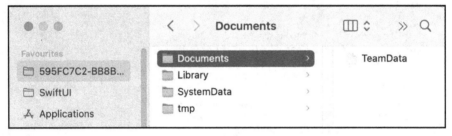

Team data

➤ In Finder, right-click **TeamData** and open the file in **TextEdit**:

```
{
  "names" : [
    "Richard",
    "Libranner",
    "Caroline",
    "Audrey",
    "Manda"
  ],
  "count" : 5
}
```

This is your structure data stored in JSON format. The identifiers are the names you used in the structure. As you can see, using `Codable`, it's very easy to store data.

Decoding

Reading the data back in is just as easy.

➤ In Team add a new method:

```
static func load() {
  // 1
  if let url = FileManager.documentURL?
    .appendingPathComponent("TeamData") {
    do {
    // 2
      let data = try Data(contentsOf: url)
      // 3
      let decoder = JSONDecoder()
      // 4
      let team = try decoder.decode(Team.self, from: data)
      print(team)
    } catch {
      print(error.localizedDescription)
    }
  }
}
```

Going through this code:

1. Get the URL.

2. Read the data from the URL into a Data type.

3. This time you're decoding, so you initialize a JSON decoder.

4. Decode the data into an instance of Team and print it to the console so that you can see what you've decoded.

➤ In CardsApp, change init() to:

```
init() {
  Team.load()
}
```

➤ Build and run, and see the new instance of Team loaded from **TeamData** printed out in the console before the **Documents** URL.

```
Team(names: ["Richard", "Libranner", "Caroline", "Audrey", "Manda"], count: 5)
file:///Users/caroline/Library/Developer/CoreSimulator/Devices/AF6C374F-808C-471E-
    B778-E90CD80DD537/data/Containers/Data/Application/4BD58B66-B793-48EE-8676-985
    46CEF4468/Documents/
```

Loaded team data

You can see that the theory of saving and loading data using Codable is very simple. But naturally, with real life data, there are always complications.

Encoding and decoding custom types

Skills you'll learn in this section: encoding; decoding; compactMap(_:)

Data types that you want to store must conform to Codable. If you check the developer documentation for the properties contained by Team, which are String and Int, you'll see they both conform to Decodable and Encodable.

Custom types which store only Codable types present no problem. But how about one of your custom types that contain types that do not conform to Codable?

Before continuing, remove the sample Team code that you created.

➤ In **CardsApp.swift**, remove init(), all of Team and teamData.

➤ Open **Transform.swift** and add this new extension:

```
extension Transform: Codable {}
```

You get a compile error: "Type Transform does not conform to protocol Decodable".

Transform contains two data types: CGSize and Angle. When you check the documentation, you'll find that CGSize conforms to Encodable and Decodable, whereas Angle does not.

When you conform your custom type to Codable, there are two required methods: init(from:) and encode(to:).

When all the types in your custom type conform to `Codable`, then all you have to do is add `Codable` conformance to your custom type, and `Codable` will automatically **synthesize** (create) the initializer and encoder methods.

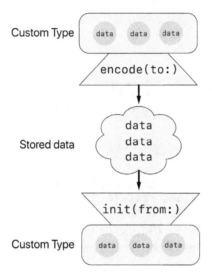

Codable synthesized methods

When the structure contains types that don't conform to `Codable`, you must implement the two synthesized methods yourself.

➤ In the **Extensions** group, create a new Swift file called **AngleExtensions.swift**.

➤ Replace the code with:

```
import SwiftUI

extension Angle: Codable {
  public init(from decoder: Decoder) throws {
    self.init()
  }

  public func encode(to encoder: Encoder) throws {
  }
}
```

You conform `Angle` to `Codable` and provide the two required methods. Because all the types used by `Transform` are now `Codable`, your code will now compile. However, the encoder and decoder methods you just created aren't doing anything useful. You'll have to tell the coders how to encode and decode every property that you want saved and loaded.

To do this, you create an enumeration that conforms to `CodingKey`, listing all the properties you want saved.

➤ Add this to the `Angle` extension:

```
enum CodingKeys: CodingKey {
  case degrees
}
```

You list only the properties that you want to save and restore. `radians` is another `Angle` property, but `Angle` can construct that internally from `degrees`, so you don't need to store it.

➤ Add this to `encode(to:)`:

```
var container = encoder.container(keyedBy: CodingKeys.self)
try container.encode(degrees, forKey: .degrees)
```

You create an encoder container using `CodingKeys`. Then you encode `degrees`, which is of type `Double`. This is a `Codable` type, so the container can encode it.

Decoding is similar.

➤ Replace the contents of `init(from:)` with:

```
let container = try decoder.container(keyedBy: CodingKeys.self)
let degrees = try container
  .decode(Double.self, forKey: .degrees)
self.init(degrees: degrees)
```

You create a decoder container to decode the data. As `degrees` is a `Double`, you decode a `Double` type. Then, you can initialize the `Angle` from the decoded degrees.

With `Angle` taken care of, and `CGSize` already conforming to `Codable`, `Transform` will now be able to synthesize the encoding and decoding methods and encode and decode itself, so your app will now compile.

You're eventually going to save a `Card`, so all types in the data hierarchy will need to to be `Codable`. Going up from `Transform` in your data structure hierarchy, the next structure that you'll tackle is `ImageElement`.

Encoding ImageElement

➤ Open **CardElement.swift** and take a look at ImageElement.

When saving an image element, you don't need to save the UUID, as it will get reconstructed when you load up the element. You'll save the transform, which is now Codable. Image and AnyShape, however, are not. At the point of loading the Image, you have access to the UIImage, and it's quite easy to save that to a file and record the filename.

➤ Add a new property to ImageElement:

```
var imageFilename: String?
```

This will hold the name of the saved image file, which will be a UUID string.

➤ Open **Card.swift** and replace addElement(uiImage:) with:

```
mutating func addElement(uiImage: UIImage) {
// 1
  let imageFilename = uiImage.save()
  let image = Image(uiImage: uiImage)
  // 2
  let element = ImageElement(
    image: image,
    imageFilename: imageFilename)
  elements.append(element)
}
```

The changes from the previous code are:

1. You now save the UIImage to a file using the provided code in **UIImageExtensions.swift**. uiImage.save() saves the **PNG** data to disk and returns a UUID string as the filename. Before saving, save() resizes large images, as you don't need to store the full resolution for the card.

2. You create the new element with both the loaded Image and the string filename.

You'll also need to remove the image file from disk when the user deletes the element.

➤ In remove(_:), add this to the top of the method:

```
if let element = element as? ImageElement {
  UIImage.remove(name: element.imageFilename)
}
```

You check that the element is an `ImageElement` and use the provided method in
UIImageExtensions.swift to remove the file from disk.

➤ Back in **CardElement.swift**, add a new extension after `ImageElement`:

```
extension ImageElement: Codable {
}
```

When adding a second initializer to the main definition of a structure, you lose the
default initializer and have to recreate it yourself. However, adding initializers to
extensions doesn't have this effect. When you conform `ImageElement` to `Codable`,
you provide the decoding initializer `init(from:)`. By adding the initializer to this
extension, you keep both the default initializer and the new decoding one.

➤ Add the `CodingKey` enumeration containing the properties to save to
`ImageElement`:

```
enum CodingKeys: CodingKey {
  case transform, imageFilename, frame
}
```

You'll save the transform, filename and frame to disk. It's unnecessary to store the
image element's id, as that can be generated when you load the element. You'll also
recreate the `Image` from the stored image file when you load the element.

➤ Add the decoder:

```
init(from decoder: Decoder) throws {
  let container = try decoder
    .container(keyedBy: CodingKeys.self)
  // 1
  transform = try container
    .decode(Transform.self, forKey: .transform)
  // 2
  imageFilename = try container.decodeIfPresent(
    String.self,
    forKey: .imageFilename)
  // 3
  if let imageFilename = imageFilename,
    let uiImage = UIImage.load(uuidString: imageFilename) {
    image = Image(uiImage: uiImage)
  } else {
    // 4
    image = Image("error-image")
  }
}
```

Going through the decoding:

1. Decode the transform. It's `Codable`, so it takes care of itself.

2. Decode the image filename. This is an optional and, if you try and decode something that does not exist, it will throw an error. Check if it exists using `decodeIfPresent(_:forKey:)`.

3. If the filename is present, load the image using the filename.

4. If there's an error loading the image, use the error image in **Assets.xcassets**.

➤ Add the encoder to the `ImageElement` `Codable` extension:

```swift
func encode(to encoder: Encoder) throws {
  var container = encoder.container(keyedBy: CodingKeys.self)
  try container.encode(transform, forKey: .transform)
  try container.encode(imageFilename, forKey: .imageFilename)
}
```

Here you're encoding the transform and the filename. `frame` is not yet `Codable`, so you'll add that in a moment.

Decoding and encoding the card

➤ Open **Card.swift** and add a new extension with the list of properties to save:

```swift
extension Card: Codable {
  enum CodingKeys: CodingKey {
    case id, backgroundColor, imageElements, textElements
  }
}
```

For `Card`, you'll save the id. This will be the name of the JSON file that you'll store all the data in, so it's important to keep track of the id to ensure data integrity. You'll store the background color in the first challenge at the end of the chapter. You'll also store image elements and text elements in two separate arrays.

➤ First add the decoder:

```swift
init(from decoder: Decoder) throws {
  let container = try decoder
    .container(keyedBy: CodingKeys.self)
  // 1
  let id = try container.decode(String.self, forKey: .id)
  self.id = UUID(uuidString: id) ?? UUID()
  // 2
```

```
    elements += try container
      .decode([ImageElement].self, forKey: .imageElements)
  }
```

Going through the decoder:

1. Decode the saved id string and restore id from the UUID string.

2. Load the array of image elements. You use the += operator to add to any elements that may already be there, just in case you load the text elements first.

As you're restoring id, you'll need to make it a var.

➤ In Card, change let id = UUID() to:

```
  var id = UUID()
```

➤ Add the encoder to Card's Codable extension:

```
func encode(to encoder: Encoder) throws {
  var container = encoder.container(keyedBy: CodingKeys.self)
  try container.encode(id.uuidString, forKey: .id)
  let imageElements: [ImageElement] =
    elements.compactMap { $0 as? ImageElement }
  try container.encode(imageElements, forKey: .imageElements)
}
```

Here you encode the id as a UUID string. You also extract all the image elements from elements using compactMap(_:)

Swift Dive: compactMap(_:)

compactMap(_:) returns an array with all the non-nil elements that match the closure. $0 represents each element.

When code is more complex than the above, you can replace the closure with:

```
  let imageElements: [ImageElement] =
    elements.compactMap { element in
    element as? ImageElement
  }
```

This replaces the non-descriptive $0 with element.

The code is equivalent to:

```
  var imageElements: [ImageElement] = []
```

```
for element in elements {
  if let element = element as? ImageElement {
    imageElements.append(element)
  }
}
```

The biggest advantage of using compactMap(_:) is that imageElements is a constant. This is safer because you can't accidentally add data to it at a later time. It's also less code and more readable once you're accustomed to using array methods such as map(_:) and filter(_:). When necessary, you can compose them them together to create arrays from complex operations. If you're more comfortable with for loops, then you can use those instead.

Saving the card

With all the coding and encoding in place, you can finally fill out save().

➤ Still in **Card.swift**, replace save() with:

```
func save() {
  do {
  // 1
    let encoder = JSONEncoder()
    // 2
    let data = try encoder.encode(self)
    // 3
    let filename = "\(id).rwcard"
    if let url = FileManager.documentURL?
      .appendingPathComponent(filename) {
      // 4
      try data.write(to: url)
    }
  } catch {
    print(error.localizedDescription)
  }
}
```

To save the data, you:

1. Set up the JSON encoder

2. Set up a Data property. This is a buffer that will hold any kind of byte data and is what you will write to disk. Fill the data buffer with the encoded Card.

3. The filename will be the card id plus a **.rwcard** extension.

4. Write the data to the file.

Perform this method whenever there are changes to the card.

➤ Add:

```
save()
```

to the end of:

- `remove(_:)`
- `addElement(uiImage:)`
- `update(_:frame:)`

You're already calling `save()` when the user presses the **Done** button and, also, when he exits the app and the scene phase changes.

➤ Build and run in the simulator.

➤ Open the **Documents** folder in Finder. The folder path prints out in the console, but you should have the folder in your **Favorites** sidebar.

➤ In the simulator, choose the green card and add a new photo. (Don't use the pink flowers as currently that file format does not work.) When the card adds the new element, it saves the photo to a **PNG** file and itself to a file with the **.rwcard** extension. In Finder, open this in TextEdit — you should just be able to double click it to open it.

```
{"id":"6D924181-ABFC-457A-A771-984E7F3805BD","imageElements":
[{"imageFilename":null,"transform":{"offset":[4,-137],"size":
[412,296],"rotation":{"degrees":-6.0000000000000009}}},
{"imageFilename":"8808F791-E832-465D-911A-A250B91A5141",
"transform":{"offset":[0,0],"size":[250,180],"rotation":
{"degrees":0}}}]}
```

You'll see something like the above. This is the JSON format as described earlier. You can see that you're saving the card `id`, which matches the filename and, also, an array of two `imageElements`. The first element will have `null` in the filename as it was provided by the preview data and never saved to a file. The second element will have the added photo with the name of the saved file.

If you want to make the output more human readable, in `save()`, after initializing encoder, you can add:

```
encoder.outputFormatting = .prettyPrinted
```

Loading Cards

> **Skills you'll learn in this section**: file enumeration; `Equatable`

Now that you've saved a card, you'll start the app by loading them.

File enumeration

To list the cards, you'll iterate through all the files with an extension of **.rwcard** and load them into the cards array.

➤ Open **CardStore.swift** and create a new extension with the method to load the files:

```swift
extension CardStore {
  // 1
  func load() -> [Card] {
    var cards: [Card] = []
    // 2
    guard let path = FileManager.documentURL?.path,
      let enumerator =
        FileManager.default.enumerator(atPath: path),
          let files = enumerator.allObjects as? [String]
    else { return cards }
    // 3
    let cardFiles = files.filter { $0.contains(".rwcard") }
    for cardFile in cardFiles {
      do {
        // 4
        let path = path + "/" + cardFile
        let data =
          try Data(contentsOf: URL(fileURLWithPath: path))
        // 5
        let decoder = JSONDecoder()
        let card = try decoder.decode(Card.self, from: data)
        cards.append(card)
      } catch {
        print("Error: ", error.localizedDescription)
      }
    }
    return cards
  }
}
```

Going through the code:

1. You'll return an array of Cards from load(). These will be all the cards in the **Documents** folder.

2. Set up the path for the **Documents** folder and enumerate all the files and folders inside this folder.

3. Filter the files so that you only hold files with the **.rwcard** extension. These are the Card files.

4. Read each file into a Data variable.

5. Decode each Card from the Data variable. You've done all the hard work of making all the properties used by Card and its subtypes Codable, so you can then simply add the decoded Card to the array you're building.

➤ Replace the implementation of init(defaultData:) with:

```
cards = defaultData ? initialCards : load()
```

Instead of using the default data, you can choose to load the cards from disk.

Adding a new card

You'll need a method to add a new card. When you add this new card to cards, it will only hold the background color.

➤ Add this new method to CardStore:

```
func addCard() -> Card {
  let card = Card(backgroundColor: Color.random())
  cards.append(card)
  card.save()
  return card
}
```

Here you create a new card with a random background color, add it to the array of cards and save it to disk.

➤ In **CardsApp.swift**, initialize store without the default data:

```
@StateObject var store = CardStore()
```

Adding a button to create a new card

Without the default data, you'll need some way of adding cards. You'll create an **Add** button that you'll enhance in the following chapter.

➤ Open **CardsView.swift**.

➤ In body, replace CardsListView() with:

```
VStack {
  Button(action: {
    viewState.selectedCard = store.addCard()
    viewState.showAllCards = false
  }, label: {
    Text("Add")
  })
  CardsListView()
}
```

You set up a temporary button to add a card. When you tap the button, you call your new addCard() method in store. This adds a new Card to the store's cards array and saves the card file to disk.

Also, you set viewState.selectedCard to be the newly created card and viewState.showAllCards to false, so only the new card is displayed.

➤ Open your app's **Documents** folder in Finder and remove all the files from the folder. This will reset your app's data.

➤ Build and run your app.

No app data

➤ Tap **Add** to add a new card. A new **.rwcard** file will appear in your app's **Documents** folder. Add a couple of photos and stickers to the card. These will get saved right away. Move them around and tap **Done** to save the transforms. Your new card will show underneath the **Add** button.

When you re-run your app, any cards you create will show up just as you created them.

Adding a card

Your app is in great shape now. There are still a couple of problems that you may have noticed. You're not yet storing the card's background color between sessions, so it reverts to the card background's default yellow. You're also not persisting any clip frames. Neither `Color` nor `AnyShape` conforms to `Codable`, and they are a little harder to persist than the previous types.

Saving the frame

AnyShape does not conform to `Codable`, as it's a custom type. To save the frame, you'll encode the index of the shape in the `shapes` array. When you decode, you'll use this index to restore the frame as an `AnyShape`.

➤ Open **CardElement.swift** and locate `ImageElement`'s `Codable` extension. Add this to the end of `encode(to:)`:

```
if let index =
  Shapes.shapes.firstIndex(where: { $0 == frame }) {
  try container.encode(index, forKey: .frame)
}
```

Here you're finding the first shape which is equal to your element's frame. You'll get an error because AnyShape doesn't conform to `Equatable`, which means that you can't compare the shape to the frame.

The Equatable protocol

Consider what equality is this case. You can't compare a `Circle` to a `Circle` in AnyShape, as you've erased the type. Inside each `Shape`, though, is a `Path`, and a `Path` type conforms to `Equatable`.

➤ Open **AnyShape.swift** and create a new extension:

```
extension AnyShape: Equatable {
}
```

➤ Compile and click the red dot next to the compile error. Click **Fix** to add protocol stubs.

```
static func == (lhs: AnyShape, rhs: AnyShape) -> Bool {
    code
}
```

This required method defines the == operator, with the left hand side and right hand side as parameters. The returned Boolean indicates whether the result is equal or not.

➤ Replace the code placeholder with:

```
let rect = CGRect(
  origin: .zero,
  size: CGSize(width: 100, height: 100))
let lhsPath = lhs.path(in: rect)
let rhsPath = rhs.path(in: rect)
return lhsPath == rhsPath
```

You create the path of the two shapes in a small rectangle. The size of the rectangle doesn't matter as long as it's not zero. You then compare the two paths to see if they are the same.

Your app will now compile, and you can compare two `AnyShapes`.

➤ Open **CardElement.swift** where you set up the encoding. You'll now do the decoding.

➤ At the end of `init(from:)` add this:

```
if let index =
  try container.decodeIfPresent(Int.self, forKey: .frame) {
  frame = Shapes.shapes[index]
}
```

Here you decode the index, if there is one, and set up the frame using the index.

➤ Build and run and test that your frames are being saved:

Saving the frames

Challenges

Challenge 1: Save the background color

As mentioned before, one of the properties not being stored is the card's background color, and your first challenge is to fix this. Instead of making `Color` `Codable`, you'll store the color data in `CGFloats`. In **ColorExtensions.swift**, there are two methods to help you:

- `colorComponents()` separates out a `Color` into red, green, blue and alpha components. These are returned in an array of four `CGFloats`. `CGFloat` conforms to `Codable`, so you'll be able to store the color.

- `color(components:)` is a static method which initializes a `Color` from four `CGFloats`. This is commonly called a **factory method**, as you're creating a new instance.

In **Card.swift**, encode and decode the background color using these two methods.

Before testing your solution, remove all files from the app's **Documents** folder. When you change the format of the file, it becomes unreadable. When adding properties to files in an app that you've already released, you would have to take this into account, as you wouldn't want to lose your users' data. Generally you'd store a version number in your files and have a startup method that does an upgrade of files if the data is an older version.

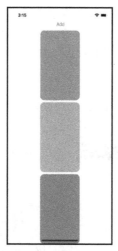

Card background colors saved

Challenge 2: Save text data

This is a super-challenging challenge that will test your knowledge of the previous chapters too. You're going to save text elements into your Card **.rwcard** file. Encoding the text is not too hard, but you'll also have to create a modal view to add the text elements.

1. Create a new SwiftUI file for your text entry modal. You will need to hold a `TextElement` binding property sent from `CardDetailView` to hold the text data temporarily, just as you've done for your other picker modals with `frame` and `stickerImage`. This time, though, in `CardDetailView`, instantiate the state property and don't make `textElement` an optional. You can check whether text is empty with `if textElement.text.isEmpty`.

2. In your new file, add an environment `presentationMode` property as you did for your other modals and replace body contents with:

```
let onCommit = {
  presentationMode.wrappedValue.dismiss()
}
TextField(
  "Enter text", text: $textElement.text, onCommit: onCommit)
```

The text field will show a placeholder and update the text String with the user's input. When the user presses **Return**, the modal will close.

3. In **CardDetailView.swift**, change sheet(item:) to add the text picker modal just as you did the other modals. In onDisappear(_:), if the text is not empty, add the new text element to the card. You'll add a new method to Card to create the TextElement, just as you did with ImageElement earlier.

4. Make TextElement Codable so that you save and restore the text with the card.

5. In Card's Codable extension, make sure that you encode and decode the text elements with the image elements.

Text entry and added text

This looks like a substantial challenge, but each step is one that you have done before, so you shouldn't have any trouble. Learning how to add features to an existing app is an important skill. If you do have any difficulties, then take a look at the project in this chapter's **challenge** folder.

When you finish this challenge, give yourself a big pat on the back, as you've now created an app that has a complex UI and persists data each time you run the app. This is the meat and vegetables of app development. The following chapters cover making your app look gorgeous and round off the meal with an exotic dessert.

Key points

- Saving data is the most important feature of an app. Almost all apps save some kind of data, and you should ensure that you save it reliably and consistently. Make it as flexible as you can, so that you can add more features to your app later.

- `ScenePhase` is useful to determine what state your app is in. Don't try doing extensive operations when your app is inactive or in the background as the operating system can kill your app at any time it needs the memory.

- JSON format is a standard for transmitting text over the internet. It's easy to read and, when you provide encoders and decoders, you can store almost anything in a JSON file.

- `Codable` encompasses both decoding and encoding. You can extend this task and format your data any way you want to.

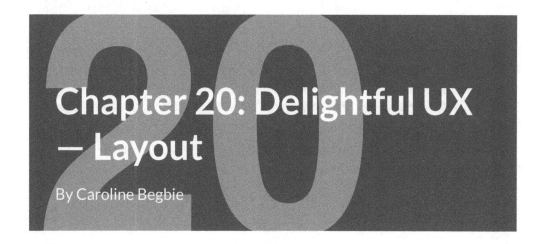

Chapter 20: Delightful UX — Layout

By Caroline Begbie

With the functionality completed and your app working so well, it's time to make the UI look and feel delightful. Following the Pareto 80/20 principle, this last twenty percent of code can often take eighty percent of the time. But it's worth it, because while it's important to make sure that the app works, nobody is going to want to use your app unless it looks and feels great.

The starter app

There are a few changes to the project since the challenge project in the last chapter. These are the major changes:

- To prevent huge, monolithic views, it's a good idea to refactor often. `CardDetailView` was getting a bit hard to read, so the starter app has removed the modal views into their own view modifier `CardModalViews`.

- The asset catalog has more pleasing random colors to use for backgrounds, as well as other colors that you'll use in these last chapters.

- `ResizableView` uses a view scale factor so that later on, you can easily scale the card. The default scale is 1, so you won't notice it to start with.

- `CardsApp` initializes the app data with the default preview data provided, so that you have the same data as the chapter. Remember to change to `@StateObject var store = CardStore()` in **CardsApp.swift** when you want to start saving your own cards again.

- Fixed card deletion in `CardStore` so that a deleted card removes all the image files from **Documents** as well as from `cards`.

- `CardDrop` has `size` and `frame` properties that you'll use in the Challenge.

This is the view hierarchy of the app you've created so far.

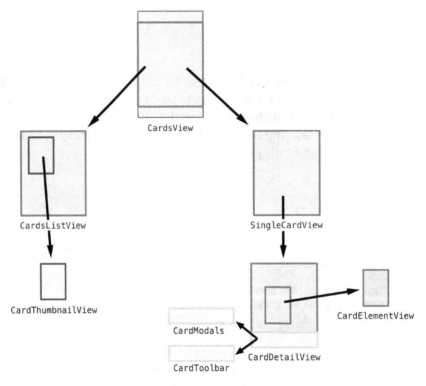

View Hierarchy

As you can see, it's very modular. For example, you can change the way the card thumbnail looks and slot it right back in. You can easily add buttons to the toolbar and add a corresponding modal.

You instantiate the one single source of truth — `CardStore` — and pass it down through all these views through bindings.

Designing the cards list

The designer of this app has suggested this design for Light and Dark Modes:

App Design

The top segmented controller will swap the display between a grid list view and a carousel. The bottom button is wide. This is the design that you'll attempt to duplicate.

Adding the list background color

➤ Before adding anything to the project, build and run the app in Simulator and choose **Device ▸ Erase All Contents and Settings…**.

This will delete all the data you have so far created for the app. For the moment, you'll use the default data provided with the app.

➤ Open **CardsView.swift**.

➤ Add a modifier to ZStack:

```
.background(
  Color("background")
    .edgesIgnoringSafeArea(.all))
```

This will use a color from the asset catalog named **background** for the background color. This is defined as light gray for light appearance and dark gray for dark appearance. By using `edgesIgnoringSafeArea(_:)`, you ensure the background covers all the screen.

➤ Preview the view. In this image, the background color is pink for clarity; yours will be light gray.

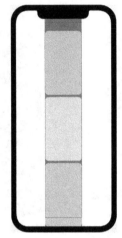

Background Color not showing up

Instead of the background color showing across the whole view, even though you're ignoring all the safe areas, the background color is only showing up in the area of the scroll view. This is because `ZStack` only takes up as much space as required by its child views.

Layout

> **Skills you'll learn in this section**: control view layout

It's time to take a deeper look at how SwiftUI handles view layout.Most of the time, SwiftUI views lay themselves out and look great, and you don't have to think about the layout at all. But then comes the time where you want exact positioning, or a view isn't behaving the way that you thought it would, and you might start fighting the system. Once you understand layout and treat it logically, then it all becomes much easier.

Layout starts from the top of the view hierarchy. The parent view tells its children, "I propose this size". Each child then takes as much room as it needs within the parent's available space and tells the parent "I only need this size". This continues all the way down the view hierarchy. The parent then resizes itself to the size of its child views.

➤ Create a new SwiftUI View file named **LayoutView.swift** to experiment with various layouts. If you still have **ContentView.swift** in your file, you can use that instead.

➤ In LayoutView_Previews, add a new modifier to LayoutView:

```
.previewLayout(.fixed(width: 500, height: 300))
```

This gives a fixed size to the preview of 500 x 300.

➤ In LayoutView, add a new modifier to Text:

```
.background(Color.red)
```

➤ Preview the view. The red color shows how much space the Text view takes up on screen.

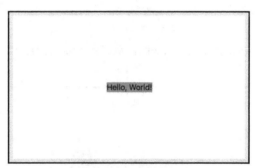

Text with red background

There are three views in the view tree hierarchy here:

```
LayoutView ► Text (modified) ► Red
```

LayoutView has a fixed size of 500 by 300 points. Text takes up the amount of space needed for the letters in the assigned font size. Color is a bit different. It's a **late binding token**, which means that the size is assigned at the last moment.

A `Color` view fills the whole space of its parent.

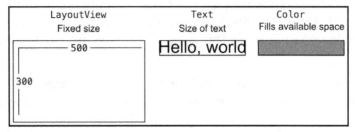

Laying out views

➤ Change `LayoutView` to:

```swift
struct LayoutView: View {
  var body: some View {
    HStack {
      Text("Hello, World!")
        .background(Color.red)
      Text("Hello, World!")
        .padding()
        .background(Color.red)
    }
    .background(Color.gray)
  }
}
```

➤ Here you create a horizontal stack with two `Text` views. The second `Text` has padding.

Laying out views

The view tree is now:

```
LayoutView ➤ HStack ➤ Text (modified) ➤ Red
                    ➤ Text (modified) ➤ Padding (modified) ➤ Red
                    ➤ Gray
```

LayoutView still has the fixed size of 500 by 300 points. HStack presents 500 by 300 points to its children. The first Text returns the space it needs, but the second text has a padding modifier, so returns its space plus the padding. HStack then takes up only the space required by its two child views plus HStack's default padding between the two child views. HStack's gray background color fills out the space taken up by HStack underneath the two Text views.

Every time you add a modifier, you create a new layer in the view hierarchy. But don't worry about the efficiency of this — SwiftUI views are lightweight and adding new views is incredibly fast.

The frame modifier

In previous code, you have changed the default size of views using `frame(width:height:alignment:)`, giving absolute values to `width` and `height`.

When you want to lay out views relative to parent view sizes, you can specify minimum and maximum widths and heights using `frame(minWidth:idealWidth:maxWidth:minHeight:idealHeight:maxHeight:alignment:)`.

➤ Before `.background(Color.gray)`, add this:

```
.frame(maxWidth: .infinity)
```

The HStack now tells its parent that it wants the maximum available width, so HStack, with its gray color, expands to the whole width of the view.

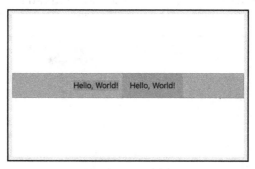

Maximum width

Remember your earlier problem with the background color only taking up the width of the ScrollView? Specifying a frame with maxWidth and maxHeight of infinity would be one way of filling up the entire available background.

GeometryReader

> **Skills you'll learn in this section**: GeometryReader; use given view size to layout child views

However, when you need to know the size of the parent so that you can lay out child views with more precision, there's another flexible view that takes up the whole available space and gives you the size in points. GeometryReader is a container view that returns its preferred size. Later, you'll use GeometryReader to determine the size of card thumbnails based upon the width of the available space.

➤ In LayoutView, embed HStack in a GeometryReader and give it a yellow background:

```
GeometryReader { proxy in
  HStack {
    ...
  }
  .frame(maxWidth: .infinity)
  .background(Color.gray)
}
.background(Color.yellow)
```

GeometryReader takes up the size of the parent, in this case the whole 500 x 300 point view. It returns a value of type GeometryProxy, which includes a size property so that you can find out exactly the size of the view. You can then lay out child views using this size.

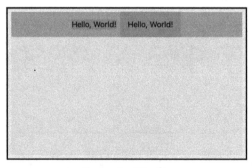

GeometryReader

Notice that GeometryReader changes alignment behavior. Instead of HStack being centered in its parent view, it is now aligned to the top left of its parent view. You'll discover more about alignment later in this chapter.

➤ Change HStack's modifiers to:

```
.frame(width: proxy.size.width * 0.8)
.background(Color.gray)
.padding(
  .leading, (proxy.size.width - proxy.size.width * 0.8) / 2)
```

frame(width:height:alignment) now uses a relative value of four fifths of the width of the available area. If the parent view gets larger, for example on device rotation, proxy.size will update and refresh the view. The view will resize to four fifths of the new parent size.

To center HStack, you calculate the leading padding, using the geometry proxy width.

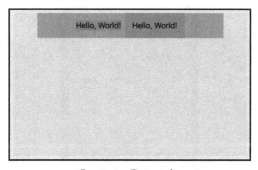

GeometryProxy size

Notice the order of the modifiers. If you change the order of any one of these, you'll get a different result. Before filling with color, you must set the size of the view. If you calculate the padding before filling with gray, then you'll center the text views but not the background gray color.

Setting the card thumbnail size

When showing a list of card thumbnails on an iPad, you have more room than on a smaller device, so the thumbnail size should be larger. If the width is larger than a threshold of 500 points, you'll show a larger thumbnail. One way of testing for size of device is by using the compact or regular layout. Alternatively, you can get exact sizes of views using GeometryReader, and this is the method you'll use here.

➤ Open **CardsListView.swift**.

➤ Embed ScrollView in GeometryReader:

```
GeometryReader { proxy in
```

```
ScrollView(showsIndicators: false) {
    ...
  }
}
```

➤ Open **CardsView.swift** and preview.

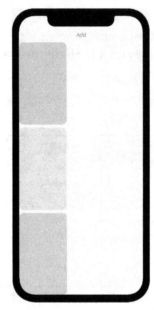

ScrollView in GeometryReader

Notice the side effects of using GeometryReader. CardsListView's parent is ZStack in **CardsView.swift**. GeometryReader takes all the available space and passes that back to ZStack. That means that ZStack's light gray background color now fills the entire screen.

The second side effect is that the central alignment of ScrollView is lost. You'll fix this when you add a grid view shortly.

➤ Open **CardsListView.swift** again.

Within ScrollView, you now have access to proxy.size which gives you the entire available space of CardsListView's parent.

➤ Change CardThumbnailView(card: card) to:

```
CardThumbnailView(card: card, size: proxy.size)
```

You now pass the size to the thumbnail, which can take appropriate action. You'll get a compile error until you fix CardThumbnailView.

➤ Open **CardThumbnailView.swift**.

➤ Add the size after the card property:

```
var size: CGSize = .zero
```

➤ Open **Settings.swift** and replace thumbnailSize with:

```
static func thumbnailSize(size: CGSize) -> CGSize {
  let threshold: CGFloat = 500
  var scale: CGFloat = 0.12
  if size.width > threshold && size.height > threshold {
    scale = 0.2
  }
  return CGSize(
    width: Settings.cardSize.width * scale,
    height: Settings.cardSize.height * scale)
}
```

The thumbnail size will scale to 12 percent of the final size of the card. When the size offered has a width or height greater than 500 points, then you scale to 20 percent of the final size.

➤ In **CardThumbnailView.swift**, replace frame(width:height:) with:

```
.frame(
  width: Settings.thumbnailSize(size: size).width,
  height: Settings.thumbnailSize(size: size).height)
```

Now that you know the screen space available to the card list, you calculate the thumbnail's frame accordingly.

➤ Build and run on both iPad and iPhone simulators and compare the two thumbnail sizes.

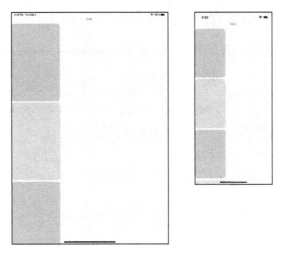

Thumbnail sizes on iPad and iPhone

The thumbnail size on the iPad is larger than that on the iPhone.

Adding a lazy grid view

> **Skills you'll learn in this section**: GeometryProxy size calculations

Instead of showing one column of scrolling cards, you'll add a LazyVGrid to show the cards in multiple columns. This should be adaptive depending on the device's current display width.

➤ Open **CardsListView.swift** and add a new method to CardsListView:

```
func columns(size: CGSize) -> [GridItem] {
  [
    GridItem(.adaptive(
      minimum: Settings.thumbnailSize(size: size).width))
  ]
}
```

This returns an array of GridItem — in this case, with one element — you can use this to tell the LazyVGrid the size and position of each row. This GridItem is adaptive, which means the grid will fit as many items as possible with the minimum size provided.

➤ In body, embed ForEach in a LazyVGrid:

```
GeometryReader { proxy in
  ScrollView(showsIndicators: false) {
    LazyVGrid(columns: columns(size: proxy.size), spacing: 30) {
      ForEach(store.cards) { card in
        ...
      }
    }
  }
}
```

You now have a flexible grid with vertical spacing of 30 points.

➤ Build and run the app on various simulators and switch from portrait to landscape to see how the columns vary.

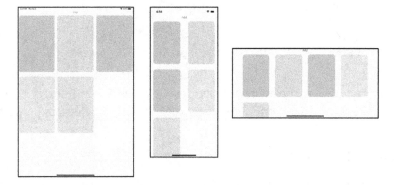

Grids on iPad and iPhones

Note: If you want to visualize how much space views take up, try adding .background(Color.red) as a modifier to the various views.

Creating the button for a new card

You'll now place a button at the foot of the screen to create a new card.

➤ Open **CardsView.swift**.

➤ In CardsView, remove VStack and its contents, so that ZStack only contains SingleCardView and its conditional:

```
ZStack {
  if !viewState.showAllCards {
```

```
      SingleCardView()
    }
  }
  .background...
```

➤ In CardsView, create a new button property:

```
var createButton: some View {
// 1
  Button(action: {
    viewState.selectedCard = store.addCard()
    viewState.showAllCards = false
  }) {
    Label("Create New", systemImage: "plus")
  }
  .font(.system(size: 16, weight: .bold))
// 2
  .frame(maxWidth: .infinity)
  .padding([.top, .bottom], 10)
// 3
  .background(Color("barColor"))
}
```

You don't always have to create new structures for views. Sometimes, if it's a simple view and you're only using it once, it's easier to keep track of views as properties or methods.

Going through this code:

1. Create a simple button using a Label format, so that you can specify a system image. When tapped, you create a new card and assign it to viewState.selectedCard. You set viewState.showAllCards to false, so that SingleCardView will show.

2. The button stretches all the way across the screen, less the padding.

3. The background color is in the asset catalog. You'll customize the button text color shortly.

You'll add the button as another layer on top of CardsListView.

➤ At the top of ZStack, add this code:

```
CardsListView()
VStack {
  Spacer()
  createButton
}
```

VStack and Spacer will place the button at the bottom of the screen.

CardsView now looks like this:

```
ZStack {
  CardsListView()
  VStack {
    Spacer()
    createButton
  }
  if !viewState.showAllCards ...
}
```

➤ Build and run (or use Live Preview) and test out your new button.

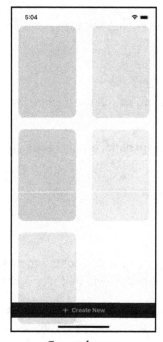

Create button

The button code has a "gotcha". Although the button frame extends all the way across the screen, only the text is tappable.

➤ In createButton, move frame(maxWidth: .infinity) from being a modifier on Button to a modifier on Label:

```
Button(action: {
...
}) {
```

```
    Label("Create New", systemImage: "plus")
        .frame(maxWidth: .infinity)
}
...
```

➤ Build and run again. The button looks the same but is tappable all the way across.

Outlining the cards

Open **CardThumbnailView.swift**.

An alternative to using a `RoundedRectangle` is to use the card background color as the view.

➤ Change `RoundedRectangle(cornerRadius:)` and `foregroundColor(_:)` to:

```
card.backgroundColor
    .cornerRadius(10)
```

This changes the corner radius to match the design, but otherwise produces the same result as before.

➤ Add a modifier to `card.background`, after `frame(width:height:alignment:)`:

```
.shadow(
    color: Color("shadow-color"),
    radius: 3,
    x: 0.0,
    y: 0.0)
```

Here you add a shadow with your specified color and a radius of 3. With the x and y positions both being zero, the shadow will be three points all around the view.

This is a very subtle outline color, but if your designer tells you to add it, trust the designer. :]

➤ Temporarily change `card.backgroundColor` to:

```
Color(UIColor.systemBackground)
```

As the card color is now the same as the screen's background color you'll be able to see the shadow.

➤ Preview the view, switching between Dark and Light color schemes in **Inspect Preview**.

Outline Colors with temporary card color

➤ Change `Color(UIColor.systemBackground)` back to:

```
card.backgroundColor
```

This restores your card's background color.

Outline Colors

Designing the card detail screen

> **Skills you'll learn in this section**: accent color; scale a fixed size view

Customizing the accent color

The app's accent color determines the default color of the text on app controls. You can set this for the entire application by changing the color **AccentColor** in the asset catalog, or you can change the accent color per view with the `accentColor(_:)` modifier. The default is blue, which doesn't work at all well for the text button:

The default accent color

➤ Open **Assets.xcassets** and choose **AccentColor**.

AccentColor is automatically created when you create a new project using the App template.

➤ Change the color to black for **Any Appearance** and white for **Dark Appearance**.

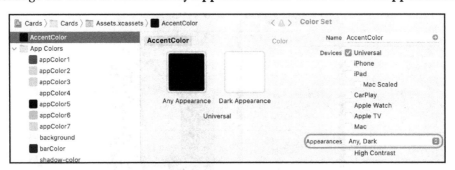

Change the accent color

This will change the default accent color of all the controls throughout the app.

➤ Open **CardsView.swift** and preview it.

The **Create** button text is now black and doesn't show on the black bar.

Black text

➤ In `createButton`, add a new modifier after `background(Color("barColor")`:

```
.accentColor(.white)
```

As the button is dark in both light and dark appearances, you set the button's accent color to always be white.

➤ Live preview the view in both Light and Dark color schemes:

Accent color

Throughout the app, text takes on **AccentColor** in **Assets.xcassets** except for where you specify `accentColor(_:)` on specific views.

Scaling the card to fit the device

Currently a card takes up the full size of the screen, no matter what device or orientation you're using. This obviously doesn't work when you've created a portrait card and then turn the device to landscape.

You're going to create cards with a fixed size of 1300 by 2000. The entire card will be visible at one time, no matter the orientation, and you'll calculate the appropriate size of the card view using a geometry reader proxy size.

➤ Open **CardDetailView.swift**.

➤ Add these new methods to `CardDetailView`:

```swift
func calculateSize(_ size: CGSize) -> CGSize {
  var newSize = size
  let ratio =
    Settings.cardSize.width / Settings.cardSize.height

  if size.width < size.height {
    newSize.height = min(size.height, newSize.width / ratio)
    newSize.width = min(size.width, newSize.height * ratio)
  } else {
    newSize.width = min(size.width, newSize.height * ratio)
    newSize.height = min(size.height, newSize.width / ratio)
  }
  return newSize
}

func calculateScale(_ size: CGSize) -> CGFloat {
  let newSize = calculateSize(size)
  return newSize.width / Settings.cardSize.width
}
```

These methods calculate the size and scale of the card view with the correct aspect ratio using a given size. This size will come from a `GeometryReader`'s `GeometryProxy`.

➤ In body, embed `content` in a `GeometryReader`:

```swift
var body: some View {
  GeometryReader { proxy in
    content
      .onChange(of: scenePhase) ...
```

You can now calculate the frame of `content` using the geometry reader proxy size.

➤ Add these modifiers to `content` after `cardModals(card:currentModal:)`:

```
// 1
.frame(
  width: calculateSize(proxy.size).width ,
  height: calculateSize(proxy.size).height)
// 2
.clipped()
// 3
.frame(maxWidth: .infinity, maxHeight: .infinity)
```

There's a lot of layout going on in these few modifiers:

1. Calculate the size of the card view given the available space.

2. The background color will spill out of the frame, so clip it.

3. Make sure that `content` takes up all of the space available to it. This will center the card view in the geometry reader.

➤ In the **Views** group, open **ResizableView.swift**.

Notice that the new changes in this file adjust all the offsets and sizes to be scaled to `viewScale`. This defaults to 1, so you don't have to specify a view scale if you don't want to.

➤ Open **CardDetailView.swift** again.

➤ In `var content`, change `resizableView(transform: bindingTransform(for: element))` to:

```
.resizableView(
  transform: bindingTransform(for: element),
  viewScale: calculateScale(size))
```

When `ResizableView` transforms the size of each element, it now uses the scale calculated using the proxy size.

Unfortunately your app fails to compile, because `proxy`'s `size` isn't available to `content`.

➤ Change `var content: some View {` to:

```
func content(size: CGSize) -> some View {
```

This changes `content` to be a method instead of a property, so that you can pass the geometry proxy size.

➤ In body, change content to:

```
content(size: proxy.size)
```

➤ Build and run on various devices and orientations and check out your newly scaled card view. The card stays in portrait and is fixed to a scaled 1300 by 2000 size.

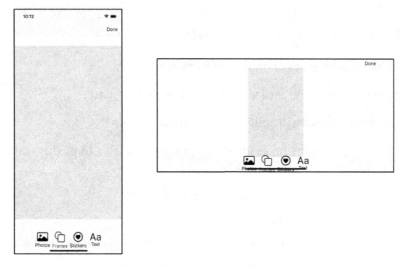

Scaled card in portrait and landscape

Unfortunately, now you have a new problem! When you add a photo, because the card is scaled, it's too small to manage.

➤ Open **Settings.swift** and change defaultElementSize to:

```
static let defaultElementSize =
  CGSize(width: 800, height: 800)
```

➤ Build and run, and now you can add elements that are appropriate to the size of the device.

The scaled card

Alignment

Skills you'll learn in this section: stack alignment

The final subject in layout that you'll cover is alignment. Take another look at the previous image. Currently, the images in your toolbar buttons are different sizes which misaligns the button text. Your attention-to-detail gene should have been crying inwardly because of this.

`VStack(alignment:spacing:)` and `HStack(alignment:spacing:)` have optional alignment parameters.

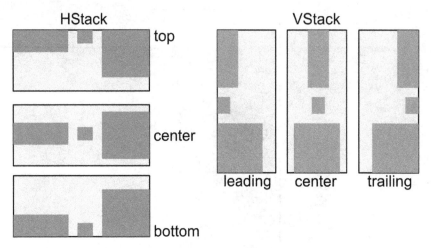

Stack Alignment

With an `HStack`, you describe how child views should align vertically, and with a `VStack`, you describe the horizontal view alignment

➤ Open **CardBottomToolbar.swift** and preview the view.

Xcode Tip: Don't forget your keyboard shortcut **Shift-Command-O** to quickly open a file by name. To see the current file in the Project navigator, press **Shift-Command-J**.

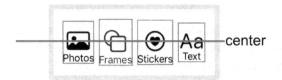

Misaligned preview of the toolbar buttons

Currently, in `CardBottomToolbar`, your toolbar buttons are in a center aligned `HStack`. This means that the `ToolbarButtonViews`, which consist of a `VStack` with an `Image` above and `Text` below, are all center aligned.

➤ In `CardBottomToolbar`, change `HStack {` to:

```
HStack(alignment: .top) {
```

This aligns the buttons at the top of the HStack.

Top aligned buttons

➤ Now try bottom alignment. Change the alignment to:

```
HStack(alignment: .bottom) {
```

This is the best result as all the text is now aligned.

Bottom aligned buttons

When you build and run the app on an iPhone and rotate to landscape, you will see that the images escape over the top of the bar and the home bar covers the text.

Escaping buttons

In Chapter 16, "Adding Assets to Your App", you used size classes for compact and regular to determine which launch image to use. Here, you'll check the size class of the device in code and use a different view for each size class. The compact size class will only show the image, whereas the regular size class will show both image and text.

➤ Still in **CardBottomToolbar.swift**, in ToolbarButtonView, add this:

```
func regularView(
  _ imageName: String,
  _ text: String
) -> some View {
  VStack(spacing: 2) {
    Image(systemName: imageName)
```

```
    Text(text)
  }
  .frame(minWidth: 60)
  .padding(.top, 5)
}
```

This is the regular size class view that shows both image and text.

➤ Add this method:

```
func compactView(_ imageName: String) -> some View {
  VStack(spacing: 2) {
    Image(systemName: imageName)
  }
  .frame(minWidth: 60)
  .padding(.top, 5)
}
```

This is the compact size class view that shows only the image.

➤ Add a new environment property to `ToolbarButtonView`:

```
@Environment(\.verticalSizeClass) var verticalSizeClass
```

This system environment property holds whether the vertical size class is currently compact or regular.

➤ Replace body with:

```
var body: some View {
  if let text = modalButton[modal]?.text,
    let imageName = modalButton[modal]?.imageName {
    if verticalSizeClass == .compact {
      compactView(imageName)
    } else {
      regularView(imageName, text)
    }
  }
}
```

This will show the correct view for the correct size class.

➤ Build and run the app on an iPhone simulator and open a card. When you rotate the simulator, both text and images show in portrait but only the images show in landscape.

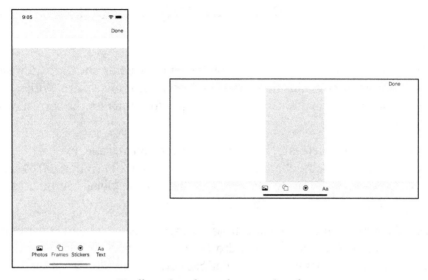

Toolbar view dependent on size class

Challenge

Challenge: Drag and drop into the correct offset

In Chapter 17, "Interfacing With UIKit", you implemented drag and drop. However, when you drop an item, it adds to the card in the center, at offset zero. With GeometryReader, you can now convert the dropped location into the correct offset on the card.

1. CardDrop, the drop delegate, now takes in a size and a frame. In CardDetailView's body, change .onDrop(of:delegate:) so that CardDrop receives the calculated size of the card and the frame in global coordinates. That's proxy.frame(in: .global).

2. In CardDrop, examine the Dispatch.main.async closure. offset is calculated for you, using info.location. The drop delegate provides this drop location. calculateOffset does various calculations between coordinate spaces.

To illustrate what a coordinate space is, all card offsets are saved with the origin being at the center of the card. The origin is location (0, 0). However, info.location is in screen coordinates, where the origin is at the top left of the screen. So you must convert from "screen space" to "card space". If you need a reminder on how to do drag and drop, take another look at Chapter 17, "Interfacing With UIKit".

Try out drag and drop on iPad, and you have an infinite number of Google images to decorate your card.

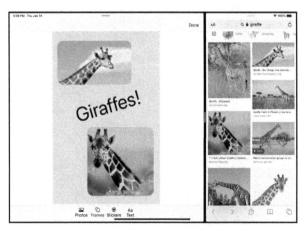

Drag and Drop

Key points

- Even though your app works, you're not finished until your app is fun to use. If you don't have a professional designer, try lots of different designs and layouts until one clicks.

- Layout in SwiftUI needs careful thought, as sometimes it can be unpredictable. The golden rule is that views take their size from their children.

- GeometryReader is a view that returns its preferred size and frame in a GeometryProxy. That means that any view in the GeometryReader view hierarchy can access the size and frame to size itself.

- Stacks have alignment capabilities. If these aren't enough, you can create your own custom alignments too. There's a great Apple WWDC video that goes into SwiftUI's layout system in depth at: https://apple.co/39uamSx

Chapter 21: Delightful UX — Final Touches

By Caroline Begbie

An iOS app is not complete without some snazzy animation. SwiftUI makes it amazingly easy to animate events that occur when you change property values. Transition animations are a breeze.

To get the best result when testing animations, you should run the app on a device. Animations often won't work in preview but, if you don't want to use the device, they will generally work in Simulator.

The starter project

➤ Open the starter project for this chapter.

• This project has an additional group called **Supporting Code**. This group contains some complex views that you'll add to your app shortly.

• Card contains two extra properties. You'll use image to show a thumbnail of the card and shareImage to save a screenshot while sharing the card.

• ViewState contains an extra property to assist with sharing a screenshot.

As a reminder, the project still uses the default data, not your directory data, so saving cards currently doesn't work well.

Animated splash screen

Skills you'll learn in this section: set up properties for animation

Sometimes in a more complex app, after showing the launch screen, your app will take a few seconds to do all the loading housekeeping. To prevent the UI from appearing to stall, the app can perform an animation to distract the user. Apps such as Twitter and Uber use animation to reflect their branding.

You'll create an animated splash screen where the letters **C-A-R-D-S** will drop down from the top and, when that animation is complete, the animation view will slide to the main cards view.

Final animation

➤ In the **Cards** group, under **CardsApp.swift**, create two new SwiftUI View files named **AppLoadingView.swift** and **SplashScreen.swift**.

➤ Open **AppLoadingView.swift**. This view will determine whether you're showing the animation or not.

➤ Create a new property in `AppLoadingView`:

```
@State private var showSplash = true
```

➤ Change body to:

```
var body: some View {
  if showSplash {
    SplashScreen()
      .edgesIgnoringSafeArea(.all)
  } else {
    CardsView()
  }
}
```

When `showSplash` is true, you'll show the splash animation, otherwise you'll show the main `CardsView`. At the moment, you never set `showSplash` to false, so `CardsView` will never show. Sometimes the live preview doesn't show animations correctly — or at all — so in order to see the animation on the simulator, you'll keep it this way until your splash animation is perfected.

➤ In `AppLoadingView_Previews`, add this modifier to `AppLoadingView`:

```
.environmentObject(CardStore(defaultData: true))
```

This sets up the card store, so that the app will still work in Live Preview.

➤ Open **CardsApp.swift** and change `CardsView()` to:

```
AppLoadingView()
```

You show the intermediate view which contains the splash screen.

➤ Build and run, and you'll see the default "Hello World" from `SplashScreen`.

Hello, World

➤ Open **SplashScreen.swift** and add this new method to `SplashScreen`:

```swift
func card(letter: String, color: String) -> some View {
  ZStack {
    RoundedRectangle(cornerRadius: 25)
      .shadow(radius: 3)
      .frame(width: 120, height: 160)
      .foregroundColor(.white)
    Text(letter)
      .fontWeight(.bold)
      .scalableText()
      .foregroundColor(Color(color))
      .frame(width: 80)
  }
}
```

Here you create a view with a shadow, that takes in a letter and a color.

➤ Change `Text("Hello, World!")` to:

```swift
card(letter: "C", color: "appColor7")
```

Here you create the view with the letter "C" and the name of a color set up in your asset catalog.

➤ Preview the view.

The card

You now have a stationary card. You'll separate out the animation movement into a new view modifier.

➤ In **SplashScreen.swift**, add a new structure:

```swift
private struct SplashAnimation: ViewModifier {
  @State private var animating = true
  let finalYPosition: CGFloat
  let delay: Double

  func body(content: Content) -> some View {
    content
      .offset(y: animating ? -700 : finalYPosition)
      .onAppear {
        animating = false
      }
  }
}
```

To drop the card from the top, you'll animate content's offset. If animating is true, then the card's offset is off the top of the screen at -700 points. When false, the offset will be the final designated position. You change animating to false when the view appears.

You'll use the delay property shortly.

➤ In `SplashScreen`, replace body with:

```
var body: some View {
  card(letter: "C", color: "appColor7")
    .modifier(SplashAnimation(finalYPosition: 200, delay: 0))
}
```

Here, you call the view modifier with the final Y position of the card.

➤ Live Preview the view, and you'll see your card 200 points below the center, but not animated yet.

The card before animation

SwiftUI Animation

> **Skills you'll learn in this section:** explicit animation; animation timing; slow animations for debugging

SwiftUI makes animating any view parameter that depends on a property incredibly easy. You simply surround the dependent property with a closure:

```
withAnimation {
    property.toggle()
}
```

And that's it! Any parameter in your entire app that depends on `property`, will animate automatically.

In `SplashAnimation`, the offset of your card depends on `animating`.

➤ In `onAppear(_:)`, change `animating = false` to:

```
withAnimation {
    animating = false
}
```

➤ Live preview the view. Your card now animates from the top and ends up at a Y offset of 200.

➤ Build and run the app in Simulator.

➤ In Simulator, choose **Debug ▸ Slow Animations**. This is a debug feature to slow down animations, so that you can see them properly. You'll now see a check mark next to the menu item.

➤ Build and run the app again to see the animation in slow motion.

➤ In `SplashScreen`, change the contents of body to:

```
ZStack {
  Color("background")
    .edgesIgnoringSafeArea(.all)
  card(letter: "S", color: "appColor1")
    .modifier(SplashAnimation(finalYPosition: 240, delay: 0))
  card(letter: "D", color: "appColor2")
    .modifier(SplashAnimation(finalYPosition: 120, delay: 0.2))
  card(letter: "R", color: "appColor3")
    .modifier(SplashAnimation(finalYPosition: 0, delay: 0.4))
  card(letter: "A", color: "appColor6")
    .modifier(SplashAnimation(finalYPosition: -120, delay: 0.6))
  card(letter: "C", color: "appColor7")
    .modifier(SplashAnimation(finalYPosition: -240, delay: 0.8))
}
```

This sets up all the card letters with their final positions and colors. The `delay` parameter doesn't do anything yet, but you'll use it shortly. The background color is in your asset catalog.

➤ Live Preview or run in Simulator. In this animation, all the cards animate downwards with the same timing, which isn't aesthetically pleasing.

Animating with the same timing

When you use `withAnimation(_:_:)`, you can specify what sort of `Animation` you want to use. You can specify the timing of the animation, the duration and whether it has a delay.

➤ In `SplashAnimation`, in `onAppear(_:)`, change `withAnimation { to`:

```
withAnimation(Animation.default.delay(delay)) {
```

Here you're using the default animation with a delay modifier. You've already set up the cards with their delay. Each card has a 0.2 second delay greater than the previous card.

➤ Live Preview the result. With the delays, the card animation is staggered.

Animation delay

An `Animation` can have various qualities. The most common are:

- **easeIn**: where the animation starts slowly, but speeds up to the end.

- **easeOut**: where the animation starts at speed but slows down toward the end.

- **easeInOut**: a combination of the previous two.

- **linear**: where the animation speed is constant all the way through.

➤ Replace `withAnimation(Animation.default.delay(delay)) {` with:

```
withAnimation(Animation.easeOut(duration: 1.5).delay(delay)) {
```

This animation lasts for 1.5 seconds and slows gradually at the end of the animation.

➤ Live Preview first to see the animation in 1.5 seconds. Then build and run on the simulator with slow animations. You can see that the cards fall closer together toward the end of the animation.

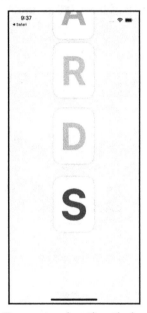

Ease out animation timing

A more interesting `Animation` is a spring, where the view bounces like a spring. You can specify how stiff it is and how fast the bouncing stops.

➤ In `SplashAnimation`, replace the `withAnimation(_:_:)` closure with:

```
withAnimation(
  Animation.interpolatingSpring(
    mass: 0.2,
    stiffness: 80,
    damping: 5,
    initialVelocity: 0.0)
  .delay(delay)) {
  animating = false
}
```

➤ Live Preview this, and you'll see that each card bounces as it hits its offset position. Experiment with the values of each of these spring properties to see how they affect the animation.

To finish off this animation, add a random rotation to each card.

➤ In `SplashAnimation`, after `offset(y:)`, add this:

```
.rotationEffect(
  animating ? .zero
    : Angle(degrees: Double.random(in: -10...10)))
```

The card animates to a random rotation between -10 and 10 degrees as it drops.

➤ Live Preview, and you'll see your final animation.

Random rotation

Explicit and implicit animation

Skills you'll learn in this section: implicit animation

withAnimation(_:_:) **explicitly** causes animations with parameters affected by the property within its closure. If you have multiple properties changing, you can explicitly change the animation for each of them.

For **implicit** animation, you animate any view with an animatable parameter automatically.

➤ In SplashAnimation, remove the withAnimation(_:_:) closure, so that onAppear(_:) is:

```
.onAppear {
  animating = false
}
```

This removes all animation.

➤ After the rotation effect modifier add this:

```
.animation(
  Animation.interpolatingSpring(
    mass: 0.2,
    stiffness: 80,
    damping: 5,
    initialVelocity: 0.0)
    .delay(delay))
```

This adds an implicit animation to the view. Whenever any animatable property affects the view, you describe the animation to use for this view.

➤ Live Preview the animation.

In this case, as you are only animating views with one animatable property, the implicit animation will appear exactly the same as the explicit animation. Explicit animations can be less code, but implicit animations give you more control by being able to animate each view depending on the animated property with different animations.

Animated transitions

Skills you'll learn in this section: transitions

You'll now transition your splash screen to the main `CardsView`. SwiftUI makes this easy with built-in transition effects, but you can also have complete control about how the view transitions.

➤ Open **AppLoadingView.swift**.

➤ After `edgesIgnoringSafeArea(.all)`, add:

```
.onAppear {
  DispatchQueue.main.asyncAfter(deadline: .now() + 1.5) {
    withAnimation(.linear(duration: 5)) {
      showSplash = false
    }
  }
}
```

Here you set `showSplash` to `false` after a delay and use explicit animation. `showSplash` controls which view shows. You want the splash screen to show for a second or two and then transition to the main view.

Slowing the animation in Simulator doesn't work well when testing this transition, so you give the transition animation a slow duration of 5 seconds to see what's happening.

➤ In Simulator, choose **Debug ▸ Slow Animations** to turn off the slow animations.

➤ As Live Preview doesn't work well with transition animations, build and run the app.

The default transition does an opacity fade from one view to another.

Fade transition

➤ In `AppLoadingView`, add a modifier to `CardsView()`:

```
.transition(.slide)
```

➤ Build and run to see the slide transition over the specified five second duration.

Slide transition

As well as `opacity` and `slide`, there are a couple more automatic transitions:

- **move**: allows you to specify the edge that the new view moves in from.

- **scale**: the new view scales up.

You can also have a different transition for each direction by using:

```
.transition(.asymmetric(insertion: .slide, removal:.scale))
```

➤ Change the transition to:

```
.transition(.scale(scale: 0, anchor: .top))
```

This will scale the new view in from the top.

➤ Replace `withAnimation(.linear(duration: 5)) {` with:

```
withAnimation {
```

This replaces the five second duration with the default transition duration.

➤ Build and run to see your completed splash screen animation and transition.

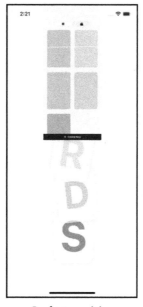

Scale transition

Transition from card list to single card

Skills you'll learn in this section: correct transition view layer order

When you tap a card in the scrolling list of cards, the transition is very abrupt.

➤ Open **CardsView.swift** and add a new modifier to `SingleCardView`:

```
.transition(.move(edge: .bottom))
```

This transition will slide the new view in from the bottom edge. If you build and run the application, no transition animation takes place yet, because you haven't configured which property to animate.

The Boolean property `ViewState.showAllCards` controls which view shows, so you'll locate where this property toggles.

➤ Open **CardsListView.swift** and, in `onTapGesture(count:perform:)`, change `viewState.showAllCards.toggle()` to:

```
withAnimation {
  viewState.showAllCards = false
}
```

When `viewState.showAllCards` changes to false, it will now trigger animation in all places that use this property.

➤ Similarly, open **CardsView.swift**, and in `createButton`, change `viewState.showAllCards = false` to:

```
withAnimation {
  viewState.showAllCards = false
}
```

Creating a new card now also performs the transition.

➤ In the **Views/Single Card Views** group, open **CardToolbar.swift** and locate the **Done** button.

➤ Replace `viewState.showAllCards.toggle()` with:

```
withAnimation {
  viewState.showAllCards = true
}
```

➤ Build and run and choose a card. Although the initial slide transition takes place, the transition when you press **Done** does not work well. The card view transitions behind the list of cards. You can slow the simulator animations to see this better.

Transition behind cards

➤ Open **CardsView.swift** and add a new modifier to `SingleCardView`:

```
.zIndex(1)
```

`zIndex` controls the order of views when they are on top of each other. A view with `zIndex` of 1 will show in front of a view with `zIndex` of 0.

The transition moves the new view behind the old view, so to keep the card view in front, you change `SingleCardView`'s `zIndex` to higher than `CardsListView`'s.

➤ Build and run, and the transition animation from card to list now takes place in front.

Fixed the transition

Supporting multiple view types

Skills you'll learn in this section: picker control

You'll add a picker view to the top of the list of cards to choose how you view the cards. You can either view them in the scrolling list or in a carousel. When you have a set of mutually exclusive values, you can use a picker control to decide between them.

There are various picker styles for mutually exclusive picking. For example, WheelPickerStyle shows the options in a scrollable wheel. Apple's Clock app uses a wheel picker for the Timer. You'll use a SegmentedPickerStyle, which is a horizontal control that holds one value at a time.

Picker with two segments

The carousel

Carousel.swift, included in the starter project in the **Supporting Code** group, is an alternative view for listing the cards. It's a an example of a TabView, similar to the one you created in Section 1.

➤ Open **Carousel.swift** and Live Preview the view. Swipe to view each card.

Carousel

Each card should take up most of the device's screen, so the code uses GeometryReader to determine the size. There should be nothing new to you in this code. One of SwiftUI's great advantages is that you can be given a view like this, and it's an easy matter to slot it into your own code.

Adding a picker

➤ In the **Views** group, under **CardsView.swift**, create a new SwiftUI View file named **ListSelectionView.swift**.

➤ Add a new Binding to ListSelectionView:

```
@Binding var selection: CardListState
```

CardListState is an enumeration in **ViewState.swift** that can take one of two values: list and carousel. selection holds the current picker selection.

➤ Update `ListSelectionView_Previews` to pass the initial selection of `list`:

```
static var previews: some View {
  ListSelectionView(selection: .constant(.list))
}
```

➤ In `ListSelectionView`, replace body with:

```
var body: some View {
  // 1
  Picker(selection: $selection, label: Text("")) {
  // 2
    Image(systemName: "square.grid.2x2.fill")
      .tag(CardListState.list)
    Image(systemName: "rectangle.stack.fill")
      .tag(CardListState.carousel)
  }
  // 3
  .pickerStyle(SegmentedPickerStyle())
  .frame(width: 200)
}
```

Going through this code:

1. You use a `Picker`, passing in the selection property to update.

2. You assign SFSymbols for each option. When the user chooses an option, the `tag(_:)` modifier will update `selection` with the specified value.

3. You tell the `Picker` what picker style to use.

➤ Preview the picker.

Segmented Picker

In the app, when you tap the right segment, the cards should display in the carousel; tapping the left segment will display them in the scrolling list.

➤ Open **CardsView.swift** and embed ZStack in a VStack.

```
VStack {
  ZStack {
    ...
  }
}
```

➤ At the top of VStack, add this code:

```
if viewState.showAllCards {
   ListSelectionView(selection: $viewState.cardListState)
}
```

If you're showing all the cards, show the picker so that you can decide how to view them.

➤ Change CardsListView() to:

```
switch viewState.cardListState {
case .list:
   CardsListView()
case .carousel:
   Carousel()
}
```

You show the scrolling list or the carousel depending on the view state.

➤ Build and run to see the picker in action.

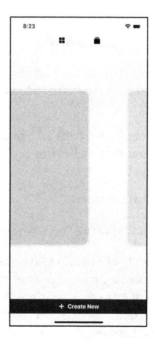

The two card list views

Sharing the card

Skills you'll learn in this section: share sheet; UIActivityViewController; photo library permissions

At the moment, when you create a card, you're the only person that can admire it. As a final feature, you'll add sharing.

You'll create a share button on the navigation bar. On tapping this button, you'll screen capture the card. You'll then use this screenshot in the built-in view controller that provides standard services, commonly called a Share view, for sharing to other apps such as email or your Photos library.

To make it easy to keep track of the sharing state, the starter project added two new properties.

- In **Card.swift**, shareImage will temporarily store the screenshot image for sharing.

- In **ViewState.swift**, shouldScreenshot will trigger a screenshot when set to true.

Currently in SwiftUI, there's not an easy way to create a screenshot, so you'll use a pre-made RenderableView with code in the starter project's **Supporting Code** group.

➤ Open **CardDetailView.swift** and, in body, embed GeometryReader in a new Container by **Command-clicking** GeometryReader and choosing **Embed...** from the resulting menu.

➤ Rename Container to:

```
RenderableView(card: $card)
```

RenderableView is a **@ViewBuilder**, where you send the content view in a closure. You already created a simple container view in Chapter 10, "Refining Your App", and other examples of @ViewBuilders are: VStack, Button and GeometryReader. With ViewModifiers, one view passes through the modifier to create a new view. With @ViewBuilders, however, you can supply multiple views inside the closure and create one new view.

You embed the card content view in `RenderableView`, and this view will take a screenshot when `viewState.shouldScreenshot` is true. `RenderableView` will also save a thumbnail image of the card to disk when the view disappears. You'll use this thumbnail later in this chapter.

➤ Locate:

```
.modifier(CardToolbar(currentModal: $currentModal))
.cardModals(card: $card, currentModal: $currentModal)
```

➤ Cut these two lines and paste them at the end of body, so that they are modifiers on `RenderableView` rather than on `content(size:)`.

Shortly, you'll create a **Share** button in `CardModalViews`, which you call from `cardModals(card:currentModal:)`. You should generally create modal views from as high a level as possible. In this case, if you leave the modifiers on `content(size:)`, the system will get confused and present a second share sheet on top of the first share sheet. You'll also get an uncomfortable message in the debug console: **Presenting view controller from detached view controller...is discouraged**.

➤ In the **Model** group, open **CardModal.swift** and add a new case to `CardModal`:

```
case shareSheet
```

➤ In the **Views ▸ Single Card Views** group, open **CardToolbar.swift**.

➤ Add this code to `toolbar(content:)` with the other `ToolbarItems`:

```
ToolbarItem(placement: .navigationBarLeading) {
  Button(action: {
    viewState.shouldScreenshot = true
    currentModal = .shareSheet
  }) {
    Image(systemName: "square.and.arrow.up")
  }
}
```

Here you create a share button on the leading edge of the navigation bar. When the user taps this button, `viewState.shouldScreenshot` triggers a screenshot in `RenderableView`, which saves the screenshot in `card.shareImage`. The button also sets the current modal to be a share sheet.

➤ In the **Views ▸ Single Card Views** group, open **CardModalViews.swift**.

➤ In body, add a new case to the switch statement:

```
case .shareSheet:
  if let shareImage = card.shareImage {
    ShareSheetView(
      activityItems: [shareImage],
      applicationActivities: nil)
    .onDisappear {
      card.shareImage = nil
    }
  }
```

Here you pass the screenshot to ShareSheetView and show the modal. This view controls a UIActivityViewController inside a UIViewControllerRepresentable and is created for you in **ShareSheetView.swift** in **Supporting Code**.

➤ Open **SingleCardView.swift** and preview the view to see your share button.

The share button

➤ Build and run the app and choose a card. Tap the share sheet icon at the top left. The card view now renders to a screenshot image, which is passed to the share sheet.

➤ Choose **Save Image** to save the image to the photo library.

The share sheet

The app will crash with an error:

```
This app has crashed because it attempted to access privacy-
sensitive data without a usage description.  The app's
Info.plist must contain an NSPhotoLibraryAddUsageDescription key
with a string value explaining to the user how the app uses this
data.
```

Whenever your app first adds an image to the photo library, you must get permission from the user and let them know how you will use the library data.

➤ In the **Project navigator**, choose the top **Cards** group. Choose the target **Cards** and **Info** along the top.

➤ Add a new key `NSPhotoLibraryAddUsageDescription`, or **Privacy - Photo Library Additions Usage Description**.

➤ In the **Value** field, add:

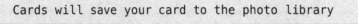

```
Cards will save your card to the photo library
```

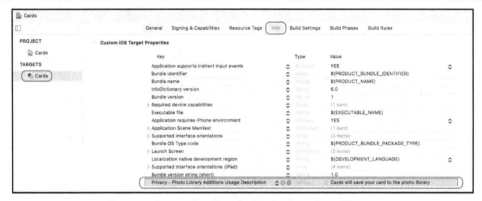

Key to ask user for permission to use photo library

This is the message your users will see, so you might add something soothing about not using their personal data for nefarious purposes.

➤ Build and run the app again and choose a card. Share the card and save the image to the photo library again. This time, the app asks for permission to save to photos, showing the message you entered in the **Info** key.

Asking user for permission to use photo library

➤ Tap **OK** and the card will save to the photo library. Check out the Photos app on the simulator to see your photo library.

Your shared card in the Photos Library

If you run the app on a device with Mail, Messages or any sharing app installed, you can share the image through those, too.

Challenges

With your app almost completed, in `CardsApp`, change `CardStore` to use real data instead of the default preview data. Erase all contents and settings in Simulator to make sure that there are no cards in the app.

Challenge 1: Load the thumbnail image

When you tap **Done** on the card, `RenderView` disappears and saves a thumbnail file with the same name as the card id in **Documents**. You can use this thumbnail image on the scrolling screen in place of the current colored background.

In **CardThumbnailView.swift**, load this image file. There's a `load(uuidString:)` method in **UIImageExtensions**. If the load is successful, show the image. If not, show the card's background color. Enclose the two alternative views in a `Group`, and place the modifiers on the group, rather than on the background color.

The thumbnail image

Challenge 2: Change the text entry modal view

In the **Supporting Code** group, you'll find an enhanced Text Entry view called **TextView.swift**, that lets users pick fonts and colors when they enter text. There is a list of some of the fonts available on iOS in **AppFonts.swift**.

First, preview and examine `TextView` and make sure you understand it. SwiftUI views look complicated, but you have encountered almost everything in this file before.

Your challenge is to add this view to the modal view `TextPicker` under the current `TextField`.

With the new font and color, style the text currently being entered in the `TextField`. Use `.font(.custom(textElement.textFont, size: 30))` to style the font.

Run the app in Simulator to test the view, as the text element does not update with the font and color in preview.

Text entry with fonts and colors

When you've completed these challenges, you should be well pleased with yourself. You've worked hard to construct an app with some very tricky features. Don't rest on your laurels, though. You still have Section 3 to work through!

Key points

- Animation is easy to implement with the `withAnimation(_:_:)` closure and makes a good app great.

- You can animate explicitly with `withAnimation(_:_:)` or implicitly per view with the `animation(_:)` modifier.

- Transitions are also easy with the `transition(_:)` modifier. Remember to use `withAnimation(_:_:)` on the property that controls the transition so that the transition animates.

- Picker views allow the user to pick one of a set of values. You can have a wheel style picker or a segmented style picker.

- Using the built-in `UIActivityViewController` inside a `UIViewControllerRepresentable`, it's easy to share or print an image.

Where to go from here?

You probably want to animate everything possible now. The book *iOS Animation by Tutorials* is available with the Pro subscription at https://bit.ly/3roiqMa and has two chapters fully dedicated to animations and transitions with SwiftUI.

A great example of an app with complex layout and animation is Apple's Fruta sample app at https://apple.co/2XE8tNF. This is a fully featured app where "Users can order smoothies, save favorite drinks, collect rewards, and browse recipes." Fruta also has various features, such as widgets, which you'll learn about in Section 3. Download the app and see if you can work out how it all fits together.

Section III: Your third app: RWFreeView

You've now built two apps with beautiful user interfaces. But, you're probably wondering how to build an app that accesses resources on the internet. Fear not! In this section, you'll build RWFreeView, an app that allows you to view all the free video episodes on raywenderlich.com. Along the way, you'll:

- Learn how to build lists of information and navigate between views using SwiftUI.

- Discover the intricacies of REST APIs and how to use them.

- Explore iOS's networking support using a Swift Playground.

- Learn to how add support for iOS Widgets to your app.

Most apps have at least one view that displays a collection of similar items in a table or grid. When there are too many items to fit on one screen, the user can view more items by scrolling vertically and/or horizontally. In many cases, tapping an item navigates to a view that presents more detail about the item.

In this section, you'll create the **RWFreeView** app. It fetches information about free raywenderlich.com video episodes and streams them for playback in the app. Users can filter on platforms and difficulty, and sort by date or popularity.

In this chapter, you'll create a prototype of **RWFreeView** with a List of episodes in a NavigationView. Tapping a list item pushes a detail view onto the navigation stack. The starter project already contains **PlayerView.swift**, which displays a VideoPlayer, like the one in HIITFit. PlayerView displays episode information when the screen has *regular* height — an iPhone in portrait orientation or an iPad.

Getting started

Open the **RWFreeView** app in the **starter** folder. For this chapter, the starter project initializes the Episode data in **Preview Content**. In Chapter 24, "Downloading Data", you'll fetch this data from api.raywenderlich.com.

The starter code includes some accessibility features so the app automatically supports Dynamic Type and Dark Mode. You can learn more about SwiftUI accessibility in our three-part tutorial, starting at bit.ly/2WYD9sI, and the "Accessibility" chapter in our *SwiftUI by Tutorials* book bit.ly/32oFTCs.

List

The SwiftUI `List` view is the easiest way to present a collection of items in a view that scrolls vertically. You can display individual views *and* loop over arrays within the same `List`. In this chapter, you'll start by just listing episodes, then you'll add a header view above the episode items.

To present a list of episodes, the syntax looks a lot like `ForEach`.

➤ In **ContentView.swift**, replace the contents of `ContentView` with the following code:

```
@StateObject private var store = EpisodeStore()

var body: some View {
  List(store.episodes, id: \.name) { episode in
    EpisodeView(episode: episode)
  }
}
```

You initialize `EpisodeStore`, which creates a sample `episodes` array. Then you tell `List` to loop over `episodes` and you provide an `id`. Like `ForEach`, `List` expects each item to have an identifier, so it knows which item is in which row. The argument `\.name` tells `List` that each item is identified by that property value.

Creating a gradient background

`EpisodeView` is already defined in **EpisodeView.swift** to display useful information about the episode. It contains an icon to indicate that selecting it will play the video. The `PlayButtonIcon` background is a custom color:

Play button icon with solid color background

It's not hard to guess what you're going to do next. You'll change the background to a gradient that goes from dark to light, horizontally across the icon.

➤ In **PlayButtonIcon.swift**, add this property to PlayButtonIcon:

```
let gradientColors = Gradient(
  colors: [Color.gradientDark, Color.gradientLight])
```

You specify the colors that make up the gradient. You can use as many colors as you like. For this small icon, two colors are enough.

> **Note:** I defined these colors in the assets catalog **Assets.xcassets/colors**. The designer picked these colors to look good in both light and dark appearance, so each custom color has only a *Universal* setting. In **ColorExtension.swift**, I add gradientDark and gradientLight to the standard Color values.

➤ Now replace .fill(Color.gradientDark) with the following:

```
.fill(
  LinearGradient(
    gradient: gradientColors,
    startPoint: .leading,
    endPoint: .trailing))
```

You supply an array of gradient colors. This is a LinearGradient, so you supply start and end *points*. These values apply the gradient along the icon's horizontal axis, grading from dark on the leading edge to light on the trailing edge.

Play button icon with gradient background

Other start and end points create gradients along different axes, for example, *vertically* from top to bottom or *diagonally* from topLeading to bottomTrailing.

There are two other types of gradient: RadialGradient grades from the start *radius* to the end *radius*, and AngularGradient grades from the start *angle* to the end *angle*.

Adapting to Dark Mode automatically

EpisodeView uses standard system and UI element colors to automatically adapt when users turn on **Dark Mode** and built-in text styles like headline to support **Dynamic Type**. Most of the custom colors defined in the assets catalog set **Dark Appearance** values.

> **Note**: Apple's **Human Interface Guidelines ▸ Visual Design ▸ Color** apple.co/39GwXvn shows system colors for dark and light modes and lists UI element colors. And **Human Interface Guidelines ▸ Visual Design ▸ Typography** apple.co/39HydhD has a table of text styles, weights and sizes.

EpisodeView also uses AdaptingStack to switch from HStack to VStack when the user selects **Larger Text** in **Settings**. AdaptingStack comes from code presented in WWDC 2019 Session 412: Debugging in Xcode 11 (apple.co/3u0kr2z).

➤ In **ContentView.swift**, use the preview inspector to switch **Color Scheme** to **Dark** or, in previews, add this modifier to ContentView():

```
.preferredColorScheme(.dark)
```

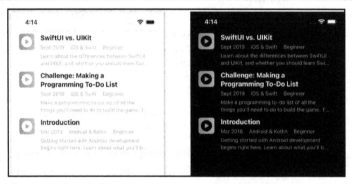

UIColor system and element colors automatically adapt to Dark Mode.

➤ Switch **Color Scheme** back to **Light** or, in previews, comment out .preferredColorScheme(.dark).

NavigationView

In Chapter 15, "Structures, Classes & Protocols", you used NavigationView so you could add toolbar buttons to CardDetailView. Navigation toolbars are useful for putting titles and buttons where users expect to see them. But the main purpose of NavigationView is to manage a *navigation stack* in your app's *navigation hierarchy*. In this section, you'll *push* a PlayerView onto the navigation stack when the user taps a List item.

Start by adding a navigation bar with a title.

➤ In **ContentView.swift**, embed List in NavigationView and modify it to set the screen's title:

```
NavigationView {
  List(store.episodes, id: \.name) { episode in
    EpisodeView(episode: episode)
  }
  .navigationTitle("Videos")
}
```

Notice navigationTitle modifies List, not NavigationView. A NavigationView can contain alternative root views, each with its own .navigationTitle and toolbars.

Note: navigationTitle replaces navigationBarTitle, which is deprecated.

➤ Refresh the preview. By default, you get a large title:

Navigation title defaults to large title.

Modifying the navigation bar

The Figma design for this app calls for a black navigation bar in both light and dark color schemes.

➤ Add the following method to `ContentView`, below body:

```
init() {
  // 1
  let appearance = UINavigationBarAppearance()
  appearance.backgroundColor = UIColor(named: "top-bkgd")
  appearance.largeTitleTextAttributes =
    [.foregroundColor: UIColor.white]
  appearance.titleTextAttributes =
    [.foregroundColor: UIColor.white]

  // 2
  UINavigationBar.appearance().tintColor = .white

  // 3
  UINavigationBar.appearance().standardAppearance = appearance
  UINavigationBar.appearance().compactAppearance = appearance
  UINavigationBar.appearance().scrollEdgeAppearance = appearance

  // 4
  UISegmentedControl.appearance()
    .selectedSegmentTintColor = UIColor(named: "list-bkgd")
}
```

As a structure, `ContentView` has a default initializer, so you usually don't have to write an `init()` method. In this case, you need to set some attributes that you can't access with SwiftUI. SwiftUI doesn't yet have an API to modify the appearance of the navigation bar, so you have to fall back on UIKit's `UINavigationBarAppearance` to configure its attributes.

1. You create an instance of `UINavigationBarAppearance` then set the background color to almost-black and, for both large and standard size titles, you set text color to white.

2. `UINavigationBarAppearance` doesn't have a `tintColor` property, so you set it in the `UIAppearance` proxy of the underlying `UINavigationBar`. This setting affects the color of the back button text and back arrow.

3. You assign your `UINavigationBarAppearance` configuration to all three appearances of `UINavigationBar`: standard-height, compact-height and when the edge of scrollable content reaches the matching edge of the navigation bar.

4. You'll soon add a header view with a segmented control. Here, you set the color of the selected segment to match the color you'll use for the list background.

➤ Refresh the preview:

Navigation bar with black background in light color mode

Now you're all set to navigate to `PlayerView` and add a toolbar button.

Navigating to a detail view

To see that back button you tinted white, you'll navigate to the video player view when the user taps a list item.

➤ In the List closure, replace EpisodeView(episode: episode) with this:

```
NavigationLink(destination: PlayerView(episode: episode)) {
  EpisodeView(episode: episode)
}
```

You embed the content view of the List row in a NavigationLink and set the destination to PlayerView.

➤ Live-preview ContentView and tap an item:

Navigation link to PlayerView

Each List row acquires a *disclosure indicator*, telling the user there's more to see.

ContentView is currently the only view in the navigation stack. When you tap an item, NavigationView *pushes* PlayerView onto the navigation stack: It's now the top view on the stack, so it's the view that's visible.

NavigationView gives you a "back" button, labeled the same as the root view's navigationTitle. Because you set UINavigationBar.appearance().tintColor to white, the back button's arrow and "Videos" label are both white.

AVPlayer takes care of streaming the video from its remote location. The episode's title slide appears when the video is ready to play.

Now PlayerView needs a navigation title.

➤ In **PlayerView.swift**, add these two modifiers to the top-level VStack:

```
.navigationTitle(episode.name)
.navigationBarTitleDisplayMode(.inline)
```

You use the episode's name as the title for this view, and you specify a centered normal size title to override the default large title.

You don't embed the VStack in NavigationView because PlayerView is in the navigation stack controlled by the NavigationView in ContentView.

If you want the *preview* of PlayerView to display the navigation title, embed it in NavigationView.

➤ In **PlayerView.swift**, in previews, wrap PlayerView in NavigationView:

```
NavigationView {
   PlayerView(episode: store.episodes[0])
}
```

The portrait-orientation preview now displays the navigation title.

➤ In **ContentView.swift**, run live-preview and tap an item:

PlayerView with navigation title

➤ Tap the back button to *pop* this view off the navigation stack, revealing `ContentView` again.

Opening the real page in a browser

There's an even easier way to play the video. Here's how you open the raywenderlich.com page in the device's default browser.

➤ In **ContentView.swift**, comment out the `NavigationLink(...) { ... }` code and type the following code in its place:

```
Link(destination: URL(string: episode.linkURLString)!) {
  EpisodeView(episode: episode)
}
```

The `Link` control opens its destination URL in the associated app. You create the URL from the `Episode` computed property `linkUrlString`, which is just a redirect URL:

```
let uri: String  // redirects to the real web page
var linkURLString: String {
  "https://www.raywenderlich.com/redirect?uri=" + uri
}
```

The associated app is Safari (in a simulator) or your device's default browser.

➤ Build and run in the simulator or on your device. Tap an item to open the video's web page in Safari or your device's default browser:

Open episode's raywenderlich.com page.

Link takes users from your app to their browser app, giving them access to their browser settings and saved passwords. They can easily sign in, explore the site and even make purchases, without sharing any secure data or history with your app.

> **Note**: If you see a note that a newer version exists, it's because this older version has been around longer, so has had more views.

➤ To return to your app, tap the **RWFreeView** back button.

➤ Comment out or delete the Link(...) { ... } code and uncomment the NavigationLink code.

Navigation toolbar button

Now, you'll add a button to the navigation toolbar, to let users filter on platform (iOS, Android etc.) and difficulty (Beginner, Intermediate, Advanced).

➤ Add this code below `.navigationTitle("Videos")`:

```
.toolbar {
  ToolbarItem {
    Button(action: { }) {
      Image(systemName: "line.horizontal.3.decrease.circle")
        .accessibilityLabel(Text("Shows filter options"))
    }
  }
}
```

Just like you did in Chapter 15, "Structures, Classes & Protocols", you add a `Button` as a `ToolbarItem` to the `toolbar`. The button uses the default placement on the trailing side of the toolbar. You'll soon fill in the button's `action`.

The button's label is an SF Symbol that represents a filter, but the `systemName` gives no indication of this purpose. You could write a comment to remind yourself what it is, but it's just as easy to supply the information as an accessibility label for VoiceOver to read out.

➤ Live-preview `ContentView`: You should see a filter icon in the upper right corner:

Filter toolbar button

Now for some action! The starter project already has a `FilterOptionsView`, and you know the drill to make the button present it as a modal sheet.

➤ First, add this `State` property to `ContentView`:

```
@State private var showFilters = false
```

➤ Then, add this `Button` action to your new toolbar button:

```
showFilters.toggle()
```

➤ Finally, add this modifier after the `toolbar` closure:

```
.sheet(isPresented: $showFilters) {
  FilterOptionsView()
}
```

➤ Live-preview `ContentView`. Tap the filter button to see the filter options:

Filter options

Selecting a button changes its color to green. You'll implement these filters in Chapter 24, "Downloading Data".

> **Note:** To support **Dynamic Type**, `FilterOptionsView` uses built-in text styles like `title2` and also uses `AdaptingStack` to switch from `HStack` to `VStack` when the user selects **Larger Text** in **Settings**.

➤ Tap the close button or **Apply** to dismiss this modal sheet.

Header view

Apps that download and display results from a server often include features like these:

1. Let users enter a search term.

2. Display any filters the user has set, and let the user remove one or all of them without showing `FilterOptionsView`.

3. Let users select the sort order: newest or most popular.

4. Display the number of fetched episodes.

A common solution is to add a header above the list. It would be natural to use a `VStack` for this:

➤ In **ContentView.swift**, embed the `List` in a `VStack`, then add `HeaderView` before the `List`:

```
VStack {
  HeaderView(count: store.episodes.count)
  List(store.episodes, id: \.name) { episode in
```

➤ Check that `navigationTitle` etc. modify `VStack`, not `List`: Collapse `ToolbarItem` to help you see where `VStack` ends, then move the closing brace of `VStack` to the line above `.navigationTitle("Videos")`.

```
var body: some View {
   NavigationView {
      VStack {
         HeaderView(count: store.episodes.count)
         List(store.episodes, id: \.name) { episode in
            NavigationLink(destination: PlayerView(episode: episode)) {
               EpisodeView(episode: episode)
            }
         }
      }
      .navigationTitle("Videos")
      .toolbar {
         ToolbarItem { ••• }
      }
   }
}
```

Move VStack closing brace.

`NavigationView` has some odd bugs that show up at this point. The easiest fix is non-intuitive.

➤ Add this modifier to `NavigationView`:

```
.navigationViewStyle(StackNavigationViewStyle())
```

➤ Refresh the preview:

VStack with HeaderView and List

Not great. `HeaderView` is way too big. You could try to address this issue with modifiers, but there's a much easier way.

Remember this `List` feature? You can display individual views *and* loop over arrays within the same `List`. The trick is to use `ForEach` to loop over `episodes`.

➤ Replace `List` with `ForEach` then replace `VStack` with `List`:

```
List {
  HeaderView(count: store.episodes.count)
  ForEach(store.episodes, id: \.name) { episode in
    NavigationLink(destination: PlayerView(episode: episode)) {
      EpisodeView(episode: episode)
    }
  }
}
```

`List` can show any list of views, but inside a `List`, you need `ForEach` to iterate over the `episodes` array. You'll soon see that `ForEach` lets you customize each row too.

➤ Refresh the preview:

List with HeaderView and ForEach

That's much better!

> **Note**: Thanks to Mojtaba Hosseini for the nifty `cornerRadius(_:corners:)` extension used to round only the bottom corners of `HeaderView`.

Your list and navigation are working. There's just one last feature to add.

Page size menu

`HeaderView` displays the number of fetched episodes. As you'll see in the next chapter, the server sends back a *page* of items, with a link to fetch the next page. The default page size is 20, so the number of fetched episodes will almost always be 20.

You'll add a menu to let users change this number.

➤ In **HeaderView.swift**, in the `HStack` containing `Text`, `Spacer` and `Picker`, add this `Menu` between `Text` and `Spacer`:

```
Menu("\(Image(systemName: "filemenu.and.cursorarrow"))") {
  Button("10 results/page") { }
  Button("20 results/page") { }
  Button("30 results/page") { }
  Button("No change") { }
}
```

`Menu` is like the `contextMenu` you used in Chapter 15, "Structures, Classes & Protocols", to delete a card element — in fact, it uses `contextMenu` under the hood — but it's a button. The user doesn't have to long-press it.

You'll fill in the button actions in Chapter 24, "Downloading Data".

➤ In **ContentView.swift**, refresh the preview and tap your new button:

Page size menu

Custom design

Now it's time to customize the list to match the Figma design.

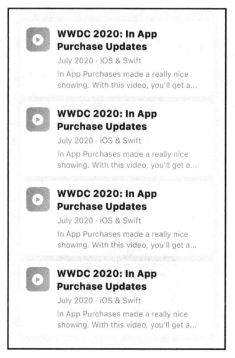

Figma design

The Figma design configures each `List` row as a "card" with rounded corners and a shadow. There's a small space between cards, but no list separator. And there are no disclosure indicators.

Creating a card

➤ In **EpisodeView.swift**, add these modifiers to the top-level HStack to make it look like a card:

```
.padding(10)
.background(Color.itemBkgd)
.cornerRadius(15)
.shadow(color: Color.black.opacity(0.1), radius: 10)
```

You add padding around the text and set the background color to white (Any Appearance) or a dark gray (Dark Appearance). This will make it, and its shadow, stand out against the List background, which you'll soon set to light gray (Any Appearance) or almost black (Dark Appearance).

You round the corners, then set a shadow.

➤ In **ContentView.swift**, refresh the preview:

List of cards

That's a good start. The items look like cards, so now you don't need the separator lines.

Hiding the list separator lines

You'll hide the list separator lines by tweaking the row content.

➤ In **ContentView.swift**, add these modifiers to `NavigationLink( ... ) { ... }`:

```
.frame(
  maxWidth: .infinity,
  maxHeight: .infinity,
  alignment: .leading)
.listRowInsets(EdgeInsets())
.padding(.bottom, 8)
.padding([.leading, .trailing], 20)
.background(Color.listBkgd)
```

Note: This is very similar to the code that extends the background color of **HeaderView** to the edges of the **List** row.

You expand the `frame` of each row and set all `EdgeInsets` to zero. Then, you add padding to separate the cards from each other and move them in from the sides. Finally, you set the `List` background to gray.

➤ Refresh the preview:

Hidden list separator lines

Great, no more separator lines!

> **Note**: Even if you didn't have to accommodate `HeaderView`, you'd need to
> switch to `List { ForEach ... }` to customize the list rows like this. `ForEach`
> functions like a view *generator*. Without `ForEach`, you can't even modify the
> row background color: `listRowBackground(_:)` has no effect unless it's
> inside a `ForEach` closure.

Now that you've customized the `List` row, it no longer changes color when the user
taps it. But the disclosure indicator on the trailing edge of each `List` row shows it's
tappable, so it's not too much of a problem.

Hiding the disclosure indicator

However... the disclosure indicator pushes the "card" out of alignment with the
header view. And the Figma design wants it gone. So here's how you hide it.

➤ In `ContentView`, replace `NavigationLink( ... ) { ... }` with the following:

```
ZStack {
  NavigationLink(destination: PlayerView(episode: episode)) {
  }
  EpisodeView(episode: episode)
}
```

You embed `NavigationLink` in a `ZStack`, making sure the separator-hiding
modifiers modify the `ZStack`, which is now the contents of the `List` row. Then you
move `EpisodeView(episode: episode)` *out* of the `NavigationLink` closure, but
still *inside* the `ZStack`.

`EpisodeView` isn't in `NavigationLink`, so doesn't have a disclosure indicator. The
`NavigationLink` destination is unchanged, so tapping the row still displays
`PlayerView`.

➤ Live-preview `ContentView` and tap an item to make sure the navigation link still works.

Hidden disclosure indicators

Actually, `NavigationLink` still displays a disclosure indicator, but it's *almost* covered by the `EpisodeView` layered on top.

➤ To reveal the disclosure indicators lurking beneath, reduce the opacity of `EpisodeView`:

```
EpisodeView(episode: episode)
    .opacity(0.2)
```

➤ Refresh the preview:

Disclosure indicator still visible

Yup, they're still there. Depending on what you present in the row, you might not cover them completely. You don't want to have to compromise your design just to hide these indicators, so here's a solution that works for whatever row content you have.

➤ Add this modifier to `NavigationLink( ... ) { ... }`:

```
.opacity(0)
```

Disclosure indicators not visible

You make the `NavigationLink` view transparent, so it's not visible at all!

➤ Remove `.opacity(0.2)` from `EpisodeView(episode: episode)`.

There are just two fine points to take care of:

1. Your future self, or someone who takes over your code, might wonder why there's nothing in the `NavigationLink` closure and might move `EpisodeView(episode: episode)` back inside.

2. There's no visual feedback when the user taps the row.

➤ To solve the first issue, add this view inside the `NavigationLink` closure:

```
EmptyView()
```

You explicitly display an empty view, so you know you did it on purpose.

➤ For the second issue, add this modifier to `NavigationLink( ... ) { ... }`:

```
.buttonStyle(PlainButtonStyle())
```

You apply `PlainButtonStyle()`, which shows a *tiny* visual effect when you tap a `List` row.

➤ Live-preview your app and try it out to make sure everything still works.

Running RWFreeView on iPad

There's just one more thing: Check how your app looks on an iPad.

➤ If you have this modifier on `NavigationView` to fix the `navigationTitle` bug, comment it out:

```
.navigationViewStyle(StackNavigationViewStyle())
```

➤ Build and run on an iPad simulator:

Default split view on iPad

The default navigation style on iPads is double-column, with the list in a sidebar. This is also the default style on Max iPhones in landscape orientation. When the app launches, it presents an almost-blank screen. You can specify an initial selected item to appear on launch.

➤ In **ContentView.swift**, add this line after `.navigationTitle("Videos")`:

```
PlayerView(episode: store.episodes[0])
```

➤ Build and run again:

App displays first video on launch.

Now the app launches with a `PlayerView` presenting the first episode.

But for RWFreeView, you'll *prevent* your app from using this default style.

➤ Delete or comment out `PlayerView(episode: store.episodes[0])` then add (or restore) this modifier to `NavigationView { ... }`:

```
.navigationViewStyle(StackNavigationViewStyle())
```

You tell the app to always use stack navigation on iPads and Max iPhones. This is the default navigation style for iPhones in portrait orientation and for non-Max iPhones in landscape orientation.

➤ Build and run again to see the List, just like on an iPhone. Then rotate to landscape:

List in landscape orientation

Yikes! In landscape orientation, the width of EpisodeView varies with the length of description. But the Figma design wants the List rows to be narrower than the iPad screen anyway, even in portrait orientation. Fixing the width at 644 allows 85 (footnote-size) characters per line, which is a comfortable reading width for most people.

➤ In **EpisodeView.swift**, add these properties to EpisodeView:

```
@Environment(\.verticalSizeClass) var
  verticalSizeClass: UserInterfaceSizeClass?
@Environment(\.horizontalSizeClass) var
  horizontalSizeClass: UserInterfaceSizeClass?
var isIPad: Bool {
  horizontalSizeClass == .regular &&
    verticalSizeClass == .regular
}
```

You check the device's vertical and horizontal size classes. If both are regular, the device is an iPad.

➤ Now add this modifier to the top-level HStack, after padding(10):

```
.frame(width: isIPad ? 644 : nil)
```

You set width to 644 if the device is an iPad. Otherwise, you let the view set its own width.

➤ Build and run again on an iPad and check portrait and landscape orientations:

Fixed-width list on iPad

Looking good! Now you're all set to learn how to download data from a server, after the next chapter, which covers some HTTP and REST API basics.

Key points

- The SwiftUI `List` view is the easiest way to present a collection of items in a view that scrolls vertically. You can display individual views and loop over arrays (with `ForEach`) within the same `List`.

- `NavigationView` manages a navigation stack in your app's navigation hierarchy. Tapping a `NavigationLink` pushes its destination view onto the navigation stack. Tapping the back button pops this view off the navigation stack.

- A `NavigationView` can contain alternative root views. You modify each with its own `navigationTitle` and toolbars.

- Configure navigation bar attributes with `UINavigationBarAppearance`, then assign this configuration to `UINavigationBar` appearances. Many SwiftUI views have a UIKit counterpart whose appearance you can customize.

- It's easy to open a web link in the device's default browser using `Link`.

Chapter 23: Just Enough Web Stuff

By Audrey Tam

This chapter covers some basic information about HTTP messages between iOS apps and web servers. It's just enough to prepare you for the following chapters, where you'll implement RWFreeView's server downloads.

There's no SwiftUI in this chapter.

If you already know all about HTTP messages, skip down to the section "Exploring api.raywenderlich.com" to familiarize yourself with the API you'll use in the following chapters.

Servers and resources

HTTP requests and responses between client and server

Many apps communicate with computers on the internet to access databases and other resources. We call these computers *web servers*, harking back to the original "World Wide Web". Or *cloud servers* because nowadays everything is "in the Cloud". "Host" is another term for "server".

Apps like Safari and RWFreeView are *clients* of these servers. A client sends a *request* to a server, which sends back a *response*. This communication consists of plain-text messages that conform to the Hypertext Transfer Protocol (**HTTP**). Hypertext is structured text that uses hyperlinks between nodes containing text. Web pages are written in HyperText Markup Language (HTML).

HTTP has several methods, including POST, GET, PUT and DELETE. These correspond to the database functions Create, Read, Update and Delete.

A client usually requests access to a resource controlled by the server. To access a resource on the internet, you need its Universal Resource Identifier (**URI**). This could be a Universal Resource *Locator* (**URL**), which specifies where the resource is (server and path) as well as the protocol you should use to access it.

For example, **https://raywenderlich.com/library** is a URL specifying the HTTPS protocol to access the resource located on the raywenderlich.com server with the path library. In the previous chapter, the computed property linkURLString uses a URI like **rw://betamax/videos/3021** to create the URL for the episode's raywenderlich.com page.

> **Note**: **HTTPS** is the secure, encrypted version of HTTP. It protects your users from eavesdropping. The underlying protocol is the same but, instead of transferring plain-text messages, everything is encrypted before it leaves the client or server.

HTTP messages

A client's HTTP **request** message contains *headers*. A POST or PUT request has a *body* to contain the new or updated data. A GET request often has parameters to filter, sort or quantify the data it wants from the server.

A server's HTTP **response** message also has headers and a body. A key part of the response is the **status code** — ideally, **200 OK** in response to a GET request or **201 Created** in response to a POST request. You don't want to see any error status codes like **404 Not Found**:

GitHub's 404 page

There are many many HTTP response status codes. You'll find a fun representation of them at http.cat. For example:

418 I'm a teapot

Mozilla (mzl.la/3o6qWNM) provides more conventional descriptions of status codes:

*The HTTP **418 I'm a teapot** client error response code indicates that the server refuses to brew coffee because it is, permanently, a teapot. A combined coffee/tea pot that is temporarily out of coffee should instead return 503. This error is a reference to Hyper Text Coffee Pot Control Protocol defined in April Fools' jokes in 1998 and 2014. Some websites use this response for requests they do not wish to handle, such as automated queries.*

> **Note**: The 1998 HTCPCP (bit.ly/3olM42q) April Fools' joke was inspired by the Trojan Room coffee pot (bit.ly/3pkCDSb), the subject of the world's first web cam. It was set up in 1991, long before the Internet of Things (IoT).

If an HTTP message has a body, it also has a **Content-Type** header. Content-Type specifies the internet media type of the data in the HTTP message body.

Usually, you'll work with three content types for *text data*, depending on the structure:

- **JSON** (JavaScript Object Notation) is the most common data format used for HTTP communication by app clients. It's a structured data format consisting of numbers, strings and arrays and dictionaries that can contain strings, numbers and nested arrays and dictionaries.

- Web forms use **form-encoded**, which looks like a query string. A query string is a collection of key-value pairs, separated by & and preceded by ?.

- Web pages are **HTML**.

When working with *binary data* some of the most used types are: PDF, image formats and multi-part form data, when the client sends any kind of binary file along with text elements.

REST API

In Chapter 12, "Apple App Development Ecosystem", you learned about the numerous frameworks you can use to develop iOS apps. An Apple framework is one kind of Application Programming Interface (**API**). It tells you how to use the standard components created by Apple engineers.

Another kind of API is the set of rules for clients to request resources from a server. Most of the APIs you'll use for your apps are REST APIs, which use HTTP. For each resource available on the server, the REST API documentation tells you how to construct a request:

- The resource's URL, called its *endpoint*.

- Which HTTP method to use.

- Which HTTP headers to include.

- What to put in the request body.

> **Note**: REST is the acronym of "REpresentational State Transfer", the name created by Roy Fielding for the architectural style underlying the World Wide Web. The term describes how a well-designed Web application works: A user selects a resource identifier from a network of Web resources (a virtual state-machine) and uses methods like GET or POST to create a state transition that transfers the resource's representation to the user.

In the next chapter, you'll set up RWFreeView to communicate with the REST API **api.raywenderlich.com**. In this chapter, you'll explore this API's documentation at raywenderlich.docs.apiary.io.

Sending and receiving HTTP messages

Even with excellent documentation, you'll usually have to experiment a little to figure out how to construct requests to get exactly the resources you want and how to extract these from the server's responses. So how do you send requests and examine responses?

Browser

The easiest way to make a simple HTTP GET request is to enter the URL in a browser app like Safari.

➤ Enter this URL in your favorite browser:

```
https://www.raywenderlich.com/library
```

This is the endpoint of the raywenderlich.com library. You get a page similar to this:

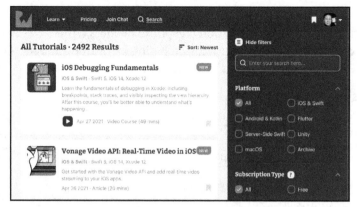

HTTP response to raywenderlich.com/library request

This is the body of the server's response, but you don't get to see the headers. And, you can't do much more than a simple GET request.

cURL

A browser is a fully-automated HTTP tool. At the other end of the spectrum is the command-line tool **cURL** (curl.se) — "the internet transfer backbone for thousands of software applications".

The documentation for a REST API often provides sample requests to show you how to use it. Very often, these use cURL.

➤ Open **Terminal** and enter this command:

```
curl https://api.github.com/zen
```

You send an HTTP request to GitHub's API server. The response is a random item from their design philosophies, like "Favor focus over features" or "Avoid administrative distraction".

There are lots more request examples at GitHub's *Getting started with the REST API* ([bit.ly/3iD717R](bit.ly/3iD717R)).

But, you exclaim, curl doesn't show any response headers either! Well, like all Unix commands, curl has a wealth of options, including --include and its shortcut -i, to include the HTTP response headers in its output.

➤ Enter this command:

```
curl -i https://api.github.com/zen
```

And you see quite a lot more output:

```
HTTP/2 200
server: GitHub.com
date: Tue, 27 Apr 2021 01:40:56 GMT
content-type: text/plain;charset=utf-8

...

x-ratelimit-limit: 60
x-ratelimit-remaining: 58
x-ratelimit-reset: 1619491224
x-ratelimit-used: 2
accept-ranges: bytes
x-github-request-id: EF14:706C:A3D763:B0E977:60876BA7

Avoid administrative distraction.
```

Headers beginning with **x-** are custom headers set up by the organization. For example, x-ratelimit-limit and x-ratelimit-used indicate how many requests a client can make in a rolling time period (typically an hour) and how many of those requests the client has already made.

The curl --verbose or -v option displays *request* headers and a *lot* more.

➤ Enter this command:

```
curl -v https://api.github.com/zen
```

Replacing -i with -v produces quite a lot more output — every handshake interaction between the terminal and the server, the encryption algorithms used, the server certificate details, as well as the response headers. The *request* headers are just the five lines that start with >:

```
> GET /zen HTTP/2
> Host: api.github.com
```

```
> User-Agent: curl/7.64.1
> Accept: */*
>
```

Lines that start with < are *response* headers, and lines that start with * are additional information provided by cURL.

You might not enjoy typing long structured command lines, especially something like this sample cURL command to create a new GitHub repository:

```
curl -i -H \
  "Authorization: token
5199831f4dd3b79e7c5b7e0ebe75d67aa66e79d4" \
  -d '{ \
    "name": "blog", \
    "auto_init": true, \
    "private": true, \
    "gitignore_template": "nanoc" \
  }' \
  https://api.github.com/user/repos
```

This POST command sends authorization data in a request header and the request body as data in JSON format. The endpoint doesn't name a specific user because GitHub knows that from the token value.

Another problem with using cURL: If the response is complex, it's hard to examine it in the terminal.

➤ Enter this command:

```
curl https://api.raywenderlich.com/api/contents
```

This is a request to the API you'll use for RWFreeView. The response is pretty mind-numbing:

Response body using cURL

If you concentrate, you *might* be able to see from this output that the response body is a dictionary where the first value `"data"` is an array of dictionaries. You can use a tool like codebeautify.org/jsonviewer to format this so it's easier to read.

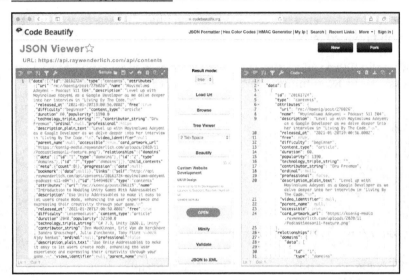

Response body at codebeautify.org/jsonviewer

But there's a better solution: apps that make your HTTP messaging easier.

Exploring api.raywenderlich.com

Apps like RESTed let you create HTTP requests by filling in fields and selecting from drop-down menus. You can pretty-print responses and use syntax highlighting.

➤ In a browser, open apple.co/3cb5CnP, click **View in Mac App Store** and install the app.

Requesting contents

➤ Open **RESTed** and replace `http://localhost:3000/` with this URL:

```
https://api.raywenderlich.com/api/contents
```

You set the *resource endpoint*. How do you know what to ask for? Look through the table of contents sidebar at raywenderlich.docs.apiary.io: In the **References** section, **/contents** sounds like the most general, highest level of data.

How do you know what to write in front of **/contents**? Select **/contents** then scroll down to find this gray field with **200 OK** and a disclosure indicator:

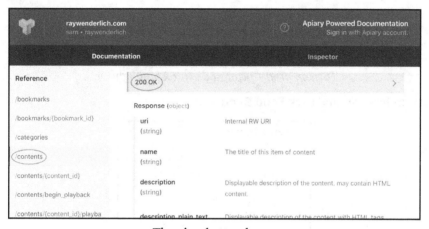

There's a button here...

➤ It's a button: click it!

The request endpoint

A sidebar opens, showing the **Request**. This sidebar has lots of features. You'll see some of them soon.

➤ Back in RESTed, leave the **GET** method selected. Open preferences and check the boxes for **Pretty-print response** and **Apply syntax highlighting**:

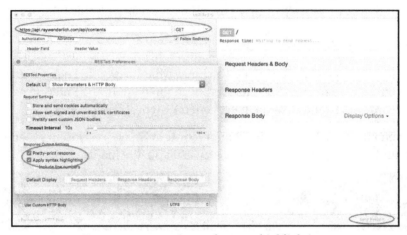

Turn on pretty-print and syntax highlighting.

➤ Close preferences and click **Send Request**.

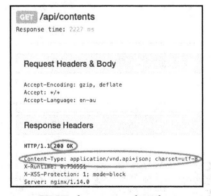

RESTed response headers

And here's the response time, the request headers, response headers with status code **200 OK**.

Content-Type is `application/vnd.api+json; charset=utf-8`. The key information here is **json**. This tells you how to decode the response body.

> **Note**: **UTF-8** string encoding is a version of Unicode that is very efficient for storing regular text, but less so for special symbols or non-Western alphabets. Still, it's the most popular way to deal with Unicode text today.

➤ Scroll down to view the **response body**.

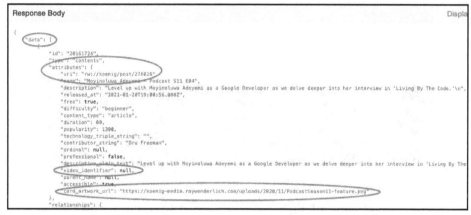

RESTed response body

Scrolling through the response body, it's much easier to see the top level dictionary with four keys: `data`, `included`, `links` and `meta`. The information you need for your app is in the `data` value, which is an array of dictionaries.

Each dictionary in the array contains the `attributes` for one content item. bit.ly/ 3sMFjdy describes these attributes. In the next chapter, you'll use `JSONDecoder` to extract the attributes you want and store them in the `Episode` structure so you can display them in RWFreeView.

Media URLs

➤ Notice that `card_artwork_url` is a URL. Go ahead and copy-paste one of these URLs in RESTed and send the request.

RESTed: Card artwork

The response header **Content-Type** is now `image/png` and the **Server** is `AmazonS3`. (The server for the contents response is `nginx`.) RESTed is able to display the image.

You've already used the `uri` attribute to open an episode in a browser from RWFreeView.

You'll use the `video_identifier` value to fetch the video url to play in `PlayerView`. For example, the `video_identifier` of "SwiftUI vs. UIKit" is 3021.

➤ Send this request in RESTed:

```
https://api.raywenderlich.com/api/videos/3021/stream
```

The response body contains this `url`:

```
"url": "https://player.vimeo.com/external/357115704.m3u8?
s=19d68c614817e0266d6749271e5432675a45c559&oauth2_token_id=89771
1146"
```

➤ This is the link you'll pass to `PlayerView`. RESTed isn't able to play it, so paste it into Safari to see it load the video.

Open video URL in Safari.

This is how the server provides access to additional resources. Images and videos aren't embedded directly into the search results, but you get a URL that allows you to access each item separately.

Sorting

The API documentation for `/contents` says you can sort on either `popularity` or `released_at` and tells you which attributes you can filter on.

➤ In RESTed, re-send the contents request:

```
https://api.raywenderlich.com/api/contents
```

➤ Scan the `released_at` values for the first few array items, and you'll see the default sort order is reverse chronological order. The first item was released most recently, and later items were released earlier.

So change the request to show you the *most popular* items first.

➤ In the parameter section, click + to add **Parameter Name sort** with **Parameter Value -popularity**:

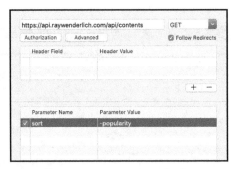

Request: sort on popularity

You ask for *reverse* numerical order because higher popularity values indicate more popular content items.

➤ Click **Send Request**.

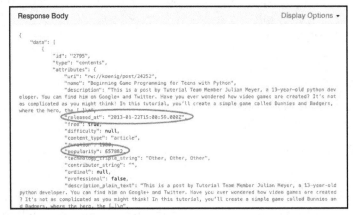

Response: sort on popularity

Now the first array item has a released_at date in 2013, and its popularity value is 657882! It's probably higher by the time you send this request.

Filtering

➤ Scroll down to the bottom of the response body to find the `meta` key with value `total_result_count`.

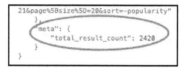

Contents meta item

2420 items match the filters in the `/contents` request. It's probably more by the time you read this. Many of these items aren't about iOS or Swift. How can you request only iOS and Swift items?

In the API documentation, the **You can filter on:** list includes **domain_ids**, which sounds like a possibility for a solution.

➤ In the sidebar of the API web page, click **/domains** then click its **200 OK** button:

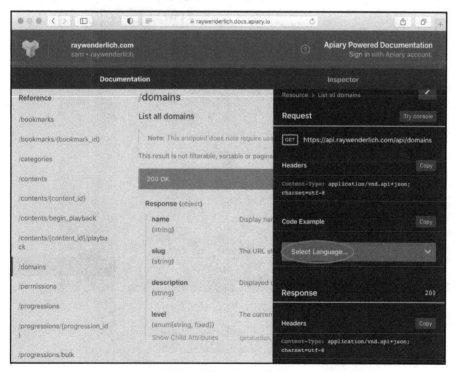

Apiary /domains sidebar

The `domains` request is already done, and you'll look at the response soon. But first...

➤ Click **Select Language…** (click the text; the disclosure arrow on this button doesn't do anything):

Apiary sidebar: Select Language…

This tool *generates code* for this HTTP request in several programming languages, including cURL and Swift!

➤ Select **Swift**:

```
Swift                                                                          >

import Foundation

// NOTE: Uncomment following two lines for use in a Playground
// import PlaygroundSupport
// PlaygroundPage.current.needsIndefiniteExecution = true

let url = URL(string: "https://api.raywenderlich.com/api/domains")!
var request = URLRequest(url: url)
request.addValue("application/vnd.api+json; charset=utf-8", forHTTPHeaderField:
"Content-Type")

let task = URLSession.shared.dataTask(with: request) { data, response, error in
  if let response = response {
    print(response)

    if let data = data, let body = String(data: data, encoding: .utf8) {
      print(body)
    }
  } else {
    print(error ?? "Unknown error")
  }
}

task.resume()
```

Apiary sidebar: generated Swift code

You'll write something similar to this in the next chapter. This tool is useful either as a starting point for your code or to check you haven't forgotten anything.

Below the **Code Example** section is **Response**.

➤ Keep scrolling to view the **Body**:

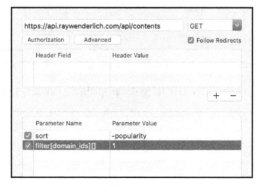

Apiary sidebar: /domains response body

It's pretty-printed and a little more colorful than RESTed. And, no surprise, "iOS & Swift" has id value 1. This is the parameter value you need to create your filter endpoint.

> **Note**: The response to the /contents request already contains this information in the value of the included key.

➤ Close the **/domains** sidebar and go back to the **/contents** documentation to see how to create the filter endpoint.

Here's the example:

```
filter[content_types][]=collection&filter[content_types][]=screencast
```

Apiary /contents: filter example

➤ So, in RESTed, add a parameter with name **filter[domain_ids][]** and value **1**:

Request: filter on domain id

➤ Add two more parameters:

- Name: **filter[content_types][]**

- Value: **episode**

And

- Name: **filter[subscription_types][]**

- Value: **free**

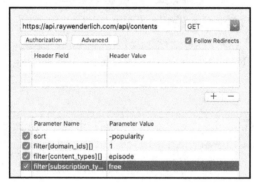

Request: filter on content and subscription types

➤ Click **Send Request**.

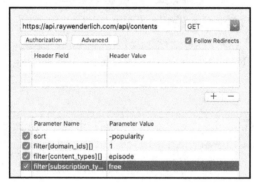

Response: most popular free iOS & Swift episodes

Now the first item is "SwiftUI vs. UIKit" with popularity value 43193.

With these parameters set up in RESTed, you can easily turn any of them off by unchecking its checkbox. Or, you can change a parameter value to retrieve a different domain or content type.

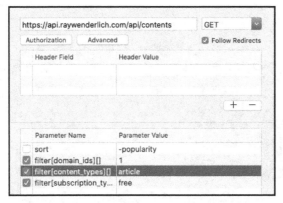

RESTed lets you edit or turn off parameters.

Apiary console

The sidebar has a feature that looks wonderful but doesn't quite work.

➤ Open the /**contents** sidebar and click **Try console** to get a form where you can add the same parameters:

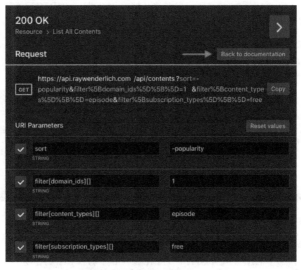

Apiary sidebar: Try console

But when you **Send request**, the response is *We encountered an error. Please try later.*

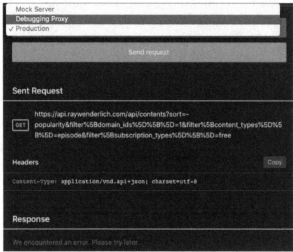

Apiary sidebar: Try console: select server

Changing **Production** to **Debugging Proxy** works, but doesn't pretty-print the response body. Using **Mock Server** works and pretty-prints, but contains no results after July 24, 2018. Also, you can't turn off just some parameters: **Reset values** deletes *all* parameters.

URL-encoding

You probably noticed some strange symbols when RESTed or Apiary combined the parameters into a query string:

```
https://api.raywenderlich.com/api/contents?
  filter%5Bsubscription_types%5D%5B%5D=free&
  filter%5Bdomain_ids%5D%5B%5D=1&
  filter%5Bcontent_types%5D%5B%5D=episode&
  sort=-popularity
```

Note: I indented these lines for readability. This string won't work as a URL.

RESTed and Apiary *URL-encoded* the square brackets you used in the parameter names to %5B and %5D. URLs sent over the internet can contain only letters, digits and these punctuation marks: –, _, . and ~.

Other punctuation marks, including /, ? and %, are encoded as a pair of hexadecimal digits preceded by the escape character %. The hexadecimal value is the character's byte value in ASCII, for example, 20 (32 in decimal) for the space character and 25 (37 in decimal) for the % character. The space character can also be encoded as +. For a non-ASCII character, URL-encoding uses its UTF-8 byte value.

When / and ? are delimiters in the URL, they don't get encoded.

Challenges

Challenge 1: Change the page size

➤ Scroll down to the bottom of the response body to find the `links` item.

Filter query response: links

The `links` value is a dictionary of five keys: `self`, `first`, `prev`, `next` and `last`. The values are query URLs. The current response is both `self` and `first`. The `prev` key has no value because there's no previous page.

Paging is controlled by two query terms that you didn't set. For example, the `next` URL includes these parameters:

```
page%5Bnumber%5D=2&page%5Bsize%5D=20
```

URL-*decoded*, this is `page[number]=2&page[size]=20`. So the `next` page has 20 items, as do the `self` and `first` pages. The `last` page has `page[number]=22` and `page[size]=20`, but actually has only 9 items because `total_result_count` is 429.

One of the features you'll implement in the next chapter is letting the user change the page size. You're probably pretty sure you'll need to set the `page[size]` parameter.

Your challenge is to **send a RESTed request that changes the page size to 5** (it'll be easier to count a small number of response items).

Note: This is all documented in the Apiary's **Introduction ▸ Pagination** section.

Here's my RESTed request and response:

Set page size = 5

The **final** folder in the project materials has saved RESTed requests for all the requests in this section.

You're now well-prepared to implement HTTP messages in RWFreeView.

Challenge 2: POST request and authentication

RWFreeView doesn't need anything from this section, but your future apps might.

RWFreeView only needs to GET resources from the server and, because it gets only free items, your users don't need to authenticate.

You usually need to implement authentication for apps that let users access restricted materials or create, update or delete server records. Consider using **Sign In with Apple**. Follow our tutorial *Sign in with Apple Using SwiftUI* bit.ly/3iHqNix.

To try out a POST request, you'll use RESTed to send something like this GitHub `curl` example:

```
curl -i -H \
  "Authorization: token
5199831f4dd3b79e7c5b7e0ebe75d67aa66e79d4" \
```

```
-d '{ \
    "name": "blog", \
    "auto_init": true, \
    "private": true, \
    "gitignore_template": "nanoc" \
  }' \
https://api.github.com/user/repos
```

This example shows how to create a new GitHub repository, so it requires GitHub-user authentication. Remember when you set up your GitHub account in Xcode, you had to generate a personal access token? You'll need one here, too.

➤ If you haven't saved a plain-text copy of your GitHub personal access token, generate a new one at bit.ly/2Y71Ofh.

➤ In RESTed, add **Header Field Authorization** with **Header Value token**. Paste **your** personal access token after "token " to complete this value:

Authorization header with (dummy) personal access token

➤ Set the endpoint to **https://api.github.com/user/repos**, the method to **POST**, then select **Form-encoded** and set parameters **name** api-test-repo, **auto_init** true, **private** false:

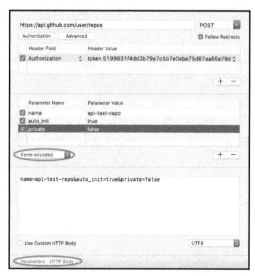

POST request parameters: Form-encoded

> **Note**: If you don't see both the parameter fields and the HTTP body, make sure both buttons are active.

Instead of appending to the endpoint, POST request parameters appear in the body field.

➤ Click **Send Request**.

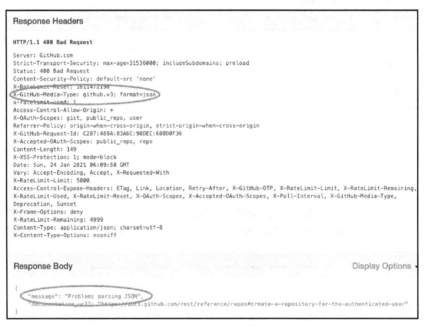

Response: 400 Bad Request. Problems parsing JSON

This was a deliberate "oops" to show you what happens if the server expects the POST request body to be in JSON but you send form-encoded data instead. Form-encoded data looks like the query string part of a URL because that's how a web form sends it.

➤ Change **Form-encoded** to **JSON-encoded**, then click **Send Request**.

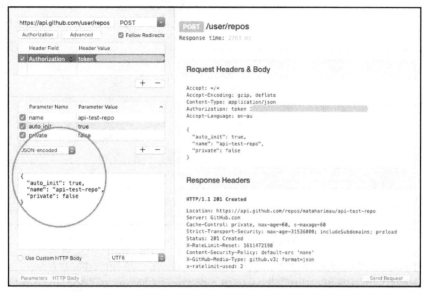

JSON-encoded parameters: Response: 201 Created

That worked! Check your GitHub account to see there really is a new repository named **api-test-repo**:

GitHub: New repository created

➤ Click **Send Request** again.

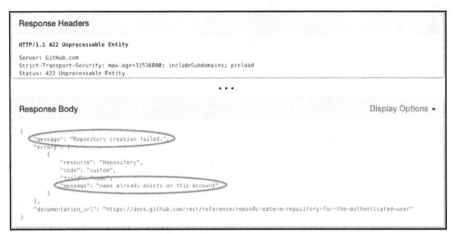

GitHub: 422 Unprocessable Entity

If you try to create the same repo again, the server returns the error message "name already exists on this account" along with a documentation_url for this endpoint.

Key points

- Client apps send HTTP requests to servers, which send back responses.

- An HTTP response contains a status code and some content. Text content is usually in JSON format and may contain URIs the client app can use to access media resources.

- HTTP requests follow the rules of the server's REST API, whose documentation specifies resource endpoints, HTTP methods and headers, and how to construct POST and PUT request bodies.

- You can send simple GET requests in a browser app. Use cURL or an app like RESTed to create and send requests and inspect responses.

- The documentation for api.raywenderlich.com includes a sidebar where you can create an HTTP request then generate Swift code for your app or send the request to a Mock Server or Debugging Proxy server.

Chapter 24: Downloading Data

By Audrey Tam

Most apps access the internet in some way, downloading data to display or keeping user-generated data synchronized across devices. Your RWFreeView app needs to create and send HTTP requests and process HTTP responses. Downloaded data is usually in JSON format, which your app needs to decode into its data model.

If your app downloads data from your own server, you might be able to ensure the JSON structure matches your app's data model. But RWFreeView needs to work with the raywenderlich.com API and its JSON structure, which is deeply nested. So in this chapter, you'll learn two ways to work with nested JSON.

Getting started

Open the **Networking** playground in the starter folder and open the **Episode** playground page. If the editor window is blank, show the Project navigator (**Command-1**) and select **Episode** there.

Open Episode playground page.

Playgrounds are useful for exploring and working out code before moving it into your app. You can quickly inspect values produced by methods and operations, without needing to build a user interface or search through a lot of debug console messages.

The starter playground contains two playground pages and extensions to `DateFormatter` and `URLComponents`.

Asynchronous functions

`URLSession` is Apple's framework for HTTP messages. Most of its methods involve network communication, so you can't predict how long they'll take to complete. In the meantime, the system must continue to interact with the user.

To make this possible, `URLSession` methods are *asynchronous*: They dispatch their work onto another *queue* and immediately return control to the *main queue*, so it can respond to user interface events. When you call the method, you supply a *completion handler*. This runs when the network task completes to process the response from the server.

> **Note**: `URLSession` and the broader topic of concurrency have their own video course at bit.ly/3x6Z8hN, and there's also a book, *Concurrency by Tutorials*, at bit.ly/3n0BSgF.

Because asynchronous tasks *appear* to finish immediately, the **Episode** and **VideoURL** playground pages contain the following code so the playground doesn't stop execution before an asynchronous task completes:

```
import PlaygroundSupport
PlaygroundPage.current.needsIndefiniteExecution = true
```

Creating a REST request

A REST request is a URL with query parameters. In the previous chapter, you saw the URL-encoded URL for a typical `contents` query:

```
https://api.raywenderlich.com/api/contents?
filter%5Bsubscription_types%5D%5B%5D=free&filter%5Bdomain_ids%5D
%5B%5D=1&filter%5Bcontent_types%5D%5B%5D=episode&sort=-
popularity
```

This URL lists query parameter names and values after the ? separator.

In this playground, you'll create this REST request for free iOS & Swift episodes, sorted by popularity. Your approach will be flexible, so you can easily change the query parameter values.

Many of the query parameter names, like `filter[domain_ids][]` contain brackets, which must be URL-encoded to %5B and %5D. You'll need to create URLs like this in your app, and you certainly don't want to do the URL-encoding yourself! Fortunately, you can hand this work over to `URLComponents` and `URLQueryItem`.

URLComponents

The `URLComponents` structure enables you to construct a URL from its parts and, also, to access the parts of a URL. Components include `scheme`, `host`, `port`, `path`, `query` and `queryItems`. The `url` itself gives you access to URL components like `lastPathComponent`.

➤ Add this code to the **Episode** playground:

```
let baseURLString = "https://api.raywenderlich.com/api/"
var urlComponents = URLComponents(
  string: baseURLString + "contents/")!
urlComponents.queryItems = [
  URLQueryItem(
    name: "filter[subscription_types][]", value: "free"),
  URLQueryItem(
    name: "filter[content_types][]", value: "episode")
]
urlComponents.url
urlComponents.url?.absoluteString
```

You set the URL string for the API's base endpoint and add the `contents` endpoint to create a `URLComponents` instance. Then, you create an array of `URLQueryItem` values. The `URLQueryItem` parameters are the parameter names and values you used in the previous chapter to construct your RESTed request.

The last line displays the final URL *string* in the sidebar. The line above it displays the final URL. What's the difference? Time to find out!

> **Note**: In a playground, you can write an expression on its own line to display its value.

➤ Click the **Execute Playground** arrow on the last line number or at the bottom of the playground:

```
6   let baseUrlString = "https://api.raywenderlich.com/api/"
7   var urlComponents = URLComponents(string: baseUrlString + "contents/")!
8   urlComponents.queryItems = [
9     URLQueryItem(name: "filter[subscription_types][]", value: "free"),
10    URLQueryItem(name: "filter[content_types][]", value: "episode")
11  ]
12  urlComponents.url
    urlComponents.url?.absoluteString
14
15
```

Execute-Playground arrows on the code line and in the bottom bar

Note: Clicking the arrow next to a line of code runs the playground only up to that line.

The sidebar displays values for some lines with buttons for **Quick Look** and **Show Result**.

➤ Click the **Show Result** button of the last code line and resize the display window that appears below the code line:

```
urlComponents.url                                    Optional(https://api.raywenderlich.com/api/contents/?filter%5Bsubscription_...
urlComponents.url?.absoluteString                    "https://api.raywenderlich.com/api/contents/?filter%5Bsubscription_types%5...
  https://api.raywenderlich.com/api/contents/?
  filter%5Bsubscription_types%5D%5B%5D=free&filter%5B
  content_types%5D%5B%5D=episode
```

Show Result of the code line.

```
"https://api.raywenderlich.com/api/contents/?
filter%5Bsubscription_types%5D%5B%5D=free&filter%5Bcontent_types
%5D%5B%5D=episode"
```

Thanks to `urlComponents`, your queries are safely URL-encoded and appended to the base URL.

➤ Now look at the `url` on the line above. Notice it's not in quotation marks, because it's not a `String`. In fact, it's an `Optional`. Click its **Show Result** button:

Playground trying to display a URL

The playground tries its best to open the URL.

You can create a URL from a String, if the String has all the right parts. Then, you can access these parts as properties of the URL instance: host, baseURL, path, lastPathComponent, query etc.

If you try to create a URL from a String that wouldn't work in a browser, the initializer returns nil. That's why urlComponents.url is an Optional and there's a url? in the last code line: If url is nil, it doesn't have an absoluteString property.

➤ Click their **Hide Result** buttons to close the result windows.

> **Note**: You can also use print(urlComponents.url?.absoluteString) to see the printed value in the Debug area below. If you're not able to see the Debug area, click the button next to the Run/Stop button or press **Shift-Command-C.**

URLComponents helper method

URLQueryItem makes it easy to add a query parameter name and value to the request URL, but your app provides lots of options for users to customize downloaded contents. And almost every selection and deselection requires a new request. You'll be writing **a lot** of code to add query items.

The name and value arguments of URLQueryItem look like dictionary key and value items, so it's easy to create a dictionary of parameter names and values, then transform this dictionary into a queryItems array. It's especially easy when Alfian Losari has already done it in bit.ly/3pRtT6t. :] It's in **Networking/Sources/URLComponentsExtension.swift** in this playground.

➤ Replace the urlComponents.queryItems definition with:

```
var baseParams = [
  "filter[subscription_types][]": "free",
  "filter[content_types][]": "episode",
  "sort": "-popularity",
  "page[size]": "20",
  "filter[q]": ""
]
urlComponents.setQueryItems(with: baseParams)
```

You create a dictionary whose keys are query parameter names. The first two are fixed: You always want to download free episodes.

You include sort, page size and q (search term) because these are single-value options. They have default values, and this dictionary lets you easily change their values. For example:

```
// when user changes page size
baseParams["page[size]"] = "30"
// when user enters a search term
baseParams["filter[q]"] = "json"
```

The `setQueryItems(with:)` helper method defined in the `URLComponents` extension creates a `URLQueryItem` for each dictionary item and sets the `queryItems` array of the `URLComponents` instance. In the next chapter, you'll append other query items to this array.

➤ Replace `urlComponents.url` with this line:

```
urlComponents.queryItems! +=
    [URLQueryItem(name: "filter[domain_ids][]", value: "1")]
```

You request only episodes in the "iOS & Swift" domain.

You don't include this query parameter in `baseParams` because you can add more than one `domain_id` query item to a RESTED request URL.

The `queryItems` array is an optional, in case `urlComponents` doesn't have any `queryItems` component. But, you just created the `queryItems` component, so it's safe to force-unwrap it.

➤ Execute the playground and show the `absoluteString` result:

Result of adding domain query item

Now you're all set to send the request URL to the raywenderlich.com API server.

URLSessionDataTask

➤ Add this code below the `absoluteString` line:

```
let contentsURL = urlComponents.url!  // 1

// 2
```

```
URLSession.shared
  .dataTask(with: contentsURL) { data, response, error in
    defer { PlaygroundPage.current.finishExecution() }  // 3
    if let data = data,
      let response = response as? HTTPURLResponse {  // 4
      print(response.statusCode)
      // Decode data and display it
    }
    // 5
    print(
      "Contents fetch failed: " +
        "\(error?.localizedDescription ?? "Unknown error")")
  }
  .resume()  // 6
```

1. You assign the `url` property of `urlComponents` to `contentsURL`. In this playground, you know this is a valid URL, so it's safe to force-unwrap it. When this code is in a method, you would do this assignment in a `guard` statement and exit if the value is `nil`.

2. You create a `dataTask` with `contentsURL`. For simple requests like this, the `shared` session with default configuration works fine. You can create a session with a custom configuration. For example, here's how you create a session that waits 300 seconds for a network connection:

```
let config = URLSessionConfiguration.default
config.waitsForConnectivity = true
config.timeoutIntervalForResource = 300
let session = URLSession(configuration: config)
```

3. The `defer` statement stops playground execution when the `dataTask` handler completes. This is convenient when the code is the last thing executed in a playground page.

4. You supply a *completion handler*. When the task completes, this handler receives three arguments. You usually name them `data`, `response` and `error`. All three are optionals, so you must unwrap them. Completion handlers usually check `response.statusCode` then decode `data`.

5. You print the `error`, if it exists, or "Unknown error". A common source of "Unknown error" is a failure to decode `data`.

6. `URLSession` tasks are created in a suspended state, so you must call `resume()` method to start them. This step is easy to forget, even for experienced iOS developers. ;]

What about that comment `Decode data and display it` after you print the status code? Most of the rest of this chapter helps you do that. If you run this code now, you'll get "Unknown error" because you haven't decoded `data` yet.

Fetching a video URL

To display a video, you actually need to run *two* download requests. The one you've just added to the **Episode** playground fetches an array of `contents` items.

One of the `contents` item attributes is `video_identifier`. It's an integer like 3021. You'll use it to fetch the URL string of the item's video.

➤ In the **VideoURL** playground page, add these lines of code:

```
let videoId = 3021
let baseURLString = "https://api.raywenderlich.com/api/videos/"
let queryURLString = baseURLString + String(videoId) + "/stream"
let queryURL = URL(string: queryURLString)!
URLSession.shared
  .dataTask(with: queryURL) { data, response, error in
    defer { PlaygroundPage.current.finishExecution() }
    if let data = data,
      let response = response as? HTTPURLResponse {
      print("\(videoId) \(response.statusCode)")
      // Decode response and display it
    }
    print(
      "Videos fetch failed: " +
        "\(error?.localizedDescription ?? "Unknown error")")
  }
  .resume()
```

You create the query URL and the `dataTask` code to send it, then print the response status code. Then, you need to `Decode response and display it`.

The JSON response for this query is simpler than for the `contents` query, so you'll decode this first.

Decoding JSON

If there's a good match between your data model and a JSON value, the default
`init(from:)` of `JSONDecoder` is poetry in motion, letting you decode complex
structures of arrays and dictionaries in a single line of code. Unfortunately,
api.raywenderlich.com sends a deeply-nested JSON structure that you probably
won't want to replicate in your app. So, it's time to learn more about `CodingKey`
enumerations and custom `init(from:)` methods.

> **Note**: Dive deeper into JSON with our tutorial *Encoding and Decoding in Swift*
> bit.ly/3bqsrBY.

Decoding JSON that (almost) matches your data model

In Chapter 19, "Saving Files", you saw how easy it is to encode and decode the `Team`
structure as JSON because all its properties are `Codable`. You were saving and
loading your app's own data model, so item names and structure in JSON format
exactly matched your `Team` structure.

JSON values sent by real-world APIs rarely match the way you want to name or
structure your app's data.

If the JSON structure matches your app's data model, but the JSON names use
`snake_case` while your property names use `camelCase`, you just tell the decoder to
do the translation:

```
let decoder = JSONDecoder()
decoder.keyDecodingStrategy = .convertFromSnakeCase
```

This takes care of translating JSON names like `released_at` and `video_identifier`
to property names `releasedAt` and `videoIdentifier`.

If the JSON structure matches your app's data model, but some of the names are
different, you simply have to define a `CodingKey` enumeration to assign JSON item
names to your data model properties. For example, `Episode` has a `description`
property, but the matching JSON item's name is `description_plain_text`:

```
enum CodingKeys: String, CodingKey {
  case description = "description_plain_text"
```

```
    case id, uri, name, ...
}
```

Unfortunately, as soon as you create a `CodingKey` enumeration for one property name, you must include **all** the property names, even those that already match JSON item names.

Decoding nested JSON

Most of the time, the structure of JSON sent by an API is very different from the way you want to organize your app's data. This is the case with api.raywenderlich.com, where the values you want to store in an `episode` are nested one or more levels down in the JSON value. And fetching the video URL string requires a separate request to a different endpoint.

Even the `videos` request has this problem. All you want is the `"url"` value, but it's buried in a nested JSON structure.

➤ Send this request with **RESTed**, or use the **Try console** of the `/videos/` `{video_id}/stream` endpoint at raywenderlich.docs.apiary.io.

```
https://api.raywenderlich.com/api/videos/3021/stream
```

You get this response body:

```
{
  "data": {
    "id": "32574",
    "type": "attachments",
    "attributes": {
      "url": "https://player.vimeo.com/external/357115704...",
      "kind": "stream"
    }
  }
}
```

The JSON value contains a dictionary named `"data"`. The value of its `"attributes"` key is another dictionary, and the value of the `"url"` key is the URL string you want to store in your `Episode` instance.

There are two approaches to decoding nested JSON:

1. Define your data model to mirror the JSON value.

2. Flatten the JSON value into your data model.

You'll do it the first way to see how nifty automatic JSON decoding can be. Then you'll do it the second way, because that's how you'll do it in your app. In exchange for more decoding work, you'll get sensible data structures that are easier and more natural to work with.

Making the data model fit the JSON

➤ In the **VideoURL** playground page, set up these structures to mirror the JSON value's hierarchy:

```
struct ResponseData: Codable {
  let data: Video
}

struct Video: Codable {
  let attributes: VideoAttributes
}

struct VideoAttributes: Codable {
  let url: String
}
```

You create separate structures with `data`, `attributes` and `url` properties. The relationships between these structures match the nesting of the JSON value's `"data"`, `"attributes"` and `"url"`.

➤ In the completion handler for the `queryURL` `dataTask`, replace the `Decode response and display it` comment with this code:

```
if let decodedResponse = try? JSONDecoder().decode(  // 1
    ResponseData.self, from: data) {  // 2
  DispatchQueue.main.async {
    print(decodedResponse.data.attributes.url)  // 3
  }
  return
}
```

1. You don't need to configure `JSONDecoder` for this task, so you just create one inline.

2. You decode the top level `ResponseData`, and this gives you access to its `data.attributes.url` property.

3. You run the `print` statement on the main queue. This isn't really necessary in a playground, but is essential in an app. You usually do something in the `dataTask` handler to update the user interface, and all UI updates **must** run on the main queue.

➤ Run the playground.

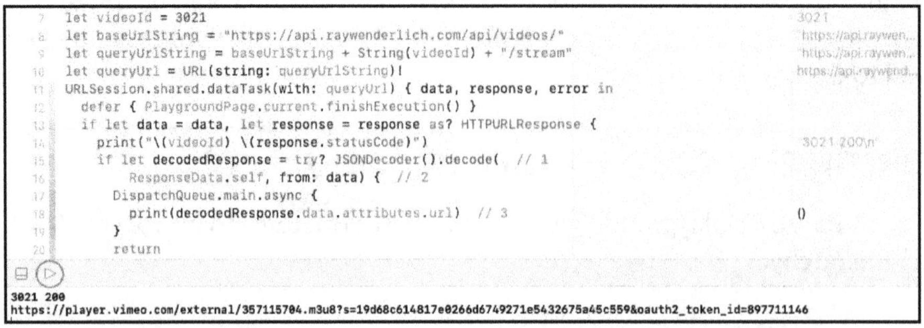

Playground execution stops after decoding URL string.

The URL string appears in the debug area, and playground execution stops.

> **Note**: You must run the whole playground if you added the `ResponseData` and other structures below the `URLSession` code. They're not "visible" if you click the run button on the `resume()` line.

➤ **Option-click** `url`:

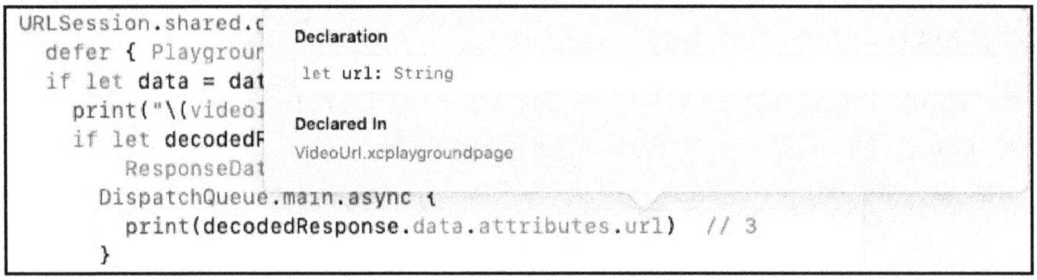

View type of url property.

Its type is `String`, as you'd expect.

➤ In `VideoAttributes`, change the type of `url`:

```
let url: URL
```

➤ Run the playground again, then check the type of url:

```
URLSession.shared.c   Declaration
  defer { Playgrour
  if let data = dat      let url: URL
    print("\(video)
    if let decodedF    Declared In
      ResponseDat      VideoUrl.xcplaygroundpage
    DispatchQueue.main.async {
      print(decodedResponse.data.attributes.url)   // 3
    }
```

Type of url property is URL.

This is one of the nifty `JSONDecoder` automagic tricks: It created a `URL` from the JSON string value.

The downside of this approach comes when you need to use `url` in your app. You don't really want to have to create a `ResponseData` instance for every video. It's much more natural to include it as one of the `Episode` properties.

Flattening the JSON response into the data model

In Chapter 19, "Saving Files", you wrote a `CodingKey` enumeration and a custom `init(from:)` to decode a `Double` value that you then used to initialize an `Angle`. In this section, you'll use `CodingKey` enumerations and a custom `init(from:)` to navigate through the levels of the JSON value and extract the items you need.

Here's the JSON value again:

```
{
  "data": {
    "id": "32574",
    "type": "attachments",
    "attributes": {
      "url": "https://player.vimeo.com/external/357115704...",
      "kind": "stream"
    }
  }
}
```

Think of `"data"` as a *container* inside the top-level *container*.

➤ Comment out the `ResponseData`, `Video` and `VideoAttributes` structures, then add this code:

```swift
struct VideoURLString {
  // data: attributes: url
  var urlString: String

  enum CodingKeys: CodingKey {
    case data
  }

  enum DataKeys: CodingKey {
    case attributes
  }
}

struct VideoAttributes: Codable {
  var url: String
}
```

This time, you mirror the JSON hierarchy in the `CodingKey` enumerations you create for the top-level and "data" containers. The cases are the JSON keys you care about: "data" in the top-level container and "attributes" in the "data" container.

Then, you create a structure to hold the "attributes" item you care about: `url`.

To flatten the JSON structure to fit your data model, you must write your own initializer.

➤ Add this code below `VideoURLAttributes`:

```swift
extension VideoURLString: Decodable {
  init(from decoder: Decoder) throws {
    let container = try decoder.container(  // 1
      keyedBy: CodingKeys.self)
    let dataContainer = try container.nestedContainer(
      keyedBy: DataKeys.self, forKey: .data)  // 2
    let attr = try dataContainer.decode(
      VideoAttributes.self, forKey: .attributes)  // 3
    urlString = attr.url  // 4
  }
}
```

> **Note**: You always put this decoding initializer in an extension. If you put it in the main `VideoURLString` structure, you lose the default initializer that Swift creates for structures.

You drill down into the JSON value, using the coding keys to create containers and access their contents.

1. First, you get the top-level container. The `case data` in `CodingKeys` matches something in this top-level container.

2. Next, you grab the nested container that matches `case data` in `CodingKeys`. The `case attributes` in `DataKeys` matches something in `dataContainer`.

3. Then, you decode the `attributes` item in `dataContainer`, mapping it to the `VideoAttributes` structure. So `attr` is an instance of `VideoAttributes`.

4. Finally, you reach the `"url"` value in the JSON hierarchy! You assign it to the top-level `urlString` property of this `VideoURLString` instance.

This is more work than just mirroring the JSON hierarchy in your data model structures, but it has two advantages:

1. Your data model structures are flatter and easier to understand. They match your mental model of your app's data.

2. If the JSON hierarchy changes, you only need to modify `CodingKey` enumerations and your custom `init(from:)`. You don't need to refactor your data model structures.

➤ Change the `JSONDecoder().decode` code to use `VideoURLString`:

```
if let decodedResponse = try? JSONDecoder().decode(
    VideoURLString.self, from: data) {
  DispatchQueue.main.async {
    print(decodedResponse.urlString)
  }
  return
}
```

➤ Run the playground again to check it still decodes the `url`:

```
 7   let videoId = 3021                                                              3021                    ▦
 8   let baseUrlString = "https://api.raywenderlich.com/api/videos/"                 "https://api.raywen...  ▦
 9   let queryUrlString = baseUrlString + String(videoId) + "/stream"                "https://api.raywen...  ▦
10   let queryUrl = URL(string: queryUrlString)!                                     https://api.raywend...  ▦
11   URLSession.shared.dataTask(with: queryUrl) { data, response, error in
12     defer { PlaygroundPage.current.finishExecution() }
13     if let data = data, let response = response as? HTTPURLResponse {
14       print("\(videoId) \(response.statusCode)")                                  3021 200\n             ▦
15       if let decodedResponse = try? JSONDecoder().decode(
16         VideoUrlString.self, from: data) {
17         DispatchQueue.main.async {
18           print(decodedResponse.urlString)                                        ()                     ▦
19         }
20         return
21       }
```

```
3021 200
https://player.vimeo.com/external/357115704.m3u8?s=19d68c614817e0266d6749271e5432675a45c559&oauth2_token_id=897711146
```

Decoding url with flattened JSON.

You'll use this `VideoURLString` decoding structure when you flatten the `contents` JSON value into the `Episode` structure.

Decoding the contents response

Now you're ready to tackle the `contents` query response. Here's one of the items returned:

```
{
  "data": [
    {
      "id": "5117655",
      "attributes": {
        "uri": "rw://betamax/videos/3021",
        "name": "SwiftUI vs. UIKit",
        "released_at": "2019-09-03T13:00:00.000Z",
        "difficulty": "beginner",
        "description_plain_text": "Learn about...\n",
        "video_identifier": 3021,
        ...
      },
      "relationships": {
        "domains": {
          "data": [
            {
              "id": "1",
              "type": "domains"
            }
          ]
        },
        ...
      }
      ...
```

```
    },
    ...
}
```

The top-level container is a dictionary. One of its keys is "data", which is an array of dictionaries. Most of the data you need to store for each Episode instance is in the "attributes" value.

You'll use the "video_identifier" value to create a VideoURLString object to fetch the URL string of the episode's video.

And the episode's domains (platforms) are listed by "id" in the "relationships" value.

One more JSONDecoder trick

You're definitely going to flatten this JSON into your Episode structure, but first, you've got to see what JSONDecoder can do with Date strings.

➤ In the **Episode** playground page, set up an EpisodeStore struct to store the episodes and a Episode structure that mirrors the JSON value:

```
struct EpisodeStore: Decodable {
  var episodes: [Episode] = []

  enum CodingKeys: String, CodingKey {
    case episodes = "data"   // array of dictionary
  }
}

struct Episode: Decodable, Identifiable {
  let id: String
  let attributes: Attributes
}

struct Attributes: Codable {
  let name: String
  let released_at: Date
}
```

In the JSON value, "released_at" is a string, but you'll set up a JSONDecoder to automatically convert it to a Date value.

FormatterExtension.swift contains two DateFormatter type properties:

```
public extension DateFormatter {
  /// Convert /contents released_at String to Date
```

```
  static let apiDateFormatter: DateFormatter = {
    let formatter = DateFormatter()
    formatter.dateFormat = "yyyy-MM-dd'T'HH:mm:ss.SSS'Z'"
    return formatter
  }()

  /// Format date to appear in EpisodeView and PlayerView
  static let episodeDateFormatter: DateFormatter = {
    let formatter = DateFormatter()
    formatter.dateFormat = "MMM yyyy"
    return formatter
  }()
}
```

The `dateFormat` in `apiDateFormatter` is the template for the `"released_at"` string.

> **Note**: This date format is an international standard defined by ISO 8601 bit.ly/3aJJSwR. You can find date format patterns and a table of date field symbols at bit.ly/3oZTuZu.

➤ In the **Episode** playground page, before the `URLSession` code, create a `JSONDecoder` and set its date decoding strategy:

```
let decoder = JSONDecoder()
decoder.dateDecodingStrategy = .formatted(.apiDateFormatter)
```

This is all you need to do to enable the decoder to convert the `"released_at"` string into a `Date` value. Then later, you'll use `episodeDateFormatter` to display the month and year of this date in `EpisodeView`.

> **Note**: There's actually a specific `ISO8601DateFormatter` and a JSON date decoding strategy `iso8601`, but the strategy doesn't include milliseconds (SSS) and doesn't let you instantiate an `ISO8601DateFormatter` to set the milliseconds option. Nor can you use `.formatted` to set a configured `ISO8601DateFormatter` as the date formatter for decoder, because it's not of type `DateFormatter`. These restrictions are only a problem if you're using standard decoding provided for you by the compiler. If you write a custom decoder — something you'll do shortly — you can use `ISO8601DateFormatter` directly.

➤ In the completion handler for `dataTask`, replace the comment `Decode data and display it` with this code:

```
if let decodedResponse = try? decoder.decode(
    EpisodeStore.self, from: data) {
  DispatchQueue.main.async {
    let date =
      decodedResponse.episodes[0].attributes.released_at
    DateFormatter.episodeDateFormatter.string(from: date)
  }
  return
}
```

You check the `Date` value created by `decoder` by converting it to the `String` you'll display in `EpisodeView`.

➤ Run the playground.

```
let decoder = JSONDecoder()                                    Foundation.JSONDecoder
decoder.dateDecodingStrategy = .formatted(.apiDateFormatter)   Foundation.JSONDecoder
// 2
URLSession.shared
  .dataTask(with: contentsURL) { data, response, error in
  defer { PlaygroundPage.current.finishExecution() }  // 3
  if let data = data,
    let response = response as? HTTPURLResponse {  // 4
    print(response.statusCode)                                 "200\n"
    if let decodedResponse = try? decoder.decode(
      EpisodeStore.self, from: data) {
      DispatchQueue.main.async {
        let date =
          decodedResponse.episodes[0].attributes.released_at   "Sep 3, 2019 at 1:00 PM"
        DateFormatter.episodeDateFormatter.string(from: date)  "Sep 2019"
      }
```

released_at string converted to Date and back to shorter string.

The date created by `decoder` is displayed in the default medium style, then `episodeDateFormatter` displays the short string you'll display in `EpisodeView`.

Flattening the contents response

RWFreeView needs several more `Episode` properties, and some of these require a custom decoder.

➤ In the **Episode** playground page, replace the `attributes` property of the `Episode` structure with all the properties you need:

```
// flatten attributes container
//1
let uri: String
let name: String
let released: String
let difficulty: String?
```

```
let description: String  // description_plain_text

// 2
var domain = ""  // relationships: domains: data: id

// send request to /videos endpoint with urlString
var videoURL: VideoURL?  // 3

// redirects to the real web page
var linkURLString: String {  // 4
  "https://www.raywenderlich.com/redirect?uri=" + uri
}
```

1. Declare the properties you're going to map from the JSON response. Fetched items that aren't episodes don't have "difficulty" values, so this is optional.

2. Most of these properties match items in the "attributes" container, but the domain "id" value is nested deep in the "relationships" dictionary.

3. You'll create a VideoURL object, which sends a request to fetch urlString.

4. In case you want to use Link to open a browser, you compute linkURLString from uri.

Decoding most of Episode's properties

Xcode is complaining Episode doesn't conform to Decodable because you haven't told it how these new properties will get values. Coming right up!

➤ First, delete Attributes. You're going to flatten it into the top level of Episode.

➤ Add these CodingKey enumerations to Episode:

```
enum DataKeys: String, CodingKey {
  case id
  case attributes
  case relationships
}

enum AttrsKeys: String, CodingKey {
  case uri, name, difficulty
  case releasedAt = "released_at"
  case description = "description_plain_text"
  case videoIdentifier = "video_identifier"
}

struct Domains: Codable {
  let data: [[String: String]]
}
```

```
enum RelKeys: String, CodingKey {
  case domains
}
```

You create `CodingKey` enumerations `DataKeys`, `AttrsKeys` and `RelKeys` for the "data", "attributes" and "relationships" containers and create a structure to hold the "domains" item you care about: `data`.

> **Note:** Swift enumeration case identifiers can include the underscore character, but raywenderlich.com code uses **SwiftLint** github.com/realm/SwiftLint, which allows only letters and digits. And the `convertFromSnakeCase` key decoding strategy only works during automatic JSON decoding.

➤ Also add this type property to `Episode`:

```
static let domainDictionary = [
  "1": "iOS & Swift",
  "2": "Android & Kotlin",
  "3": "Unity",
  "5": "macOS",
  "8": "Server-Side Swift",
  "9": "Flutter"
]
```

You'll use this to convert `domains id` values to platform names.

➤ Finally, add this extension to **FormatterExtension.swift**:

```
public extension Formatter {
  /// Creates ISO8601DateFormatter that formats milliseconds
  static let iso8601: ISO8601DateFormatter = {
    let formatter = ISO8601DateFormatter()
    formatter.formatOptions = [
      .withInternetDateTime,
      .withFractionalSeconds
    ]
    return formatter
  }()
}
```

You create an `ISO8601DateFormatter` and set its options to include `withFractionalSeconds`. Using this date formatter, you don't need to type out the date format string, where it's so easy to make a mistake that breaks the decoder.

To flatten the JSON structure into `Episode`, you must write your own initializer in an extension.

➤ Start by decoding the JSON items. Add this extension in the **Episode** playground page:

```
extension Episode {
  init(from decoder: Decoder) throws {
    let container = try decoder.container(  // 1
      keyedBy: DataKeys.self)
    let id = try container.decode(String.self, forKey: .id)

    let attrs = try container.nestedContainer(  // 2
      keyedBy: AttrsKeys.self, forKey: .attributes)
    let uri = try attrs.decode(String.self, forKey: .uri)
    let name = try attrs.decode(String.self, forKey: .name)
    let releasedAt = try attrs.decode(
      String.self, forKey: .releasedAt)
    let releaseDate = Formatter.iso8601.date(  // 3
      from: releasedAt)!
    let difficulty = try attrs.decode(
      String?.self, forKey: .difficulty)
    let description = try attrs.decode(
      String.self, forKey: .description)
    let videoIdentifier = try attrs.decode(
      Int?.self, forKey: .videoIdentifier)

    let rels = try container.nestedContainer(
      keyedBy: RelKeys.self, forKey: .relationships)  // 4
    let domains = try rels.decode(
      Domains.self, forKey: .domains)
    if let domainId = domains.data.first?["id"] {  // 5
      self.domain = Episode.domainDictionary[domainId] ?? ""
    }
  }
}
```

1. Here, the top-level container is `"data"`. It contains the items named in `DataKeys`: `"id"`, `"attributes"` and `"relationships"`.

2. You grab the nested container that matches `case attributes` in `DataKeys`, then decode the six values you want to store in `Episode`.

3. For the `releasedAt` coding key, you decode the `String`, then convert it to a `Date` with your millisecond-handling `iso8601` formatter.

4. Similarly, you get the `"relationships"` container and decode the `"domains"` item.

5. Finally, you get a `domainId` value and convert it to a platform name. The `"domains"` item is an array because an episode could be relevant to more than one domain. You take the first array item. This is an optional because an array can be empty. The value of the `"id"` key is also an optional, in case there's no such key. If you can unwrap these optionals, you look up the matching platform name in `domainDictionary` and assign it to the `domain` property.

You'll use these decoded values to initialize each `Episode`. For most properties, you'll just assign the decoded value to the property. But you'll convert the `releaseDate Date` to a `String` value, and you need a way to use `videoIdentifier` to fetch a video URL string.

VideoURL class

You'll soon decode `video_identifier` from the `contents` response and use it to create a `VideoURL` object.

➤ In the **VideoURL** playground page, remove the code below `let videoId = 3021`, but not the structures and extension, if you added them there.

➤ Now, add the following code:

```
class VideoURL {
  var urlString = ""

  init(videoId: Int) {
    let baseURLString =
      "https://api.raywenderlich.com/api/videos/"
    let queryURLString =
      baseURLString + String(videoId) + "/stream"
    guard let queryURL = URL(string: queryURLString)   // 1
    else { return }
    URLSession.shared
      .dataTask(with: queryURL) { data, response, error in
        defer { PlaygroundPage.current.finishExecution() }
        if let data = data,
          let response = response as? HTTPURLResponse {
          print("\(videoId) \(response.statusCode)")
          if let decodedResponse = try? JSONDecoder().decode(
            VideoURLString.self, from: data) {
            DispatchQueue.main.async {
              self.urlString = decodedResponse.urlString   // 2
              print(self.urlString)
            }
          }
          return
```

```
        }
      }
      print(
        "Videos fetch failed: " +
          "\(error?.localizedDescription ?? "Unknown error")")
    }
    .resume()
  }
}
```

This moves the code you had before inside the `VideoURL` class with a couple of small changes:

1. Now that you're in a method, you can exit if something goes wrong, so you create `queryURL` safely in a `guard` statement instead of force-unwrapping the URL.

2. Assign the decoded JSON to the `urlString` property of this `VideoURL` object, then print that value.

➤ Now replace `let videoId = 3021` with this:

```
VideoURL(videoId: 3021)
```

You create a `VideoURL` object to test your new class.

➤ Run the playground and check it's still fetching the video URL:

```
 7   VideoUrl(videoId: 3021)                                                      VideoUrl        
 8   class VideoUrl {  // 1
 9     var urlString = ""
10
11     init(videoId: Int) {
12       let baseUrlString = "https://api.raywenderlich.com/api/videos/"          https://api.raywen...
13       let queryUrlString = baseUrlString + String(videoId) + "/stream"         https://api.raywen...
14       guard let queryUrl = URL(string: queryUrlString) else { return }  // 2
15       URLSession.shared.dataTask(with: queryUrl) { data, response, error in
16         defer { PlaygroundPage.current.finishExecution() }  // 3
17         if let data = data, let response = response as? HTTPURLResponse {
18           print("\(videoId) \(response.statusCode)")                           3021 200\n
19           if let decodedResponse = try? JSONDecoder().decode(
20             VideoUrlString.self, from: data) {
21             DispatchQueue.main.async {
22               self.urlString = decodedResponse.urlString  // 4
23               print(self.urlString)                                            'https://player.vime...

3021 200
https://player.vimeo.com/external/357115704.m3u8?s=19d68c614817e0266d6749271e5432675a45c559&oauth2_token_id=897711146
```

VideoURL(videoId: 3021)

➤ Copy VideoURL, the structures and extension to the **Episode** playground page. Comment out or delete the defer statement in init(videoId:):

```
//defer { PlaygroundPage.current.finishExecution() }
```

You don't want to stop playground execution after decoding the first video URL!

Everything's now in place to finish initializing Episode.

➤ Add the following code to the end of the init(from:) method in the Episode extension:

```
self.id = id
self.uri = uri
self.name = name
self.released = DateFormatter.episodeDateFormatter.string(   //
1
  from: releaseDate)
self.difficulty = difficulty
self.description = description
if let videoId = videoIdentifier {   // 2
  self.videoURL = VideoURL(videoId: videoId)
}
```

When you write your own decoder initializer, you lose JSONDecoder's automatic operation. So you must initialize every property, even if you just assign a decoded value to a property.

Two properties require more work than just assigning the local value to the property:

1. You use DateFormatter.episodeDateFormatter to convert the releaseDate date into the self.released string you'll display in EpisodeView.

2. If you decoded a videoIdentifier value, you initialize a VideoURL instance with this value and assign its urlString property to self.videoURLString.

➤ Now scroll to the URLSession code, where the compiler is complaining **'Episode' has no member 'attributes'**. Replace all the code in the dataTask handler's main queue closure with the following:

```
print(decodedResponse.episodes[0].released)
print(decodedResponse.episodes[0].domain)
```

You print some of your newly-decoded properties.

➤ Run the playground.

```
26    URLSession.shared.dataTask(with: contentsUrl) {
27      data, response, error in
28      defer { PlaygroundPage.current.finishExecution() }  // 3
29      if let data = data,
30        let response = response as? HTTPURLResponse {  // 4
31        print(response.statusCode)                                              "200\n"
32        if let decodedResponse = try? decoder.decode(
33            EpisodeStore.self, from: data) {
34          DispatchQueue.main.async {
35            print(decodedResponse.episodes[0].released)                        "Sep 2019\n"
36            print(decodedResponse.episodes[0].domain)                          "iOS & Swift\n"
37          }

200
Sep 2019
iOS & Swift
```

Custom decoding of contents response

➤ Scroll to see that `init(from:)` ran 20 times:

```
extension Episode {
  init(from decoder: Decoder) throws {
    let container = try decoder.container(keyedBy: DataKeys.self)  // 1      (20 times)
    let id = try container.decode(String.self, forKey: .id)                  (20 times)

    let attrs = try container.nestedContainer(                               (20 times)
      keyedBy: AttrsKeys.self, forKey: .attributes)  // 2
    let uri = try attrs.decode(String.self, forKey: .uri)                    (20 times)
    let name = try attrs.decode(String.self, forKey: .name)                  (20 times)
    let releasedAt = try attrs.decode(String.self, forKey: .releasedAt)      (20 times)
    let releaseDate = Formatter.iso8601.date(from: releasedAt)!  // 3        (20 times)
    let difficulty = try attrs.decode(String?.self, forKey: .difficulty)     (20 times)
    let description = try attrs.decode(String.self, forKey: .description)     (20 times)
    let videoIdentifier = try attrs.decode(Int?.self, forKey:                (20 times)
      .videoIdentifier)

    let rels = try container.nestedContainer(                                (20 times)
      keyedBy: RelKeys.self, forKey: .relationships)  // 4
    let domains = try rels.decode(Domains.self, forKey: .domains)            (20 times)
    if let domainId = domains.data.first?["id"] {  // 5
      self.domain = Episode.domainDictionary[domainId] ?? ""
    }
```

Episode init(from:) ran 20 times.

Your JSON decoding is all working, and this is as much as you can test in a playground. You're ready to copy and adapt all this code into your app to make everything work!

Key points

- Playgrounds are useful for working out code. You can quickly inspect values produced by methods and operations.

- `URLComponents` query items help you create URL-encoded URLs for REST requests.

- Use `URLSession dataTask` to send an HTTP request and process the HTTP response.

- Decode nested JSON values either by mirroring the JSON structure in your app's data model, or by flattening the JSON structure into your data model.

- Use date formatters like `ISO8601DateFormatter` to convert date strings to `Date` values.

Chapter 25: Implementing Filter Options

By Audrey Tam

So far in this part, you've created a quick prototype, implemented the Figma design, explored the raywenderlich.com REST API and worked out the code to send a REST request and decode its response. In this chapter, you'll copy and adapt the playground code into your app. Then, you'll build on this to implement all the filters and options that let your users customize which episodes they fetch. Your final result will be a fully-functioning app you can use to sample all our video courses.

Getting started

Open the RWFreeView starter project. It contains code you'll use to keep the filter buttons synchronized between `FilterOptionsView` and `HeaderView`. And `EpisodeStore` is now an `EnvironmentObject`, used by `ContentView`, `FilterOptionsView`, `HeaderView` and `SearchField`.

Swift playground

Open the **Networking** playground in the starter folder or continue with your playground from the previous chapter. You'll adapt code from the **Episode** playground into a fetchContents() method in **EpisodeStore.swift** and replace the old prototype Episode with the new Episode structure and extension. And, you'll create a new Swift file — **VideoURL.swift** — for the VideoURL class and make it conform to ObservableObject.

Some of the new Episode properties are slightly different, so you'll fix a few errors that appear in **EpisodeView.swift** and **PlayerView.swift**.

The starter project already contains **FormatterExtension.swift** and **URLComponentsExtension.swift**.

From playground to app

The playground code is enough to get your app downloading popular free episodes. You'll implement query options and filters in the second half of this chapter.

➤ In **Project navigator**, in the **Preview Content** group, delete **EpisodeStoreDevData.swift**. You're about to change the Episode structure, and you'll initialize the episodes array from a URLSession response.

➤ In **EpisodeStore.swift**, replace init() with this code:

```
func fetchContents() {}

init() {
  fetchContents()
}
```

You'll copy playground code to implement fetchContents(), and init() simply calls fetchContents().

Adapting EpisodeStore code

Now start copying and adapting code from the **Episode** playground page into **EpisodeStore.swift**.

➤ Replace `func fetchContents() {}` with the following code:

```
// 1
let baseURLString = "https://api.raywenderlich.com/api/contents"
var baseParams = [
  "filter[subscription_types][]": "free",
  "filter[content_types][]": "episode",
  "sort": "-popularity",
  "page[size]": "20",
  "filter[q]": ""
]
// 2
func fetchContents() {
  guard var urlComponents = URLComponents(string: baseURLString)
  else { return }
  urlComponents.setQueryItems(with: baseParams)
  guard let contentsURL = urlComponents.url else { return }
}
```

1. You copy `baseURLString` and `baseParams` into `EpisodeStore` as properties.

2. You create `urlComponents` as a local variable in `fetchContents()`, then call `urlComponents.setQueryItems(with:)`. Now that you're in a method, you create `urlComponents` and `contentsURL` in guard statements, so you can exit if one fails.

➤ Now copy the `URLSession` code into `fetchContents()` and modify what happens on the main queue:

```
URLSession.shared
  .dataTask(with: contentsURL) { data, response, error in
    // defer { PlaygroundPage.current.finishExecution() }  // 1
    if let data = data,
      let response = response as? HTTPURLResponse {
      print(response.statusCode)
      if let decodedResponse = try? JSONDecoder().decode(  // 2
        EpisodeStore.self, from: data) {
        DispatchQueue.main.async {
          self.episodes = decodedResponse.episodes  // 3
        }
        return
      }
    }
    print(
```

```
      "Contents fetch failed: " +
        "\(error?.localizedDescription ?? "Unknown error")")
  }
  .resume()
```

1. Delete the `PlaygroundPage` line of code. It won't work here anyway.

2. You create a default `JSONDecoder`. You don't need to configure it because you'll be providing a custom `init(from:)`.

3. In the `DispatchQueue.main` closure, you set `episodes` from the decoded response.

Xcode complains that `EpisodeStore` doesn't conform to `Decodable`, so start fixing that now.

➤ Add this code to `EpisodeStore` below the `init()` method:

```
// 1
enum CodingKeys: String, CodingKey {
  case episodes = "data"   // array of dictionary
}
// 2
init(from decoder: Decoder) throws {
  let container = try decoder.container(
    keyedBy: CodingKeys.self)
  episodes = try container.decode(
    [Episode].self, forKey: .episodes)
}
```

1. In the next step, you'll declare `EpisodeStore` to be `Decodable`, so you copy `CodingKeys` from the playground to satisfy that protocol.

2. In your app, `EpisodeStore` publishes an array and two dictionaries. `Published` properties aren't `Decodable`, so you must explicitly decode at least one of them to conform to `Decodable`.

➤ Scroll up and replace the `class EpisodeStore` line with this:

```
final class EpisodeStore: ObservableObject, Decodable {
```

When you add the `init(from:)` initializer, an Xcode error might tell you to mark it as `required`. This keyword indicates that every subclass of `EpisodeStore` must implement this initializer. You won't be subclassing `EpisodeStore`, so you apply the `final` keyword to the class to make this fact explicit. This gets rid of the error message.

Having added `CodingKeys` and `init(from:)`, you can now declare that `EpisodeStore` conforms to `Decodable`.

Copying Episode code

Now the `Decodable` issue moves to `Episode`, so you'll fix that next. The code you need is already in the playground. There's a lot of it, so you'll put it in its own file.

➤ Delete `Episode` in **EpisodeStore.swift**, then create a new **Swift file** named **Episode.swift** with the playground code for `struct Episode` and `extension Episode`.

And now you need to supply the `VideoURL` class.

Copying VideoURL & VideoURLString code

➤ Create a new **Swift file** named **VideoURL.swift** and add this code to it:

```
class VideoURL: ObservableObject {
  @Published var urlString = ""
}
```

Instead of the simple `class` and `var` in the playground, `VideoURL` in your app is an `ObservableObject`. It *publishes* `urlString` because there's a network delay between initializing a `VideoURL` object and assigning a non-empty value to `urlString`.

➤ Below `VideoURL`, copy `VideoURLString` and its extension, and `VideoAttributes` from the playground.

➤ Now copy the `init(videoId:)` method from the playground into `VideoURL` and modify the `dataTask` completion handler:

```
init(videoId: Int) {
  let baseURLString =
    "https://api.raywenderlich.com/api/videos/"
  let queryURLString =
    baseURLString + String(videoId) + "/stream"
  guard let queryURL = URL(string: queryURLString)
  else { return }
  URLSession.shared
    .dataTask(with: queryURL) { data, response, error in
      if let data = data,
        let response = response as? HTTPURLResponse {
        // 1
        if response.statusCode != 200 {
          print("\(videoId) \(response.statusCode)")
```

```
        return
      }
      if let decodedResponse = try? JSONDecoder().decode(
        VideoURLString.self, from: data) {
        // 2
        self.urlString = decodedResponse.urlString
      }
    } else {
      print(
        "Videos fetch failed: " +
          "\(error?.localizedDescription ?? "Unknown error")")
    }
  }
  .resume()
}
```

1. To reduce the number of debug messages, you only print the status code if it's not **200 OK**. The status code is **404 Not found** if an item doesn't have a video URL. As there's no data to decode, you exit, leaving `urlString` with the value "".

2. You don't need to print the `urlString`.

Using changed Episode properties

The `difficulty` property is now optional, so the app won't compile. If Xcode hasn't already complained, press **Command-B** to build the app, and error flags will appear. Two errors are about this line of code:

```
Text(String(episode.difficulty).capitalized)
```

It appears in **EpisodeView.swift** and in **PlayerView.swift**.

➤ In **EpisodeView.swift**, click the red error button to see Xcode's suggestions and select the first fix "Coalesce using '??'...".

Xcode suggests fixes for optional.

➤ Use "" for the default value:

```
Text(String(episode.difficulty ?? "").capitalized)
```

➤ Do the same to fix the error in **PlayerView.swift**.

Another error appears in the first line of body in **PlayerView.swift**:

```
if let url = URL(string: episode.videoURLString) {
```

➤ The `videoURLString` in the simple `Episode` structure of Chapter 22, "Lists & Navigation", is now `videoURL?.urlString`. It's an optional, so replace this line using the same coalescing trick:

```
if let url = URL(string: episode.videoURL?.urlString ?? "") {
```

Debugging with a breakpoint

And your app is ready!

➤ Build and run. If it runs very slowly in a simulator, install it on an iOS device. Then, scroll down and examine the **Introduction** episodes:

Notice something odd about these Introduction episodes?

They're all the same! Tap them to make sure: Yes, the videos are all the same too.

If you send the same request in RESTed, you'll see the same number of **Introduction** episodes, but they're all different. So how can you see what's happening in your app?

Breakpoints to the rescue! In Chapter 9, "Saving History Data", you learned how to insert a breakpoint on a line of code where you want execution to pause while you inspect the current values. This time, you'll just print out values every time that line executes without pausing the app.

In this case, it's useful to see the `videoIdentifier` and `description` values of each decoded **Introduction** episode.

➤ In **Episode.swift**, in `extension Episode`, add a breakpoint to the line `self.id = id` in `init(from:)`, then right-click the blue breakpoint arrow and select **Edit Breakpoint...**.

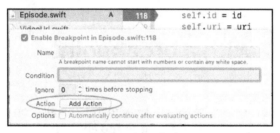

Breakpoint window

➤ In the breakpoint window, click **Add Action** and set the **Action** to **Log Message**. In the **Condition** field, type **name == "Introduction"** and, in the message field, type **@videoIdentifier@ @description@**. Finally, check the box to **Automatically continue after evaluating actions**.

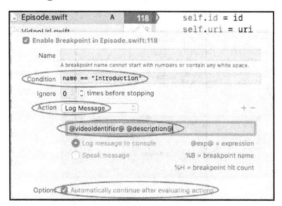

Edit breakpoint to show Introduction details.

➤ Build and run.

```
1450  "Getting started with Android development begins right here. Learn about what you\'ll be making in this course.\n"
2056  "Let\'s take a look at what you\'ll be learning in this part of the course, and why it\'s important.\n"
2978  "Getting started with Android development begins right here. Learn about what you\'ll be making in this course.\n"
1707  "Let\'s review what you will be learning in this course, beginning with a brief history of RxSwift.\n"
3146  "Welcome to Programming in Swift! Let\'s go over what you\'ll be learning in this course, and why it\'s important.\n"
1977  "Table views are an integral part of iOS. In this video, you\'ll get an overview of them and what this course will cover.\n"
2451  "In this introductory episode, find out what we\'ll cover in the course, and familiarize yourself with Big O Notation.\n"
2245  "Let\'s review what you will be learning in this course, including a brief discussion of benefits of MVVM and the course sample project.\n"
3243  "Welcome to the SwiftUI course. In this section you\'re going to learn the basics of building out interfaces using SwiftUI.\n"
```

Breakpoint messages

The debug console displays videoIdentifier and description for several episodes, and they're all different. So, there's nothing wrong with the server response or with your app's decoding.

Notice the first **Introduction** episode is the one that gets repeated in the running app.

➤ Click the breakpoint arrow to disable it.

Your app decodes several different **Introduction** episodes into your episodes array, but displays only the first one, again and again. This is the work of the loop in **ContentView.swift**, so this is the next place to look for the problem.

```
ForEach(store.episodes, id: \.name) { episode in
```

Oh! id: \.name means every episode with the same name is the same episode, so the first **Introduction** episode is **the** episode.

Easy to forget but also easy to fix. :]

➤ In **ContentView.swift**, delete the id: \.name parameter from ForEach.

```
ForEach(store.episodes) { episode in
```

Episode now has an id property, which ForEach and List use by default, unless you specify some other value for the id argument. This id property is different for each episode, even if they have the same name.

➤ Build and run.

RWFreeView running!

Much better!

Improving the user experience

Congratulations, your app is working! Now you can look for opportunities to improve your users' experience. Your app should enable them to complete tasks and achieve goals without confusion or interruptions. You don't want users scratching their heads wondering what's happening or what to do next.

Exercise: Display parentName

➤ Take another look at those **Introduction** episodes. Even if a user reads the description, it doesn't always tell them enough to decide whether to play the video. Sometimes, there are several **Conclusion** episodes, too. Can you add more information to these episodes?

In the raywenderlich.com API, the attributes key parent_name tells you the course an episode is in. You can improve your users' experience by adding a parentName property to Episode, then display it when name is "Introduction" or "Conclusion".

Try this exercise on your own before reading my list of steps below or looking at the final project.

➤ In **Episode.swift**, in Episode, add parentName: String? to the list of properties. It's rare, but possible, for parent_name to be null.

➤ Add case parentName = "parent_name" to AttrsKeys.

➤ Decode it with let parentName = try attrs.decode(String?.self, forKey: .parentName).

➤ Still in init(from:), set the property with the decoded value self.parentName = parentName.

➤ In **EpisodeView.swift**, display parentName below name:

```
if episode.name == "Introduction" ||
   episode.name == "Conclusion" {
  Text(episode.parentName ?? "")
    .font(.subheadline)
    .foregroundColor(Color(UIColor.label))
    .padding(.top, -5.0)
}
```

Negative padding squeezes it up closer to the episode name.

➤ Build and run, then scroll down to see the **Introduction** episodes now display more information:

Introduction episodes display parent name.

Indicating activity

The list is blank while the `dataTask` is running. Users expect to see an activity indicator until the list appears.

ActivityIndicator.swift contains the spinner activity indicator from Sarah's article bit.ly/3cVlzif, modified to use your app's gradient colors.

➤ In **EpisodeStore.swift**, add this property to control whether the spinner appears:

```
@Published var loading = false
```

➤ In `fetchContents()`, add this line before the `URLSession` code:

```
loading = true
```

➤ And in the `dataTask` handler, add this at the beginning, where you had the `defer` closure to finish playground execution:

```
defer {
  DispatchQueue.main.async {
```

```
        self.loading = false
    }
}
```

You set `loading` to `true` before starting `dataTask` and set it to `false` after receiving and decoding the network response. Using the `defer` block ensures you hide the activity indicator in both success and failure cases.

Now you've set the value of `loading` in all the necessary places, you'll use its value to show or hide `ActivityIndicator()`.

➤ In **ContentView.swift**, add this line after `HeaderView(count:)`

```
if store.loading { ActivityIndicator() }
```

➤ Build and run to see your spinner.

Spinner activity indicator

It looks pretty cool! After you've implemented all the query options, you'll make the list do something even cooler while it loads the new episodes.

What if there's no video?

While writing this chapter, sometimes one or more *placeholder* episodes appeared in the contents query results. These don't have a video, so PlayerView is blank — not a good user experience. I created a PlaceholderView to display when there's no video URL.

It turns out these placeholders shouldn't be included in results, and they've been deleted now. But you should still check for a video URL. You might, for example, decide to allow non-episode content types, which don't have videos (but forget to provide an appropriate viewer).

In **PlayerView.swift**, you'll display a "No video" message when there's no video URL.

➤ In **PlayerView.swift**, click the gutter next to GeometryReader to fold it so you can see where the if let url closure ends:

```
var body: some View {
  if let url = URL(string: episode.videoUrl?.urlString ?? "") {
    GeometryReader { ••• }
  }|
  }
}
```

Fold GeometryReader to see closing } of if.

➤ Replace the if closure's closing brace with this else closure:

```
} else {
  PlaceholderView()
}
```

To test this, you need to temporarily change the content_types value.

➤ In **EpisodeStore.swift**, in baseParams, change "episode" to "article":

```
"filter[content_types][]": "article"
```

➤ Build and run, then tap any item:

Articles don't have videos.

➤ In **EpisodeStore.swift**, in baseParams, change "article" back to "episode":

```
"filter[content_types][]": "episode"
```

OK, your app's basic download function is working well, delivering a great user experience. Now, it's time to implement all those options and filters, so your users can customize their query results.

Implementing HeaderView options

HeaderView provides these options for users to customize downloaded contents:

- Clear some or all filter options.

- Enter a search term.

- Change the page size.

- Switch sorting between **Popular** and **New**.

You'll manage the filter options in the next two sections.

In this section, you'll implement the last three actions, which correspond to the last three keys in the baseParams dictionary in EpisodeStore:

```
var baseParams = [
  "filter[subscription_types][]": "free",
  "filter[content_types][]": "episode",
  "sort": "-popularity",
  "page[size]": "20",
  "filter[q]": ""
]
```

For each of these three user actions, you'll write code to change the appropriate value and send a new request.

Entering a search term

In **HeaderView.swift**, add this property to SearchField:

```
@EnvironmentObject var store: EpisodeStore
```

You'll pass the user's search term to the baseParams dictionary in EpisodeStore.

➤ In body, replace TextField("", text: $queryTerm) with the following:

```
TextField(
  "",
  text: $queryTerm,
  onEditingChanged: { _ in },
  onCommit: {
    store.baseParams["filter[q]"] = queryTerm
    store.fetchContents()
  }
)
```

When the user taps the keyboard's **return** key, the onCommit code runs. You set the value of the query filter to the user's search term, then call fetchContents().

➤ Build and run, then enter a search term like **map**:

Search for episodes about map

You can tell it worked. The episode names have changed, some of the descriptions mention MapKit or "map", and there are only 8 episodes instead of 20.

Changing the page size

Next, implement the page size menu.

➤ Scroll up to the page size menu buttons and add actions:

```
Button("10 results/page") {
  store.baseParams["page[size]"] = "10"
  store.fetchContents()
}
Button("20 results/page") {
  store.baseParams["page[size]"] = "20"
  store.fetchContents()
}
Button("30 results/page") {
  store.baseParams["page[size]"] = "30"
  store.fetchContents()
}
Button("No change") { }
```

Depending on the selected button, you set the value of the page size key, then call `fetchContents()`.

➤ Build and run, then select 10 or 30 results per page:

Change the page size

I included 10 results/page in the menu because it's easy to count to 10 to see if it's working. ;]

Switching the sort order

And now, get the sort order control working.

➤ In **HeaderView.swift**, change the initial value of `sortOn`:

```
@State private var sortOn = "none"
```

This value doesn't match either segment `tag`, so neither segment shows as selected until the user taps one.

➤ Add this modifier to `Picker("", selection: $sortOn)`:

```
.onChange(of: sortOn) { _ in
  store.baseParams["sort"] = sortOn == "new" ?
    "-released_at" : "-popularity"
  store.fetchContents()
}
```

When the `sortOn` value changes, you set the `baseParams` value for the `"sort"` key, then call `fetchContents()`.

➤ Build and run. Notice the date of the first item is **Sep 2019**, then select **New** in the picker:

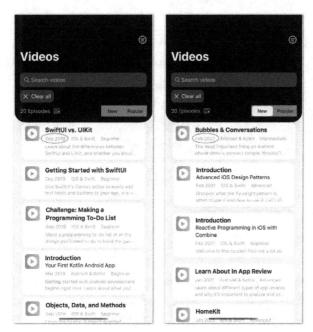

Sort by release date

Now the items all have recent release dates.

You've implemented every `HeaderView` option except clearing query filters. Before you can clear a query filter, you need a way to add them to `HeaderView`. So first, you'll implement query filters in `FilterOptionsView`.

Implementing filters in FilterOptionsView

In `FilterOptionsView`, users can select or deselect filter options then tap **Apply** or **X** to combine the selected options into a new request.

There are two types of query filters: **Platforms** (called domains in the API) and **Difficulty**. Users can select one or more of each type — Android & Kotlin *and* Flutter, Beginner *and* Intermediate — so you can't store their selections in a dictionary like `baseParams`, where each key is a unique query parameter name.

Query filter dictionaries

To keep track of selected query filter options, the starter project contains two query filter dictionaries in **EpisodeStore.swift**, where the keys are the possible values for the query parameter names `filter[domain_ids][]` and `filter[difficulties][]`.

```swift
@Published var domainFilters: [String: Bool] = [
  "1": true,
  "2": false,
  "3": false,
  "5": false,
  "8": false,
  "9": false
]
@Published var difficultyFilters: [String: Bool] = [
  "advanced": false,
  "beginner": true,
  "intermediate": false
]
```

A query filter dictionary value is `true` if the user has selected the query filter matching that key. In the starter project, the iOS & Swift domain and beginner difficulty are already selected but not yet implemented.

Tapping a query filter button in `FilterOptionsView` toggles its value in one of these query filter dictionaries. For example:

```swift
Button("iOS & Swift") { store.domainFilters["1"]!.toggle() }
```

This value also switches the color of the query filter button in `FilterOptionsView`: green when `true`, gray when `false`.

```
.buttonStyle(
   FilterButtonStyle(
      selected: store.domainFilters["1"]!, width: nil))
```

When your users tap query filter buttons to make their selections, then tap the **X** or **Apply** button, here's what your code needs to do.

➤ In **FilterOptionsView.swift**, add this line to the actions of the xmark and **Apply** buttons, before the line that dismisses this sheet:

```
store.fetchContents()
```

That's all! You'll soon update `fetchContents()` to combine all the user's selections into a single query URL.

Clearing all query filters

In `FilterOptionsView`, the user might tap **Clear All**. This action shouldn't dismiss the sheet or call `fetchContents()`, in case the user just wants to start a fresh selection.

➤ In **FilterOptionsView.swift**, set the **Clear All** button's action:

```
store.clearQueryFilters()
```

➤ And in **EpisodeStore.swift**, add this method to `EpisodeStore`:

```
func clearQueryFilters() {
   domainFilters.keys.forEach { domainFilters[$0] = false }
   difficultyFilters.keys.forEach {
      difficultyFilters[$0] = false
   }
}
```

You only need to set all the values to `false` in both query filter dictionaries. You created a method to do this because you'll also call it in `HeaderView`.

➤ Build and run, show the filter options view, then select some query filters. The buttons turn green. Now tap **Clear All** to see them turn gray.

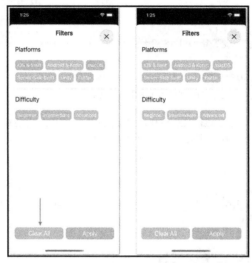

Clear all query filters

Filtering and mapping query filters

Tapping **Apply** won't change your results yet. You have to add the corresponding query items to your contentsURL.

➤ Still in **EpisodeStore.swift**, replace the guard let contentsURL line in fetchContents() with this code:

```
let selectedDomains = domainFilters.filter {
  $0.value
}
.keys
let domainQueryItems = selectedDomains.map {
  queryDomain($0)
}

let selectedDifficulties = difficultyFilters.filter {
  $0.value
}
.keys
let difficultyQueryItems = selectedDifficulties.map {
  queryDifficulty($0)
}

urlComponents.queryItems! += domainQueryItems
urlComponents.queryItems! += difficultyQueryItems
```

```
guard let contentsURL = urlComponents.url else { return }
print(contentsURL)
```

You filter for domainFilters keys with value true, producing a collection of domain keys. Then you call the queryDomain(_:) method on each key, producing an array of URLQueryItem. You do the same for difficultyFilters, also producing an array of URLQueryItem. Then you append each array to urlComponents.queryItems to create your contents query URL.

➤ Build and run. Notice all the results are for **iOS & Swift Beginner**, even though the header view doesn't display these buttons.

➤ Show the filter options sheet and select or deselect some query filters. Tap **Apply** or the xmark:

Apply filters

These filter buttons work. Now to get the HeaderView buttons in sync.

Implementing query filters in HeaderView

When the user selects query filters in FilterOptionsView, their buttons should appear in HeaderView. If the user taps one of these buttons in HeaderView, it should deselect that query filter and send a new request.

Clearing all in HeaderView

Before you set up these query filter buttons, implement the **Clear all** button to clear the query filters and the search term.

➤ In **HeaderView.swift**, add this code as the action for the **Clear all** button:

```
queryTerm = ""
store.baseParams["filter[q]"] = queryTerm
store.clearQueryFilters()
store.fetchContents()
```

You empty the search TextField value and set the value of the query parameter to this empty string. Then, you clear the domain and difficulty query filters and call fetchContents().

Showing the query filter buttons

This display is trickier than FilterOptionsView because the number of buttons is variable. Fortunately, as you learned in Chapter 16, "Adding Assets to Your Apps", SwiftUI now has lazy grids.

➤ First, set up a three-column layout. Add this property to HeaderView:

```
let threeColumns = [
  GridItem(.flexible(minimum: 55)),
  GridItem(.flexible(minimum: 55)),
  GridItem(.flexible(minimum: 55))
]
```

➤ **Clear all** is one of the buttons in this grid, so replace its enclosing HStack with the following:

```
HStack {
  LazyVGrid(columns: threeColumns) {  // 1
    Button("Clear all") {
      queryTerm = ""
      store.baseParams["filter[q]"] = queryTerm
      store.clearQueryFilters()
```

```
      store.fetchContents()
    }
    .buttonStyle(HeaderButtonStyle())
    ForEach(
      Array(
        store.domainFilters.merging(   // 2
          store.difficultyFilters) { _, second in second
        }
        .filter {   // 3
          $0.value
        }
        .keys), id: \.self) { key in
      Button(store.filtersDictionary[key]!) {   // 4
        if Int(key) == nil {   // 5
          store.difficultyFilters[key]!.toggle()
        } else {
          store.domainFilters[key]!.toggle()
        }
        store.fetchContents()   // 6
      }
      .buttonStyle(HeaderButtonStyle())
    }
  }
  Spacer()
}
```

1. A LazyVGrid fills in items horizontally, row by row. The first button is always **Clear all**.

2. The dictionary method merging merges the two query filter dictionaries into a new, temporary dictionary. You specify _, second in second to resolve any key clashes in favor of the second dictionary. (You know there won't be any key clashes, but Xcode doesn't.) To use ForEach, you create an Array from the resulting collection of keys.

3. You filter for query filter keys with value true, just like in fetchContents().

4. For each selected key, you create a Button. To display the correct label, filtersDictionary is Episode.domainDictionary plus difficulty items.

5. You can create an Int from a domainFilters key but not from a difficultyFilters key, so this test tells you which query filter dictionary to update.

6. Every button calls fetchContents() to send the new request.

➤ Build and run. Now the header view displays buttons for **Beginner** and **iOS & Swift**, and these match the green buttons in `FilterOptionsView`:

Filter buttons in HeaderView

➤ Close the filter options sheet. In the header, tap **iOS & Swift**:

Deselecting filter in HeaderView

And now you get **Beginner** episodes for **Android & Kotlin** too. And the **iOS & Swift** button in `FilterOptionsView` is now gray.

One last thing...

Your activity spinner appears whenever the user changes a query filter or option. The previous list persists until the spinner stops. Instead, why not show *redacted* items?

➤ In **ContentView.swift**, edit the condition for showing `ActivityIndicator()`:

```
if store.loading && store.episodes.isEmpty {
  ActivityIndicator()
}
```

When the app launches, `store.episodes` is empty while the app decodes the initial request data. After the initial download, it's possible to select filter options that return 0 episodes, so you keep `store.loading` in the condition to stop the spinner even when there aren't any episodes to show.

Also add this modifier to `FilterOptionsView()` when you present it:

```
.environmentObject(store)
```

You pass the environment object to the modal sheet explicitly. When you present a view as a modal sheet, it isn't actually in the view tree of `ContentView`. In spite of this, `FilterOptionsView` works pretty well, until it doesn't. It's possible to create conditions for a run-time error, complaining the modal view doesn't have the environment object from an ancestor view. The app crashes. Passing `store` explicitly prevents this problem.

➤ Then modify the `ForEach` closure with this:

```
.redacted(reason: store.loading ? .placeholder : [])
```

While your app is decoding the response data into the `episodes` array, you display a placeholder view for each item. This replaces text with rounded rectangles of the same size and color. When loading finishes, you remove the `reason` for redaction, so your items appear as normal.

As a final touch, make sure the `PlayButtonIcon` for each icon *isn't* redacted.

➤ In **EpisodeView.swift**, add `unredacted` modifier to `PlayButtonIcon`:

```
PlayButtonIcon(width: 40, height: 40, radius: 6)
  .unredacted()
```

➤ Build and run and wait for the list to load. Then, change any query option to see your redacted placeholders:

Redacted placeholder views

It looks so professional!

Your RWFreeView is now a fully-functional real live app. Install it on your iOS device and enjoy exploring all our free episodes. One of the joys of writing this chapter was watching Ray's "SwiftUI vs. UIKit" video multiple times — just to make sure the app was still working, of course. ;] And check out the next (final) chapter to create an RWFreeView widget.

Key points

- `Published` properties aren't `Decodable`, so you must explicitly decode at least one of them to make an `ObservableObject` conform to `Decodable`.

- After adding a breakpoint to a line of code, you can edit it to print out values without pausing the app every time that line executes.

- Remember to let `ForEach` and `List` use the `id` property of an `Identifiable` type.

- Look for opportunities to improve your users' experience and head off "huh?" moments.

Chapter 26: Widgets

By Audrey Tam

Ever since Apple showed off its new home screen widgets in the 2020 WWDC Platforms State of the Union, everyone has been creating them. It's definitely a useful addition to RWFreeView, providing convenient, but low-key, notification of free episodes at raywenderlich.com. And, it gives your users quick access to your app.

> **Note**: The WidgetKit API continues to evolve at the moment, which may result in changes that break your code. Apple's template code has changed a few times since the WWDC demos. You might still experience some instability. That said, Widgets are cool and a ton of fun!

Getting started

Open the starter project or continue with your app from the previous chapter.

WidgetKit

WidgetKit is Apple's API for adding widgets to your app. The *widget extension* template helps you create a *timeline* of *entries*. You decide what app data you want to display and the time interval between entries.

And, you define a view for each size of widget — small, medium, large — you want to support.

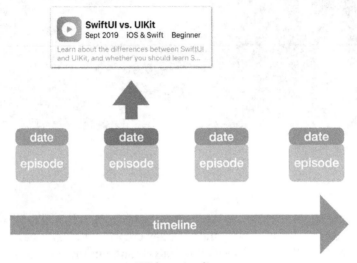

Widget timeline

Here's a typical workflow for creating a widget:

1. Add a widget extension to your app. Configure the widget's display name and description.

2. Select or adapt a data model type from your app to display in the widget. Create a timeline entry structure: a Date plus your data model type. Create sample data for snapshot and placeholder entries.

3. Decide whether to support all three widget sizes. Create small, medium and/or large views to display one or more data model values.

4. Create a timeline to deliver timeline entries. Decide on the *refresh policy*.

Adding a widget extension

➤ Start by adding a widget extension with **File ▸ New ▸ Target…**.

Create a new target.

➤ Search for "widget", select **Widget Extension** and click **Next**:

Search for 'widget'.

➤ Name it **RWFreeViewWidget**, select your team and make sure **Include Configuration Intent** is **not** checked:

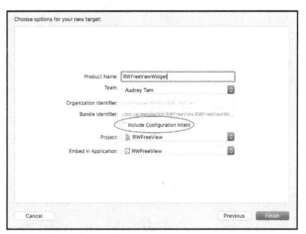

Don't select Include Configuration Intent.

There are two widget configurations: **Static** and **Intent**. A widget with `IntentConfiguration` uses Siri intents to let the user customize widget parameters. Your RWFreeView widget will be static.

> **Note:** `IntentConfiguration` is covered in our tutorial *Getting Started With Widgets* [bit.ly/2MS7K9U](bit.ly/2MS7K9U)

➤ Click **Finish** and agree to the activate-scheme dialog:

Activate scheme for new widget extension.

Configuring your widget

A new target group named **RWFreeViewWidget** appears in the Project navigator. It contains a single Swift file.

➤ Open **RWFreeViewWidget.swift**, then find RWFreeViewWidget and edit the last two modifiers: configuration display name and description.

```
@main  // 1
struct RWFreeViewWidget: Widget {
  let kind: String = "RWFreeViewWidget"

  var body: some WidgetConfiguration {
    StaticConfiguration(
      kind: kind,
      provider: Provider()  // 2
    ) { entry in
      RWFreeViewWidgetEntryView(entry: entry)  // 3
    }
    // 4
    .configurationDisplayName("RW Free View")
    .description("View free raywenderlich.com video episodes.")
  }
}
```

1. The @main attribute means this is the widget's entry point. The structure's name and its kind property are the name you gave it when you created it.

2. You'll define your widget's timeline, snapshot and placeholder entries in Provider.

3. You'll create your widget view(s) in RWFreeViewWidgetEntryView.

4. In this structure, you only need to customize the name to **RW Free View** and the description to **View free raywenderlich.com video episodes.** Your users will see these in the widget gallery.

Doing a trial run

The widget template provides a lot of boilerplate code you simply have to customize. It works right out of the box, so you can try it out now to make sure everything runs smoothly when you're ready to test your code.

➤ You can try out your widget in a simulator. If you want to install your app on your iOS device, you need to sign both targets. In the **Project** navigator, select the top level **RWFreeView** folder. Use your organization instead of "com.raywenderlich" in the bundle identifiers and set the team for each target.

> **Note**: Your widget's bundle ID prefix must be the same as your app's. This isn't a problem with RWFreeView but, if your project has different bundle IDs for Debug, Release and Beta, you'll need to edit your widget's bundle ID prefix to match.

➤ RWFreeViewWidget is a second target and it's probably the currently selected scheme. Make sure you select the **RWFreeView** scheme, then build and run. Tap the **Home** button in the simulator tool bar to close the app, then press on some empty area of your home window until the icons start to jiggle.

➤ Tap + in the upper left corner, then scroll down to find **RWFreeView**:

Widget gallery in simulator

If you've installed the app on a device, your gallery looks something like this:

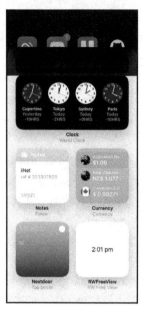

Widget gallery on iPhone

➤ Select it to see snapshots of the three sizes:

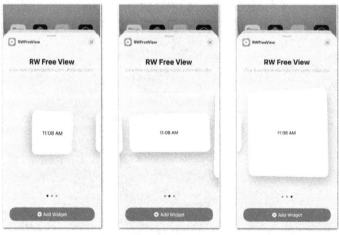

Snapshots of the three widget sizes.

➤ Tap **Add Widget** to see your widget on the screen:

Your widget on the home screen.

➤ Tap **Done** in the upper right corner.

➤ Tap the widget to reopen RWFreeView.

Your widget works! Now, you simply have to make it display information from RWFreeView.

➤ Close the app then long-press the widget to open its menu and select **Remove Widget**. Get into the habit of removing the widget after you've confirmed it's working. This is especially important if you've installed the app on your device. While you're developing your widget, it will display a new view every three seconds, and that's a real drain on your battery.

Creating entries from your app's data

It makes sense for your widget to display some of the information your app shows for each episode. These properties are in the `Episode` structure.

➤ In **RWFreeViewWidget.swift**, find `SimpleEntry`. Add this line below `date`:

```
let episode: Episode
```

An Xcode error appears, because the widget doesn't know about `Episode`. You need to add **Episode.swift** to the widget target.

➤ In Project navigator, select **Episode.swift**. Show the File inspector and check the **Target Membership** box for **RWFreeViewWidgetExtension**:

Add Episode.swift to widget target.

`Episode` has a property of type `VideoURL` and uses `Formatter.iso8601` to create `releaseData`, so error messages might now appear in **Episode.swift**.

➤ Also add **VideoURL.swift** and **FormatterExtension.swift** to the widget target.

Now the error messages in **RWFreeViewWidget.swift** are the expected ones about `Missing argument for parameter 'episode' in call`. The missing `Episode` arguments are for creating `SimpleEntry` instances in `placeholder(in:)`, `getSnapshot(in:completion:)`, `getTimeline(in:completion:)` and down in the preview.

First, you need a sample episode for the parameter value.

➤ In **RWFreeViewWidget.swift**, add this property to `Provider`:

```
let sampleEpisode = Episode(
  id: "5117655",
  uri: "rw://betamax/videos/3021",
  name: "SwiftUI vs. UIKit",
  parentName: nil,
  released: "Sept 2019",
  difficulty: "beginner",
  description: "Learn about the differences between SwiftUI and"
```

```
        + "UIKit, and whether you should learn SwiftUI, UIKit, or "
        + "both.\n" ,
   domain: "iOS & Swift")
```

The widget doesn't actually need `uri`, but the default `Episode` initializer requires this parameter.

➤ Now fix the errors one by one, or use this handy shortcut for **Editor ▸ Fix All Issues**: **Control-Option-Command-F**. Then replace all the `Episode` placeholders in `Provider` with `sampleEpisode` and replace the one in `RWFreeViewWidget_Previews` with `Provider().sampleEpisode`.

Placeholder & snapshot

Adding the `Episode` property to `SimpleEntry` caused errors in the `Provider` structure, which creates two `SimpleEntry` instances. Its methods are called by WidgetKit, not by any code you write.

To display your widget for the first time, WidgetKit calls `placeholder(in:)` and applies the same `redacted(reason: .placeholder)` modifier you used at the end of the previous chapter to mask the view's contents. This method is *synchronous*: Nothing else can run on its queue until it finishes. So don't do any network downloads or complex calculations in this method.

WidgetKit calls `getSnapshot(in:completion:)` whenever the widget is in a transient state, waiting for data or appearing in the widget gallery.

Creating widget views

Now you've decided what data to display, you need to define views to display it.

➤ First, in **RWFreeViewWidget.swift**, in `RWFreeViewWidgetEntryView`, add this environment property:

```
@Environment(\.widgetFamily) var family
```

You'll use this to customize the widget view for small, medium and large widget sizes.

➤ Still in `RWFreeViewWidgetEntryView`, replace the body contents with this code:

```
VStack(alignment: .leading, spacing: 6) {
  HStack {
    PlayButtonIcon(width: 50, height: 50, radius: 10)
      .unredacted()
    VStack(alignment: .leading) {
      Text(entry.episode.name)
        .font(.headline)
        .fontWeight(.bold)
      if family != .systemSmall {
        HStack {
          Text(entry.episode.released + "   ")
          Text(entry.episode.domain + "   ")
          Text(String(entry.episode.difficulty ?? "")
            .capitalized)
        }
      } else {
        Text(entry.episode.released + "   ")
      }
    }
  }
  .foregroundColor(Color(UIColor.label))

  if family != .systemSmall {
    Text(entry.episode.description)
      .lineLimit(2)
  }
}
.padding(.horizontal)
.background(Color.itemBkgd)
.font(.footnote)
.foregroundColor(Color(UIColor.systemGray))
```

This is just a mini-version of your app's `EpisodeView`, allowing more space for the description. The small widget size doesn't have much space, so you only display the episode `name` and `released` properties.

Again, you need to add some app files to your widget target, to get rid of the error messages.

➤ Add these files to the widget target: **PlayButtonIcon.swift** and, for `Color.itemBkgd`, **ColorExtension.swift** and **Assets.xcassets**. If the error messages don't go away, press **Command-B** to rebuild the project.

Widget sizes

➤ Now preview your widget.

Preview of small size widget

> **Note**: Don't worry if the playback button icon doesn't look right. I experienced an intermittent preview bug that displayed just an orange gradient. It looked fine in a simulator or on a device.

Not bad, but it looks a little crowded, and a longer title wouldn't fit at all. Try the medium size.

➤ In `RWFreeViewWidget_Previews`, replace the contents of `previews` with:

```
let view = RWFreeViewWidgetEntryView(
  entry: SimpleEntry(
    date: Date(),
    episode: Provider().sampleEpisode))
view.previewContext(WidgetPreviewContext(family: .systemSmall))
view.previewContext(WidgetPreviewContext(family: .systemMedium))
view.previewContext(WidgetPreviewContext(family: .systemLarge))
```

Now you can preview all three sizes at once:

Preview all three widget sizes

If you think one of the sizes looks best, or if you definitely don't want to support one of the sizes, you can restrict your widget to specific size(s).

For RWFreeView, the medium size looks best, so you'll only support that size.

➤ In `RWFreeViewWidget`, add this modifier to `StaticConfiguration`, below `description(_:)`:

```
.supportedFamilies([.systemMedium])
```

➤ Build and run, then close the app. If you had a small or large widget installed before this, it's now gone. And when you add a widget, the only choice now is medium size.

Medium size widget in simulator

Note: If your widget doesn't appear in the gallery, or doesn't work correctly, delete the app then build and run again. If the problem persists, restart the simulator or device.

Providing a timeline of entries

The heart of your widget is the `Provider` method `getTimeline(in:completion:)`. It delivers an array of time-stamped entries for WidgetKit to display. The template code creates an array of five entries one hour apart.

```
let currentDate = Date()
for hourOffset in 0 ..< 5 {
  let entryDate = Calendar.current.date(
    byAdding: .hour,
    value: hourOffset,
    to: currentDate)!
  let entry = SimpleEntry(
    date: entryDate,
    episode: sampleEpisode)
  entries.append(entry)
}
```

This code creates each entry with the same `sampleEpisode`. You'll modify the method so it displays items in the `episodes` array. Waiting an hour between entries is no good for testing purposes, so you'll shorten the interval to a few seconds.

First, you must populate your `episodes` array.

Creating a local EpisodeStore

The quickest way — fewest lines of code — to get episodes is to create an `EpisodeStore` in the widget.

➤ In **RWFreeViewWidget.swift**, add this property to `Provider`:

```
let store = EpisodeStore()
```

➤ Add **EpisodeStore.swift** and **URLComponentsExtension.swift** to the widget target.

➤ Now, in `getTimeline(in:completion:)`, replace the `for` loop with the following code:

```
let interval = 3
for index in 0 ..< store.episodes.count {
  let entryDate = Calendar.current.date(
    byAdding: .second,
    value: index * interval,
    to: currentDate)!
  let entry = SimpleEntry(
```

```
    date: entryDate,
    episode: store.episodes[index])
  entries.append(entry)
}
```

You use the `episodes` array in `EpisodeStore` to create an array of `SimpleEntry` values, three seconds apart.

➤ Back in **EpisodeStore.swift**, add this `import` statement:

```
import WidgetKit
```

`fetchContents()` needs to call a `WidgetCenter` method to reload your widget's timeline.

➤ In `fetchContents()`, add this line to the `DispatchQueue.main.async` closure

```
WidgetCenter.shared.reloadTimelines(ofKind: "RWFreeViewWidget")
```

Initializing `EpisodeStore` calls `fetchContents()` to create the `episodes` array, but this is an asynchronous task, so a user might install the widget while its `episodes` array is empty. You tell the widget to reload its timeline when the array is ready.

➤ Build and run, then close the app. Look for your widget and add it. Then watch it display your 20 free popular episodes:

Widget showing Popular episodes

➤ Tap the widget to reopen your app. Select **New,** wait for the list to reload, then close the app. Your widget is still displaying popular episodes:

Widget still showing Popular episodes

Your widget's EpisodeStore is separate from your app's EpisodeStore, so it's still using the initial options. You need to decide between these two design options:

1. Keep the widget's array in sync with the app's.

2. Allow the user to set different query options for the widget.

Later in this chapter, you'll implement a deep link from the widget into your app to open the player view of the widget's entry. This won't make sense if the widget's array could be different from the app's array. So this chapter chooses the first design option.

> **Note:** The second option requires you to create a widget with an
> IntentConfiguration, covered in our tutorial *Getting Started With Widgets*
> bit.ly/2MS7K9U

Creating an App Group

Xcode Tip: App group containers allow apps and targets to share resources.

Whenever the user changes a query option in your app, `fetchContents()` downloads and decodes a new `episodes` array. To share this array with your widget, you'll create an app group. Then, in **EpisodeStore.swift**, you'll write a file to this app group, which you'll read from in **RWFreeViewWidget.swift**.

➤ If you haven't signed the targets yet, do it now. In the Project navigator, select the top level **RWFreeView** folder. For each target, change the bundle identifier prefix to your organization instead of "com.raywenderlich" and set the team.

➤ Now select the **RWFreeView** target. In the **Signing & Capabilities** tab, click + **Capability**, then drag **App Groups** into the window. Click + to add a new container.

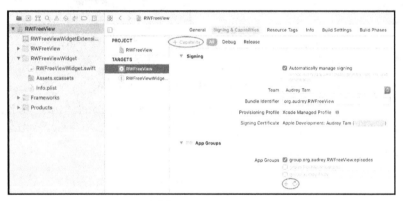

Add new app group.

➤ Name your container **group.your.prefix.RWFreeView.episodes**. Be sure to replace **your.prefix** with your bundle identifier prefix. Click the reload button if the color of your group doesn't change from red to black.

➤ Now select the **RWFreeViewWidgetExtension** target and add the **App Groups** capability. If necessary, scroll through the **App Groups** to find and select **group.your.prefix.RWFreeView.episodes**.

Writing the app group file

➤ At the top of **EpisodeStore.swift**, just below the `import WidgetKit` statement, add this code:

```
extension FileManager {
  static func sharedContainerURL() -> URL {
    return FileManager.default.containerURL(
      forSecurityApplicationGroupIdentifier:
        "group.your.prefix.RWFreeView.episodes"
    )!
  }
}
```

This is simply some standard code for getting the app group container's URL. Be sure to substitute *your* bundle identifier prefix.

It makes sense to write this app group file just after you've decoded the `contents` response into the `episodes` array. To write an array to a file, you JSON-encode it. Then the widget JSON-decodes the file contents. But you can't reuse the JSON decoding code you've built into `Episode` because that's expecting the nested JSON structure sent by the API server.

Your widget only needs a few `Episode` properties, so you'll create a `MiniEpisode` type for it to use.

➤ In **Episode.swift**, add this code at the end of the file, outside of all other curly braces:

```
struct MiniEpisode: Codable {
  let id: String
  let name: String
  let released: String
  let domain: String
  let difficulty: String
  let description: String
}
```

Every property is a `String` so you don't need any custom encoding or decoding code.

➤ In **EpisodeStore.swift**, add this property to `EpisodeStore`:

```
var miniEpisodes: [MiniEpisode] = []
```

➤ Also add this helper method to `EpisodeStore`:

```
func writeEpisodes() {
```

```
    let archiveURL = FileManager.sharedContainerURL()
      .appendingPathComponent("episodes.json")
print(">>> \(archiveURL)")

    if let dataToSave = try? JSONEncoder().encode(miniEpisodes) {
      do {
        try dataToSave.write(to: archiveURL)
      } catch {
        print("Error: Can't write episodes")
      }
    }
  }
}
```

Here, you convert your array of `MiniEpisode` values to JSON and save it to the app group's container.

➤ In `fetchContents()`, add this code to the `DispatchQueue.main.async` closure, **before** the call to `WidgetCenter`:

```
self.miniEpisodes = self.episodes.map {
  MiniEpisode(
    id: $0.id,
    name: $0.name,
    released: $0.released,
    domain: $0.domain,
    difficulty: $0.difficulty ?? "",
    description: $0.description)
}
self.writeEpisodes()
```

You map your array of `Episode` values into an array of `MiniEpisode` values, then write this array into your app group file. The existing call to `WidgetCenter` now tells the widget to reload its timeline whenever your app has downloaded and decoded a new array of episodes.

Next, go and set up the widget to read this file.

Reading the episodes file

➤ Open **RWFreeViewWidget.swift**.

You need to replace `Episode` with `MiniEpisode`.

➤ Replace the definition of `sampleEpisode` with this code

```
let sampleEpisode = MiniEpisode(
  id: "5117655",
  name: "SwiftUI vs. UIKit",
```

```
  released: "Sept 2019",
  domain: "iOS & Swift",
  difficulty: "beginner",
  description: "Learn about the differences between SwiftUI and"
    + "UIKit, and whether you should learn SwiftUI, UIKit, or "
    + "both.\n")
```

`MiniEpisode` contains only the parameters the widget needs, in a slightly different order.

➤ In `SimpleEntry`, replace `let episode: Episode` with the following:

```
let episode: MiniEpisode
```

➤ Now, in `RWFreeViewWidgetEntryView`, `difficulty` isn't an optional anymore, so remove the nil coalescing operator:

```
Text(String(entry.episode.difficulty)
  .capitalized)
```

Now, you can read your `episodes` array from the app group file.

➤ Add this helper method to `Provider`:

```
func readEpisodes() -> [MiniEpisode] {
  var episodes: [MiniEpisode] = []
  let archiveURL =
    FileManager.sharedContainerURL()
    .appendingPathComponent("episodes.json")
  print(">>> \(archiveURL)")

  if let codeData = try? Data(contentsOf: archiveURL) {
    do {
      episodes = try JSONDecoder()
        .decode([MiniEpisode].self, from: codeData)
    } catch {
      print("Error: Can't decode contents")
    }
  }
  return episodes
}
```

This reads the `MiniEpisode` values from the file `fetchContents()` saved into the app group's container.

➤ Delete this line from `Provider`:

```
let store = EpisodeStore()
```

You won't be using a local `EpisodeStore` anymore.

➤ In `getTimeline(in:completion:)`, replace the `for` loop with the following code:

```
let episodes = readEpisodes()
for index in 0 ..< episodes.count {
  let entryDate = Calendar.current.date(
    byAdding: .second,
    value: index * interval,
    to: currentDate)!
  let entry = SimpleEntry(
    date: entryDate,
    episode: episodes[index])
  entries.append(entry)
}
```

You read the `episodes` array from the app group file and use it instead of `store.episodes`.

> **Note**: If you changed the bundle identifier, you'll end up having two apps. Delete the old one before running the project.

➤ Build and run, then close the app. Look for your widget and add it. Watch it display a few of your 20 free popular episodes, then tap the widget to reopen your app. Select **New**, wait for the list to reload, then close the app. Your widget is now displaying recent episodes:

Widget reloaded with New episodes

Your widget's working well, and you could happily install it on your device now. If you want to do so, skip down to the end of this chapter to change the timeline back to one-hour intervals.

The next section adds a feature many users expect: When you tap the widget, the app should display the PlayerView for the current widget entry.

Deep-linking into your app

You can set up your widget with a deep link to activate a NavigationLink that opens a PlayerView with the widget entry's episode. Here's your workflow:

1. Create a URL scheme.

2. Modify the top level container view of your widget view with widgetURL(_:).

3. In your app, implement onOpenURL(perform:) to activate a NavigationLink with the correct destination view.

Creating a URL scheme

"URL scheme" sounds very grand and a little scary but, because it's just between your widget and your app, it can be quite simple. You're basically creating a tiny API between widget and app. The widget needs to send enough information to the app, so the app knows which view to display. Formatting this information as a URL lets you use URL or URLComponents properties to extract the necessary values.

For this app, the id property of Episode uniquely identifies it. So the URL to open "SwiftUI vs. UIKit" is simply:

```
URL(string: "rwfreeview://5117655")
```

And you can access this id value as the host property of the URL. So simple!

In your widget

➤ In **RWFreeViewWidget.swift**, in RWFreeViewWidgetEntryView, add this modifier to the top-level VStack:

```
.widgetURL(URL(string: "rwfreeview://\(entry.episode.id)"))
```

> **Note**: In the medium and large widget sizes, you can use
> Link(_:destination:) to attach links to different parts of the view.

In your app

In your app, you implement .onOpenURL(perform:) to process the widget URL. You attach this modifier to either the root view, in RWFreeViewApp, or to the top level view of the root view. For RWFreeView, you'll attach this to the NavigationView in ContentView, because the perform closure must assign a value to a @State property of ContentView.

First, you need to trigger NavigationLink programmatically. You'll use its tag-selection initializer to activate it when you set a value for the selection argument.

➤ In **ContentView.swift**, add this @State property to ContentView:

```
@State private var selectedEpisode: Episode?
```

This is the selection argument. You can activate NavigationLink by assigning a value to this property.

➤ Then, replace the ZStack in the ForEach closure with the following:

```
ZStack {
  NavigationLink(
    destination: PlayerView(episode: episode),
    tag: episode,
    selection: $selectedEpisode) {
    EmptyView()
  }
  .opacity(0)
  .buttonStyle(PlainButtonStyle())
  EpisodeView(episode: episode)
    .onTapGesture {
      selectedEpisode = episode
    }
}
```

This NavigationLink activates whenever you set selectedEpisode. But just tapping an item will no longer activate NavigationLink. So you modify EpisodeView with onTapGesture to set the value of selectedEpisode.

Xcode complains that Episode doesn't conform to Hashable, so head over to **Episode.swift** to make it so.

➤ In **Episode.swift**, add this extension:

```
extension Episode: Hashable {
  static func == (lhs: Episode, rhs: Episode) -> Bool {
    lhs.id == rhs.id
  }

  func hash(into hasher: inout Hasher) {
    hasher.combine(id)
  }
}
```

Here you made Episode conform to Hashable by implementing the equatable static function, ==(_:_:), and hash(into:).

➤ Back in **ContentView.swift**, add this modifier to the NavigationView:

```
.onOpenURL { url in
  if let id = url.host,
    let widgetEpisode = store.episodes.first(
      where: { $0.id == id }) {
    selectedEpisode = widgetEpisode
  }
}
```

You extract the id value from the widget URL, then find the first episode with the same id value.

➤ Build and run, wait for the list to load, then close the app and add your widget. Tap an entry to see it open the `PlayerView` with that video:

Deep link opens widget entry's episode.

> **Note**: This doesn't work every time. Often, when a deep link doesn't open `PlayerView`, tapping the item in the app doesn't open `PlayerView` either. This happens on a device as well as in the simulator. `NavigationLink` has a history of buggy behavior.

One last thing

You've been using a three second interval in your timeline to make testing simpler. You definitely don't want to release your widget with such a short interval.

Refresh policy

In `getTimeline(in:completion:)`, after the `for` loop, you create a `Timeline(entries:policy:)` instance. The template sets `policy` to `.atEnd`, so WidgetKit creates a new timeline after the last date in the current timeline. The new timeline doesn't start immediately. See for yourself.

➤ In **EpisodeStore.swift**, set "page[size]": "5" in baseParams so the timeline ends soon after you install the widget. Build and run, then add your widget. When it reaches the fifth item, wait for the first item to reappear. In the simulator on my Mac, it took between one and two minutes.

Of course, your current timeline fires at 3-second intervals, which is far from normal. With a more normal interval, like one hour, you probably won't notice any delay.

➤ In **EpisodeStore.swift**, set "page[size]" back to **20**.

There are two other TimelineReloadPolicy options:

• after(_:) : Specify a Date when you want WidgetKit to refresh the timeline. Like atEnd, this is more a suggestion to WidgetKit than a hard deadline.

• never: Use this policy if your app uses WidgetCenter to tell WidgetKit when to reload the timeline. This is a good option for RWFreeView. You've already seen the timeline reload almost immediately when you change a query option in your app. You could add code to your app to call fetchContents() at the same time every day, and this would also refresh your widget's timeline.

Using normal timing

If you want to use RWFreeView on your device as a real app, set up the timeline to change every hour instead of every three seconds.

> **Note**: The project in the final folder still displays every three seconds.

➤ In **RWFreeViewWidget.swift**, in getTimeline(in:completion:), change the entryDate code to this:

```
let entryDate = Calendar.current.date(
  byAdding: .hour,
  value: index,
  to: currentDate)!
```

You're restoring the template code's original timing. Now, your widget will display episodes one hour apart. You can add it to your device's home screen with no worries about excessive battery use.

You can also remove the declaration of interval as Xcode so helpfully suggests since you're no longer using it.

Key points

- WidgetKit is a new API. You might experience some instability. You can fix many problems by deleting the app or by restarting the simulator or device.

- To add a widget to your app, decide what app data you want to display and the time interval between entries. Then, define a view for each size of widget — small, medium, large — you want to support.

- Add app files to the widget target and adapt your app's data structures and views to fit your widgets.

- Create an app group to share data between your app and your widget.

- Deep-linking from your widget into your app is easy to do.

Conclusion

We hope you're excited by the new world of iOS and SwiftUI development that lies before you!

By completing this book, you've gained the knowledge and tools you need to build beautiful iOS apps. Set your imagination free and couple your creativity with your newfound knowledge to create some impressive apps of your own.

There is so much more to the iOS ecosystem and raywenderlich.com has the resources to help your continued growth as an iOS developer:

- *SwiftUI by Tutorials* will expand your knowledge of SwiftUI and explores more advanced developer topics.

- *iOS App Distribution & Best Practices* will guide you through the process of publishing your app on the App Store.

- The many video courses and free tutorials on raywenderlich.com explore diverse topics from MapKit to Core Data to animation and much more.

If you have any questions or comments as you work through this book, please stop by our forums at https://forums.raywenderlich.com and look for the particular forum category for this book.

Thank you again for purchasing this book. Your continued support is what makes the tutorials, books, videos, conferences and other things we do at raywenderlich.com possible, and we truly appreciate it!

— Audrey, Caroline, Libranner and Richard

The *SwiftUI Apprentice* team

CPSIA information can be obtained
at www.ICGtesting.com
Printed in the USA
BVHW012339300821
615624BV00026B/174